A HARMONY OF THE GOSPELS FOR STUDENTS OF THE LIFE OF CHRIST

A HARMONY OF THE GOSPELS FOR STUDENTS OF THE LIFE OF CHRIST

Based on the Broadus Harmony in the Revised Version

BY

A. T. ROBERTSON, M.A., D.D., LL.D, LITT.D.

GYAN

Published by

Gyan Publishing House
5, Ansari Road
Daryaganj, New Delhi-110002
Phone: 011-47034999, 9811692060
E-mail: books@gyanbooks.com

Distribution Network
gyanbooks.com
India, USA, Canada, UK, Australia

ISBN: 978-81-212-7703-7 (PB)
First Published, 1922

2nd Impression 2024

Printed at: Gyan Press, Delhi.

A HARMONY OF THE GOSPELS FOR STUDENTS OF THE LIFE OF CHRIST
Author: A. T. ROBERTSON

A HARMONY OF THE GOSPELS
FOR STUDENTS OF THE LIFE OF CHRIST

A. T. ROBERTSON, M.A., D.D., LL.D., Litt. D.

BY PROFESSOR A. T. ROBERTSON

A HARMONY OF THE GOSPELS FOR STUDENTS OF THE LIFE OF CHRIST. Based on the BROADUS HARMONY.

A GRAMMAR OF THE GREEK NEW TESTAMENT IN THE LIGHT OF HISTORICAL RESEARCH. Third Edition. Pages 1538.

A SHORT GRAMMAR OF THE GREEK NEW TESTAMENT. Fifth Edition. Pages 284. Translation in Dutch, French, German and Italian.

PRACTICAL AND SOCIAL ASPECTS OF CHRISTIANITY. The Wisdom of James. Second Edition. Pages 271.

PAUL THE INTERPRETER OF CHRIST. Second Edition. Pages 155.

TYPES OF PREACHERS IN THE NEW TESTAMENT. Pages 238.

EPOCHS IN THE LIFE OF JESUS. Pages 212. Numerous Editions.

EPOCHS IN THE LIFE OF PAUL. Numerous Editions. Pages 337.

JOHN THE LOYAL: Studies in the Ministry of the Baptist. Pages 327. Several editions.

THE PHARISEES AND JESUS. The Stone (Princeton) Lectures. The Studies in Theology Series. Pages 201.

LUKE THE HISTORIAN IN THE LIGHT OF RESEARCH. Pages 267.

THE NEW CITIZENSHIP. Pages 157. Second Edition.

THE GLORY OF THE MINISTRY. Pages 243. Second Edition.

MAKING GOOD IN THE MINISTRY. A sketch of John Mark. Pages 174. Second Edition.

PAUL'S JOY IN CHRIST. Studies in Philippians. Pages 267. Second Edition.

THE DIVINITY OF CHRIST IN THE GOSPEL OF JOHN. Pages 173. Second Edition.

THE STUDENT'S CHRONOLOGICAL NEW TESTAMENT. Second Edition.

COMMENTARY ON THE GOSPEL ACCORDING TO MATTHEW. The Bible for Home and School. Pages 308.

STUDIES IN MARK'S GOSPEL. Pages 158.

STUDIES IN THE NEW TESTAMENT. Many editions. Pages 284.

THE TEACHING OF JESUS CONCERNING GOD THE FATHER. The Teaching of Jesus Series. Pages 190.

KEYWORDS IN THE TEACHING OF JESUS. Pages 127. Several Editions.

LIFE AND LETTERS OF JOHN A. BROADUS. Pages 476. Numerous Editions.

SYLLABUS FOR NEW TESTAMENT STUDY. Pages 207. Fourth Edition.

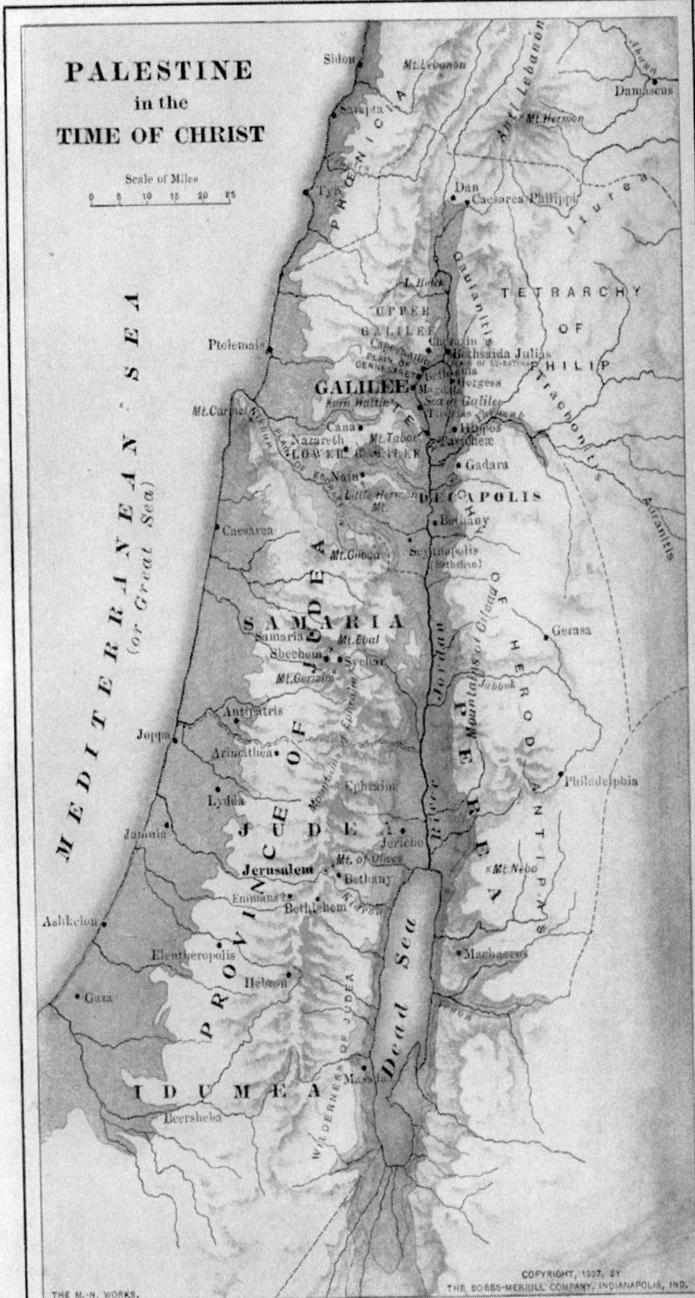

PALESTINE
in the
TIME OF CHRIST
Scale of Miles
0 5 10 15 20 25
MEDITERRANEAN SEA
(or Great Sea)
Sidon
Mt. Lebanon
Anti Lebanon
Damascus
Mt. Hermon
Sarepta
PHOENICIA
Tyre
Dan
Caesarea Philippi
Iturea
L. Huleh
UPPER
GALILEE
TETRARCHY
OF
PHILIP
Gaulanitis
Ptolemais
Capernaum
Chorazin
Bethsaida Julias
Bethsaida
Gergesa
Trachonitis
GALILEE
Magdala
Sea of Galilee
Mt. Carmel
Cana
Mt. Tabor
Hippos
Nazareth
Tarichese
LOWER GALILEE
Nain
Gadara
Little Hermon
DECAPOLIS
Auranitis
Caesarea
Mt. Gilboa
Scythopolis
(Bethshan)
SAMARIA
Samaria
Mt. Ebal
Shechem
Sychar
Mt. Gerizim
Gerasa
Jordan
Jabbok
Antipatris
Joppa
Arimathea
Philadelphia
Ephraim
Lydda
JUDEA
Jamnia
Jericho
River
PEREA
Mt. of Olives
Jerusalem
Bethany
Mt. Nebo
Emmaus
Bethlehem
Ashkelon
Dead Sea
Eleutheropolis
Machaerus
Hebron
Gaza
PROVINCE OF JUDEA
WILDERNESS OF JUDEA
IDUMEA
Masada
Beersheba
THE M.-N. WORKS
COPYRIGHT, 1907, BY
THE BOBBS-MERRILL COMPANY, INDIANAPOLIS, IND.

A HARMONY OF THE GOSPELS FOR STUDENTS OF THE LIFE OF CHRIST

Based on the Broadus Harmony in the Revised Version

BY

A. T. ROBERTSON, M.A., D.D., LL.D., LITT.D.

CHAIR OF NEW TESTAMENT INTERPRETATION
SOUTHERN BAPTIST THEOLOGICAL SEMINARY
LOUISVILLE, KENTUCKY

"Take my yoke upon you, and learn of me."

NEW YORK
GEORGE H. DORAN COMPANY

TO

ELIZA S. BROADUS

ELDEST DAUGHTER OF JOHN A. BROADUS
AN ELECT LADY BELOVED IN MANY LANDS

PREFACE

It is now just thirty years since one day his young assistant suggested to Dr. John A. Broadus that he prepare a harmony of the Gospels that should depart from the old plan of following the feasts as the turning points in the life of Jesus. He acted on the hint and led the way that all modern harmonies have followed. The book has gone through a dozen large editions and has become the standard harmony for many thousands of students all over the world. Broadus was concerned to bring out "the inner movements of the history, towards that long-delayed, but foreseen and inevitable collision, in which, beyond all other instances, the wrath of man was made to praise God." This he succeeded in doing with marvelous power.

A generation has passed by and it is meet that the work of Broadus should be reviewed in the light of modern synoptic criticism and research into every phase of the life of Christ. So I have made a new analysis that preserves Broadus's real purpose, but with new sections and new notes. The notes at the end of the old volume, written by me for the first edition, have been thoroughly revised and brought up to date. The Old Testament passages referred to in the Gospels are given in the text. The Gospel of Mark appears in the first column, then Matthew, Luke, and John. It is now known that Matthew and Luke made use of Mark for the framework of their Gospels. This change simplifies amazingly the unfolding of the narrative.

There is still dispute concerning the historical worth of the Gospel of John, but the Johannine authorship is not disproved. It still holds the field in my opinion. Dr. C. H. Burney's theory of an Aramaic original is already giving a new turn to Johannine criticism.

A harmony of the Gospels cannot meet every phase of modern criticism. The data are given, as free from bias as circumstances allow, so that all students can use the book and interpret the facts according to their various theories. Numerous historical items call for notes of various kinds that throw light on the passage in question. No effort is made to reconcile all the divergent statements of various details in the different Gospels. The differences challenge the student's interest as much as the correspondences and are natural marks of individual work. The notes and appendices at the end of the volume are meant for students who wish help for historical study of the life of Christ. A harmony cannot give all the aid that one needs, but it is the one essential book for the serious study of the life of Jesus. Students in colleges, theological seminaries, Young Men's Christian Association and Young Women's Christian Association classes, Sunday School teachers and pupils, preachers, all who read the Gospels intelligently must have a modern harmony of the Gospels. One who has never read a harmony will be amazed at the flood of light that flashes from the parallel and progressive records of the life of Jesus Christ.

Broadus began teaching the life of Jesus in 1859 and kept it up till his death in 1895. I began like work in 1888 and have kept on without a break till now. I count it one of the crowning mercies of my life that I have led so many successive classes of young ministers and young women (some five thousand in all) through the study of Christ's life. If only one can pass on to others in all their freshness and power the teachings of Jesus, he cannot fail. There was a time when men hung in wonder upon the words of Jesus, listening with awe and rapture as he spoke. The Figure of Christ fills the world today as never before. Back to Christ the world has come, the Christ of Faith and of Experience, the Jesus of History, the Man of Galilee, the Hope of Today, the Jesus Christ of the Four Gospels, in the full blaze of modern critical and historical study.

A. T. ROBERTSON.

Louisville,
Kentucky.

CONTENTS

CHIEF DIVISIONS OF THE HARMONY

ANALYTICAL OUTLINE OF THE HARMONY

PART I: THE SOURCES OF THE GOSPELS

PART II: THE PRE-EXISTENT STATE OF CHRIST AND HIS INCARNATION

PART III: THE TWO GENEALOGIES IN MATTHEW AND LUKE

PART IV: THE BIRTH AND CHILDHOOD OF THE BAPTIST AND OF JESUS

SECTIONS 4–19

PART V: THE BEGINNING OF THE BAPTIST'S MINISTRY

SECTIONS 20–23

PART VI: THE BEGINNING OF CHRIST'S PUBLIC MINISTRY

SECTIONS 24–36

PART VII: THE GREAT GALILEAN MINISTRY

SECTIONS 37–71

Eight Groups in the Period

PART VIII: THE SPECIAL TRAINING OF THE TWELVE IN DISTRICTS AROUND GALILEE

SECTIONS 72–95

PART IX: THE LATER JUDEAN MINISTRY

SECTIONS 96-111

PART X: THE LATER PEREAN MINISTRY

SECTIONS 112–127

PART XI: THE LAST PUBLIC MINISTRY IN JERUSALEM

SECTIONS 128–139

PART XII: IN THE SHADOW WITH JESUS

SECTIONS 139–152

PART XIII: THE ARREST, TRIAL, CRUCIFIXION, AND BURIAL OF JESUS

SECTIONS 153–168

PART XIV: THE RESURRECTION, APPEARANCES, AND ASCENSION OF CHRIST

SECTIONS 169–184

TABLE FOR FINDING ANY PASSAGE IN THE HARMONY

MARK

Chap.	Verse	Section	Page	Chap.	Verse	Section	Page
1	1	20	15	8	13–26	81	98
1	2–6	21	15	8	27–30	82	99
1	7–8	23	17	8	31–37	83	100
1	9–11	24	19	8	38–9: 1	84	101
1	12–13	25	20	9	2–8	85	102
1	14	34	27	9	9–13	86	103
1	14–15	37	31	9	14–29	87	104
1	16–20	41	33	9	30–32	88	107
1	21–28	42	34	9	33–37	90	108
1	29–34	43	34	9	38–50	91	109
1	35–39	44	35	10	1–12	122	141
1	40–45	45	36	10	13–16	123	143
2	1–12	46	37	10	17–31	124	143
2	13–17	47	39	10	32–45	125	146
2	18–22	48	40	10	46–52	126	148
2	23–28	50	44	11	1–11	128b	152
3	1–6	51	45	11	12–18	129	156
3	7–12	52	46	11	19–25	131	159
3	13–19	53	47	11	27–12:12	132	160
3	19–30	61	61	12	13–17	133	164
3	31–35	63	63	12	18–27	134	165
4	1–2	64	64	12	28–34	135	167
4	3–25	64	64	12	35–37	136	168
4	26–29	64	67	12	38–40	137	169
4	30–32	64	68	12	41–44	138	172
4	33–34	64	68	13	1–37	139	173
4	35–41	65	70	14	1–2	140	186
5	1–20	66	71	14	3–9	141	187
5	21–43	67	74	14	10–11	142	188
6	1–6	69	77	14	12–16	143	189
6	6–13	70	78	14	17	144	190
6	14–29	71	82	14	18–21	146	191
6	30–44	72	85	14	27–31	147	194
6	45–46	73	88	14	22–25	148	196
6	47–52	74	89	14	26, 32–42	152	201
6	53–56	75	90	14	43–52	153	205
7	1–23	77	92	14	53, 55–65	155	209
7	24–30	78	94	14	54, 66–72	156	212
7	31–8: 9	79	95	15	1	157	215
8	10–12	80	97	15	1–5	159	216

MARK—Continued

Chap.	Verse	Section	Page	Chap.	Verse	Section	Page
15	6–15	161	220	16	1	169	239
15	16–19	162	226	16	2–8	171	240
15	20–23	163	226	16	9–11	173	243
15	24–32	164	228	16	12–13	176	244
15	33–37	165	232	16	14	178	245
15	38–41	166	234	16	15–18	181	249
15	42–46	167	235	16	19–20	184	251
15	47	168	237				

MATTHEW

Chap.	Verse	Section	Page	Chap.	Verse	Section	Page
1	1–17	3	3	9	35–11:1	70	78
1	18–25	9	9	11	2–19	57	57
2	1–12	14	11	11	20–30	58	59
2	13–18	15	12	12	1–8	50	44
2	19–23	16	13	12	9–14	51	45
3	1–6	21	15	12	15–21	52	46
3	7–10	22	16	12	22–37	61	61
3	11–12	23	17	12	38–45	62	62
3	13–17	24	19	12	46–50	63	63
4	1–11	25	20	13	1–3	64	64
4	12	34	27	13	3–23	64	64
4	13–16	40	32	13	24–30	64	68
4	17	37	31	13	31–32	64	68
4	18–22	41	33	13	33–35	64	68
4	23–25	44	35	13	36–43	64	69
5	1–2	54	48	13	44	64	69
5	3–12	54	48	13	45–46	64	69
5	13–20	54	49	13	47–50	64	70
5	21–48	54	50	13	51–53	64	70
6	1–18	54	51	13	54–58	69	77
6	19–34	54	52	14	1–12	71	82
7	1–6	54	53	14	13–21	72	85
7	7–12	54	54	14	22–23	73	88
7	13–8: 1	54	54	14	24–33	74	89
8	2–4	45	36	14	34–36	75	90
8	5–13	55	55	15	1–20	77	92
8	14–17	43	34	15	21–28	78	94
8	18, 23–27	65	70	15	29–38	79	95
8	19–22	93	112	15	39–16:4	80	97
8	28–34	66	71	16	5–12	81	98
9	1–8	46	37	16	13–20	82	99
9	9–13	47	39	16	21–26	83	100
9	14–17	48	40	16	27–28	84	101
9	18–26	67	74	17	1–8	85	102
9	27–34	68	77	17	9–13	86	103

MATTHEW—Continued

Chap.	Verse	Section	Page	Chap.	Verse	Section	Page
17	14–20	87	104	26	17–19	143	189
17	22–23	88	107	26	20	144	190
17	24–27	89	107	26	21–25	146	191
18	1–5	90	108	26	31–35	147	194
18	6–14	91	109	26	26–29	148	196
18	15–35	92	111	26	30, 36–46	152	201
19	1–12	122	141	26	47–56	153	205
19	13–15	123	143	26	57, 59–68	155	209
19	16–20:16	124	143	26	58, 69–75	156	212
20	17–28	125	146	27	1	157	215
20	29–34	126	148	27	3–10	158	215
21	1–11, 14–17	128 b	152	27	2, 11–14	159	216
21	{ 18–19	129	156	27	15–26	161	220
	12–13, }			27	27–30	162	226
21	19–22	131	159	27	31–34	163	226
21	23–22:14	132	160	27	35–44	164	228
22	15–22	133	164	27	45–50	165	232
22	23–33	134	165	27	51–56	166	234
22	34–40	135	167	27	57–60	167	235
22	41–46	136	168	27	61–66	168	237
23	1–39	137	169	28	1	169	239
24 and }	......	139	173	28	2–4	170	240
25 }				28	5–8	171	241
26	1–5	140	186	28	9–10	174	243
26	6–13	141	187	28	11–15	175	244
26	14–16	142	188	28	16–20	811	249

LUKE

Chap.	Verse	Section	Page	Chap.	Verse	Section	Page
1	1–4	1	1	3	15–18	23	17
1	5–25	4	5	3	19–20	34	27
1	26–38	5	6	3	21–23	24	20
1	39–45	6	7	3	23–38	3	3
1	46–56	7	7	4	1–13	25	20
1	57–80	8	8	4	14	34	27
2	1–7	10	9	4	14–15	37	31
2	8–20	11	10	4	16–31	39	31
2	21	12	10	4	31–37	42	34
2	22–38	13	10	4	38–41	43	34
2	39	16	13	4	42–44	44	35
2	40	17	13	5	1–11	41	33
2	41–50	18	13	5	12–16	45	36
2	51	19	14	5	17–26	46	37
3	1–2	20	15	5	27–32	47	39
3	3–6	21	15	5	33–39	48	40
3	7–14	22	16	6	1–5	50	44

LUKE—CONTINUED

Chap.	Verse	Section	Page	Chap.	Verse	Section	Page
6	6–11	51	45	17	11–37	120	139
6	12–16	53	47	18	1–14	121	140
6	17–19	54	48	18	15–17	123	143
6	20–26	54	48	18	18–30	124	143
6	27–36	54	51	18	31–34	125	146
6	37–42	54	53	18	35–43	126	148
6	43–49	54	54	19	1–28	127	150
7	1–10	55	55	19	29–44	128b	152
7	11–17	56	56	19	45–48	129	156
7	18–35	57	57	21	37–38	131	159
7	36–50	59	60	20	1–19	132	160
8	1–3	60	61	20	20–26	133	164
8	4	64	64	20	27–40	134	165
8	5–18	64	64	20	41–44	136	168
8	19–21	63	63	20	45–47	137	169
8	22–25	65	70	21	1–4	138	172
8	26–39	66	71	21	5–36	139	173
8	40–56	67	74	22	1–2	140	186
9	1–6	70	78	22	3–6	142	188
9	7–9	71	82	22	7–13	143	189
9	10–17	72	85	22	{ 14–16, 24–30 }	144	190
9	18–21	82	99				
9	22–25	83	100	22	21–23	146	191
9	26–27	84	101	22	31–38	147	194
9	28–36	85	102	22	17–20	148	195
9	36	86	103	22	39–46	152	201
9	37–43	87	104	22	47–53	153	205
9	43–45	88	107	22	54, 63–65	155	209
9	46–48	90	108	22	54–62	156	212
9	49–50	91	109	22	66–71	157	215
9	51–56	95	113	23	1–5	159	216
9	57–62	93	112	23	6–12	160	220
10	1–24	102	120	23	13–25	161	221
10	25–37	103	122	23	26–33	163	226
10	38–42	104	122	23	33–43	164	228
11	1–13	105	123	23	44–46	165	232
11	14–36	106	123	23	45, 47–49	166	234
11	37–54	107	125	23	50–54	167	235
12	1–59	108	126	23	55–56	168	237
13	1–9	109	128	24	1–8	171	240
13	10–21	110	129	24	9–12	172	242
13	22–35	113	131	24	13–32	176	244
14	1–24	114	132	24	33–35	177	245
14	25–35	115	133	24	36–43	178	245
15	1–32	116	134	24	44–49	183	250
16	1–17:10	117	135	24	50–53	184	251

JOHN

Chap.	Verse	Section	Page
1	1-18	2	2
1	19-28	26	22
1	29-34	27	22
1	35-51	28	23
2	1-11	29	24
2	12	30	24
2	13-22	31	25
2	23-3:21	32	25
3	22-36	33	26
4	1-4	34	27
4	5-42	35	27
4	43-45	36	29
4	46-54	38	31
5	1-47	49	42
6	1-14	72	85
6	14-15	73	88
6	16-21	74	89
6	22-71	76	90
7	1	77	92
7	2-9	94	112
7	10	95	113
7	11-52	96	114
7	53-8:11	97	115
8	12-20	98	116
8	21-59	99	116
9	1-41	100	118
10	1-21	101	119
10	22-39	111	129
10	40-42	112	131
11	1-44	118	137
11	45-54	119	139
11	55-12:1, 9-11	128 a	152
12	12-19	128 b	152
12	20-50	130	157
12	2-8	141	187
13	1-20	145	190
13	21-30	146	191
13	31-38	147	193
14	......	149	197
15 and 16	......	150	198
17	......	151	200
18	1	152	201
18	2-12	153	205
18	12-14, 19-23	154	209
18	24	155	209
18	15-18, 25-27	156	212
18	28-38	159	216
18	39-19:16	161	221
19	16-17	163	226
19	18-27	164	228
19	28-30	165	232
19	31-42	167	235
20	1	171	240
20	2-10	172	242
20	11-18	173	242
20	19-25	178	245
20	26-31	179	247
21	......	180	247

NOTE:—The verses that are omitted in the Canterbury Revision do not appear in this Harmony. They are Mark 7:16; 9:44, 46; 11:26; 15:28; Matthew 17:21; 18:11; 23:14; Luke 17:36; 23:17; John 5:4.

In addition to the Gospels use is made of

Acts 1:3-8 in § 183, page 250.
Acts 1:9-12 in § 184, page 251.
Acts 1:18-19 in § 158, page 215.
1 Cor. 11:23-26 in § 148, page 195.
1 Cor. 15:5 in § 177, page 245.
1 Cor. 15:5 in § 179, page 247.
1 Cor. 15:6 in § 181, page 249.
1 Cor. 15:7 in § 182, page 250.

A HARMONY OF THE GOSPELS
FOR STUDENTS OF THE LIFE OF CHRIST

PART I

THE SOURCES OF THE GOSPELS

§ 1. IN THE DEDICATION LUKE EXPLAINS HIS METHOD OF RESEARCH*

Luke 1:1–4

1 FORASMUCH as many have taken in hand to draw up a narrative con-
2 cerning those matters which have been [1]fulfilled among us, even as they
delivered them unto us, which from the beginning were eyewitnesses
3 and ministers of the word, it seemed good to me also, having traced the
course of all things accurately from the first, to write unto thee in order,
4 most excellent Theophilus;† that thou mightest know the certainty con-
cerning the [2]things [3]wherein thou wast instructed.

[1] Or, *fully established.* [2] Gr. *words.* [3] Or, *which thou wast taught by word of mouth.*

---

* Luke is the first critic of the life of Christ whose criticism has been preserved to us. Others had drawn up narratives of certain portions of Christ's work. Others still had been eyewitnesses of the ministry of Jesus and gave Luke their oral testimony. Luke sifted it all with care and produced an orderly and reasonably full narrative of the earthly ministry of Jesus. We cannot reproduce all the sources that Luke had at his command, but it is clear that he followed in the main our Gospel of Mark, as any one can see for himself by comparing the two Gospels in this Harmony. Both Matthew and Luke made use of Mark. But they had other sources also. See note 2 on Synoptic Criticism at the close of the Harmony. See also Chapter IV, "Luke's Method of Research" in my *Luke the Historian in the Light of Research.*

† Luke alone follows the method of ancient historians in dedicating his Gospel, as also the Acts (1:1), to a patron who probably met the expense of publication. So Luke as a Gentile Christian writes an historical introduction in literary (*Koiné*) Greek after the fashion of Thucydides and Plutarch. Mark had no formal introduction. Matthew's introduction is genealogical because he is writing for Jewish readers to prove that Jesus is the Messiah of Jewish hope. John, writing last of all, has a theological introduction to meet the Gnostic and philosophical misconceptions concerning the Person of Christ. Thus he pictures Christ as the Eternal Logos, with God in his pre-incarnate state, who became flesh and thus revealed the Father to men.

PART II

THE PRE-EXISTENT STATE OF CHRIST AND HIS INCARNATION

§ 2. IN HIS INTRODUCTION JOHN PICTURES CHRIST AS THE WORD (LOGOS)

John 1:1–18

1 In the beginning was the Word,* and the Word was with God, and
2 the Word was God. The same was in the beginning with God. All
3 things were made [1]by him; and without him [2]was not anything made
4 that hath been made. In him was life; and the life was the light of men.
5 And the light shineth in the darkness; and the darkness [3]apprehended
6 it not. There came a man, sent from God, whose name was John. The
7 same came for witness, that he might bear witness of the light, that all
8 might believe through him. He was not the light, but *came* that he
9 might bear witness of the light. [4]There was the true light, *even the light*
10 which lighteth [5]every man, coming into the world. He was in the world,
and the world was made [1]by him, and the world knew him not. He
11 came unto [6]his own, and they that were his own received him not. But
12 as many as received him, to them gave he the right to become children
13 of God, *even* to them that believe on his name: which were [7]born, not
of [8]blood, nor of the will of the flesh, nor of the will of man, but of God.
14 And the Word* became flesh, and [9]dwelt among us (and we beheld his
glory, glory as of [10]the only begotten from the Father), full of grace and
15 truth. John beareth witness of him, and crieth, saying, [11]This was he
of whom I said, He that cometh after me is become before me: for he
16 was [12]before me. For of his fulness we all received, and grace for grace.
17 For the law was given [1]by Moses; grace and truth came [1]by Jesus Christ.
18 No man hath seen God at any time; [13]the only begotten Son, which is in
the bosom of the Father, he hath declared *him*.

[1] Or, *through*. [2] Or, *was not anything made. That which hath been made was life in him; and the life, &c.* [3] Or, *overcame*. [4] Or, *The true light, which lighteth every man, was coming*. [5] Or, *every man as he cometh*. [6] Gr. *his own things*. [7] Or, *begotten*. [8] Gr. *bloods*. [9] Gr. *tabernacled*. [10] Or, *an only begotten from a father*. [11] Some ancient authorities read *this was he that said*. [12] Gr. *first in regard of me*. [13] Many very ancient authorities read *God only begotten*.

---

* The Fourth Gospel makes no further use of the term Logos (Word) for Christ. No other Gospel employs the term, but in 1 John 1:1 we find "the Word of life" in this sense and in Rev. 19:14 we have: "and his name is called the Word of God." The Greek word has a double sense (reason and speech) and John seems to have both ideas in mind (1:18). Christ is the Idea of God and the Expression of God. The Stoics followed Plato in the philosophical use of Logos. Philo took it up and made it familiar to Jewish readers who were already used to the Hebrew *Mêmra* (Word) in a personal sense. But John carried the term further than any of his predecessors and placed it on a par with Messiah, Son of God, Son of Man, and other phrases that portray aspects of the Person of Christ. John writes his Gospel to prove the deity of Jesus (John 20:31) against Gnostics (Cerinthian) who denied it, as he wrote his First Epistle (1 John 1:1–4) to prove the humanity of Jesus against Docetic Gnostics who disclaimed it. See note 3 at end of Harmony.

PART III

THE TWO GENEALOGIES IN MATTHEW AND LUKE

§ 3. APPARENTLY JOSEPH'S GENEALOGY IN MATTHEW AND MARY'S IN LUKE*

Matt. 1:1–17. (*Cf.* 1 Chron. 1:34; 2:1–15; 3:1–19.)

1 [1]The book of the [2]generation
of Jesus Christ, the son of David,
the son of Abraham.
2 Abraham begat Isaac; and Isaac
begat Jacob; and Jacob begat Ju-
3 dah and his brethren; and Judah
begat Perez and Zerah of Tamar;
and Perez begat Hezron; and Hez-
4 ron begat [3]Ram; and [3]Ram begat
Amminadab; and Amminadab
begat Nahshon: and Nahshon
5 begat Salmon; and Salmon begat
Boaz of Rahab; and Boaz begat
6 Obed of Ruth; and Obed begat
Jesse; and Jesse begat David the
king.
And David begat Solomon of
her *that had been the wife* of Uriah;
7 and Solomon begat Rehoboam;
and Rehoboam begat Abijah;
8 and Abijah begat [4]Asa; and [4]Asa
begat Jehoshaphat; and Jehosh-
aphat begat Joram; and Joram
9 begat Uzziah; and Uzziah begat
Jotham; and Jotham begat Ahaz;
10 and Ahaz begat Hezekiah; and
Hezekiah begat Manasseh; and
Manasseh begat [5]Amon; and
11 [5]Amon begat Josiah; and Josiah
begat Jechoniah and his breth-
ren, at the time of the [6]carrying
away to Babylon.
12 And after the [6]carrying away

Luke 3:23–38. (*Cf.* 1 Chron. 1:1–4, 24–28; 2:1–15; 3:17; Ruth 4:18–22.)

Being the son (as was supposed)
24 of Joseph, the *son* of Heli, the
son of Matthat, the *son* of Levi,
25 the *son* of Jannai, the *son* of Jo-
seph, the *son* of Matthias, the
son of Amos, the *son* of Nahum,
the *son* of Esli, the *son* of Nag-
26 gai, the *son* of Maath, the son of
Mattathias, the *son* of Semein,
the *son* of Josech, the *son* of
27 Joda, the *son* of Joanan, the *son*
of Rhesa, the *son* of Zerubbabel,
the *son* of [7]Shealtiel, the *son* of
28 Neri, the *son* of Melchi, the *son*
of Addi, the *son* of Cosam, the
29 *son* of Elmadam, the *son* of Er,
the *son* of Jesus, the *son* of Elie-
zer, the *son* of Jorim, the *son* of
30 Matthat, the *son* of Levi, the *son*
of Symeon, the *son* of Judas, the
son of Joseph, the *son* of Jonam,
31 the *son* of Eliakim, the *son* of
Melea, the *son* of Menna, the *son*
of Mattatha, the *son* of Nathan,
32 the *son* of David, the *son* of Jesse,
the *son* of Obed, the *son* of Boaz,
the *son* of [8]Salmon, the *son* of
33 Nahshon, the *son* of Amminadab,
[9]the *son* of [10]Arni, the *son* of Hez-
34 ron, the *son* of Perez, the *son* of
Judah, the *son* of Jacob, the *son*
35 of Isaac, the *son* of Abraham, the
son of Terah, the *son* of Nahor,

---

* This view is not accepted by all scholars, though it is found as early as Eusebius (*Hist. Eccl.* i, 7). See note 5 at end of Harmony.

Matt. 1:1–17

to Babylon, Jechoniah begat
[7]Shealtiel; and [7]Shealtiel begat
13 Zerubbabel; and Zerubbabel be-
gat Abiud; and Abiud begat Eli-
14 akim; and Eliakim begat Azor;
and Azor begat Sadoc; and Sa-
15 doc begat Achim; and Achim
begat Eliud; and Eliud begat
Eleazar; and Eleazar begat Mat-
than; and Matthan begat Jacob;
16 and Jacob begat Joseph the hus-
band of Mary, of whom was born*
Jesus, who is called Christ.

Luke 3:23–38

the *son* of Serug, the *son* of Reu,
the *son* of Peleg, the *son* of Eber,
36 the *son* of Shelah, the *son* of Cai-
nan, the *son* of Arphaxad, the
son of Shem, the *son* of Noah,
37 the *son* of Lamech, the *son* of
Methuselah, the *son* of Enoch,
the *son* of Jared, the *son* of Ma-
38 halaleel, the *son* of Cainan, the
son of Enos, the *son* of Seth, the
son of Adam, the *son* of God.

17 So all the generations from Abraham unto David are fourteen generations; and from David to the [6]carrying away to Babylon fourteen generations; and from the [6]carrying away to Babylon unto the Christ fourteen generations.†

[1] Or, *The Genealogy of Jesus Christ.* [2] Or, *the birth;* as in ver. 18. [3] Gr. *Aram.* [4] Gr. *Asaph.* [5] Gr. *Amos.* [6] Or, *removal to Babylon.* [7] Gr. *Salathiel.* [8] Some ancient authorities write *Sala.* [9] Many ancient authorities insert *the son of Admin;* and one writes *Admin* for *Amminadab.* [10] Some ancient authorities write *Aram.*

* The Sinaitic Syriac, against all the early Greek manuscripts, reads in Matt. 1:16: "But Joseph, to whom the Virgin Mary was betrothed, begat Jesus." This ancient Ebionitic text is followed by Von Soden in his *Griechisches Neues Testament* and by Moffatt in his *New Translation of the New Testament*, but it is difficult to believe it genuine, for in Matt. 1:18–22 the writer pictures Joseph as on the point of putting Mary away privily. The two reports in the Sinaitic Syriac flatly contradict each other. Those who accept it say that the writer of the Virgin Birth view in 1:18–20 overlooked 1:16 (certainly a serious oversight). It is easier to think that an Ebionitic scribe in copying altered 1:16, but passed by 1:18–20. The Ebionites denied the deity of Jesus. Both Matthew and Luke (1:26–38) give the Virgin Birth of Jesus, but they preserve separate traditions on the subject.

† Observe that Matthew's three divisions of the genealogy represent three great periods in the history of Israel. See note 5 at end of Harmony for discussion of the differences between the genealogies in Matthew and in Luke.

PART IV

THE BIRTH AND CHILDHOOD OF THE BAPTIST AND OF JESUS

Probably B.C. 7 to A.D. 7

§§ *4–19. These sections include the annunciations, the birth, infancy, and childhood of both John and Jesus.*

§ 4. THE ANNUNCIATION* OF THE BIRTH OF THE BAPTIST TO ZACHARIAS

Jerusalem, in the Temple. Probably B.C. 7

Luke 1:5–25†

5 There was in the days of Herod, king of Judea, a certain priest named
Zacharias, of the course of Abijah: and he had a wife of the daughters
6 of Aaron, and her name was Elisabeth. And they were both righteous
before God, walking in all the commandments and ordinances of the
7 Lord blameless. And they had no child, because that Elisabeth was
barren, and they both were *now* [1]well stricken in years.
8 Now it came to pass, while he executed the priest's office before God
9 in the order of his course, according to the custom of the priest's office,
10 his lot was to enter into the [2]temple of the Lord and burn incense. And
the whole multitude of the people were praying without at the hour of
11 incense. And there appeared unto him an angel of the Lord standing
12 on the right side of the altar of incense. And Zacharias was troubled
13 when he saw *him*, and fear fell upon him. But the angel said unto him,
Fear not, Zacharias: because thy supplication is heard, and thy wife
14 Elisabeth shall bear thee a son, and thou shalt call his name John. And
15 thou shalt have joy and gladness; and many shall rejoice at his birth. For
he shall be great in the sight of the Lord, and he shall drink no wine nor
[3]strong drink [*see Num. 6:3; Judg. 13:4–6; 1 Sam. 1:11*]; and he shall
16 be filled with the [4]Holy Ghost, even from his mother's womb. And many
17 of the children of Israel shall he turn unto the Lord their God. And
he shall [5]go before his face in the spirit and power of Elijah, to turn the
hearts of the fathers to the children [*see Mal. 3:1; 4:5–6*], and the disobedient

---

* There are three annunciations: (1) to Zacharias § 4, (2) to Mary § 5, (3) to Joseph § 9. Luke gives the first two and Matthew the third. The Angel Gabriel is named by Luke (1:19, 26), but Matthew simply has "an angel of the Lord" (1:20).

† It is certain that Luke tells the infancy stories from the standpoint of Mary while Matthew writes from the standpoint of Joseph. Matthew gives the public account while Luke tells the private story from Mary herself (Ramsay, *Was Christ Born at Bethlehem?* p. 79). Luke could have seen Mary, if still alive, or could have obtained it from one of Mary's circle either orally or in manuscript form. Some scholars even suggest "Gospel of Mary" and even, "Gospel of the Baptist" as a written source for Luke in 1:5–2:52. Sanday (*The Life of Christ in Recent Research*, p. 166) says: "These two chapters—whatever the date at which they were first committed to writing—are essentially the most archaic thing in the whole New Testament" Certainly Luke reveals the use of Aramaic or Hebrew sources by the sudden changes in his style from 1:1–4. Luke, if familiar with the current account as seen in Matthew, apparently felt that he owed it to Mary to record her story of her great experience.

Luke 1:5–25

to walk in the wisdom of the just; to make ready for the Lord a people pre-
18 pared *for him*. And Zacharias said unto the angel, Whereby shall I
know this? for I am an old man, and my wife [6]well stricken in years.
19 And the angel answering said unto him, I am Gabriel, that stand in the
presence of God [*see Dan. 8:16; 9:21*]; and I was sent to speak unto thee,
20 and to bring thee these good tidings. And behold, thou shalt be silent
and not able to speak, until the day that these things shall come to pass,
because thou believedst not my words, which shall be fulfilled in their
21 season. And the people were waiting for Zacharias, and they marvelled
22 [7]while he tarried in the [2]temple. And when he came out, he could not
speak unto them: and they perceived that he had seen a vision in the
[2]temple: and he continued making signs unto them, and remained dumb.
23 And it came to pass, when the days of his ministration were fulfilled, he
departed unto his house.
24 And after these days Elisabeth his wife conceived; and she hid her-
25 self five months, saying, Thus hath the Lord done unto me in the days
wherein he looked upon *me*, to take away my reproach among men.

[1] Gr. *advanced in their days*. [2] Or, *sanctuary* [3] Gr. *sikera*. [4] Or, *Holy Spirit;* and so throughout all the Gospels. [5] Some ancient authorities read *come nigh before his face*. [6] Gr. *advanced in her days*. [7] Or, *at his tarrying*.

§ 5. THE ANNUNCIATION TO THE VIRGIN MARY OF THE BIRTH OF JESUS

Nazareth. Probably B.C. 7 or 6

Luke 1:26–38

26 Now in the sixth month the angel Gabriel was sent from God unto
27 a city of Galilee, named Nazareth, to a virgin betrothed to a man whose
name was Joseph, of the house of David; and the virgin's name was Mary.
28 And he came in unto her, and said, Hail, thou that art [1]highly favoured,
29 the Lord *is* with thee.[2] But she was greatly troubled at the saying, and
30 cast in her mind what manner of salutation this might be. And the
angel said unto her, Fear not, Mary: for thou hast found [3]favour with
31 God. And behold, thou shalt conceive in thy womb, and bring forth a
32 son, and shalt call his name Jesus [*see Isa. 7:14*]. He shall be great, and
shall be called the Son of the Most High: and the Lord God shall give unto
33 him the throne of his father David [*see 2 Sam. 7:12–17*]: and he shall reign
over the house of Jacob [4]forever; and of his kingdom there shall be no end.
34 And Mary said unto the angel, How shall this be, seeing I know not a
35 man? And the angel answered and said unto her, The Holy Ghost shall
come upon thee, and the power of the Most High shall overshadow thee:
wherefore also [5]that which [6]is to be born [7]shall be called holy [*see Ex. 13:12*],
36 the Son of God. And behold, Elisabeth thy kinswoman, she also hath
37 conceived a son in her old age: and this is the sixth month with her that
38 [8]was called barren. For no word from God shall be void of power [*see Gen. 18:14*]. And Mary said, Behold, the [9]handmaid of the Lord; be it unto
me according to thy word. And the angel departed from her.

[1] Or, *endued with grace*. [2] Many ancient authorities add *blessed* art *thou among women*. (See ver. 42.) [3] Or, *grace*. [4] Gr. *unto the ages*. [5] Or, *the holy thing which is to be born shall be called the son of God*. [6] Or, *is begotten*. [7] Some ancient authorities insert *of thee*. [8] Or, *is*. [9] Gr. *bondmaid*.

§6. THE SONG* OF ELISABETH TO MARY UPON HER VISIT

Hill Country of Judea

Luke 1:39–45

39 And Mary arose in these days and went into the hill country with
40 haste, into a city of Judah; and entered into the house of Zacharias and
41 saluted Elisabeth. And it came to pass, when Elisabeth heard the sal-
utation of Mary, the babe leaped in her womb; and Elisabeth was filled
42 with the Holy Ghost; and she lifted up her voice with a loud cry, and
said, Blessed *art* thou among women, and blessed *is* the fruit of thy womb.
43 And whence is this to me, that the mother of my Lord should come unto
44 me? For behold, when the voice of thy salutation came into mine ears,
45 the babe leaped in my womb for joy. And blessed *is* she that [1]believed;
for there shall be a fulfilment of the things which have been spoken to
her from the Lord.

[1] Or, *believed that there shall be.*

§7. THE MAGNIFICAT OF MARY

Hill Country of Judea

Luke 1:46–56

And Mary said,

46 My soul doth magnify the Lord [*see 1 Sam. 2:1–10*],
47 And my spirit hath rejoiced in God my Saviour.
48 For he hath looked upon the low estate of his [1]handmaiden:
For behold, from henceforth all generations shall call me blessed [*see 1 Sam 1:11*].
49 For he that is mighty hath done to me great things;
And holy is his name [*see 1 Sam. 2:2*].
50 And his mercy is unto generations and generations
On them that fear him [*see Ps. 103:17*].
51 He hath shewed strength with his arm;
He hath scattered the proud [2]in the imagination of their heart [*see 1 Sam. 2:4; Ps. 89:10*].
52 He hath put down princes from *their* thrones,
And hath exalted them of low degree [*see Job 5:11; 12:19*].
53 The hungry he hath filled with good things;
And the rich he hath sent empty away [*see Ps. 107:9*].
54 He hath holpen Israel his servant,
That he might remember mercy [*see Isa. 41:8–9*].
55 (As he spake unto our fathers)
Toward Abraham and his seed for ever [*see Gen. 17:7; Mic. 7:20*].
56 And Mary abode with her about three months, and returned unto her house.

[1] Gr. *bondmaiden.* [2] Or, *by.*

* This hymn or psalm springs from the omen to Elisabeth.

§8. THE BIRTH AND CHILDHOOD OF THE BAPTIST, AND HIS DESERT LIFE

Hill Country of Judea. B.C. 7 or 6

Luke 1:57–80

57 Now Elisabeth's time was fulfilled that she should be delivered; and
58 she brought forth a son. And her neighbors and her kinsfolk heard
that the Lord had magnified his mercy toward her; and they rejoiced
59 with her. And it came to pass on the eighth day, that they came to
circumcise the child; and they would have called him Zacharias, after
60 the name of his father. And his mother answered and said, Not so;
61 but he shall be called John. And they said unto her, There is none of
62 thy kindred that is called by this name. And they made signs to his
63 father, what he would have him called. And he asked for a writing
64 tablet, and wrote, saying, His name is John. And they marvelled all.
And his mouth was opened immediately, and his tongue *loosed*, and he
65 spake, blessing God. And fear came on all that dwelt round about them:
and all these sayings were noised abroad throughout all the hill country
66 of Judea. And all that heard them laid them up in their heart, saying,
What then shall this child be? For the hand of the Lord was with him.

67 And his father Zacharias was filled with the Holy Ghost, and prophesied, saying,

68 Blessed *be* the Lord, the God of Israel;
For he hath visited and wrought redemption for his people [*see Ps. 72:18; 111:9*],
69 And hath raised up a horn of salvation for us
In the house of his servant David [*see 1 Sam. 2:10; Ps. 18:3*],
70 (As he spake by the mouth of his holy prophets which have been since the world began),
71 Salvation from our enemies, and from the hand of all that hate us [*see Ps. 106:10*];
72 To show mercy towards our fathers,
And to remember his holy convenant;
73 The oath which he sware unto Abraham our father [*see Gen. 17:7; Lev. 26:42; Ps. 105:8; Mic. 7:20*],
74 To grant unto us that we being delivered out of the hand of our enemies
Should serve him without fear,
75 In holiness and righteousness before him all our days.
76 Yea and thou, child, shalt be called the prophet of the Most High:
For thou shalt go before the face of the Lord to make ready his ways [*see Mal. 3:1*];
77 To give knowledge of salvation unto his people
In the remission of their sins,
78 Because of the [1]tender mercy of our God,
[2]Whereby the dayspring from on high [3]shall visit us [*see Mal. 4:2*],
79 To shine upon them that sit in darkness and the shadow of death;
To guide our feet into the way of peace [*see Isa. 8:22; 9:2*].

80 And the child grew, and waxed strong in spirit, and was in the deserts till the day of his shewing unto Israel.*

[1] Or, *heart of mercy*. [2] Or, *Wherein*. [3] Many ancient authorities read *hath visited us*.

* Dwell on this summary statement as to John's retired life in the wild regions of Judea, whence he will come forth thirty years later.

§ 9. THE ANNUNCIATION TO JOSEPH OF THE BIRTH OF JESUS

Nazareth

Matt. 1:18–25

18 Now the [1]birth [2]of Jesus Christ was on this wise: When his mother
Mary had been betrothed to Joseph, before they came together she was
19 found with child of the [3]Holy Ghost. And Joseph her husband, being
a righteous man, and not willing to make her a public example, was
20 minded to put her away privily. But when he thought on these things,
behold, an angel of the Lord appeared unto him in a dream, saying,
Joseph, thou son of David, fear not to take unto thee Mary thy wife:
21 for that which is [4]conceived in her is of the Holy Ghost. And she shall
bring forth a son; and thou shalt call his name JESUS; for it is he that shall
22 save his people from their sins. Now all this is come to pass, that it
might be fulfilled which was spoken by the Lord through the prophet,
saying,
23 Behold, the virgin shall be with child, and shall bring forth a son [*see
Isa. 7:14*], And they shall call his name [5]Immanuel;
24 which is, being interpreted, God with us. And Joseph arose from his
sleep, and did as the angel of the Lord commanded him, and took unto
25 him his wife; and knew her not till she had brought forth a son: and he
called his name Jesus.

[1] Or, *generation*: as in ver. 1 in § 3 [2] Some ancient authorities read *of the Christ*. [3] Or, *Holy Spirit*. [4] Gr. *begotten*. [5] Gr. *Emmanuel*.

§ 10. THE BIRTH OF JESUS

Bethlehem. Probably B.C. 6 or 5

Luke 2:1–7

1 Now it came to pass in those days, there went out a decree from Cæsar
2 Augustus, that all the [1]world should be enrolled. This was the first
3 enrolment made when Quirinius was governor of Syria. And all went
to enrol themselves, every one to his own city.* And Joseph also went
4 up from Galilee, out of the city of Nazareth, into Judea, to the city of
5 David, which is called Bethlehem, because he was of the house and family
of David; to enrol himself with Mary, who was betrothed to him, being
6 great with child. And it came to pass, while they were there, the days
7 were fulfilled that she should be delivered. And she brought forth her
firstborn son; and she wrapped him in swaddling clothes, and laid him in a
manger, because there was no room for them in the inn.

[1] Gr. *inhabited earth*.

---

*Observe how the ruler of the civilized world is unconsciously bringing it about that the Messiah, the son of David, shall be born at Bethlehem, though his mother's home was Nazareth. All the previous history of Rome and of Israel gathers about this manger. As to Quirinius, and as to the probable time of the Saviour's birth, see note 6 at the end of the book. The vindication of Luke's historical statements in these verses is one of the triumphs of modern research, as is shown in that note.

§ 11. THE PRAISE OF THE ANGELS AND THE HOMAGE OF THE SHEPHERDS

Near Bethlehem

Luke 2:8–20

8 And there were shepherds in the same country abiding in the field,
9 and keeping [1]watch by night over their flock. And an angel of the Lord
stood by them, and the glory of the Lord shone round about them, and
10 they were sore afraid. And the angel said unto them, Be not afraid;
11 for behold, I bring you good tidings of great joy which shall be to all the
people: for there is born to you this day in the city of David, a Saviour
12 which is [2]Christ the Lord. And this *is* the sign unto you; Ye shall find a
13 babe wrapped in swaddling clothes, and lying in a manger. And suddenly
there was with the angel a multitude of the heavenly host praising* God,
and saying,
14 Glory to God in the highest,
And on earth [3]peace among [4]men in whom he is well pleased.
15 And it came to pass, when the angels went away from them into heaven,
the shepherds said one to another, Let us now go even unto Bethlehem,
and see this [5]thing that is come to pass, which the Lord hath made known
16 unto us. And they came with haste, and found both Mary and Joseph,
17 and the babe lying in the manger. And when they saw it, they made
known concerning the saying which was spoken to them about this child.
18 And all that heard it wondered at the things which were spoken unto
19 them by the shepherds. But Mary kept all these [6]sayings, pondering
20 them in her heart. And the shepherds returned, glorifying and praising
God for all the things that they had heard and seen, even as it was spoken
unto them.

[1] Or, *night-watches*. [2] Or, *Anointed Lord*. [3] Many ancient authorities read *peace, good pleasure among men*. [4] Gr. *men of good pleasure*. [5] Or, *saying*. [6] Or, *things*.

§ 12. THE CIRCUMCISION OF JESUS

Bethlehem

Luke 2:21

21 And when eight days were fulfilled for circumcising him [*see Gen. 17:12; Lev. 12:3*], his name was called JESUS, which was so called by the angel before he was conceived in the womb.

§ 13. THE PRESENTATION IN THE TEMPLE WITH THE HOMAGE OF SIMEON AND ANNA

Jerusalem

Luke 2:22–38

22 And when the days of their purification according to the law of Moses
23 were fulfilled, they brought him up to Jerusalem, to present him to the

* The Gloria in Excelsis.

Luke 2:22–38

Lord (as it is written in the law of the Lord, Every male that openeth the
womb, shall be called holy to the Lord) [*see Ex. 13:2, 12, 15; Lev. 12:1–8*],
24 and to offer a sacrifice according to that which is said in the law of the
25 Lord, A pair of turtledoves, or two young pigeons. And behold, there was
a man in Jerusalem, whose name was Simeon; and this man was righteous
and devout, looking for the consolation of Israel: and the Holy Spirit
26 was upon him. And it had been revealed unto him by the Holy Spirit,
27 that he should not see death, before he had seen the Lord's Christ. And
he came in the Spirit into the temple: and when the parents brought in
the child Jesus, that they might do concerning him after the custom of the
28 law, then he received him into his arms, and blessed God and said,*

29 Now lettest thou thy [1]servant depart, O [2]Lord,
According to thy word, in peace;
30 For mine eyes have seen thy salvation [*see Isa. 52:10*].
31 Which thou hast prepared before the face of all the peoples;
32 A light for [3]revelation to the Gentiles,
And the glory of thy people Israel [*see Isa. 42:6; 49:6*].

33 And his father and his mother were marvelling at the things which
34 were spoken concerning him; and Simeon blessed them, and said unto
Mary his mother, Behold, this *child* is set for the falling and rising up
35 of many in Israel; and for a sign which is spoken against; yea and a sword
shall pierce through thine own soul; that thoughts out of many hearts
36 may be revealed. And there was one Anna, a prophetess, the daughter
of Phanuel, of the tribe of Asher (she was [4]of a great age, having lived
37 with a husband seven years from her virginity, and she had been a widow
even for four-score and four years), which departed not from the temple,
38 worshipping with fastings and supplications night and day. And coming
up at that very hour she gave thanks unto God, and spake of him to all
them that were looking for the redemption of Jerusalem.

[1] Gr. *bond-servant.* [2] Gr. *Master.* [3] Or, *the unveiling of the Gentiles.* [4] Gr. *advanced in many days.*

§ 14. MAGI VISIT THE NEW-BORN KING OF THE JEWS

Jerusalem and Bethlehem

Matt. 2:1–12

1 Now when Jesus was born in Bethlehem of Judea in the days of Herod
2 the king, behold, [1]wise men from the east [*see Num. 24:17*] came to
Jerusalem, saying, [2]Where is he that is born King of the Jews? for we saw
3 his star in the east, and are come to worship him. And when Herod the
4 king heard it, he was troubled, and all Jerusalem with him. And gather-
ing together all the chief priests and scribes of the people, he inquired
5 of them where the Christ should be born. And they said unto him, In
Bethlehem of Judea: for thus it is written [3]by the prophet,

* The four New Testament psalms, given by Luke, breathe the atmosphere of Old Testament piety, quite in contrast to the formalism of the Pharisees and yet thoroughly Jewish in background and Christian in sentiment. But it is primitive Christian feeling. Section 7 gives the Magnificat of Mary in response to the song of Elisabeth in § 6. In § 8 we have the *Benedictus* of Zacharias and in § 13 The *Nunc Dimittis* of Simeon.

Matt. 2:1-12

6 And thou Bethlehem, land of Judah,
Art in no wise least among the princes of Judah;
For out of thee shall come forth a governor [*see Mic. 5:1-2*],
Which shall be shepherd of my people Israel.
7 Then Herod privily called the [1]wise men, and learned of them carefully
8 [4]what time the star appeared. And he sent them to Bethlehem, and said,
Go and search out carefully concerning the young child; and when ye
have found *him*, bring me word, that I also may come and worship him.
9 And they, having heard the king, went their way; and lo, the star, which
they saw in the east, went before them, till it came and stood over where
10 the young child was. And when they saw the star, they rejoiced with
11 exceeding great joy. And they came into the house and saw the young
child with Mary his mother; and they fell down and worshipped him; and
opening their treasures they offered unto him gifts, gold and frankincense
12 and myrrh. And being warned *of God* in a dream that they should not
return to Herod, they departed into their own country another way.

[1] Gr. *Magi*. Compare Esther 1:13; Dan. 2:12. [2] Or, *Where is the King of the Jews that is born?* [3] Or, *through*. [4] Or, *the time of the star that appeared*.

§ 15. THE CHILD JESUS CARRIED TO EGYPT, AND THE CHILDREN AT BETHLEHEM SLAIN

Probably B.C. 5

Matt. 2:13-18

13 Now when they were departed, behold, an angel of the Lord appeareth
to Joseph in a dream, saying, Arise and take the young child and his
mother, and flee into Egypt, and be thou there until I tell thee: for Herod
14 will seek the young child to destroy him. And he arose and took the
young child by night, and departed into Egypt; and was there until the
15 death of Herod: that it might be fulfilled which was spoken by the Lord
through the prophet, saying, Out of Egypt did I call my son [*see Hos. 11:1*].
16 Then Herod, when he saw that he was mocked of the [1]wise men, was
exceeding wroth, and sent forth, and slew all the male children that were
in Bethlehem, and in all the borders thereof, from two years old and under,
according to the time which he had carefully learned of the [1]wise men.
17 Then was fulfilled that which was spoken [2]by Jeremiah the prophet,
saying [*see Jer. 31:15*],
18 A voice was heard in Ramah,
Weeping and great mourning
Rachel weeping for her children;
And she would not be comforted, because they are not.

[1] Gr. *Magi*. [2] Or, *through*.

§ 16. THE CHILD BROUGHT FROM EGYPT TO NAZARETH

Probably B.C. 4

Matt. 2:19–23

19 But when Herod was dead, behold, an angel
of the Lord appeareth in a dream to Joseph in
20 Egypt, saying, Arise and take the young child
and his mother, and go into the land of Israel:
21 for they are dead that sought the young child's
life. And he arose and took the young child
and his mother, and came into the land of Is-
22 rael. But when he heard that Archelaus was
reigning over Judea in the room of his father
Herod, he was afraid to go thither; and being
23 warned *of God* in a dream, he withdrew into
the parts of Galilee, and came and dwelt in a
city called Nazareth; that it might be fulfilled
which was spoken [1]by the prophets,* that he
should be called a Nazarene.

Luke 2:39

39 And when they had accomplished all things that were according to the law of the Lord, they returned into Galilee, to their own city Nazareth.

[1] Or, *through*.

§ 17. THE CHILDHOOD OF JESUS AT NAZARETH

Probably B.C. 4 to A.D. 7

Luke 2:40

40 And the child grew, and waxed strong, †filled with wisdom; and the grace of God was upon him.

§ 18. THE VISIT OF THE BOY JESUS TO JERUSALEM WHEN TWELVE YEARS OLD

Probably A.D. 7 or 8

Luke 2:41–50

41 And his parents went every year to Jerusalem at the feast of the pass-
42 over [*see Ex. 23:14–17; Deut. 16:1–8*]. And when he was twelve years old,
43 they went up after the custom of the feast; and when they had fulfilled
the days, as they were returning, the boy Jesus tarried behind in Jerusalem;
44 and his parents knew it not; but supposing him to be in the company, they
went a day's journey; and they sought for him among their kinsfolk
45 and acquaintance: and when they found him not, they returned to Jeru-

* *Cf.* Isa. 11:1 where the Messiah is called *Netzer*, a Branch, though Nazareth is not mentioned in the Old Testament.

† This simple statement of Luke tells more in one sentence than all the apocryphal Gospels of the Infancy, with their silly legends about the miraculous prowess of the child Jesus.

Luke 2: 41–50

46 salem, seeking for him. And it came to pass, after three days they found
him in the temple, sitting in the midst of the [1]doctors, both hearing them,
47 and asking them questions: and all that heard him were amazed at his
48 understanding and his answers. And when they saw him, they were
49 astonished: and his mother said unto him, [2]Son, why hast thou thus dealt
50 with us? behold, thy father and I sought thee sorrowing. And he said
unto them, How is it that ye sought me? wist ye not that I must be [3]in my
Father's house? And they understood not the saying which he spake
unto them.

[1] Or, *teachers.* [2] Gr. *Child.* [3] Or, *about my Father's business.*

§ 19. THE EIGHTEEN YEARS* AT NAZARETH

Probably A.D. 7 to A.D. 26 (or 6 to 25)

Luke 2:51–52

51 And he went down with them, and came to Nazareth; and he was subject unto them: and his mother kept all *these* [1]sayings in her heart.

52 And Jesus advanced in wisdom and [2]stature, and in [3]favor with God and men [*see 1 Sam. 2:26*].

[1] Or, *things.* [2] Or, *age.* [3] Or, *grace.*

* After the return to Nazareth, we know nothing of Jesus' life at that place beyond the general statements of Luke 2:52, with the knowledge and dispositions indicated in the narrative of § 18 and the fact that he was a carpenter, until he comes forth to be baptized by John, his forerunner. The social and political conditions of this period in Galilee are described by Edersheim, D. Smith, and other writers on the Life of Jesus, and briefly stated in Broadus's Commentary on Matthew, p. 30 f. Dwell on the general statement of Luke 2:52. Other passages throw light on the life in Nazareth as to habits of worship (Luke 4:16), the family group of brothers and sisters (Mark 6:3 = Matt. 13:55 f.), work as carpenter (*ibid.*). A helpful book on this obscure period is Ramsay's *The Education of Christ*.

PART V

THE BEGINNING OF THE BAPTIST'S MINISTRY

Probably six months and in A.D. 25. In the Wilderness of Judea and beside the Jordan, §§ 20–23

§ 20. THE TIME OF THE BEGINNING

Mark 1:1

1 The beginning of the gospel of Jesus Christ [1]the Son of God.

Luke 3:1–2

1 Now in the fif-
teenth *year of the
reign of Tiberius
Cæsar, Pontius Pi-
late being governor
of Judea, and Herod
being tetrarch of
Galilee, and his
brother Philip tet-
rarch of the region
of Ituræa and Trach-
onitis, and Lysanias†
tetrarch of Abilene,
2 in the highpriest-
hood of Annas and
Caiaphas, the word
of God came unto
John the son of Zach-
arias in the wilder-
ness.

[1] Some ancient authorities omit *the son of God*.

§ 21. THE MESSAGE AND THE MESSENGER

Mark 1:2–6

2 Even as it is writ-
ten [1]in Isaiah the
prophet,

Behold, I send my
messenger before
thy face [*see*
Mal. 3:1],

Matt. 3:1–6

1 And in those days
cometh John the
Baptist, preaching in
the wilderness of
2 Judea, saying‡ Re-
pent ye; for the king-
dom of heaven is at

Luke 3:3–6

3 And he came into
all the region round
about Jordan, preach-
ing the baptism of
repentance unto re-
4 mission of sins; as it
is written in the book

* See note 6 at end of Harmony.

† See note 6. Luke follows the custom of ancient historians in dating events by the names of the rulers. As the son of a priest John was probably thirty years old when he came forth.

‡ See Mark 1:15 (= Matt. 4:17); Matt. 10:7; Acts 2:38.

Mark 1:2–6

Who shall prepare
thy way;
3 The voice of one
crying in the wil-
derness [*see Isa. 40: 3*],
Make ye ready the
way of the Lord,
Make his paths
straight;
4 John came, who bap-
tized in the wilder-
ness and preached
the baptism of re-
pentance unto re-
5 mission of sins. And
there went out unto
him all the country
of Judea, and all
they of Jerusalem;
and they were bap-
tized of him in the
river Jordan, con-
fessing their sins.
6 And John was cloth-
ed with camel's hair,
and *had* a leathern
girdle about his loins,
and did eat locusts
and wild honey.

Matt. 3:1–6

3 hand. For this is he
that was spoken of
[2]by Isaiah the proph-
et, saying,
The voice of one
crying in the wil-
derness,
Make ye ready the
way of the Lord,
Make his paths
straight.
4 Now John himself
had his raiment of
camel's hair, and a
leathern girdle about
his loins; and his
food was locusts and
5 wild honey. Then
went out unto him
Jerusalem, and all
Judea, and all the
region round about
6 Jordan; and they
were baptized of him
in the river Jordan,
confessing their sins.

Luke 3:3–6

of the words of Isaiah
the prophet,
The voice of one
crying in the wil-
derness,
Make ye ready the
way of the Lord,
Make his paths
straight.
5 Every valley shall
be filled,
And every moun-
tain and hill shall
be brought low;
And the crooked
shall become
straight,
And the rough
ways smooth;
6 And all flesh shall
see the salvation
of God [*see Isa. 40:4–5*].

[1] Some ancient authorities read *in the prophets*. [2] Or, *through*

§ 22. A SPECIMEN* OF JOHN'S PREACHING

Matt. 3:7–10

7 But when he saw many of the
Pharisees and Sadducees coming
to his baptism, he said unto them,
Ye offspring of vipers, who warned
you to flee from the wrath to
8 come? Bring forth therefore fruit
9 worthy of [1]repentance: and think
not to say within yourselves, We
have Abraham to our father: for
I say unto you, that God is able
of these stones to raise up children

Luke 3:7–14

7 He said therefore to the multi-
tude that went out to be baptized
of him, Ye offspring of vipers, who
warned you to flee from the wrath
8 to come? Bring forth therefore
fruits worthy of [1]repentance; and
begin not to say within yourselves,
We have Abraham to our father:
for I say unto you, that God is
able of these stones to raise up
9 children unto Abraham. And

* Here we see Matthew and Luke preserving a non-Markan section, as so frequently hereafter, an example of the so-called Logia (Discourses).

Matt. 3:10–10

10 unto Abraham. And even now
is the axe laid unto the root of the
trees: every tree therefore that
bringeth not forth good fruit is
hewn down, and cast into the fire.

Luke 3:9–14

even now is the axe also laid unto
the root of the trees: every tree
therefore that bringeth not forth
good fruit is hewn down, and cast
10 into the fire. And the multitudes
asked him, saying, What then must
11 we do? And he answered and
said unto them, He that hath two
coats, let him impart to him that
hath none; and he that hath food,
12 let him do likewise. And there
came also [2]publicans to be bap-
tized, and they said unto him,
13 [3]Master, what must we do? And
he said unto them, Extort no more
than that which is appointed
14 you. And [4]soldiers also asked
him, saying, And we, what must
we do? And he said unto them,
Do violence to no man, neither
[5]exact *anything* wrongfully; and be
content with your wages.

[1] Or, *your repentance.* [2] That is, *collectors or renters of Roman taxes.* [3] Or, *Teacher.* [4] Gr. *Soldiers in service.* [5] Or, *accuse any one.*

§ 23. THE FORERUNNER'S PICTURE OF THE MESSIAH BEFORE SEEING HIM

Mark 1:7–8

7 And he preached,
saying, There com-
eth after me he that
is mightier than I,
the latchet of whose
shoes I am not [2]wor-
thy to stoop down
8 and unloose. I bap-
tized you [1]with wa-
ter; but he shall bap-
tize you [1]with the
Holy Ghost.

Matt. 3:11–12

11 I indeed baptize
you [1]with water unto
repentance: but he
that cometh after me
is mightier than I,
whose shoes I am not
[2]worthy to bear: he
shall baptize you
[1]with the Holy Ghost
12 and *with* fire: whose
fan is in his hand,
and he will throughly
cleanse his threshing-
floor; and he will
gather his wheat into
the garner, but the
chaff he will burn up
with unquenchable
fire.

Luke 3:15–18

15 And as the peo-
ple were in expec-
tation, and all men
reasoned in their
hearts concerning
John, whether haply
he were the Christ;
16 John answered, say-
ing unto them all, I
indeed baptize you
with water; but there
cometh he that is
mightier than I, the
latchet of whose
shoes I am not [2]wor-
thy to unloose: he
shall baptize you
[1]with the [3]Holy Ghost
and *with* fire: whose
17 fan is in his hand,

Luke 3:15–18
throughly to cleanse
his threshing-floor,
and to gather the
wheat into his garner:
but the chaff he will
burn up with un-
quenchable fire.
18 With many other
exhortations there-
fore preached he
[4]good tidings unto
the people.*

[1] Or, *in*. [2] Gr. *sufficient*. [3] Or, *Holy Spirit*. [4] Or, *the gospel*.

* One can easily put together all that we are told of John the Baptist in John 1:6–15 and in Sections 4, 6, 8, 20, 21, 22, 23, 24, 26, 27, 28, 33, 34, 49, 57, 84, 133. See also Acts 1:5, 22; 10:37; 13:24; 18:25; 19:1–7. For a full discussion of the Baptist see my *John the Loyal*. These months of John's ministry prepared the way for the Messiah.

PART VI

THE BEGINNING OF CHRIST'S PUBLIC MINISTRY

The Year of Obscurity*

Probably Part of A.D. 26 and 27

In all parts of the Holy Land (the first Perean Ministry, the first Galilean Ministry, the first Judean Ministry, the first Samaritan Ministry). §§ 24–36. This early ministry includes the baptism, the temptation, John's witness to Jesus, the first disciples, the first miracle and work in Galilee, the first work in Judea, the arrest of John, the work in Samaria, and the return to Galilee.

§ 24. JESUS BAPTIZED BY JOHN IN THE JORDAN

Bethany beyond Jordan. Probably A.D. 26

Mark 1:9–11

9 And it came to pass in those days, that Jesus came from Nazareth of Galilee, and was baptized of John in the Jordan.

Matt. 3:13–17

13 Then cometh Jesus from Galilee to the †Jordan unto John, to be baptized of him.
14 But John would have hindered him, saying, I have need to be baptized of thee, and comest thou to
15 me? But Jesus answering said unto him, Suffer it now: for thus it becometh us to fulfil all righteousness. Then he

Luke 3:21–23

---

* The precise duration of this early ministry cannot be determined. Our Lord's baptism must have been at least two months *before* the Passover, and may have been some weeks or months earlier. Then the highly successful ministry in Judea *after* the Passover must have lasted several months (John 3:22; 4:1–3). If the "yet four months" in John 4:35 be understood to be not a common saying as to the usual interval between seedtime and harvest, but a statement that it was *then* just four months before harvest, that would make the Judean ministry extend eight months after the Passover. But this interpretation is upon the whole improbable, and we can only say that the opening ministry lasted several months. The time occupied makes very little difference for our understanding the events and discourses. All of the incidents during this period after the temptation are given in John's Gospel. But for the Fourth Gospel we should not know that Jesus did not plunge at once into the great Galilean Ministry.

† The Gospel of the Hebrews (one of the apocryphal gospels) is quoted by Jerome (*adv. Pelag.* iii. 2) as having the following: "Behold, the Lord's mother and His brethren were saying to Him, John the Baptist baptizes unto the remission of sins; let us go and be baptized by him. But he said unto them, What sin have I done, that I should go and be baptized by him? unless perchance this very thing which I have said is an ignorance."

Mark 1:9–11

10 And straightway
coming up out of the
water, he saw the
heavens rent asunder,
and the Spirit as a
dove descending up-
11 on him: and a voice
came out of the
heavens, Thou art
my beloved Son, in
thee I am well pleas-
ed [*see Ps. 2:7; Isa.
42:1*].

Matt. 3:13–17

16 suffereth [1]him. And
Jesus, when he was
baptized, went up
straightway from the
water: and lo, the
heavens were opened
[2]unto him, and he
saw the Spirit of
God descending as
a dove, and coming
17 upon him; and lo, a
voice out of the heav-
ens, saying, [3]This is
my beloved Son, in
whom I am well
pleased.

Luke 3:21–23

21 Now it came to
pass, when all the
people were baptized,
that Jesus also hav-
ing been baptized,
and praying, the
heaven was opened,
22 and the Holy Ghost
*descended in a bod-
ily form, as a dove,
upon him [*see John
1:32–34*], and a
voice came out of
heaven, Thou art my
beloved Son; in thee
†I am well pleased.
23 And Jesus himself,
when he began
to teach, was about
thirty years of age.

[1] Or, *me*. [2] Some ancient authorities omit *unto him*. [3] Or, *This is my son; my beloved in whom I am well pleased*. [4] Gr. *into*.

§ 25. THE THREE TEMPTATIONS‡ OF JESUS

The Wilderness of Judea. Probably A.D. 26

Mark 1:12–13

12 And straightway
the Spirit driveth him
forth into the wilder-
13 ness. And he was
in the wilderness
forty days tempted
of Satan; and he
was with the wild
beasts;

Matt. 4:1–11

1 Then was Jesus led
up of the Spirit into
the wilderness to be
tempted of the devil.
2 And when he had
fasted forty days and
forty nights, he af-
terward hungered.
3 And the tempter
came and said unto
him, If thou art the
Son of God, com-

Luke 4:1–13

1 And Jesus, full of
the Holy Spirit, re-
turned from the Jor-
dan, and was led [4]by
the Spirit in the wil-
derness during forty
2 days, being tempted
of the devil [*see Heb.
4:15*]. And he did eat
nothing in those days:
and when they were
completed, he hun-

* The Gospel of John does not describe the baptism of Jesus, but refers to the event in a way that shows knowledge of the Synoptic Gospels.

† Codex Bezae (D) reads in Luke: "Thou art my beloved son, to-day have I begotten thee." The Gospel of the Ebionites has: "Thou art my beloved son, in thee I am well pleased, to-day I have begotten thee."

See §85 for similar language at the Transfiguration.

‡ Mark gives only a summary account while the Logia (the oldest known record) tells the temptations in detail. This early document reveals the Messianic consciousness of Jesus as distinctly as it appears in the Gospel of John. The record of the baptism in § 24 and of the temptation in § 25 goes back to the two oldest strata of the Gospel sources (Mark or the Memoirs of Peter and the Logia of Matthew) and shows that Jesus enters upon his Messianic work knowing that he had his Father's approval and the power of the Holy Spirit upon him.

Matt. 4:1–11

mand that these
stones become [1]bread.
4 But he answered and
said, It is written [*see
Deut. 8:3*], Man shall
not live by bread
alone, but by every
word that proceed-
eth out of the mouth
5 of God. Then the
devil taketh him into
the holy city; and
he set him on the
[2]pinnacle of the tem-
6 ple, and saith unto
him, If thou art the
Son of God, cast thy-
self down: for it is
written [*see Ps. 91:11–
12*],

He shall give his
angels charge
concerning thee:
And on their hands
they shall bear
thee up,
Lest haply thou
dash thy foot
against a stone.

7 Jesus said unto him,
Again it is written
[*see Deut. 6:16*], Thou
shalt not tempt the
8 Lord thy God. Again
the devil taketh him
unto an exceeding
high mountain, and
sheweth him all the
kingdoms of the
world, and the glory
9 of them; and he said
unto him, All these
things will I give
thee, if thou wilt fall
down and worship
10 me. Then saith Jesus
unto him, Get thee
hence, Satan: for it is
written [*see Deut. 6:
13*], Thou shalt wor-

Luke 4:1–13

3 gered. And the devil
said unto him, If
thou art the Son of
God, command this
stone that it become
4 [4]bread. And Jesus
answered unto him,
It is written [*see Deut.
8:3*], Man shall not
live by bread alone.
5 And he led him up,
and shewed him all
the kingdoms of [5]the
world in a moment
6 of time. And the
devil said unto him,
To thee will I give
all this authority, and
the glory of them:
for it hath been de-
livered unto me; and
to whomsoever I will
7 I give it. If thou
therefore wilt worship
before me, it shall
8 all be thine. And
Jesus answered and
said unto him, It is
written [*see Deut. 6:
13*], Thou shalt wor-
ship the Lord thy God,
and him only shalt
9 thou serve. And he
led him to Jerusalem,
and set him on the
pinnacle of the tem-
ple, and said unto
him, If thou art the
Son of God, cast thy-
self down from hence:
10 for it is written [*see
Ps. 91:11–12*],

He shall give his
angels charge
concerning thee,
to guard thee:
11 And on their hands
they shall bear
thee up,
Lest haply thou

Mark 1:12–13	Matt. 4:1–11	Luke 4:1–13
	ship the Lord thy God, and him only shalt thou serve.	dash thy foot against a stone.
		12 And Jesus answering said unto him, It is said [*see Deut. 6:16*], Thou shalt not tempt the Lord thy God.
and the angels ministered unto him.	11 Then the devil leaveth him; and behold angels came and ministered unto him.	13 And when the devil had completed every temptation, he departed from him [6]for a season.

[1] Gr. *loaves.* [2] Gr. *wing.* [3] Gr. *in.* [4] Or, *a loaf.* [5] Gr. *the inhabited earth.* [6] Or, *until.*

§ 26. THE TESTIMONY OF THE BAPTIST TO THE COMMITTEE OF THE SANHEDRIN

At Bethany beyond Jordan

John 1:19–28

19 And this is the witness of John, when the Jews sent unto him from
20 Jerusalem priests and Levites to ask him, Who art thou? And he con-
21 fessed, and denied not: and he confessed, I am not the Christ. And
they asked him, What then? Art thou Elijah? And he saith, I am not.
22 Art thou the prophet? And he answered, No. They said therefore
unto him, Who art thou? that we may give an answer to them that sent
23 us. What sayest thou of thyself? He said, I am the voice of one crying
24 in the wilderness Make straight the way of the Lord, as said Isaiah the
25 prophet [*see Isa. 40:3*]. [1]And they had been sent from the Pharisees.* And
they asked him, and said unto him, Why then baptizest thou, if thou
art not the Christ, neither Elijah, neither the prophet? John answered
26 them, saying, I baptize [2]with water: in the midst of you standeth one
whom ye know not, *even* he that cometh after me, the latchet of whose
27 shoe I am not worthy to unloose. These things were done in [3]Bethany
28 beyond Jordan, where John was baptizing.

[1] Or, *And certain had been sent from among the Pharisees.* [2] Or, *in.* [3] Many ancient authorities read *Bethabarah*, some *Betharabah*.

§ 27. JOHN'S IDENTIFICATION OF JESUS AS THE MESSIAH

At Bethany beyond the Jordan

John 1:29–34

29 On the morrow he seeth Jesus coming unto him, and saith, Behold,
30 the Lamb of God, which [1]taketh away the sin of the world [*see Isa. 53:7*]!
This is he of whom I said, After me cometh a man which is become before

* In 1:19 the priests and Levites are Sadducees. The idea seems to be that the Pharisees had the Sadducees sent on this embassy (*cf.* § 22). Later Jesus will say that John was Elijah that was to come; some will even take Jesus to be Elijah.

John 1:29–34

31 me: for he was [2]before me. And I knew him not; but that he should be
32 made manifest to Israel, for this cause came I baptizing [3]with water.
And John bare witness, saying, I have beheld the Spirit descending as
33 a dove out of heaven; and it abode upon him. And I knew him not:
but he that sent me to baptize [3]with water, he said unto me, Upon whomsoever
thou shalt see the Spirit descending, and abiding upon him, the
34 same is he that baptizeth [3]with the Holy Spirit. And I have seen, and
have borne witness that this is the son of God.*

[1] Or, *beareth the sin*. [2] Gr. *first in regard of me*. [3] Or, *in*.

§ 28. JESUS MAKES HIS FIRST† DISCIPLES

At Bethany beyond the Jordan

John 1:35–51

35 Again on the morrow John was standing, and two of his disciples;
36 and he looked upon Jesus as he walked, and saith, Behold, the Lamb
37 of God [*see Isa. 53:7*]! And the two disciples heard him speak, and they
38 followed Jesus. And Jesus turned, and beheld them following, and saith
unto them, What seek ye? And they said unto him, Rabbi (which is to
39 say, being interpreted, [1]Master), where abidest thou? He saith unto
them, Come, and ye shall see. They came therefore and saw where he
abode; and they abode with him that day: it was about the tenth hour.
40 One of the two that heard John *speak*, and followed him, was Andrew,
41 Simon Peter's brother. He findeth first his own brother Simon, and
saith unto him, We have found the Messiah (which is, being interpreted,
42 [2]Christ). He brought him unto Jesus. Jesus looked upon him, and
said, thou art Simon the son of [3]John: thou shalt be called Cephas (which
is by interpretation, [4]Peter).
43 On the morrow he was minded to go forth into Galilee, and he findeth
Philip: and Jesus saith unto him, Follow me. Now Philip was from
44 Bethsaida, of the city of Andrew and Peter. Philip findeth Nathanael,
45 and saith unto him, We have found him, of whom Moses in the law,
46 and the prophets, did write, Jesus of Nazareth, the son of Joseph. And
Nathanael said unto him, Can any good thing come out of Nazareth?
47 Philip saith unto him, Come and see. Jesus saw Nathanael coming to
him, and saith of him, Behold, an Israelite indeed, in whom is no guile!
48 Nathanael saith unto him, Whence knowest thou me? Jesus answered
and said unto him, Before Philip called thee, when thou wast under the
49 fig tree, I saw thee. Nathanael answered him, Rabbi, thou art the son

* Put together the Baptist's testimonies to Jesus in sections 21, 22, 23, 24, 26, 27, 28, 33, 57. Add John 1:6–15. Note also the four testimonies of Jesus to John, sections 49, 57, 85, 133. Observe the four successive days here in John 1:19, 29, 35, 43, and the third day from the last in John 2:1, making a week that is covered in detail (*cf.* the Passion Week at the close). We have other glimpses of special days in the ministry, as the Busy Day of the blasphemous accusation and the parables (Matt. 12 and 13). In John 1:39 the very hour is preserved, probably Roman time (ten in the morning), as John writes long after the destruction of Jerusalem and outside of Palestine and uses the Roman reckoning (midnight to midnight) in John 20:19. But see note 11 at end of Harmony for Ramsay's objections to this view.

† Notice here a series of First Things; first testimony of John, first disciples, first miracle, first residence at Capernaum, first passover during his ministry, first extended discourse.

John 1:35-51

50 of God; thou art King of Israel* [*see 2 Sam. 7:14; Ps. 2:7*]. Jesus answered
and said unto him, Because I said unto thee, I saw thee underneath the
51 fig tree, believest thou? thou shalt see greater things than these. And he
saith unto him, Verily, verily, I say unto you, Ye shall see the heaven
opened, and the angels of God ascending and descending upon the Son
of man† [*see Gen. 28:12*].

[1] Or, *Teacher*. [2] That is, *Anointed*. [3] Gr. *Joanes:* called in Matt. 16:17 *Jonah*. [4] That is, *Rock or Stone*.

§ 29. JESUS WORKS HIS FIRST MIRACLE

At Cana in Galilee

John 2:1-11

1 And the third day there was a marriage in Cana of Galilee: and the
2 mother of Jesus was there: and Jesus also was bidden, and his disciples,
3 to the marriage. And when the wine failed, the mother of Jesus saith
4 unto him, They have no wine. And Jesus saith unto her, Woman, what
5 have I to do with thee? mine hour is not yet come. His mother saith
6 unto the servants, Whatsoever he saith unto you, do it. Now there
were six waterpots of stone set there after the Jews' manner of purifying,
7 containing two or three firkins apiece. Jesus saith unto them, Fill the
8 waterpots with water. And they filled them up to the brim. And he
saith unto them, Draw out now, and bear unto the [1]ruler of the feast.
9 And they bare it. And when the ruler of the feast tasted the water [2]now
become wine, and knew not whence it was (but the servants which had
drawn the water knew), the ruler of the feast calleth the bridegroom,
10 and saith unto him, Every man setteth on first the good wine; and when
men have drunk freely, *then* that which is worse: thou hast kept the good
11 wine until now. This beginning of his signs did Jesus in Cana of Galilee,
and manifested his glory; and his disciples believed on him.

[1] Or, *steward*. [2] Or, *that it had become*.

§ 30. JESUS MAKES A FIRST SOJOURN AT CAPERNAUM, ACCOMPANIED BY HIS KINDRED AND HIS EARLY DISCIPLES

(Later Capernaum will become his home)

John 2:12

12 After this he went down to Capernaum, he, and his mother, and *his*
brethren, and his disciples: and there they abode not many days.

* Notice that these first disciples at once believed that Jesus was the Messiah (ver. 41, 45, 49). Compare the confession of Jesus (§ 35) to the Woman at Jacob's well and the confessions of Peter in Matt. 14:33; John 6:69; Matt. 16:16 (§§ 74, 76, 83).

† *Cf.* the close of the temptation in the wilderness and the experience in the Garden of Gethsemane.

§ 31. THE FIRST* CLEANSING OF THE TEMPLE AT THE PASSOVER

Jerusalem.† Probably A.D. 27

John 2:13–22

13 And the passover‡ of the Jews was at hand, and Jesus went up to
14 Jerusalem. And he found in the temple those who sold oxen and sheep
15 and doves, and the changers of money sitting: and he made a scourge
of cords, and cast all out of the temple, both the sheep and the oxen;
16 and he poured out the changers' money, and overthrew their tables;
and to them that sold the doves he said, Take these things hence; make
17 not my Father's house a house of merchandise. His disciples remembered
18 that it was written, The zeal of thine house shall eat me up [*see Ps. 69:9*].
The Jews therefore answered and said unto him, What sign shewest
19 thou unto us, seeing thou doest these things? Jesus answered and said
unto them, Destroy this [1]temple, and in three days I will raise it up.
20 The Jews therefore said, Forty and six years was this [1]temple in building,
21 and wilt thou raise it up in three days? But he spake of the [1]temple of
22 his body. When therefore he was raised from the dead, his disciples
remembered that he spake this; and they believed the scripture, and
the word which Jesus had said.

[1] Or, *sanctuary*.

§ 32. THE INTERVIEW OF NICODEMUS WITH JESUS

At Jerusalem during the Passover

John 2:23 to 3:21

23 Now when he was in Jerusalem at the passover, during the feast, many
24 believed on his name, beholding his signs which he did. But Jesus did
25 not trust himself unto them, for that he knew all men, and because he
needed not that any one should bear witness concerning [1]man: for he
himself knew what was in man.
1 Now there was a man of the Pharisees, named Nicodemus,§ a ruler
2 of the Jews: the same came unto him by night, and said to him, Rabbi,
we know that thou art a teacher come from God: for no man can do
3 these signs that thou doest, except God be with him. Jesus answered
and said unto him, Verily, verily, I say unto thee, Except a man be born

* Many scholars consider this the same incident as that in the Synoptic Gospels and placed by them in Passion Week (§ 129) probably on Monday. It is urged that Jesus would not have repeated such an act and hence one must follow either the order of John or of the Synoptics. But there is no inherent difficulty in the repetition of such an act when one reflects on the natural indignation of Jesus at the desecration of the temple on his visit during his ministry and considers that Jesus may have wished to make one last protest at the close of his ministry. Certainty, of course, is not possible in such an argument one way or the other.

† Observe the successive *scenes* of this early ministry—beside the Jordan, on the eastern side, at Cana of Galilee, at Capernaum, at Jerusalem, in Judea, in Samaria.

‡ This is the first of the passovers in John's Gospel (2:13; 6:4; 13:1). There may have been another.

§ Nicodemus appears as an exception to the statement of 2:24, as one whom Jesus did trust, and who amid all difficulties of temperament and station proved not unworthy of the trust.

John 2:23 to 3:21

4 [2]anew, he cannot see the kingdom of God. Nicodemus saith unto him,
How can a man be born when he is old? can he enter a second time into
5 his mother's womb, and be born? Jesus answered, Verily, verily, I say
unto thee, Except a man be born of water and the Spirit, he cannot enter
6 into the kingdom of God. That which is born of the flesh is flesh; and
that which is born of the Spirit is spirit. Marvel not that I said unto
7 thee, Ye must be born [2]anew. [3]The wind bloweth where it listeth, and
8 thou hearest the voice thereof, but knowest not whence it cometh, and
9 whither it goeth: so is every one that is born of the Spirit. Nicodemus
10 answered and said unto him, How can these things be? Jesus answered
and said unto him, Art thou the teacher of Israel, and understandest not
11 these things? Verily, verily, I say unto thee, We speak that we do know,
12 and bear witness of that we have seen; and ye receive not our witness. If
I told you earthly things, and ye believe not, how shall ye believe, if I
13 tell you heavenly things? And no man hath ascended into heaven, but
he that descended out of heaven, *even* the Son of man, [4]which is in heaven.
14 And as Moses lifted up the serpent in the wilderness [*see Num. 21:8-9*],
even so must the Son of man be lifted up: that whosoever [5]believeth may
15 in him have eternal life.
16 For God so loved the world, that he gave his only begotten Son, that
whosoever believeth on him should not perish, but have eternal life.
17 For God sent not the Son into the world to judge the world; but that
18 the world should be saved through him. He that believeth on him is
not judged; he that believeth not has been judged already, because he
19 hath not believed on the name of the only begotten Son of God. And this
is the judgment, that the light is come into the world, and men loved the
20 darkness rather than the light; for their works were evil. For every one
that [6]doeth ill hateth the light, and cometh not to the light, lest his works
21 should be [7]reproved. But he that doeth the truth cometh to the light,
that his works may be made manifest, [8]that they have been wrought in
God.

[1] Or, *a man, for . . . the man.* [2] Or, *from above.* [3] Or, *The Spirit breatheth.* [4] Many ancient authorities omit *which is in heaven.* [5] Or, *believeth in him may have.* [6] Or, *practiseth.* [7] Or, *convicted.* [8] Or, *because.*

§ 33. THE PARALLEL *MINISTRY OF JESUS AND JOHN WITH JOHN'S LOYALTY TO JESUS

John 3:22-36

22 After these things came Jesus and his disciples into the land of Judea;
23 and there he tarried with them, and baptized. And John also was baptiz-
ing in Ænon near to Salim, because there [1]was much water there; and
24 they came, and were baptized. For John was not yet cast into prison.
25 There arose therefore a questioning on the part of John's disciples with a
26 Jew about purifying. And they came unto John, and said to him, Rabbi,
he that was with thee beyond Jordan, to whom thou hast borne witness,
27 behold, the same baptizeth, and all men come to him. John answered and

* Jesus gained his first disciples from John at Bethany beyond Jordan and many in Jerusalem. Now he is surpassing John. On John's loyalty to Jesus see my *John the Loyal.*

John 3:22-36

said, A man can receive nothing, except it have been given him from
28 heaven. Ye yourselves bear me witness, that I said, I am not the Christ,
29 but, that I am sent before him. He that hath the bride is the bridegroom:
but the friend of the bridegroom, which standeth and heareth him, re-
joiceth greatly because of the bridegroom's voice: this my joy therefore is
30 fulfilled. He must increase, but I must decrease.
31 He that cometh from above is above all: he that is of the earth is of
the earth, and of the earth he speaketh: [2]he that cometh from heaven
32 is above all. What he hath seen and heard, of that he beareth witness;
33 and no man receiveth his witness. He that hath received his witness
34 hath set his seal to *this*, that God is true. For he whom God hath sent
speaketh the words of God: for he giveth not the Spirit by measure.
35 The Father loveth the Son, and hath given all things into his hand. He
36 that believeth on the Son hath eternal life; but he that [3]obeyeth not the
Son shall not see life, but the wrath of God abideth on him.

[1] Gr. *were many waters*. [2] Some ancient authorities read *he that cometh from heaven beareth witness of what he hath seen and heard*. [3] Or, *believeth not*.

§ 34. CHRIST'S REASONS FOR LEAVING JUDEA

John 4:1-4

1 When therefore the Lord knew how that the Pharisees had heard that
2 Jesus was making and baptizing more disciples than John (although
3 Jesus himself baptized not, but his disciples), he left Judea, and departed
4 again into Galilee. And he must needs pass through Samaria.

Luke 3:19, 20

19 But Herod the tetrarch, being reproved by him for Herodias his
brother's wife, and for all the evil things which Herod had done, added
20 yet this above all, that he shut up John in prison.*

Mark 1:14	Matt. 4:12	Luke 4:14
14 Now after that John was delivered up Jesus came into Galilee.	12 Now when he heard that John was delivered up he withdrew into Galilee.	14 And Jesus returned in the power of the Spirit into Galilee.

§ 35. JESUS IN SAMARIA.†

At Jacob's Well and in Sychar

John 4:5-42

5 So he cometh to a city of Samaria, called Sychar, near to the parcel of
ground that Jacob gave to his son Joseph: and Jacob's [1]well was there
6 [*see Josh. 24:32*]. Jesus therefore, being wearied with his journey, sat [2]thus

* The place of John's imprisonment was Machærus, east of the Dead Sea. See Josephus, *War*, Ch. VII, vi. In *Antiquities*, Ch. XVIII, v, 2 Josephus gives the public and political reason for John's imprisonment because of Herod's fear of a revolution. He "feared lest the great influences John had over the people might put it into his power and inclination to raise a rebellion."

† Notice that John also had recently been preaching to Samaritans (§ 33) and compare hereafter Philip's work in the city of Samaria (Acts 8:5 ff.)

John 4:5-42

7 by the well.[1] It was about the sixth hour. There cometh a woman of
8 Samaria to draw water: Jesus saith unto her, Give me to drink. For
9 his disciples were gone away into the city to buy food. The Samaritan
woman therefore saith unto him, How is it that thou, being a Jew, askest
drink of me, which am a Samaritan woman? ([3]For Jews have no dealings
10 with Samaritans.) Jesus answered and said unto her, If thou knewest
the gift of God, and who it is that saith to thee, Give me to drink; thou
wouldest have asked of him, and he would have given thee living water.
11 The woman saith unto him, [4]Sir, thou hast nothing to draw with, and the
12 well is deep: from whence then hast thou that living water? Art thou
greater than our father Jacob, which gave us the well, and drank thereof
13 himself, and his sons, and his cattle? Jesus answered and said unto her,
14 Every one that drinketh of this water shall thirst again: but whosoever
drinketh of the water that I shall give him shall never thirst; but the water
that I shall give him shall become in him a well of water springing up unto
15 eternal life. The woman saith unto him, [4]Sir, give me this water, that
16 I thirst not, neither come all the way hither to draw. Jesus saith unto
17 her, Go, call thy husband, and come hither. The woman answered and
18 said unto him, I have no husband. Jesus saith unto her, Thou saidst well,
I have no husband: for thou hast had five husbands; and he whom thou
19 now hast is not thy husband: this hast thou said truly. The woman
20 saith unto him, [4]Sir, I perceive that thou art a prophet. Our fathers
worshipped in this mountain; and ye say, that in Jerusalem is the place
21 where men ought to worship. Jesus saith unto her, Woman, believe me,
the hour cometh, when neither in this mountain, nor in Jerusalem, shall
22 ye worship the Father. Ye worship that which ye know not; we worship
23 that which we know: for salvation is from the Jews. But the hour cometh,
and now is, when the true worshippers shall worship the Father in spirit
24 and truth: [5]for such doth the Father seek to be his worshippers. [6]God is a
25 Spirit: and they that worship him must worship in spirit and truth. The
woman saith unto him, I know that Messiah cometh (which is called
26 Christ): when he is come, he will declare unto us all things. Jesus saith
unto her, I that speak unto thee am *he*.

27 And upon this came his disciples; and they marvelled that he was
speaking with a woman; yet no man said, What seekest thou? or, Why
28 speakest thou with her? So the woman left her waterpot, and went
29 away into the city, and saith to the men, Come, see a man, which told
30 me all things that *ever* I did: can this be the Christ? They went out of
31 the city, and were coming to him. In the mean while the disciples
32 prayed him, saying, Rabbi, eat. But he said to them, I have meat to
33 eat that ye know not. The disciples therefore said one to another, Hath
34 any man brought him *aught* to eat? Jesus saith unto them, My meat is
35 to do the will of him that sent me, and to accomplish his work. Say not
ye, There are yet four months, and *then* cometh the harvest? behold, I
say unto you, Lift up your eyes, and look on the fields, that they are
36 [7]white already unto harvest. He that reapeth receiveth wages, and
gathereth fruit unto life eternal; that he that soweth and he that reapeth
37 may rejoice together. For herein is the saying true, One soweth and
38 another reapeth. I sent you to reap that whereon ye have not laboured:
others have laboured, and ye are entered into their labour.

John 4:5–42

39 And from that city many of the Samaritans believed on him *because
of the word of the woman, who testified, He told me all things that *ever* I
40 did. So when the Samaritans came unto him, they besought him to abide
41 with them: and he abode there two days. And many more believed
42 because of his word; and they said to the woman, Now we believe, not
because of thy speaking: for we have heard for ourselves, and know that
this is indeed the Saviour of the world.†

[1] Gr. *spring:* and so in ver. 14; but not in ver. 11, 12. [2] Or, *as he was.* [3] Some ancient authorities omit *For Jews have no dealings with Samaritans.* [4] Or, *Lord.* [5] Or, *for such the Father also seeketh.* [6] Or, *God's spirit.* [7] Or, *white unto harvest. Already he that reapeth, &c.*

§ 36. THE ARRIVAL OF JESUS IN GALILEE

John 4:43–45

43 And after the two days he went forth from thence into Galilee. For
44 Jesus himself testified, that a prophet hath no honour in his own country
45 [*see Luke 4:24; Mark 6:4; Matt. 13:57*]. So when he came into Galilee, the
Galileans received him, having seen all the things that he did in Jerusalem
at the feast: for they also went unto the feast.

* See note on p. 27.

† In this early ministry Jesus allowed himself to be regarded as the Messiah by his first disciples (§ 28), and personally declared that he was the Messiah to the woman at the well (§ 35) (John 4:26), which many other Samaritans also personally believed (John 4:39, 42). He never declared this to the Jewish rulers at Jerusalem till the very end (§ 156), doubtless because such an avowal would lead them to kill him, and so must not be made till his work in teaching the people and training his disciples should be completed. Compare what he says later to Peter in Matt. 16:17–20 (§ 82). At the baptism and the temptation of Jesus it was clear that Jesus knew that he was the Son of God, the Messiah, and was so regarded by the Baptist. Events in Judea and Galilee change the early policy of Jesus and lead to silence on his part in the use of the word Messiah, though many of the people know that he makes Messianic claims and the rulers in Jerusalem come to suspect him and to fear him. See my volume on *The Pharisees and Jesus.*

PART VII

THE GREAT GALILEAN MINISTRY

Probably* Autumn of A.D. 27 to Spring of 29

(Apparently about a year and a half)

§§ *37–71. Great fulness of detail in Mark for this period and condensed report in Luke while Matthew is chiefly topical in this portion. Mark's Gospel plunges at once into the Great Galilean Ministry (cf. Peter's summary of Christ's life in Acts 10:36–43 to the household of Cornelius). The mass of material makes clear grouping difficult, but there is progress† in the development of events.*

1. The Rejection at Nazareth and the New Home in Capernaum, §§ 37–43.
2. The First Tour of Galilee with the Four Fishermen and the Call of Matthew (Levi) on the Return with the Growing Fame of Jesus, §§ 44–48.
3. The Sabbath Controversy in Jerusalem and in Galilee, §§ 49–51.
4. The Choice of the Twelve and the Sermon on the Mount, §§ 52–54.
5. The Spread of Christ's Influence and the Inquiry from John in Prison, §§ 55–59.
6. The Second Tour of Galilee (now with the Twelve) and the Intense Hostility of the Pharisees, §§ 60–63.
7. The First Great Group of Parables with the Visit to Gerasa (Khersa) and to Nazareth (final one), §§ 64–69.
8. The Third Tour of Galilee (Following the Twelve) and the Effect on Herod Antipas, §§ 70–71.

---

* We cannot confidently determine the length of the ministry in Galilee. We are not sure whether it *began* in summer or late autumn (see footnote 7 in Explanatory Notes at end of Harmony). If the feast of John 5:1 was a passover or there is an unknown passover, the Galilean ministry lasted at least sixteen months, for it *ended* when another passover was near (John 6:4). Otherwise we should not certainly know that it lasted more than some six or eight months. About the two subsequent periods of our Lord's ministry we shall find no room to question that each lasted six months; but *here* we have to admit much uncertainty as to the time. After all, a determination of the time employed would be a matter of very little importance to our study of this period. But the immense amount of material in this period argues for a length of over a year.

† Throughout this great ministry in Galilee, and the periods that will follow after, the reader ought to trace carefully the *progress* of the history along several lines: (1) the Saviour's progressive self-manifestation; (2) the gradual training of the Twelve who are to carry on his teaching and work after his death; (3) the deepening and spreading hostility of the Jewish influential classes and official rulers. By constantly observing these parallel lines of progress, it will be seen that the history and teachings of our Lord exhibit a vital growth, moving on to an end by him foreseen (Luke 12:50), when the hostility of the rulers will culminate as he before the Sanhedrin avows himself to be the Messiah, and the Twelve will be almost prepared to succeed him.

§ 37. GENERAL ACCOUNT OF HIS TEACHING IN GALILEE

Mark 1:14–15

14 [Now after that
John was delivered
up, Jesus came into
Galilee], preaching
the gospel of God,
15 and saying, The
time is fulfilled, and
the kingdom of God
is at hand: repent
ye, and believe in
the gospel.

Matt. 4:17

17 From that time be-
gan Jesus to preach,
and to say, Repent
ye; for the kingdom
of heaven is at hand.

Luke 4:14–15

14 [And Jesus return-
ed in the power of
[*see John 4:3, 43*] the
Spirit into Galilee]:
and a fame went out
concerning him
through all the region
15 round about. And
he taught in their
synagogues, being
glorified of all.

In sections 38–43 (the Rejection at Nazareth and the New Home in Capernaum) Jesus revisits Cana and Nazareth, recalls the four fishermen by the Sea of Galilee, and begins his ministry of teaching and healing in Capernaum.

§ 38. THE HEALING AT CANA OF THE SON OF A COURTIER OF CAPERNAUM

John 4:46–54

46 He came therefore again unto Cana of Galilee, where he made the
47 water wine. And there was a certain [1]nobleman, whose son was sick at
Capernaum. When he heard that Jesus was come out of Judea into
Galilee, he went unto him, and besought *him* that he would come down,
48 and heal his son; for he was at the point of death. Jesus therefore said
49 unto him, Except ye see signs and wonders, ye will in no wise believe.
50 The [1]nobleman saith unto him. [2]Sir, come down ere my child die. Jesus
saith unto him, Go thy way; thy son liveth. The man believed the word
51 that Jesus spake unto him, and he went his way. And as he was now
52 going down, his [3]servants met him, saying, that his son lived. So he
inquired of them the hour when he began to amend. They said therefore
53 unto him, Yesterday at the seventh hour the fever left him. So the
father knew that *it was* at that hour in which Jesus said unto him, Thy
54 son liveth: and himself believed, and his whole house. This is again the
second sign that Jesus did, having come out of Judea into Galilee.

[1] Or, *king's officer*. [2] Or, *Lord*. [3] Gr. *bond-servants*.

§ 39. THE FIRST REJECTION AT NAZARETH

Luke 4:16–31

16 And he came to Nazareth, where he had been brought up: and he
entered, as his custom was, into the synagogue on the sabbath day, and
17 stood up to read. And there was delivered unto him [1]the book of the

Luke 4:16–31

prophet Isaiah. And he opened the [2]book, and found the place where
it was written,
18 The Spirit of the Lord is upon me,
[3]Because he anointed me to preach [4]good tidings to the poor:
He hath sent me to proclaim release to the captives,
And recovering of sight to the blind,
To set at liberty them that are bruised
19 To proclaim the acceptable year of the Lord [*see Isa. 58:6; 61:1–2*].
20 And he closed the [2]book, and gave it back to the attendant, and sat down:
21 and the eyes of all in the synagogue were fastened on him. And he
began to say unto them, To-day hath this scripture been fulfilled in your
22 ears. And all bare him witness, and wondered at the words of grace
which proceeded out of his mouth: and they said, Is not this Joseph's son?
23 And he said unto them, Doubtless ye will say unto me this parable, Physi-
cian, heal thyself [*see John 6:42; 7:15*]: whatsoever we have heard done
24 at Capernaum, do also here in thine own country. And he said, Verily
I say unto you, No prophet is acceptable in his own country [*see John 4:44*].
25 But of a truth I say unto you, There were many widows in Israel in the
days of Elijah, when the heaven was shut up three years and six months,
when there came a great famine over all the land [*see 1 Kings 17:1; 18:1–2*];
26 and unto none of them was Elijah sent, but only to [5]Zarephath, in the
land of Sidon, unto a woman that was a widow [*see 1 Kings 17:8–9*]. And
27 there were many lepers in Israel in the time of Elisha the prophet; and
none of them was cleansed, but only Naaman the Syrian [*see 2 Kings 5:1, 14*].
28 And they were all filled with wrath in the synagogue, as they heard these
29 things; and they rose up, and cast him forth out of the city, and led him
unto the brow of the hill whereon their city was built, that they might
30 throw him down headlong. But he passing through the midst of them
31 went his way. And he came down to Capernaum, a city of Galilee.

[1] Or, *a roll.* [2] Or, *roll.* [3] Or, *wherefore.* [4] Or, *the gospel.* [5] Gr. *Sarepta.*

§ 40. THE NEW HOME IN CAPERNAUM

Matt. 4:13–16

13 And leaving Nazareth* he came and dwelt in Capernaum, which is by
14 the sea, in the borders of Zebulun and Naphtali; that it might be fulfilled
which was spoken [1]by Isaiah the prophet [*see Isa. 8:23; 9:1–2*], saying,
15 The land of Zebulun and the land of Naphtali,
[2]Toward the sea, beyond Jordan,
Galilee of the [3]Gentiles,
16 The people which sat in darkness
Saw a great light
And to them which sat in the region and shadow of death,
To them did light spring up.

[1] Or, *through.* [2] Gr. *the way of the sea.* [3] *Nations*, and so elsewhere.

* Nazareth was never the Saviour's residence during his public ministry. After the wedding at Cana he lived a short time at *Capernaum*, and henceforth that city will be his abode, till he leaves Galilee six months before the crucifixion—most of the time, however, being actually spent in several journeys throughout Galilee, together with a trip to Jerusalem, and retirement to districts around Galilee.

§41. JESUS FINDS FOUR FISHERS OF MEN IN FOUR FISHERMEN*

By the Sea of Galilee, near Capernaum

Mark 1:16–20

16 And passing along
by the sea of Galilee,
he saw Simon and
Andrew the brother
of Simon casting a
net in the sea: for
they were fishers.
17 And Jesus said unto
them, Come ye after
me, and I will make
you to become fishers
18 of men. And straight-
way they left the
nets, and followed
19 him. And going on
a little further, he
saw James the *son* of
Zebedee, and John
his brother, who were
also in the boat mend-
20 ing the nets. And
straightway he called
them: and they left
their father Zebedee
in the boat with the
hired servants, and
went after him.

Matt. 4:18–22

18 And walking by
the sea of Galilee, he
saw two brethren,
Simon who is called
Peter, and Andrew
his brother, casting
a net into the sea;
for they were fishers.
19 And he saith unto
them, Come ye after
me, and I will make
you fishers of men.
20 And they straight-
way left the nets, and
21 followed him. And
going on from thence
he saw other two
brethren, [1]James the
son of Zebedee, and
John his brother, in
the boat with Zebedee
their father, mending
their nets; and he
22 called them. And they
straightway left the
boat and their father,
and followed him.*

Luke 5:1–11

1 Now it came to
pass, while the mul-
titude pressed upon
him, and heard the
word of God, that he
was standing by the
lake of Gennesaret;
2 and he saw two boats
standing by the lake:
but the fishermen had
gone out of them, and
were washing their
3 nets. And he entered
into one of the boats,
which was Simon's,
and asked him to
put out a little from
the land. And he
sat down and taught
the multitudes out of
4 the boat. And when
he had left speaking,
he said unto Simon,
Put out into the
deep, and let down
your nets for a
5 draught. And Simon
answered and said,
Master, we toiled all
6 night, and took nothing: but at thy word I will let down the nets. And
when they had this done, they inclosed a great multitude of fishes; and
7 their nets were breaking; and they beckoned unto their partners in the
other boat, that they should come and help them. And they came, and
8 filled both the boats, so that they began to sink. But Simon Peter, when
he saw it, fell down at Jesus' knees, saying, Depart from me; for I am a
9 sinful man, O Lord. For he was amazed, and all that were with him,
10 at the draught of the fishes which they had taken; and so were also James
and John, sons of Zebedee, which were partners with Simon. And Jesus
11 said unto Simon, Fear not; from henceforth thou shalt [2]catch men. And
when they had brought their boats to land, they left all, and followed him.

[1] Or, *Jacob:* and so elsewhere. [2] Gr. *take alive.*

* Three of these two pairs of brothers (Andrew and Peter, John and James) had already become disciples of Jesus at Bethany beyond Jordan (James probably soon afterwards), but now they leave their prosperous fish business and follow Jesus continuously as many business men since have given up a lucrative business for the ministry. They, along with Philip and Nathaniel, had been with Jesus in the early ministry (the year of obscurity).

§ 42. THE EXCITEMENT IN THE SYNAGOGUE BECAUSE OF THE TEACHING OF JESUS AND THE HEALING OF A DEMONIAC ON THE SABBATH

Mark 1:21-28

21 And they go into Capernaum;
and straightway on the sabbath
day he entered into the syna-
22 gogue and taught. And they
were astonished at his teaching:
for he taught them as having au-
thority, and not as the scribes.
23 And straightway there was in
their synagogue a man with an
unclean spirit, and he cried out,
24 saying, What have we to do with
thee, thou Jesus of Nazareth?
art thou come to destroy us? I
know thee who thou art, the
25 Holy One of God. And Jesus re-
buked [1]him, saying, hold thy
peace, and come out of him.
26 And the unclean spirit, [2]tearing
him and crying with a loud voice,
27 came out of him. And they were
all amazed, insomuch that they
questioned among themselves, say-
ing, What is this? a new teach-
ing! with authority he command-
eth even the unclean spirits, and
28 they obey him. And the report of
him went out straightway every-
where into all the region of Galilee
round about.

Luke 4:31-37

31 [And he came down to Caper-
naum, a city of Galilee.] And he
was teaching them on the sab-
32 bath day: and they were aston-
ished at his teaching; for his
33 word was with authority. And
in the synagogue there was a
man, which had a spirit of an
unclean [3]devil; and he cried out
34 with a loud voice, [4]Ah! what have
we to do with thee, thou Jesus of
Nazareth? art thou come to de-
stroy us? I know thee who thou
art [*see Ps. 16:10*], the Holy One
of God.
35 And Jesus rebuked him, saying,
Hold thy peace, and come out of
him. And when the [3]devil had
thrown him down in the midst, he
came out of him, having done him
36 no hurt. And amazement came
upon all, and they spake together,
one with another, saying, What
is [5]this word? for with authority
and power he commandeth the
unclean spirits, and they come
37 out. And there went forth a
rumour concerning him into every
place of the region round about.

[1] Or, *it*. [2] Or, *convulsing*. [3] Gr. *demon*. [4] Or, *let alone*. [5] Or, *this word, that with authority—come out?*

§ 43. HE HEALS PETER'S MOTHER-IN-LAW AND MANY OTHERS

At Capernaum, in Peter's Home

Mark 1:29-34

29 And straightway
[3]when they were come
out of the synagogue,
they came into the
house of Simon and
Andrew, with James
30 and John. Now Si-

Matt. 8:14-17

Luke 4:38-41

38 And he rose up
from the synagogue
and entered into the
house of Simon. And
Simon's wife's moth-
er was holden with a

Mark 1:29–34

mon's wife's mother
lay sick of a fever;
and straightway they
31 tell him of her: and
he came and took
her by the hand, and
raised her up; and
the fever left her,
and she ministered
unto them.
32 And at even, when
the sun did set,
they brought unto
him all that were
sick, and them that
were [1]possessed with
33 devils. And all the
city was gathered together
at the door.
34 And he healed many
that were sick with
divers diseases, and
cast out many [4]devils;
and he suffered not
the [4]devils to speak,
because they knew
him.[5]

Matt. 8:14–17

14 And when Jesus
was come into Peter's
house, he saw
his wife's mother lying
sick of a fever.
15 And he touched her
hand, and the fever
left her; and she
arose, and ministered
unto him.
16 And when even was
come, they brought
unto him many [1]possessed
with devils:
and he cast out the
spirits with a word,
and healed all that
17 were sick: that it
might be fulfilled
which was spoken
[2]by Isaiah the prophet
[*see Isa. 53:4*], saying,
Himself took our
infirmities, and bare
our diseases.

Luke 4:38–41

great fever; and they
besought him for
39 her. And he stood
over her, and rebuked
the fever; and it left
her: and immediately
she rose up and ministered
unto them.
40 And when the sun
was setting, all they
that had any sick
with divers diseases
brought them unto
him; and he laid his
hands on every one
of them, and healed
41 them. And [4]devils
also came out from
many, crying out, and
saying, Thou art the
Son of God. And
rebuking them, he
suffered them not to
speak, because they
knew that he was
the Christ.

[1] Or, *demoniacs*. [2] Or, *through*. [3] Some ancient authorities read *when he was come out of the synagogue, he came, &c.* [4] Gr. *demons*. [5] Many ancient authorities add *to be Christ*. See Luke 4:41.

In sections 44–52 Jesus makes his first tour of Galilee with the Four Fishermen whom he has now called to follow him continuously. On the return to Capernaum Matthew is called and various miracles arouse the enthusiasm of the multitudes and the hostility of the Pharisees to Christ's teachings.

§44. THE FIRST TOUR OF GALILEE WITH THE FOUR FISHERMEN

Mark 1:35–39

35 And in the morning,
a great while
before day, he rose
up and went out,
and departed into a
desert place, and

Luke 4:42–44

42 And when it was
day, he came out and
went into a desert
place: and the multitudes
sought after
him, and came unto

Mark 1:35–39

36 there prayed. And
Simon and they that
were with him fol-
37 lowed after him; and
they found him, and
say unto him, All
are seeking thee.
38 And he saith unto
them, Let us go else-
where into the next
towns, that I may
preach there also; for
to this end came I
39 forth. And he went
into their syna-
gogues throughout
all Galilee, preach-
ing and casting out
[4]devils.

Matt. 4:23–25

23 And [1]Jesus went
about in all Galilee,*
teaching in their
synagogues, and
preaching the [2]gos-
pel of the kingdom,
and healing all man-
ner of disease and all
manner of sickness
24 among the people. And the report
of him went forth into all Syria:
and they brought unto him all that
were sick, holden with divers
diseases and torments, [3]possessed
with devils, and epileptic, and
25 palsied; and he healed them. And
there followed him great multi-
tudes from Galilee and Decapolis
and Jerusalem and Judea and
from beyond Jordan.

Luke 4:42–44

him, and would have
stayed him, that he
should not go from
43 them. But he said
unto them, I must
preach the [5]good ti-
dings of the king-
dom of God to the
other cities also; for
therefore was I sent.
44 And he was preach-
ing in the synagogues
of [6]Galilee.

[1] Some ancient authorities read *he*. [2] Or, *good tidings*: and so elsewhere. [3] Or, *demoniacs* [4] Gr. *demons*. [5] Or, *Gospel*. [6] Very many ancient authorities read *Judea*.

§ 45. A LEPER HEALED, AND MUCH POPULAR EXCITEMENT

Mark 1:40–45

40 And there cometh to
him a leper, beseech-
ing him, [1]and kneel-
ing down to him,
and saying unto him,
If thou wilt, thou
canst make me clean.
41 And being moved
with compassion, he

Matt. 8:2–4

2 And behold, there
came to him a leper
and worshipped him,
saying, Lord, if thou
wilt thou canst make
me clean,
3 And he stretched
forth his hand, and

Luke 5:12–16

12 And it came to
pass, while he was
in one of the cities,
behold, a man full of
leprosy: and when
he saw Jesus, he fell
on his face, and be-
sought him, saying,
Lord, if thou wilt,

* This journey about all Galilee included a *great mass* of teaching and healing (dwell on Matt. 4:23–25), of which only a few specimens are recorded, and these apparently occurred at Capernaum, his headquarters. The journey given by Luke only (8:1–3) is probably distinct from this, and if so it would be a *second*, while that of Luke 9:1–6(=Mark 6:6–13=Matt. 9:35, 11:1), which is quite certainly distinct, would then be a *third* journey about Galilee. The reader ought to expand his imagination and take in these extended labors.

Mark 1:40–45

stretched forth his
hand, and touched
him, and saith unto
him, I will; be thou
42 made clean. And
straightway the lep-
rosy departed from
him, and he was
43 made clean. And he
[2]strictly charged him,
and straightway sent
44 him out, and saith
unto him, See thou
say nothing to any
man: but go thy way,
shew thyself to the
priest, and offer for
thy cleansing the
things which Moses
commanded, for a
testimony unto them.

45 But he went out, and
began to publish it
much, and to spread
abroad the [3]matter,
insomuch that [4]Jesus
could no more openly
enter into [5]a city,
but was without in
desert places: and
they came to him
from every quarter.

Matt. 8:2–4

touched him, saying, I will; be thou made clean. And straightway his leprosy was cleansed.

4 And Jesus saith unto
him, See thou tell
no man; but go thy
way, shew thyself to
the priest, and offer
the gift that Moses
commanded, for a
testimony unto them.

Luke 5:12–16

thou canst make me
13 clean. And he stretch-
ed forth his hand,
and touched him, say-
ing, I will; be thou
made clean. And
straightway the lep-
rosy departed from
him.
14 And
he charged him to
tell no man: but go
thy way, and shew
thyself to the priest,
and offer for thy
cleansing, according
as Moses command-
ed, for a testimony
unto them [*see Lev. 13: 49; 14:2–32*].
15 But so much the
more went abroad the
report concerning
him: and great multi-
tudes came together
to hear, and to be
healed of their in-
16 firmities. But he
withdrew himself in
the deserts, and
prayed.

[1] Some ancient authorities omit *and kneeling down to him.* [2] Or, *sternly.* [3] Gr. *word.* [4] Gr. *he.* [5] Or, *the city.*

§46. THRONGED IN CAPERNAUM, HE HEALS A PARALYTIC LOWERED THROUGH THE ROOF OF PETER'S HOUSE

Mark 2:1–12

1 And when he en-
tered again into Ca-
pernaum after some
days, it was noised
that he was [1]in the
2 house. And many
were gathered to-
gether, so that there

Matt. 9:1–8

1 And he entered into a boat, and crossed over, and came into his own city.

Luke 5:17–26

17 And it came to pass on one of those days, that he was teaching; and there were Pharisees and doctors of the law sitting by, which were come out of every

Mark 2:1–12	Matt. 9:1–8	Luke 5:17–26
was no longer room *for them*, no, not even about the door: and he spake the word un-		village of Galilee and Judea and Jerusalem: and the power of the Lord was with him
3 to them. And they come bringing unto him a man sick of the palsy, borne of four. 4 And when they could not [5]come nigh unto him for the crowd, they uncovered the roof where he was: and when they had broken it up, they let down the bed whereon the sick of the	2 And behold they brought to him a man sick of the palsy, lying on a bed;	18 [6]to heal. And behold, men bring on a bed a man that was palsied: and they sought to bring him in, and to lay him 19 before him. And not finding by what *way* they might bring him in because of the multitude, they went up to the housetop, and let him down through the tiles with his couch into the midst before Jesus.
5 palsy lay. And Jesus seeing their faith saith unto the sick of 6 the palsy, [1]Son, thy sins are forgiven. But there were certain of the scribes sitting there, and reasoning in their hearts, 7 Why doth this man thus speak? he blasphemeth: who can forgive sins but one,	and Jesus seeing their faith said unto the sick of the palsy, [1]Son, be of good cheer; thy sins are 3 forgiven. And behold, certain of the scribes said within themselves, This man blasphemeth.	20 And seeing their faith, he said, Man, thy sins are forgiven 21 thee. And the scribes and the Pharisees began to reason, saying, Who is this that speaketh blasphemies? Who can forgive sins but God alone?
8 *even* God? And straightway Jesus, perceiving in his spirit that they so reasoned within themselves, saith unto them, Why reason ye these things in your hearts?	4 And Jesus [2]knowing their thoughts said, Wherefore think ye evil in your hearts?	22 But Jesus perceiving their reasonings, answered and said unto them, [7]What reason ye in your hearts?
9 Whether is easier, to say to the sick of the palsy, Thy sins are forgiven; or to say, Arise, and take up thy bed, and walk?	5 For whether is easier, to say, Thy sins are forgiven; or to say, 6 Arise and walk? But	23 Whether is easier to say, Thy sins are forgiven thee; or to say, Arise and walk?
10 But that ye may know that the Son of man hath [3]power	that ye may know that the Son of man hath [3]power on earth	24 But that ye may know that the Son of man hath [3]power

Mark 2:1–12	Matt. 9:1–8	Luke 5:17–26
on earth to forgive sins (he saith to the sick of the palsy),* I 11 say unto thee, Arise, take up thy bed, and go unto thy house.	to forgive sins (then saith he to the sick of the palsy), Arise, and take up thy bed, and go unto thy	on earth to forgive sins (he said unto him that was palsied), I say unto thee, Arise, and take up thy couch, and go 25 unto thy house. And
12 And he arose, and straightway took up the bed, and went forth before them all; insomuch that they were all amazed, and glorified God, saying, We never saw it on this fashion.	7 house. And he arose, and departed to his house. 8 But when the multitudes saw it, they were afraid, and glorified God, which had given such [3]power unto men.	immediately he rose up before them, and took up that whereon he lay, and departed to his house, 26 glorifying God. And amazement took hold on all, and they glorified God; and they were filled with fear, saying, We have seen strange things to-day.

[1] Gr. *Child*. [2] Many ancient authorities read *seeing*. [3] Or, *authority*. [4] Or, *at home*. [5] Many ancient authorities read *bring him unto him*. [6] Gr. *that he should heal*. Many ancient authorities read *that* he *should heal them*. [7] Or, *Why*.

§ 47. THE CALL OF MATTHEW (LEVI) AND HIS RECEPTION IN HONOR OF JESUS

Capernaum

Mark 2:13–17	Matt. 9:9–13	Luke 5:27–32
13 And he went forth again by the sea side; and all the multitude resorted unto him, and he taught them. 14 And as he passed by, he saw Levi the *son* of Alphæus sitting at the place of toll, and he saith unto him, Follow me. And he arose and followed	9 And as Jesus passed by from thence, he saw a man, called Matthew, sitting at the place of toll: and he saith unto him, Follow me. And he arose, and followed him.	27 And after these things he went forth, and beheld a publican, named Levi, sitting at the place of toll, and said unto him, Follow me. 28 And he forsook all, and rose up and followed him.
15 him. And it came to pass, that he was sitting at meat in his house, and many	10 And it came to pass, as he [1]sat at meat in the house, behold, many publi-	29 And Levi made him a great feast in his house: and there was

* Note the parenthetic explanation of the writers in the middle of the saying of Jesus. It is proof that each of the Gospels had the same written source here or rather, as we know otherwise, that Matthew and Luke had Mark before them.

Mark 2:13–17	Matt. 9:9–13	Luke 5:27–32
[4]publicans and sinners sat down with Jesus and his disciples: for there were many, and they followed him.	cans and sinners came and sat down with Jesus and his disciples.	a great multitude of publicans and of others that were sitting at meat with them.
16 And the scribes[5] of the Pharisees, when they saw that he was eating with the sinners and publicans, said unto his disciples, [6]He eateth [7]and drinketh with publicans and sinners.	11 And when the Pharisees saw it, they said unto his disciples, Why eateth your [2]Master with the publicans and sinners?	30 And [8]the Pharisees and their scribes murmured against his disciples, saying, Why do ye eat and drink with the publicans and sinners?
17 And when Jesus heard it, he saith unto them, They that are [3]whole have no need of a physician, but they that are sick: I came not to call the righteous but sinners.	12 But when he heard it, he said, They that are [3]whole have no need of a physician, but they that are 13 sick. But go ye and learn what *this* meaneth,* I desire mercy, and not sacrifice: for I came not to call the righteous, but sinners.	31 And Jesus answering said unto them, They that are [3]whole have no need of a physician; but they that are sick. 32 I am not come to call the righteous but sinners to repentance.

[1] Gr. *reclined:* and so always. [2] Or, *Teacher.* [3] Gr. *strong.* [4] That is, *collectors or renters of Roman taxes:* and so elsewhere. [5] Some ancient authorities read *and the Pharisees.* [6] Or, *how is it that he eateth . . . sinners?* [7] Some ancient authorities omit *and drinketh.* [8] Or, *the Pharisees and the scribes among them.*

§ 48. JESUS IN THREE PARABLES DEFENDS HIS DISCIPLES FOR FEASTING† INSTEAD OF FASTING

Mark 2:18–22	Matt. 9:14–17	Luke 5:33–39
18 And John's disciples and the Pharisees were fasting: and they come and say unto him, Why do John's disciples and the disciples of the Pharisees fast, but thy disciples fast not?	14 Then come to him the disciples of John, saying, Why do we and the Pharisees fast [1]oft, but thy disciples	33 And they said unto him, The disciples of John fast often, and make supplications; likewise also the *disciples* of the Pharisees; but thine 34 eat and drink.
19 And Jesus said unto them, Can the sons of the bride-chamber	15 fast not? And Jesus said unto them, Can the sons of the bride-chamber mourn, as	And Jesus said unto them, Can ye make the sons of the bride-chamber fast while

* Hos. 6:6.

† It was probably the presence of the disciples of Christ at Matthew's feast on one of the Jewish fast days that occasioned the complaint of John's disciples and the Pharisees. It is sad to see disciples of John aligned with the Pharisees against Jesus.

Mark 2:18–22

fast, while the bride-groom is with them? as long as they have the bride-groom with them they cannot
20 fast. But the days will come, when the bride-groom shall be taken away from them, and then they will fast in that day.

21 No man seweth a piece of undressed cloth on an old garment; else that which should fill it up taketh from it, the new from the old, and a worse rent
22 is made. And no man putteth new wine into old [2]wine-skins: else the wine will burst the skins, and the wine perisheth, and the skins: but *they put* new wine into fresh wine-skins.

Matt. 9:14–17

long as the bride-groom is with them?

But the days will come, when the bride-groom shall be taken away from them, and then will they fast.

16 And no man putteth a piece of undressed cloth upon an old garment; for that which should fill it up taketh from the garment, and a worse rent is made.
17 Neither do *men* put new wine into old [2]wine-skins: else the skins burst and the wine is spilled, and the skins perish; but they put new wine into fresh wine-skins, and both are preserved.

Luke 5:33–39

the bride-groom is with them?

35 But the days will come; and when the bride-groom shall be taken away from them, then will they fast in those days.
36 And he spake also a parable* unto them; No man rendeth a piece from a new garment and putteth it upon an old garment; else he will rend the new, and also the piece from the new will not agree
37 with the old. And no man putteth new wine into old [2]wine-skins; else the new wine will burst the skins, and itself will be spilled, and the skins will perish.
38 But new wine must be put into fresh
39 wine-skins. And no man having drunk old *wine* desireth new: for he saith, The old is [3]good.

[1] Some ancient authorities omit *oft*. [2] That is, *skins used as bottles*. [3] Many ancient authorities read *better*.

In sections 49 to 51 we see the Pharisees attacking Jesus both in Jerusalem and in Galilee with great hostility and with the purpose of killing him because of violation of the Pharisaic regulations about the Sabbath. Jesus defends himself and his disciples by various arguments and personal claims.

* Note the use of the term parable in Luke. There are three parables (the sons of the bride-chamber, the new patch on an old garment, the new wine in old wine-skins) here together. A few isolated ones have already occurred as in John 2:19.

§ 49. AT A FEAST IN JERUSALEM (POSSIBLY THE PASSOVER) JESUS HEALS A LAME MAN ON THE SABBATH AND DEFENDS THIS ACTION TO THE PHARISEES IN A GREAT DISCOURSE

John 5:1–47

1 After these things there was [1]a feast* of the Jews; and Jesus went up
to Jerusalem.†
2 Now there is in Jerusalem by the sheep *gate* a pool, which is called in
3 Hebrew [2]Bethesda, having five porches. In these lay a multitude of them
5 that were sick, blind, halt, withered.[3] And a certain man was there,
6 which had been thirty and eight years in his infirmity. When Jesus saw
him lying, and knew that he had been now a long time *in that case*, he
7 saith unto him, Wouldst thou be made whole? The sick man answered
him, [4]Sir, I have no man, when the water is troubled, to put me into the
8 pool: but while I am coming, another steppeth down before me. Jesus
9 saith unto him, Arise, take up thy bed, and walk. And straightway the
man was made whole, and took up his bed and walked.
10 Now it was the sabbath on that day. So the Jews said unto him that
was cured, It is the sabbath, and it is not lawful for thee to take up thy
11 bed [*see Ex. 20:10; Deut. 5:14*]. But he answered them, He that made me
12 whole, the same said unto me, Take up thy bed, and walk. They asked
13 him, Who is the man that said unto thee, Take up *thy bed*, and walk? But
he that was healed wist not who it was: for Jesus had conveyed himself
14 away, a multitude being in the place. Afterward Jesus findeth him in
the temple, and said unto him, Behold, thou art made whole: sin no more,
15 lest a worse thing befall thee. The man went away, and told the Jews
16 that it was Jesus which had made him whole. And for this cause did the
Jews persecute Jesus, because he did these things on the sabbath. But
17 Jesus answered them, My Father worketh even until now, and I work.
18 For this cause therefore the Jews sought the more to kill him, because he
not only brake the sabbath, but also called God his own Father, making
himself equal with God.
19 Jesus therefore answered and said unto them,
Verily, verily, I say unto you, The Son can do nothing of himself, but
what he seeth the Father doing: for what things soever he doeth, these
20 the Son also doeth in like manner. For the Father loveth the Son, and
sheweth him all things that himself doeth; and greater works than these
21 will he shew him, that ye may marvel. For as the Father raiseth the dead
and quickeneth them, even so the Son also quickeneth whom he will.

* This feast of John 5:1 was *most probably* a Passover (see note at end of volume, note 7). If so, we should know that our Lord's public ministry lasted three years and a fraction, and that the great ministry in Galilee lasted some 18 to 20 months. Otherwise, we should know of only two years and a fraction for the former, and 6 to 8 months for the latter; as John gives three passovers beyond question (John 2:13; 6:4; 12:1), and our Lord's ministry began some time before the first of these. If the feast of 5:1 was not a passover, it is quite impossible to determine what other feast it was. While one would be glad to settle these questions, if it were possible, yet it really does not matter as regards understanding our Lord's *recorded* history and teachings during the great ministry in Galilee, the only point of difference being that if this feast was a Passover (or if there is an unmentioned Passover) we should conceive of the three journeys about Galilee as occupying a longer time, and including more extensive *unrecorded* labors in preaching and healing.

† It is to be noted that John's Gospel gives the Jerusalem Ministry of Jesus almost entirely except Galilee in ch. 2, Samaria and Galilee in ch. 4, Galilee in ch. 6 and again in ch. 21. It seems clear that John wrote with full knowledge of the Synoptic Gospels and supplements them at certain points. Both Luke and John were thus critics of the Gospel records.

John 5:1–47

22 For neither doth the Father judge any man, but he hath given all judge-
ment unto the Son; that all may honour the Son, even as they honour the
23 Father. He that honoureth not the Son honoureth not the Father which
24 sent him. Verily, verily, I say unto you, He that heareth my word, and
believeth him that sent me, hath eternal life, and cometh not into judge-
25 ment, but hath passed out of death into life. Verily, verily, I say unto
you, The hour cometh, and now is, when the dead shall hear the voice
26 of the Son of God; and they that hear shall live. For as the Father hath
life in himself, even so gave he to the Son also to have life in himself: and
27 he gave him authority to execute judgement, because he is [5]the Son of
28 man. Marvel not at this: for the hour cometh, in which all that are in
29 the tombs shall hear his voice, and shall come forth; they that have done
good, unto the resurrection of life; and they that have [6]done ill, unto the
resurrection of judgement.

30 I can of myself do nothing: as I hear, I judge: and my judgement is
righteous; because I seek not mine own will, but the will of him that sent
31 me. If I bear witness of myself, my witness is not true. It is another
32 that beareth witness of me; and I know that the witness which he wit-
33 nesseth of me is true. Ye have sent unto John, and he hath borne witness
34 unto the truth. But the witness which I receive is not from man: howbeit
35 I say these things, that ye may be saved. He was the lamp that burneth
36 and shineth: and ye were willing to rejoice for a season in his light. But the
witness which I have is greater than *that* of John: for the works which the
Father hath given me to accomplish, the very works that I do, bear
37 witness of me, that the Father hath sent me. And the Father which sent
me, he hath borne witness of me. Ye have neither heard his voice at any
38 time, nor seen his form. And ye have not his word abiding in you: for
39 whom he sent, him ye believe not. [7]Ye search the scriptures, because
ye think that in them ye have eternal life; and these are they which bear
40 witness of me; and ye will not come to me, that ye may have life. I
41 receive not glory from men. But I know you, that ye have not the love
42 of God in yourselves. I am come in my Father's name, and ye receive
43 me not; if another shall come in his own name, him ye will receive. How
44 can ye believe, which receive glory one of another, and the glory that
45 *cometh* from [8]the only God ye seek not? Think not that I will accuse you
to the Father: there is one that accuseth you, *even* Moses, on whom ye have
46 set your hope. For if ye believed Moses, ye would believe me; for he wrote
47 of me. But if ye believe not his writings, how shall ye believe my words?*

[1] Many ancient authorities read *the feast*. [2] Some ancient authorities read *Bethsaida*, others *Bethzatha*. [3] Many ancient authorities insert, wholly or in part, *waiting for the moving of the water: 4 for an angel of the Lord went down at certain seasons into the pool, and troubled the water: whosoever then first after the troubling of the water stepped in was made whole, with whatsoever disease he was holden.* [4] Or, *Lord.* [5] Or, *a son of man.* [6] Or, *practised.* [7] Or, *Search the scriptures.* [8] Some ancient authorities read *the only one.*

---

* Observe that here more than a year before the crucifixion, and probably two years (*i.e.* if the feast of 5:1 was a passover or if an unnamed passover is granted), the hostility of the Jews *at Jerusalem* (comp. John 4:1) has reached the point of a desire to kill him, as a sabbath breaker and a blasphemer (5:16–18). So we shall find him staying away from Jerusalem at the passover of John 6:4, and until the Tabernacles six months before the crucifixion (John 7:1–10). Meantime, the hostility will go on increasing in other parts of the country (Mark 3:6, etc.).—Notice also that in this discourse at Jerusalem our Lord repeatedly declares himself in a high sense the Son of God, and the appointed judge of mankind (ver. 27), and says that Moses wrote concerning him (ver. 46). All this indicated that he was the Messiah, but he did not here expressly assert it as he did in Samaria (John 4:26). That would have precipitated the collision, for to claim to be the Messiah would in the view of the Jewish rulers involve *political* consequences. Comp. John 11:48.

§ 50. ANOTHER SABBATH CONTROVERSY WITH THE PHARISEES WHEN THE DISCIPLES PLUCK EARS OF GRAIN IN THE FIELDS

Probably in Galilee on the Way Back from Jerusalem*

Mark 2:23–28

23 And it came to
pass, that he was go-
ing on the sabbath
day through the corn-
fields; and his dis-
ciples [3]began, as they
went, to pluck the
24 ears of corn. And
the Pharisees said
unto him, Behold,
why do they on the
sabbath day that
which is not lawful?
25 And he said
unto them, Did ye
never read what Da-
vid did, when he had
need, and was an
hungred, he, and
they that were with
26 him? How he en-
tered into the house
of God [4]when Abia-
thar was high priest,
and did eat the shew-
bread, which is not
lawful to eat, save
for the priests, and
gave also to them
that were with him?

27 And he said
unto them, The sab-

Matt. 12:1–8

1 At that season Jesus
went on the sabbath-
day through the corn-
fields: and his dis-
ciples were an hun-
gred, and began to
pluck ears of corn,
2 and to eat. But the
Pharisees, when they
saw it, said unto
him, Behold, thy dis-
ciples do that which
it is not lawful to do
upon the sabbath.
3 But he said unto
them, Have ye not
read what David did,
when he was an hun-
gred, and they that
were with him; how
4 he entered into the
house of God, and
[1]did eat the shew-
bread, which it was
not lawful for him
to eat, neither for
them that were with
them, but only for
5 the priests? Or have
ye not read in the
law, how that on
the sabbath day the
priests in the temple
profane the sabbath
[*see Num. 28:9–10*],
6 and are guiltless?
But I say unto you,
that [2]one greater than
7 the temple is here.
But if ye had known
what this meaneth
[*see Hos. 6:6*], I

Luke 6:1–5

1 Now it came to
pass, on a [5]sabbath,
that he was going
through the corn-
fields [*see Deut. 23:
25*]; and his disciples
plucked the ears of
corn, and did eat,
rubbing them in their
2 hands. But certain
of the Pharisees said,
Why do ye that which
it is not lawful to do
on the sabbath day
[*see John 5:10; Ex. 20:
3 10; Deut. 5:14*]? And
Jesus answering them
said, Have ye not
read even this, what
David did, when he
was an hungred, he,
and they that were
with him [*see Lev. 24:
9; 1 Sam. 21:1–6*]; how
4 he entered into the
house of God, and
did take and eat the
shewbread, and gave
also to them that
were with him; which
it is not lawful to eat
save for the priests
alone?

* Because in Mark 3:7 Jesus withdraws to the Sea of Galilee.

Mark 2:23–28

bath was made for
man, and not man for
28 the sabbath: so that
the Son of man is
lord even of the sab-
bath.*

Matt. 12:1–8

desire mercy, and not
sacrifice, ye would not
have condemned the
8 guiltless. For the
Son of man is lord of
the sabbath.

Luke 6:1–5

5 And he said
unto them, The Son
of man is lord of the
sabbath.

[1] Some ancient authorities read *they did eat.* [2] Gr. *a greater thing.* [3] Gr. *began to make their way plucking.* [4] Some ancient authorities read *in the days of Abiathar the high priest.* [5] Many ancient authorities insert *second-first.*

§ 51. A THIRD† SABBATH CONTROVERSY WITH THE PHARISEES OVER THE HEALING OF A MAN WITH A WITHERED HAND IN A SYNAGOGUE

In Galilee

Mark 3:1–6

1 And he entered
again into the syna-
gogue; and there was
a man there which
had his hand withered

2 And they watched
him, whether he
would heal him on
the sabbath day; that
they might accuse
him.
3 And he
saith unto the man
that had his hand
withered, [1]Stand
4 forth. And he saith
unto them, Is it law-
ful on the sabbath
day to do good, or
to do harm? to save
a life, or to kill? But
they held their peace.
5 And when he had
looked round about

Matt. 12:9–14

9 And he departed
thence, and went into
10 their synagogue; and
behold, a man having
a withered hand.

And
they asked him, say-
ing, Is it lawful to
heal on the sabbath
day? that they might
accuse him.
11 And he
said unto them, What
man shall there be
of you, that shall
have one sheep, and
if this fall into a pit
on the sabbath day,
will he not lay hold
on it, and lift it out?
12 How much then is a
man of more value
than a sheep! Where-
fore it is lawful to do

Luke 6:6–11

6 And it came to
pass on another sab-
bath, that he entered
into the synagogue
and taught: and there
was a man there,
and his right hand
7 was withered. And
the scribes and the
Pharisees watched
him, whether he
would heal on the
sabbath; that they
might find how to
8 accuse him. But he
knew their thoughts;
and he said to the
man that had his
hand withered, Rise
up, and stand forth
in the midst. And
he arose and stood
9 forth. And Jesus
said unto them, I ask
you, Is it lawful on

* Note the five arguments made by Jesus in defence of the conduct of the disciples on the Sabbath (the historical appeal in the conduct of David, the appeal to the law about the temple service, the voice of prophecy, the purpose of God in the Sabbath, and the lordship of the Messiah over the Sabbath). Jesus had already (John 5:17) argued that he was equal to the Father and hence had the right to do certain things (acts of mercy) on the Sabbath.

† On three other later occasions controversies arise with the Pharisees concerning Sabbath observance (John 9:1–34; Luke 13:10–21; 14:1–24). In John 7:20–24 Jesus refers to the miracle in John 5 and adds another argument (circumcision on the Sabbath) for his conduct on the Sabbath.

Mark 3:1–6

on them with anger,
being grieved at the
hardening of their
hearts, he saith unto
the man, Stretch
forth thy hand. And
he stretched it forth:
and his hand was restored.

6 And the Pharisees went out and
straightway with the
Herodians took counsel against him, how
they might destroy
him.*

Matt. 12:9–14

good on the sabbath
day.

13 Then saith he to the
man, Stretch forth
thy hand. And he
stretched it forth; and
it was restored whole,
14 as the other. But
the Pharisees went
out, and took counsel
against him, how they
might destroy him.

Luke 6:6–11

the sabbath to do
good, or to do harm?
to save a life, or to
10 destroy it? And he
looked round about
on them all, and said
unto him, Stretch
forth thy hand. And
he did *so:* and his
hand was restored.
11 But they were filled
with [2]madness; and
communed one with
another what they
might do to Jesus.

[1] Gr. *Arise into the midst.* [2] Or, *foolishness.*

In sections 52 to 54 we see Christ choosing the Twelve Apostles and delivering the Sermon on the Mount to them and to the multitudes.

§ 52. JESUS TEACHES AND HEALS GREAT MULTITUDES BY THE SEA OF GALILEE

Mark 3:7–12

7 And Jesus with his disciples
withdrew to the sea: and a great
multitude from Galilee followed:
8 and from Judea, and from Jerusalem, and from Idumæa, and
beyond Jordan, and about Tyre
and Sidon,† a great multitude,
hearing [2]what great things he
9 did, came unto him. And he
spake to his disciples, that a little boat should wait on him because of the crowd, lest they
10 should throng him, for he had
healed many; insomuch that as
many as had [3]plagues [4]pressed
upon him that they might touch
11 him. And the unclean spirits,
whensoever they beheld him, fell
down before him, and cried,

Matt. 12:15–21

15 And Jesus perceiving *it,* withdrew from thence: and many followed him;
16 and he healed them all,

* Here at some point near the sea of Galilee, there is already a plot to kill him, as some had wished to do in Jerusalem (comp. on § 49).

† Note the wide territory from which the crowds now come, from Idumea in the south to Phœnicia in the north and from Perea in the east.

Mark 3:7–12

saying, Thou art the Son of God.
12 And he charged them much
that they should not make him
known.

Matt. 12:15–21

and
charged them that they should
17 not make him known: that it
might be fulfilled which was spoken
[1]by Isaiah* the prophet, saying,
18 Behold, my servant whom I have chosen;
My beloved in whom my soul is well pleased:
I will put my Spirit upon him,
And he shall declare judgement to the Gentiles.
19 He shall not strive, nor cry aloud;
Neither shall any one hear his voice in the streets.
20 A bruised reed shall he not break,
And smoking flax shall he not quench,
Till he send forth judgement unto victory.
21 And in his name shall the Gentiles hope.

[1] Or, *through*. [2] Or, *all the things that he did*. [3] Gr. *scourges*. [4] Gr. *fell*.

§ 53. AFTER A NIGHT OF PRAYER, JESUS SELECTS TWELVE APOSTLES

Mark 3:13–19

13 And he goeth up into the moun-
tain, and calleth unto him whom
he himself would: and they went
14 unto him. And he appointed
twelve[1], that they might be with
him, and that he might send
15 them forth to preach, and to have
16 authority to cast out [2]devils; [3]and
17 Simon he surnamed Peter; and
James the *son* of Zebedee, and
John the brother of James; and
them he surnamed Boanerges,
18 which is, Sons of thunder: and

Luke 6:12–16

12 And it came to pass in these
days, that he went out into the
mountain to pray; and he con-
tinued all night in prayer to
13 God. And when it was day, he
called his disciples: and he chose
from them twelve, whom also
he named Apostles;†
14 Simon,
whom he also named Peter, and
Andrew his brother, and James
and John, and Philip and Bar-
tholomew,

* Isaiah 42:1–4.
† Matthew postpones giving the names of the Twelve till they are sent out to preach in Galilee (Matt. 10:1–4. § 70). There is a fourth list in Acts 1:13. See the four compared in note at the end of this volume, note 8.

Mark 3:13–19

Andrew, and Philip, and Bar-
tholomew, and Matthew, and
Thomas, and James the *son* of
Alphæus, and Thaddæus, and Si-
mon the [4]Cananæan,
19 and Judas
Iscariot, which also betrayed
him.

Luke 6:12–16

15 and Matthew and
Thomas, and James *the son* of
Alphæus, and Simon which was
16 called the Zealot, and Judas, *the*
son of [5]James, and Judas Iscariot,
which was the traitor.

[1] Some ancient authorities add *whom also he named apostles*. See Luke 6:13. [2] Gr. *demons*. [3] Some ancient authorities insert *and he appointed twelve*. [4] Or, *Zealot*. See Luke 6:15; Acts 1:13. [5] Or, *brother*. See Jude 1.

§ 54. THE SERMON ON THE MOUNT. PRIVILEGES AND REQUIREMENTS OF THE MESSIANIC REIGN. CHRIST'S STANDARD OF RIGHTEOUSNESS

*Matthew, chapters 5–7. Luke 6:17–49.**

A level place on a mountain, not far from Capernaum

The Place and the Audience

Matt. 5:1–2

1 And seeing the multitudes, he
went up into the mountain: and
when he had sat down, his disci-
2 ples came unto him: and he open-
ed his mouth and taught them,
saying,

Luke 6:17–19

17 And he came down with them,
and stood on a level place, and a
great multitude of his disciples,
and a great number of the peo-
ple from all Judea and Jerusalem,
and the sea coast of Tyre and
Sidon, which came to hear him,
and to be healed of their diseases;
18 and they that were troubled
with unclean spirits were healed.
19 And all the multitude sought to
touch him: for power came forth
from him, and healed *them* all.

1. *The Introduction: The Beatitudes and the Woes. Privileges of the Messiah's Subjects*

Matt. 5:3–12

3 Blessed are the poor in spirit:
for theirs is the kingdom of
4 heaven. [1]Blessed are they that

Luke 6:20–26

20 And he lifted up his eyes on
his disciples, and said, Blessed
are ye poor: for yours is the

* There is little doubt that the discourses given by Matthew and Luke are the same, Matthew locating it on "the mountain," and Luke "on a level place," which might easily be a level spot on a mountain. (See note at end of this book, note 9.) Observe that they begin and end alike, and pursue the same general order. Luke omits various matters of special interest to Matthew's Jewish readers (*e.g.* Matt. 5:17–42), and other matters that he himself will give elsewhere (*e.g.* Luke 11:1–4; 12:22–31); while Luke has a few sentences (as ver. 24–26, 38–40), which are not given by Matthew.

Matt. 5:3-12

mourn [*see Isa. 61:3*]: for they shall
5 be comforted. Blessed are the
meek: for they shall inherit the
6 earth [*see Ps. 37:11*]. Blessed are
they that hunger and thirst after
righteousness: for they shall be
7 filled [*see Ps. 55*]. Blessed are the
merciful: for they shall obtain
mercy [*see Ps. 18:25; Prov. 11:17*].
8 Blessed are the pure in heart: for
they shall see God [*see Ps. 24:3-5*].
9 Blessed are the peacemakers: for
they shall be called sons of God.
10 Blessed are they that have been
persecuted for righteousness' sake:
for theirs is the kingdom of
11 heaven. Blessed are ye when
men shall reproach you, and
persecute you, and say all manner
of evil against you falsely, for my
12 sake. Rejoice, and be exceeding
glad: for great is your reward in
heaven: for so persecuted they the
prophets which were before you.

Luke 6:20-26

21 kingdom of God. Blessed *are*
ye that hunger now: for ye shall
be filled. Blessed *are* ye that
weep now: for ye shall laugh.
22 Blessed are ye, when men shall
hate you, and when they shall
separate you *from their company*,
and reproach you, and cast out
your name as evil, for the Son of
23 man's sake. Rejoice in that day,
and leap *for joy*: for behold, your
reward is great in heaven: for in
the same manner did their fath-
24 ers unto the prophets. But woe
unto you that are rich! for ye
have received your consolation.
25 Woe unto you, ye that are full
now! for ye shall hunger. Woe *unto
you*, ye that laugh now! for ye
26 shall mourn and weep. Woe
unto you, when all men shall
speak well of you! for in the same
manner did their fathers to the
false prophets.

[1] Some ancient authorities transpose verses 4 and 5.

2. *The Theme of the Sermon: Christ's Standard of Righteousness in Contrast with that of the Scribes and Pharisees*

Matt. 5:13-20

13 Ye are the salt of the earth: but if the salt have lost its savour, where-
with shall it be salted? it is thenceforth good for nothing, but to be cast
14 out and trodden under foot of men [*see Mark 9:50; Jesus often repeated his*
15 *sayings*]. Ye are the light of the world. A city set on a hill cannot be
hid. Neither do *men* light a lamp, and put it under the bushel, but on
16 the stand; and it shineth unto all that are in the house [*see Mark 4:21;
Luke 8:16*]. Even so let your light shine before men, that they may see
your good works, and glorify your Father which is in heaven.
17 Think not that I came to destroy the law or the prophets: I came not
18 to destroy but to fulfil. For verily I say unto you, Till heaven and
earth pass away, one jot or one tittle shall in no wise pass away from the
19 law, till all things be accomplished. Whosoever therefore shall break
one of these least commandments, and shall teach men so, shall be called
least in the kingdom of heaven: but whosoever shall do and teach them,
20 he shall be called great in the kingdom of heaven. For I say unto you,
that except your righteousness shall exceed *the righteousness* of the scribes
and Pharisees, ye shall in no wise enter into the kingdom of heaven.

3. *Christ's Ethical Teaching Superior to that of the Scribes (both the Old Testament and the Oral Law) in Six Items or Illustrations (Murder, Adultery, Divorce, Oaths, Retaliation, Love of Enemies)*

Matt. 5:21–48

21 Ye have heard that it was said to them of old time, Thou shalt not
22 kill; and whosoever shall kill shall be in danger of the judgement [*see Ex.
20:13; Deut. 5:17]: but I say unto you, that every one who is angry with
his brother [1]shall be in danger of the judgement: and whosoever shall say
to his brother [2]Raca, shall be in danger of the council; and whosoever shall
23 say, [3]Thou fool, shall be in danger [4]of the [5]hell of fire. If therefore thou
art offering thy gift at the altar, and there rememberest that thy brother
24 hath aught against thee, leave there thy gift before the altar, and go thy
way, first be reconciled to thy brother, and then come and offer thy gift.
25 Agree with thine adversary quickly, whiles thou art with him in the way;
lest haply the adversary deliver thee to the judge, and the judge [6]deliver
26 thee to the officer, and thou be cast into prison. Verily I say unto thee,
Thou shalt by no means come out thence, till thou have paid the last
farthing.
27 Ye have heard that it was said, Thou shalt not commit adultery [*see Ex.*
28 *20: 14; Deut. 5:18*]: but I say unto you, that every one that looketh on a
woman to lust after her hath committed adultery with her already in his
29 heart. And if thy right eye causeth thee to stumble, pluck it out, and cast
it from thee; for it is profitable for thee that one of thy members should
30 perish, and not thy whole body be cast into [7]hell. And if thy right hand
causeth thee to stumble, cut it off, and cast it from thee: for it is profitable
for thee that one of thy members should perish, and not thy whole body
31 go into [7]hell. It was said also, Whosoever shall put away his wife, let
32 him give her a writing of divorcement [*see Deut. 24:1*]: but I say unto you,
that every one that putteth away his wife, saving for the cause of fornication,
maketh her an adulteress: and whosoever shall marry her when she
is put away committeth adultery.*
33 Again, ye have heard that it was said to them of old time, Thou shalt
34 not forswear thyself, but shalt perform unto the Lord thine oaths [*see Lev.
19:12; Num. 30:2; Ex. 20:7; Deut. 5:11; 23:21*]: but I say unto you, Swear
not at all [*see Matt. 26: 63–64*]; neither by the heaven, for it is the throne
35 of God; nor by the earth, for it is the footstool of his feet; nor [8]by Jerusalem,
36 for it is the city of the great King [*see Isa. 66:1*]. Neither shalt thou
swear by thy head, for thou canst not make one hair white or black
37 [*see Ps. 48:2*]. [9]But let your speech be, Yea, yea; Nay, nay: and whatsoever
is more than these is of [10]the evil *one.*
38 Ye have heard that it was said, An eye for an eye, and a tooth for a
39 tooth [*see Ex. 21:24; Lev. 24:20; Deut. 19:21*]: but I say unto you, Resist not
40 [11]him that is evil; but whosoever smiteth thee on thy right cheek, turn
to him the other also [*see John 18:23*]. And if any man would go to law with
41 thee, and take away thy coat, let him have thy cloke also. And whosoever
42 shall [12]compel thee to go one mile, go with him twain. Give to him that
asketh thee, and from him that would borrow of thee turn not thou away.
43 Ye have heard that it was said, Thou shalt love thy neighbour [*see Lev. 19:
18; Deut. 23:6; 25:19*].

* See further Mark 9:43–47; 10:11–12; Matt. 18:8–9; 19:9.

Matt. 5:21-48

44 and hate thine enemy: But I say un-
to you [*see Luke 23:34*], Love your
enemies, and pray for them that
45 persecute you; that ye may be sons
of your Father which is in heaven:
for he maketh his sun to rise on the
evil and the good, and sendeth
rain on the just and the unjust.

46 For if ye love them that love
you, what reward have ye? do
not even the [13]publicans the
47 same? And if you salute your
brethren only, what do ye more
than others? do not even the
48 Gentiles the same? Ye therefore
shall be perfect, as your heavenly
Father is perfect.

Luke 6:27-30, 32-36

27 But I say
unto you which hear, Love your
enemies, do good to them that
28 hate you, bless them that curse
you, pray for them that despite-
29 fully use you. To him that
smiteth thee on the *one* cheek
offer also the other; and from
him that taketh away thy cloke
withhold not thy coat also.
30 Give to every one that asketh
thee; and of him that taketh
away thy goods ask them not
32 again. And if ye love them
that love you, what thank have
ye? for even sinners love those
33 that love them. And if ye do
good to them that do good to
you, what thank have ye? for
34 even sinners do the same. And
if ye lend to them of whom ye
hope to receive, what thank have
ye? even sinners lend to sinners,
35 to receive again as much. But
love your enemies, and do *them*
good, and lend, [14]never despair-
ing; and your reward shall be
great, and ye shall be sons of the
Most High: for he is kind toward
36 the unthankful and evil. Be ye
merciful, even as your Father is
merciful.

[1] Many ancient authorities insert *without cause*. [2] An expression of contempt. [3] Or, *Moreh*, a Hebrew expression of condemnation. [4] Gr. *unto* or *into*. [5] Gr. *Gehenna of fire*. [6] Some ancient authorities omit *deliver thee*. [7] Gr. *Gehenna*. [8] Or, *toward*. [9] Some ancient authorities read *But your speech* shall be. [10] Or, *evil*: as in ver. 39; 6:13. [11] Or, *evil*. [12] Gr. *impress*. [13] That is, *collectors or renters of Roman taxes*: and so elsewhere. [14] Some ancient authorities read, *despairing of no man*.

4. *The Practice of Real Righteousness unlike the Ostentatious Hypocrisy of the Pharisees, as in Almsgiving, Prayer, Fasting*

Matt. 6:1-18

1 Take heed that ye do not your righteousness before men, to be seen of
them: else ye have no reward with your Father which is in heaven.
2 When therefore thou doest alms, sound not a trumpet before thee, as
the hypocrites do in the synagogues and in the streets, that they may
have glory of men. Verily I say unto you, They have received their
3 reward. But when thou doest alms, let not thy left hand know what
4 thy right hand doeth: that thine alms may be in secret: and thy Father
which seeth in secret shall recompense thee.

Matt. 6:1–18

5 And when ye pray, ye shall not be as the hypocrites: for they love to
stand and pray in the synagogues and in the corners of the streets, that
they may be seen of men. Verily I say unto you, They have received
6 their reward. But thou, when thou prayest, enter into thine inner
chamber, and having shut thy door, pray to thy Father which is in secret,
7 and thy Father which seeth in secret shall recompense thee. And in
praying use not vain repetitions, as the Gentiles do: for they think that
8 they shall be heard for their much speaking. Be not therefore like unto
them: for [1]your Father knoweth what things ye have need of, before ye
9 ask him. After this manner therefore pray ye: Our Father which art in
10 heaven, Hallowed by thy name. Thy kingdom come. Thy will be done,
11 as in heaven, so on earth. Give us this day [2]our daily bread. And
12 forgive us our debts, as we also have forgiven our debtors. And bring us
13 not into temptation, but deliver us from [3]the evil *one*. [4]For if ye forgive
14 men their trespasses, your heavenly Father will also forgive you. But
15 if ye forgive not men their trespasses, neither will your Father forgive
your trespasses.

16 Moreover when ye fast, be not, as the hypocrites, of a sad countenance:
for they disfigure their faces, that they may be seen of men to fast.
17 Verily I say unto you, They have received their reward. But thou,
18 when thou fastest, anoint thy head, and wash thy face; that thou be not
seen of men to fast, but of thy Father which is in secret: and thy
Father, which seeth in secret, shall recompense thee.

[1] Some ancient authorities read *God your Father.* [2] Gr. *our bread for the coming day.* [3] Or, *evil.* [4] Many authorities, some ancient, but with variations, add *For thine is the kingdom, and the power, and the glory, for ever, Amen.*

5. *Single-hearted Devotion to God, as Opposed to Worldly Aims and Anxieties*

Matt. 6:19–34

19 Lay not up for yourselves treasures upon the earth, where moth and
20 rust doth consume, and where thieves [1]break through and steal: but lay
up for yourselves treasures in heaven, where neither moth nor rust doth
21 consume, and where thieves do not [1]break through nor steal: for where
22 thy treasure is, there will thy heart be also. The lamp of the body is the
eye: if therefore thine eye be single, thy whole body shall be full of light.
23 But if thine eye be evil, thy whole body shall be full of darkness. If
therefore the light that is in thee be darkness, how great is the darkness!
24 No man can serve two masters: for either he will hate the one, and love
the other; or else he will hold to one, and despise the other. Ye cannot
25 serve God and mammon. Therefore I say unto you, Be not anxious for
your life, what ye shall eat, or what ye shall drink; nor yet for your body,
what ye shall put on. Is not the life more than the food, and the body
26 than the raiment? Behold, the birds of the heaven, that they sow not,
neither do they reap, nor gather into barns; and your heavenly Father
27 feedeth them. Are not ye of much more value than they? And which
28 of you by being anxious can add one cubit unto his [2]stature? And why
29 are ye anxious concerning raiment? Consider the lilies of the field, how
they grow; they toil not, neither do they spin: yet I say unto you, that

Matt. 6:19–34

30 even Solomon in all his glory was not arrayed like one of these. But if
God doth so clothe the grass of the field, which to-day is, and to-morrow
is cast into the oven, *shall he* not much more *clothe* you, O ye of little faith?
31 Be not therefore anxious, saying, What shall we eat? or, What shall we
32 drink? or, Wherewithal shall we be clothed? For after all these things do
the Gentiles seek; for your heavenly Father knoweth that ye have need of
33 all these things. But seek ye first his kingdom, and his righteousness;
34 and all these things shall be added unto you. Be not therefore anxious
for the morrow: for the morrow will be anxious for itself. Sufficient unto
the day is the evil thereof.

[1] Gr. *dig through*. [2] Or, *age*.

6. *Captious Criticism, or Judging Others*

Matt. 7:1–6

1 Judge not, that ye be not judg-
2 ed. For with what judgement ye
judge, ye shall be judged: and
with what measure ye mete, it
shall be measured unto you.
3 And why beholdest thou the
mote that is in thy brother's eye,
but considerest not the beam that
4 is in thine own eye? Or how wilt
thou say to thy brother, Let me
cast out the mote out of thine
eye; and lo, the beam is in thine
5 own eye? Thou hypocrite, cast
out first the beam out of thine
own eye; and then shalt thou see
clearly to cast out the mote out
of thy brother's eye.
6 Give not that which is holy un-
to the dogs, neither cast your
pearls before the swine, lest hap-
ly they trample them under their feet, and turn and rend you.

Luke 6:37–42

37 And judge not, and ye shall not
be judged: and condemn not, and
ye shall not be condemned: re-
lease, and ye shall be released:
38 give, and it shall be given unto
you; good measure, pressed down,
shaken together, running over,
shall they give into your bosom.
For with what measure ye mete
it shall be measured to you again.
39 And he spake also a parable
unto them, Can the blind guide
the blind? shall they not both
40 fall into a pit? The disciple is
not above his [1]master: but every
one when he is perfected shall
41 be as his [1]master. And why be-
holdest thou the mote that is in
thy brother's eye, but consider-
est not the beam that is in thine
42 own eye? Or how canst thou say
to thy brother, Brother, let me
cast out the mote that is in thine
eye, when thou thyself beholdest
not the beam that is in thine own
eye? Thou hypocrite, cast out
first the beam out of thine own
eye, and then shalt thou see
clearly to cast out the mote that
is in thy brother's eye.

[1] Or, *teacher*.

7. *Prayer, and the Golden Rule*

Matt. 7:7–12

7 Ask, and it shall be given you: seek, and ye shall find: knock, and it
8 shall be opened unto you, for every one that asketh receiveth; and he
9 that seeketh findeth; and to him that knocketh it shall be opened. Or
what man is there of you, who, if his son shall ask him for a loaf, will give
10 him a stone; or if he shall ask for a fish, will give him a serpent?
11 If ye then, being evil, know how to give good gifts unto your children,
how much more shall your Father which is in heaven give good things
12 to them that ask him? All things
therefore whatsoever ye would
that men should do unto you,
even so do ye also unto them: for
this is the law and the prophets.

Luke 6:31

31 And as ye would that men
should do to you, do ye also to
them likewise.

8. *The Conclusion of the Sermon. The Lesson of Personal Righteousness Driven Home by Powerful Parables*

Matt. 7:13 to 8:1.

13 Enter ye in by the narrow gate: for wide [1]is the gate, and broad is
the way, that leadeth to destruction, and many be they that enter in
14 thereby. [2]For narrow is the gate, and straitened the way, that leadeth
unto life, and few be they that find it.
15 Beware of false prophets, which come to you in sheep's clothing,
16 but inwardly are ravening wolves. By their fruits ye shall know
17 them. Do *men* gather grapes of thorns, or figs of thistles? Even so
every good tree bringeth forth
good fruit: but the corrupt tree
18 bringeth forth evil fruit. A good
tree cannot bring forth evil fruit,
neither can a corrupt tree bring
19 forth good fruit. Every tree that
bringeth not forth good fruit is
hewn down, and cast into the fire.
20 Therefore by their fruits ye shall
21 know them. Not every one that
saith unto me, Lord, Lord, shall
enter the kingdom of heaven; but
he that doeth the will of my Father
22 which is in heaven. Many will say
to me in that day, Lord, Lord, did
we not prophesy by thy name, and
by thy name cast out [3]devils, and
by thy name do many [4]mighty
23 works? And then will I profess
unto them, I never knew you: depart from me, ye that work
iniquity.

Luke 6:43–49

43 For there is no good tree that
bringeth forth corrupt fruit; nor
again a corrupt tree that bring-
44 eth forth good fruit. For each
tree is known by its own fruit.
For of thorns men do not gather
figs, nor of a bramble bush gather
45 they grapes. The good man out
of the good treasure of his heart
bringeth forth that which is good.
and the evil *man* out of the evil
treasure bringeth forth that which
is evil; for out of the abundance of
the heart his mouth speaketh.
46 And why call ye me, Lord, Lord,
and do not the things which I say?

Matt. 7:13 to 8:1

24 Every one therefore which
heareth these words of mine, and
doeth them, shall be likened un-
to a wise man, which built his
25 house upon the rock: and the
rain descended, and the floods
came, and the winds blew, and
beat upon that house; and it fell
not: for it was founded upon
26 the rock. And every one that
heareth these words of mine,
and doeth them not, shall be
likened unto a foolish man,
which built his house upon the
27 sand: and the rain descended,
and the floods came, and the
winds blew, and smote upon that
house; and it fell: and great was
the fall thereof.
28 And it came to pass, when Je-
sus ended these words, the mul-
titudes were astonished at his
29 teaching: for he taught them as
one having authority, and not as
their scribes.
1 And when he was come down
from the mountain, great multi-
tudes followed him.

Luke 6:43-49

47 Every one that cometh unto
me, and heareth my words, and
doeth them, I will shew you to
48 whom he is like: he is like a man
building a house, who digged and
went deep, and laid a foundation
upon the rock: and when a flood
arose, the stream brake against
that house, and could not shake
it: [5]because it had been well
49 builded. But he that heareth,
and doeth not, is like a man that
built a house upon the earth
without a foundation; against
which the stream brake, and
straightway it fell in; and the
ruin of that house was great.

[1] Some ancient authorities omit *is the gate.* [2] Many ancient authorities read *How narrow is the gate, &c.* [3] Gr. *demons.* [4] Gr. *powers.* [5] Many ancient authorities read *for it had been founded upon the rock:* as in Matt. 7:25.

*In sections 55 to 58 we see the rapid spread of Christ's influence and the inquiry from the Baptist in prison.**

§55. JESUS HEALS A CENTURION'S SERVANT AT CAPERNAUM

Matt. 8:5-13

5 And when he was entered into
Capernaum, there came unto him
a centurion,

Luke 7:1-10

1 After he had ended all his say-
ings in the ears of the people, he
entered into Capernaum.
2 And a certain centurion's [1]serv-
ant, who was [2]dear unto him,
was sick and at the point of
3 death. And when he heard
concerning Jesus, he sent unto
him elders of the Jews, asking

* Here we have only Matthew and Luke, a block from the Logia of Matthew.

Matt. 8:5-13

6 beseeching him, and
saying, Lord, my [1]servant lieth
in the house sick of the palsy,
grievously tormented.

7 And he saith
unto him, I will come and heal
him.

8 And the centurion answered
and said, Lord, I am not [2]worthy
that thou shouldest come under
my roof: but only [3]say the word,
and my [1]servant shall be healed.

9 For I also am a man [4]under author-
ity, having under myself soldiers:
and I say to this one, Go, and he
goeth; and to another, Come,
and he cometh; and to my [5]serv-
ant, Do this, and he doeth it.
10 And when Jesus heard it,
he marvelled, and said to them
that followed, Verily I say unto
you, [6]I have not found so great
11 faith, no, not in Israel. And I
say unto you, that many shall
come from the east and the west,
and shall [7]sit down with Abraham,
and Isaac, and Jacob, in the kingdom
12 of heaven [*see Ps. 107:3; Isa. 49:12*]: but the sons of the kingdom
shall be cast forth into the outer
darkness: there shall be weeping
13 and gnashing of teeth. And Jesus
said unto the centurion, Go thy
way; as thou hast believed *so* be
it done unto thee. And the
[1]servant was healed in that hour.

Luke 7:1-10

him that he would come and
4 save his [5]servant. And they,
when they came to Jesus, be-
sought him earnestly, saying,
He is worthy that thou shouldst
5 do this for him: for he loveth
our nation, and himself built us
6 our synagogue. And Jesus went
with them. And when he was
now not far from the house, the
centurion sent friends to him,
saying unto him, Lord, trouble
not thyself: for I am not [2]worthy
that thou shouldst come under
7 my roof: wherefore neither
thought I myself worthy to come
unto thee: but [3]say the word,
and my [1]servant shall be healed.
8 For I also am a man set under
authority, having under myself
soldiers: and I say to this one,
Go, and he goeth; and to another,
Come, and he cometh; and to my
[5]servant, Do this, and he doeth
9 it. And when Jesus heard these
things, he marvelled at him, and
turned and said unto the multi-
tude that followed him, I say
unto you, I have not found so
great faith, no, not in Israel.

10 And they that were sent, re-
turning to the house, found the
[5]servant whole.

[1] Or, *boy*. [2] Gr. *sufficient*. [3] Gr. *say with a word*. [4] Some ancient authorities insert *set*: as in Luke 7:8. [5] Gr. *bond-servant*. [6] Many ancient authorities read *With no man in Israel have I found so great faith*. [7] Gr. *recline*. [8] Or, *precious to him*; or, *honourable with him*.

§ 56. HE RAISES A WIDOW'S SON AT NAIN

Luke 7:11-17

11 And it came to pass [1]soon afterwards, that he went to a city called
12 Nain; and his disciples went with him, and a great multitude. Now

Luke 7:11–17

when he drew near to the gate of the city, behold, there was carried out
one that was dead, the only son of his mother, and she was a widow:
13 and much people of the city was with her. And when the Lord
saw her, he had compassion on her, and said unto her, Weep not.
14 And he came nigh and touched the bier: and the bearers stood still.
15 And he said, Young man, I say unto thee, Arise. And he that was
dead sat up, and began to speak. And he gave him to his mother.
16 And fear took hold on all; and they glorified God, saying, A great prophet
17 is arisen among us: and, God hath visited his people. And this report
went forth concerning him in the whole of Judea, and the region round
about.

[1] Many ancient authorities read *on the next day*.

§ 57. THE MESSAGE* FROM THE BAPTIST AND THE EULOGY OF JESUS

Galilee

Matt. 11:2–19

2 Now when John heard in the
prison† the works of the Christ,
he sent by his disciples, and said
3 unto him, Art thou he that com-
eth, or look we for another?

4 And Jesus answered and said
unto them, Go your way and tell
John the things which ye do
5 hear and see: the blind receive
their sight, and the lame walk,
the lepers are cleansed, and the
deaf hear, and the dead are
raised up, and the poor have
[1]good tidings preached to them.
6 And blessed is he, whosoever
shall find none occasion of stum-
bling in me.

Luke 7:18–35

18 And the disciples of John told
19 him all of these things. And
John calling unto him [10]two of
his disciples sent them to the
Lord, saying, Art thou he that
cometh, or look we for another?
20 And when the men were come
unto him, they said, John the
Baptist hath sent us unto thee,
saying, Art thou he that cometh,
21 or look we for another? In that
hour he cured many of diseases
and [11]plagues and evil spirits;
and on many that were blind he
22 bestowed sight. And he answer-
ed and said unto them, Go your
way, and tell John what things
ye have seen and heard [*see Isa.
2: 18-19; 35:5-6; 61:1*]: the blind
receive their sight, the lame
walk, the lepers are cleansed,
and the deaf hear, the dead are
raised up, the poor have [1]good
23 tidings preached to them. And
blessed is he, whosoever shall find
none occasion of stumbling in me.

* Observe that his fame as having raised the dead, and as being "a great prophet," spread widely, and reaching John, led to his message of inquiry (connect Luke 7:17 and 18).

† John's prison was at Machærus, east of the Dead Sea. Jesus was somewhere in Galilee, probably near Nain, which was in the southern part of Galilee.

Matt. 11:2–19

7 And as these went their way,
Jesus began to say unto the mul-
titudes concerning John, What
went ye out into the wilderness
to behold? a reed shaken with
8 the wind? But what went ye
out for to see? a man clothed
in soft *raiment?* Behold, they
that wear soft *raiment* are in
9 kings' houses. [2]But wherefore
went ye out? to see a prophet?
Yea, I say unto you, and much
10 more than a prophet. This is he,
of whom it is written,

Behold, I send my messenger
before thy face,
Who shall prepare thy way be-
fore thee.

11 Verily I say unto you, Among
them that are born of women
there hath not arisen a greater
than John the Baptist: yet he
that is [3]but little in the kingdom
of heaven is greater than he.
12 And from the days of John the
Baptist until now the kingdom of
heaven suffereth violence, and
men of violence take it by force
13 [*see Luke 16:17*]. For all the proph-
ets and the law prophesied until
14 John. And if ye are willing to re-
15 ceive [4]*it*, this is Elijah, which is to
come [*see Mal. 4:5*]. He that hath
ears [5]to hear, let him hear.

16 But whereunto
shall I liken this generation? It
is like* unto children sitting in
the marketplaces, which call un-
17 to their fellows, and say, We
piped unto you, and ye did not
dance; we wailed, and ye did not
[6]mourn.

Luke 7:18–35

24 And when the messengers of
John were departed, he began
to say unto the multitudes con-
cerning John, What went ye out
into the wilderness to behold? a
25 reed shaken with the wind? But
what went ye out to see? a man
clothed in soft raiment? Behold,
they which are gorgeously ap-
parelled, and live delicately, are
26 in kings' courts. But what went
ye out to see? a prophet? Yea,
I say unto you, and much more
27 than a prophet. This is he of
whom it is written,

Behold, I send my messenger
before thy face.
Who shall prepare thy way
before thee [*see Mal. 3:1*].

28 I say unto you, Among them
that are born of women there is
none greater than John: yet he
that is [9]but little in the kingdom
of God is greater than he.

29 And all the
people when they heard, and the
publicans, justified God, [12]being
baptized with the baptism of
30 John. But the Pharisees and
the lawyers rejected for them-
selves the counsel of God [13]being
31 not baptized of him. Whereunto
then shall I liken the men of
this generation, and to what are
32 they like? They are like unto
children that sit in the market-
place, and call one to another;
which say, We piped unto you,
and ye did not dance; we wailed,

* Parable of the Children Playing in the Market Place.

Matt. 11:2-19

18 For John came
neither eating nor drinking, and
19 they say, He hath a [7]devil. The
Son of man came eating and
drinking, and they say, Behold, a
gluttonous man, and a winebibber,
a friend of publicans and sinners!

And wisdom [8]is justified by her
[9]works.

Luke 7:18-35

33 and ye did not weep. For John
the Baptist is come eating no
bread nor drinking wine; and ye
34 say, He hath a [7]devil. The Son
of man is come eating and drink-
ing; and ye say, Behold, a glut-
tonous man, and a winebibber, a
friend of publicans and sinners!
35 And wisdom [8]is justified of all
her children.

[1] Or, *the gospel.* [2] Many ancient authorities read *But what went ye out to see? a prophet?* [3] Gr. *lesser.* [4] Or, *him.* [5] Some ancient authorities omit *to hear.* [6] Gr. *beat the breast.* [7] Gr. *demon.* [8] Or, *was.* [9] Many ancient authorities read *children:* as in Luke vii, 35. [10] Gr. *certain two.* [11] Gr. *scourges.* [12] Or, *having been.* [13] Or, *not having been.*

§ 58. WOES UPON THE CITIES OF OPPORTUNITY. THE CLAIMS OF CHRIST AS THE TEACHER ABOUT THE FATHER.

Galilee

Matt. 11:20-30

20 Then began he to upbraid the cities wherein most of his mighty works
21 were done, because they repented not. Woe unto thee, Chorazin! woe
unto thee, Bethsaida! for if the [1]mighty works had been done in Tyre and
Sidon which were done in you, they would have repented long ago in sack-
22 cloth and ashes. Howbeit I say unto you, it shall be more tolerable
23 for Tyre and Sidon in the day of judgement, than for you [*see Isa. 14:13-15*].
And thou, Capernaum, shalt thou be exalted unto heaven? thou shalt [2]go
down unto Hades: for if the [1]mighty works had been done in Sodom which
24 were done in thee, it would have remained until this day. Howbeit I
say unto you, that it shall be more tolerable for the land of Sodom in the
day of judgement, than for thee [*see Gen. 19:24*].
25 At that season Jesus answered and said, I [3]thank thee, O Father [*see John 3:35; 17:2*], Lord of heaven and earth, that thou didst hide these things
26 from the wise and understanding, and didst reveal them unto babes: yea,
27 Father, [4]for so it was well-pleasing in thy sight. All things have been
delivered unto me of my Father: and no one knoweth the Son, save the
Father: neither doth any know the Father, save the Son, and he to whom-
28 soever the Son willeth to reveal *him*. Come unto me, all ye that labour
29 and are heavy laden, and I will give you rest. Take my yoke* upon you,
and learn of me; for I am meek and lowly in heart: and ye shall find rest
30 unto your souls. For my yoke is easy, and my burden is light [*see Jer. 6:16; Sirach 51:23*].

[1] Gr. *powers.* [2] Many ancient authorities read *be brought down.* [3] Or, *praise.* [4] Or, *that.*

* Rabbinical figure for going to school. Jesus thus definitely pictures himself as the expert on God in a Johannean passage (*cf.* Luke 10:21-24). He conceives himself as the Teacher who alone is able to interpret the Father.

§ 59. THE ANOINTING* OF CHRIST'S FEET BY A SINFUL WOMAN IN THE HOUSE OF SIMON A PHARISEE. THE PARABLE OF THE TWO DEBTORS

Galilee

Luke 7:36–50

36 And one of the Pharisees desired him that he would eat with him.
37 And he entered into the Pharisee's house, and sat down to meat. And
behold, a woman which was in the city, a sinner; and when she knew
that he was sitting at meat in the Pharisee's house, she brought [1]an
38 alabaster cruse of ointment, and standing behind at his feet, weeping,
she began to wet his feet with her tears, and wiped them with the hair
of her head, and [2]kissed his feet, and anointed them with the ointment.
39 Now when the Pharisee which had bidden him saw it, he spake within
himself, saying, This man, if he were [3]a prophet, would have perceived
who and what manner of woman this is which toucheth him, that she is
40 a sinner. And Jesus answering said unto him, Simon, I have somewhat
41 to say unto thee. And he saith, [4]Master, say on. A certain lender had
two debtors: the one owed five hundred [5]pence, and the other fifty.
42 When they had not *wherewith* to pay, he forgave them both. Which
43 of them therefore will love him most? Simon answered and said, He, I
44 suppose, to whom he forgave the most. And he said unto him, Thou
hast rightly judged. And turning to the woman, he said unto Simon,
Seest thou this woman? I entered into thine house, thou gavest me no
water for my feet: but she hath wetted my feet with her tears, and wiped
45 them with her hair. Thou gavest me no kiss: but she, since the time I
46 came in, hath not ceased to [6]kiss my feet. My head with oil thou didst
47 not anoint: but she hath anointed my feet with ointment. Wherefore I
say unto thee, Her sins, which are many, are forgiven: for she loved much:
48 but to whom little is forgiven, *the same* loveth little. And he said unto
49 her, Thy sins are forgiven. And they that sat at meat with him began
50 to say [7]within themselves, Who is this that even forgiveth sins? And he
said unto the woman, Thy faith hath saved thee; go in peace.

[1] Or, *a flask*. [2] Gr. *kissed much*. [3] Some ancient authorities read *the prophet*. See John 1:21, 25. [4] Or, *Teacher*. [5] The word in the Greek denotes a coin worth about seventeen cents. [6] Gr. *kiss much*. [7] Or, *among*.

In sections 60 to 63 Jesus makes a second (three in all) tour of Galilee, this time with all the Twelve. Intense hostility of the Pharisees is aroused by the work. They make the blasphemous accusation that Jesus is in league with Satan. Even the kindred of Jesus fear that he is beside himself because of the excitement and the charges.

* This anointing in Galilee must be distinct from the anointing at Bethany, near Jerusalem, more than a year later. This sinful and penitent woman is represented by a very late tradition as being Mary Magdalene, and hence all the popular uses of the term Magdalen. But that notion has no historical support whatever, and it becomes violently improbable when we find that in the very next paragraph Luke introduces Mary Magdalene as a new figure in the history. Some men even identify Mary of Bethany with this woman that was a sinner and also with Mary Magdalen, a medley of medieval mysticism.

§60. THE SECOND TOUR OF GALILEE

Luke 8:1-3

1 And it came to pass soon afterwards, that he went about through
cities and villages, preaching and bringing the [1]good tidings of the king-
2 dom of God, and with him the twelve, and certain women which had been
healed of evil spirits and infirmities, Mary that was called Magdalene,
3 from whom seven [2]devils had gone out, and Joanna the wife of Chuza
Herod's steward, and Susanna, and many others, which ministered unto
[3]them of their substance.

[1] Or, *gospel*. [2] Gr. *demons*. [3] Many ancient authorities read *him*.

*Notice that the events of §§61–66 all occurred on the same day, called the Busy Day**

§61. BLASPHEMOUS ACCUSATION OF LEAGUE WITH BEELZEBUB

Galilee

Mark 3:19–30

19 And he cometh into a house.
20 And the multitude cometh to-
gether again, so that they could
21 not so much as eat bread. And
when his friends heard it, they
went out to lay hold on him: for
they said, He is beside himself.

22 And the scribes which came
down from Jerusalem said, He
hath Beelzebub, and, [3]By the
prince of the [2]devils casteth he
23 out the [2]devils. And he called
them unto him, and said unto
them in parables, How can Satan
24 cast out Satan? And if a king-
dom be divided against itself,
25 that kingdom cannot stand. And
if a house be divided against it-
self, that house will not be able

Matt. 12:22–37

22 Then was brought unto him
[1]one possessed with a devil, blind
and dumb: and he healed him,
insomuch that the dumb man
23 spake and saw. And all the mul-
titudes were amazed, and said,
24 Is this the son of David? But
when the Pharisees heard it,
they said, †This man doth not
cast out [2]devils, but [3]by Beelze-
bub the prince of the [2]devils
25 [*see John 7:20; 8:48, 52; 10:20*].
And knowing their thoughts he said
unto them, Every kingdom di-

* This "Busy Day" is just one of many such days in the Master's Ministry. See, for instance, the last day of his public ministry in the temple in Jerusalem. Observe Jesus in the *forenoon* teaching a crowded audience (Mark 3:19), some of whom insult and blaspheme him, and others demand a sign, and at length his mother and brethren try to carry him off as insane (comp. Mark 3:21); in the *afternoon* giving a group of most remarkable parables, several of which he interprets; towards night crossing the Lake in a boat, so tired and worn that he sleeps soundly amid the alarming storm; then healing the Gadarene demoniacs, and returning by boat, apparently the same evening. What a day of toil and trial.

† Luke (11:14–36) gives another blasphemous accusation later in Judea. Matthew (9:27–34) also has another blasphemous accusation. Note Christ's use of parables in replying to the accusations.

Mark 3:19–30

26 to stand. And if Satan hath
risen up against himself, and is
divided, he cannot stand, but
hath an end.

27 But no one can
enter into the house of the strong
man, and spoil his goods, except he
first bind the strong *man;* and then
he will spoil his house.

28 Verily I say unto
you, All their sins shall be for-
given unto the sons of men, and
their blasphemies wherewith so-
29 ever they shall blaspheme: but
whosoever shall blaspheme
against the Holy Spirit hath
never forgiveness, but is guilty
30 of an eternal sin: because they
said, He hath an unclean spirit.

Matt. 12:22–37

vided against itself is brought
to desolation; and every city or
house divided against itself shall
26 not stand: and if Satan casteth
out Satan, he is divided against
himself; how then shall his king-
27 dom stand? And if I [3]by Beelze-
bub cast out [2]devils, [3]by whom
do your sons cast them out? there-
fore shall they be your judges.
28 But if I [3]by the Spirit of God cast
out [2]devils, then is the kingdom of
29 God come upon you. Or how can
one enter into the house of the
strong *man*, and spoil his goods,
except he first bind the strong
man? and then he will spoil his
30 house. He that is not with me
is against me; and he that gather-
31 eth not with me scattereth. There-
fore I say unto you, every sin and
blasphemy shall be forgiven [4]unto
men; but the blasphemy against
the Spirit shall not be forgiven.
32 And whosoever shall speak a
word against the Son of man, it
shall be forgiven him; but whoso-
ever shall speak against the Holy
Spirit it shall not be forgiven
him, neither in this [5]world, nor
33 in that which is to come. Either make the tree good, and its fruit good;
or make the tree corrupt, and its fruit corrupt: for the tree is known by
34 its fruit. Ye offspring of vipers, how can ye, being evil, speak good
35 things? for out of the abundance of the heart the mouth speaketh. The
good man out of his own good treasure bringeth forth good things: and the
36 evil man out of his evil treasure bringeth forth evil things. And I say
unto you, that every idle word that men shall speak, they shall give
37 account thereof in the day of judgement. For by thy words thou shalt
be justified, and by thy words thou shalt be condemned.

[1] Or, *a demoniac.* [2] Gr. *demons.* [3] Or, *in.* [4] Some ancient authorities read *unto you men.* [5] Or, *age.*

§ 62. SCRIBES AND PHARISEES DEMAND A SIGN

Same day. Galilee

Matt. 12:38–45

38 Then certain of the scribes and Pharisees answered him, saying, [1]Master,
39 we would see a sign from thee. But he answered and said unto them,
An evil and adulterous generation seeketh after a sign; and there shall no

Matt. 12:38–45

40 sign be given to it but the sign of Jonah the prophet: for as Jonah was
three days and three nights in the belly of the [2]whale; so shall the Son of
man be three days and three nights in the heart of the earth [*see Jonah 1:17;*
41 *2:1–2; 3:5; 4:3; 1 Kings 10:1–10*]. The men of Nineveh shall stand up
in the judgement with this generation, and shall condemn it: for they re-
pented at the preaching of Jonah; and behold, [3]a greater than Jonah is
42 here. The queen of the south shall rise up in the judgement with this
generation, and shall condemn it: for she came from the ends of the earth
to hear the wisdom of Solomon; and behold, [3]a greater than Solomon is
43 here. But the unclean spirit, when [4]he is gone out of the man, passeth
44 through waterless places, seeking rest, and findeth it not. Then [4]he
saith, I will return into my house whence I came out; and when [4]he is
45 come, [4]he findeth it empty, swept, and garnished. Then goeth [4]he, and
taketh with [5]himself seven other spirits more evil than [5]himself, and they
enter in and dwell there: and the last state of that man becometh worse
than the first. Even so shall it be also unto this evil generation

[1] Or, *Teacher*. [2] Gr. *sea-monster*. [3] Gr. *more than*. [4] Or, *it*. [5] Or, *itself*.

§63. CHRIST'S MOTHER AND BRETHREN SEEK TO TAKE HIM HOME

Same day. Galilee

Mark 3:31–35

31 And there come his mother and his brethren; and, standing without, they sent unto him, calling him.
32 And a multitude was sitting about him; and they say unto him, Behold, thy mother and thy brethren without seek
33 for thee. And he answereth them, and saith, Who is my mother and my brethren?
34 And looking round on them which sat round about him, he saith, Behold, my mother and my brethren!

Matt. 12:46–50

46 While he was yet speaking to the multitudes, behold, his mother and his brethren stood without, seeking to speak to
47 him. [1]And one said unto him, Behold, thy mother and thy brethren stand without, seeking to speak to thee.
48 But he answered and said unto him that told him, Who is my mother? and who are my
49 brethren? And he stretched forth his hand towards his disciples, and said, Behold, my mother and
50 my brethren! For

Luke 8:19–21

19 And there came to him his mother and brethren, and they could not come at him for the crowd.
20 And it was told him, Thy mother and thy brethren stand without, desiring to see thee.
21 But he answered and said unto them,

Mark 3:31–35	Matt. 12:46–50	Luke 8:19–21
35 For whosoever shall do the will of God, the same is my brother, and sister, and mother.	whosoever shall do the will of my Father which is in heaven, he is my brother, and sister, and mother.	My mother and my brethren are these which hear the word of God, and do it [*see John 15:14*].

[1] Some ancient authorities omit ver. 47.

In §§ 64 to 69 we have the first great group of Parables with the visit to Gerasa and the return to Nazareth

§ 64. THE FIRST GREAT GROUP OF PARABLES*

Same day. Beside the Sea of Galilee. Introduction to the Group

Mark 4:1, 2	Matt. 13:1–3	Luke 8:4
1 And again he be- gan to teach by the sea side. And there is gathered unto him a very great multi- tude, so that he en- tered into a boat, and sat in the sea; and all the multitude were by the sea on the land. 2 And he taught them many things in par- ables, and said unto them in his teaching, Hearken:	1 On that day went Jesus out of the house, and sat by the 2 sea side. And there were gathered unto him great multitudes, so that he entered into a boat, and sat; and all the multitude stood on the beach. 3 And he spake to them many things in par- ables, saying,	4 And when a great multitude came to- gether, and they of every city resorted unto him, he spake by a parable:

1. *To the Crowds by the Sea*

(*a*) Parable of the Sower

Mark 4:3–25	Matt. 13:3–23	Luke 8:5–18
3 Behold, the sower went forth to sow; 4 and it came to pass, as he sowed, some *seed* fell by the way side, and the birds came and devoured 5 it. And other fell on the rocky *ground*, where it had not	3 Behold, the sower went forth to sow; 4 and as he sowed, some *seeds* fell by the way side, and the birds came and de- 5 voured them; and others fell upon the rocky places, where they had not much	5 The sower went forth to sow his seed and as he sowed some fell by the way side; and it was trodden under foot, and the birds of the heaven 6 devoured it. And other fell on the rock; and as soon as it

* We have met various *separate* parables heretofore, but here is a *group* of at least ten. Two other great groups will occur hereafter, one group given in Luke only, and the last group during the last week of our Lord's public ministry.

Mark 4:3-25

much earth: and
straightway it sprang
up, because it had no
6 deepness of earth: and
when the sun was
risen, it was scorch-
ed; and because it
had no root, it with-
7 ered away. And
other fell among the
thorns, and the thorns
grew up, and choked
it, and it yielded no
8 fruit. And others fell
into the good ground,
and yielded fruit,
growing up and in-
creasing; and brought
forth, thirtyfold, and
sixtyfold, and a hun-
9 dredfold. And he
said, Who hath ears
to hear, let him hear.
10 And when he was
alone, they that were
about him with the
twelve asked of him
the parables.
11 And he
said unto them, Un-
to you is given the
mystery of the king-
dom of God: but unto
them that are with-
out, all things are
done in parables: that
12 seeing they may see,
and not perceive; and
hearing they may
hear, and not under-
stand; lest haply they

Matt. 13:3-23

earth: and straight-
way they sprang up,
because they had no
deepness of earth:
6 and when the sun
was risen, they were
scorched; and because
they had no root,
they withered away.
7 And others fell upon
the thorns; and the
thorns grew up, and
choked them: and
8 others fell upon the
good ground, and
yielded fruit, some a
hundredfold, some
sixty, some thirty.
9 He that hath ears[1],
let him hear.
10 And the disciples
came, and said unto
him, Why speakest
thou unto them in
parables?
11 And he
answered and said
unto them, Unto you
it is given to know
the mysteries of the
kingdom of heaven,
but to them it is not
12 given. For whoso-
ever hath, to him
shall be given, and he
shall have abundance:
but whosoever hath
not, from him shall
be taken away even
that which he hath.
13 Therefore speak I to
them in parables; be-
cause seeing they see
not, and hearing they
hear not, neither do
14 they understand. And
unto them is fulfilled

Luke 8:5-18

grew, it withered
away, because it had
no moisture.
7 And
other fell amidst the
thorns; and the thorns
grew with it, and
8 choked it. And oth-
er fell into the good
ground, and grew,
and brought forth
fruit a hundredfold.
As he said these
things, he cried,
He that hath
ears to hear, let him
hear.
9 And his disciples
asked him what this
parable might be.
10 And he said, Unto
you it is given to
know the mysteries
of the kingdom of
God: but to the rest
in parables; that see-
ing they may not see,
and hearing they may
11 not understand. Now
the parable is this:

Mark 4:3-25

should turn again,
and it should be for-
13 given* them. And
he saith unto them,
Know ye not this
parable? and how
shall ye know all the
14 parables? The sow-
er soweth the word.
15 And these are they
by the way side,
where the word is
sown; and when they
have heard, straight-
way cometh Satan,
and taketh away the
word which hath been
16 sown in them. And
these in like manner
are they that are

Matt. 13:3-23

the prophecy of
Isaiah, which saith,
By hearing ye shall
hear, and shall
in no wise under-
stand;
And seeing ye shall
see, and shall
in no wise per-
ceive:
15 For this people's
heart is waxed
gross,
And their ears are
dull of hearing,
And their eyes they have closed
Lest haply they should perceive with their
eyes,
And hear with their ears,
And understand with their heart,
And should turn again,
And I should heal them [*see Isa. 6:9-10*];
16 But blessed are your eyes, for they see; and your ears, for they hear.
17 For verily I say unto you, that many prophets and righteous men desired
to see the things which ye see, and saw them not; and to hear the things
18 which ye hear, and heard them not. Hear then ye the parable of the
19 sower. When any one heareth the word of the kingdom, and under-
standeth it not, *then* cometh the evil *one*, and snatcheth away that
which hath been sown in his heart. This is he that was sown by the

Luke 8:5-18

12 The seed is the word
of God. And those
by the way side are
they that have heard;
then cometh the dev-
il, and taketh away
the word from their
heart, that they may
not believe and be
saved.

Mark

sown upon the rocky
places, who, when
they have heard the
word, straightway re-
17 ceive it with joy; and
they have no root in
themselves, but en-
dure for a while;
then, when tribula-
tion or persecution
ariseth because of the
word, straightway
18 they stumble. And
others are they that
are sown among the
thorns; these are they

Matt.

20 way side. And he
that was sown upon
the rocky places, this
is he that heareth the
word, and straight-
way with joy receiv-
21 eth it; yet hath he
not root in himself,
but endureth for a
while; and when trib-
ulation or persecution
ariseth because of the
word, straighway he
22 stumbleth. And he
that was sown among
the thorns, this is he
that heareth the

Luke

13 And
those on the rock *are*
they which, when
they have heard, re-
ceive the word with
joy; and these have
no root, which for a
while believe, and in
time of temptation
fall away.
14 And that which fell
among the thorns,
these are they that
have heard, and as

* Observe that Jesus spoke these words just after the blasphemous accusation and on the same day (Matt. 13:1).

Mark 4:3–25

that have heard the
19 word, and the cares
of the [2]world, and the
deceitfulness of riches,
and the lusts of other
things entering in,
choke the word, and
it becometh unfruit-
20 ful. And those are
they that were sown
upon the good
ground; such as hear
the word, and accept
it, and bear fruit,
thirtyfold, and sixty-
fold, and a hundred-
fold.

Matt. 13:3–23

word; and the care
of the [2]world, and the
deceitfulness of riches,
choke the
word, and he becom-
23 eth unfruitful. And
he that was sown up-
on the good ground,
this is he that heareth
the word, and un-
derstandeth it: who
verily beareth fruit,
and bringeth forth,
some a hundredfold,
some sixty, some
thirty.

Luke 8:5–18

they go on their way
they are choked with
cares and riches and
pleasures of *this* life,
and bring no fruit to
perfection.
15 And that in the good
ground, these are
such as in an honest
and good heart, hav-
ing heard the word,
hold it fast, and bring
forth fruit with pa-
tience.

Mark

21 And he said unto them, Is the
[*]lamp brought to be put under
the bushel, or under the bed, *and*
not to be put on the stand?
22 For there is nothing
hid, save that it should be mani-
fested; neither was *anything* made
23 secret, but that it should come to
light. If any man hath ears to
24 hear, let him hear. And he said
unto them, Take heed what ye
hear: with what measure ye mete
it shall be measured unto you: and
25 more shall be given unto you. For
he that hath, to him shall be
given: and he that hath not, from
him shall be taken away even that
which he hath.

Luke

16 And no man, when he hath
lighted a lamp, covereth it with a
vessel, or putteth it under a bed;
but putteth it on a stand, that they
which enter in may see the light.
17 For nothing is hid, that shall not
be made manifest; nor *anything*
secret, that shall not be known and
18 come to light. Take heed there-
fore how ye hear: for whosoever
hath, to him shall be given, and
whosoever hath not, from him
shall be taken away even that
which he [3]thinketh he hath.

[1] Some ancient authorities add here, and in ver. 43, *to hear:* as in Mark 4:9; Luke 8:8. [2] Or, *age.* [3] Or, *seemeth to have.*

(*b*) Parable of the Seed Growing of Itself

Mark 4:26–29

26 And he said, So is the kingdom of God, as if a man should cast seed
27 upon the earth; and should sleep and rise night and day, and the seed
28 should spring up and grow, he knoweth not how. The earth [1]beareth
fruit of herself; first the blade, then the ear, then the full corn in the ear.

[*] Note here another brief parable of the lamp to enforce the lesson of the parable of the Sower. Preachers to-day sometimes tell one story to illustrate another.

Mark 4:26–29

29 But when the fruit [2]is ripe, straightway he [3]putteth forth the sickle, be-
cause the harvest is come [*see Joel 3:13*].

[1] Or, *yieldeth.* [2] Or, *alloweth.* [3] Or, *sendeth forth.*

(*c*) Parable of the Tares

Matt. 13:24–30

24 Another parable set he before them, saying, The kingdom of heaven
25 is likened unto a man that sowed good seed in his field: but while men
slept, his enemy came and sowed [1]tares also among the wheat, and went
26 away. But when the blade sprang up, and brought forth fruit, then
27 appeared the tares also. And the [2]servants of the householder came and
said unto him, Sir, didst thou not sow good seed in thy field? whence then
28 hath it tares? And he said unto them, [3]An enemy hath done this. And
the [2]servants say unto him, Wilt thou then that we go and gather them
29 up? But he saith, Nay; lest haply while ye gather up the tares, ye root
30 up the wheat with them. Let both grow together until the harvest:
and in the time of the harvest I will say to the reapers, Gather up first
the tares, and bind them in bundles to burn them: but gather the wheat
into my barn.

[1] Or, *darnel.* [2] Gr. *bond-servants.* [3] Gr. *A man that is an enemy.*

(*d*) Parable of the Mustard Seed

Mark 4:30–32

30 And he said, How shall we liken
the kingdom of God? or in what
31 parable shall we set it forth? [1]It
is like a grain of mustard seed,
which, when it is sown upon the
earth, though it be less than all
the seeds that are upon the earth,
32 yet when it is sown, groweth up,
and becometh greater than all
the herbs, and putteth out great
branches; so that the birds of
the heaven can lodge under the
shadow thereof.

Matt. 13:31–32

31 Another parable set he before
them, saying, The kingdom of
heaven is like unto a grain of
mustard seed, which a man took,
32 and sowed in his field: which in-
deed is less than all seeds: but
when it is grown, it is greater
than the herbs, and becometh a
tree [*see Dan. 4:12, 21*], so that the
birds of the heaven come and
lodge in the branches thereof.

[1] Gr. *As, unto.*

(*e*) Parable of the Leaven and many such Parables

Mark 4:33–34

33 And with many* such parables

Matt. 13:33–35

33 Another parable spake he unto
them; The kingdom of heaven is
like unto leaven, which a woman
took, and hid in three [1]measures
of meal, till it was all leavened.
34 All these things spake Jesus

* See note, p. 69.

Mark 4:33-34	Matt. 13:33-35
spake he the word unto them, as 34 they were able to hear it: and without a parable spake he not unto them: but privately to his disciples he expounded all things.	in parables unto the multitudes; and without* a parable spake he 35 nothing unto them: that it might be fulfilled which was spoken [2]by the prophet, saying, I will open my mouth in parables; I will utter things hidden from the foundation [3]of the world [*see Ps. 78:2*].

[1] The word in the Greek denotes the Hebrew seah, a measure containing nearly a peck and a half. [2] Or, *through*. [3] Many ancient authorities omit *of the world*.

2. *To the Disciples in the House*

(*a*) Explanation of the Parable of the Tares

Matt. 13:36-43

36 Then he left the multitudes, and went into the house: and his disciples
came unto him, saying, Explain unto us the parable of the tares of the
37 field. And he answered and said, He that soweth the good seed is the
38 Son of man; and the field is the world; and the good seed, these are the
39 sons of the kingdom; and the tares are the sons of the evil *one;* and the
enemy that sowed them is the devil: and the harvest is [1]the end of the
40 world; and the reapers are angels. As therefore the tares are gathered
41 up and burned with fire; so shall it be in the end of the world. The Son
of man shall send forth his angels, and they shall gather out of his kingdom
all things that cause stumbling, and them that do iniquity, and shall
42 cast them into the furnace of fire: there shall be the weeping and gnashing
43 of teeth. Then shall the righteous shine forth as the sun in the kingdom
of their Father [*see Dan. 12:3*]. He that hath ears, let him hear.

[1] Or, *the consummation of the age*.

(*b*) The Parable of the Hid Treasure

Matt. 13:44

44 The kingdom of heaven is like unto a treasure hidden in the field;
which a man found, and hid; and [1]in his joy he goeth and selleth all that
he hath, and buyeth that field.

[1] Or, *for joy thereof*.

(*c*) The Parable of the Pearl of Great Price

Matt. 13:45-46

45 Again, the kingdom of heaven is like unto a man that is a merchant
46 seeking goodly pearls: and having found one pearl of great price, he went
and sold all that he had, and bought it.

* Note the expression. Matthew gives nine in Chapter 13 and Mark another. There may have been still others on this day.

(*d*) The Parable of the Net

Matt. 13:47–50

47 Again, the kingdom of heaven is like unto a [1]net, that was cast into
48 the sea, and gathered of every kind: which, when it was filled, they drew
up on the beach; and they sat down, and gathered the good into vessels,
49 but the bad they cast away. So shall it be in [2]the end of the world:
the angels shall come forth, and sever the wicked from among the right-
50 eous, and shall cast them into the furnace of fire: there shall be the weep-
ing and gnashing of teeth.

[1] Gr. *dragnet*. [2] Or, *consummation of the age*.

(*e*) The Parable of the Householder

Matt. 13:51–53

51 Have ye understood all these things? They say unto him, Yea.
52 And he said unto them, Therefore every scribe who hath been made a
disciple to the kingdom of heaven is like unto a man that is a
householder, which bringeth forth out of his treasure things new and old.
53 And it came to pass, when Jesus had finished these *parables, he de-
parted thence.

§ 65. IN CROSSING THE LAKE, JESUS STILLS THE TEMPEST

Same day. Sea of Galilee

Mark 4:35–41

35 And on that day, when even was come, he saith unto them, Let us go over unto the other side.

36 And leaving the multitude, they take him with them, even as he was, in the boat. And other boats were with him.

Matt. 8:18, 23–27

18 Now when Jesus saw great multitudes about him, he gave commandment to depart unto the other side.

23 And when he was entered into a boat, his disciples followed him.

Luke 8:22–25

22 Now it came to pass on one of those days, that he entered into a boat, himself and his disciples; and he said unto them, Let us go over to the other side of the lake: and they launched
23 forth. But as they sailed he fell asleep:

* Eight of these ten parables go in pairs (the sower and the seed growing of itself, the tares and the net, the mustard seed and the leaven, the hid treasure and the pearl of great price). But nothing can be made out of the number of the parables spoken on this day. We do not even know what the number was. Jesus had spoken various shorter and more or less isolated parables before this occasion. An immediate occasion for the use of so many and such extended parables at this point was the hostility of the Pharisees and the need of special instruction for the disciples who were taught by Jesus how to interpret parables, though they had much difficulty later in applying the instruction about the parabolic teaching.

Mark 4:35–41

37 And there ariseth a
great storm of wind,
and the waves beat
into the boat, inso-
much that the boat
38 was now filling. And
he himself was in the
stern, asleep on the
cushion: and they
awake him, and say
unto him, Master,
carest thou not that
39 we perish? And he
awoke, and rebuked
the wind, and said
unto the sea, Peace,
be still. And the
wind ceased, and
there was a great
40 calm. And he said
unto them, Why are
ye fearful? have ye
not yet faith?
41 And
they feared exceed-
ingly, and said one
to another, Who then
is this, that even the
wind and the sea
obey him?

Matt. 8:18, 23–27

24 And behold,
there arose a great
tempest in the sea,
insomuch that the
boat was covered
with the waves: but
25 he was asleep. And
they came to him,
and awoke him, say-
ing, Save, Lord; we
perish.
26 And he
saith unto them, Why
are ye fearful, O ye
of little faith? Then
he arose, and re-
buked the winds and
the sea; and there
was a great calm.
27 And the men mar-
velled, saying, What
manner of man is
this, that even the
winds and the sea
obey him?

Luke 8:22–25

and there came down
a storm of wind on
the lake: and they
were filling *with water*,
and were in jeopardy.
24 And
they came to him,
and awoke him, say-
ing, Master, master,
we perish, And he
awoke, and rebuked
the wind and the
raging of the water:
and they ceased, and
there was a calm.
25 And he said unto
them, Where is your
faith?
And being
afraid they marvelled,
saying one to an-
other, Who then is
this, that he com-
mandeth even the
winds and the water,
and they obey him?

§ 66. BEYOND THE LAKE JESUS HEALS THE GERASENE* DEMONIAC†

Gerasa (Khersa). Same day

Mark 5:1–20

1 And they came to
the other side of the
sea, into the country
2 of the Gerasenes.
And when he was
come out of the boat,
straightway there

Matt. 8:28–34

28 And when he was
come to the other
side into the country
of the Gadarenes,
there met him two
[1]possessed with dev-
ils, coming forth out

Luke 8:26–39

26 And they arrived
at the country of the
[4]Gerasenes, which is
over against Galilee.
27 And when he was
come forth upon the
land, there met him

* The long famous instance of "discrepancy" as to the *place* in this narrative has been cleared up in recent years by the decision of textual critics that the correct text in Luke is Gerasenes, as well as in Mark, and by Dr. Thomson's discovery of a ruin on the lake shore, named Khersa (Gerasa). If this village was included (a very natural supposition) in the district belonging to the city of Gadara, some miles south-eastward, then the locality could be described as either in the country of the Gadarenes, or in the country of the Gerasenes.

† Matthew mentions two demoniacs, Mark and Luke describe one, who was probably the prominent and leading one.

Mark 5:1–20

met him out of the
tombs a man with
3 an unclean spirit, who
had his dwelling in
the tombs: and no
man could any more
bind him, no, not
4 with a chain; because
that he had been
often bound with fet-
ters and chains, and
the chains had been
rent asunder by him,
and the fetters broken
in pieces: and no man
had strength to tame
5 him. And always,
night and day, in the
tombs and in the
mountains, he was
crying out, and cut-
ting himself with
6 stones. And when
he saw Jesus from
afar, he ran and wor-
7 shipped him; and cry-
ing out with a loud
voice, he saith, What
have I to do with
thee, Jesus, thou Son
of the Most High
God? I adjure thee
by God, torment me
8 not. For he said un-
to him, Come forth,
thou unclean spirit,
out of the man.

9 And he asked
him, What is thy
name? And he saith
unto him, My name
is Legion; for we are

Matt. 8:28–34

of the tombs, exceed-
ing fierce, so that no
man could pass by
that way.

29 And behold,
they cried out, say-
ing, What have we
to do with thee, thou
Son of God? art thou
come hither to tor-
ment us before the
time?

Luke 8:26–39

a certain man out of
the city, who had
[2]devils; and for a long
time he had worn no
clothes, and abode
not in *any* house, but
in the tombs.

28 And
when he saw Jesus,
he cried out, and fell
down before him,
and with a loud voice
said, What have I to
do with thee, Jesus,
thou Son of the Most
High God? I be-
seech thee, torment
29 me not. For he com-
manded the unclean
spirit to come out
of the man. For [4]oft-
entimes it had seized
him: and he was kept
under guard, and
bound with chains
and fetters; and
breaking the bands
asunder, he was driv-
en of the [2]devil into
30 the deserts. And
Jesus asked him,
What is thy name?
And he said, Legion;
for many [2]devils were
entered into him.

Mark 5:1-20

10 many. And he be-
sought him much that
he would not send
them away out of
11 the country. Now
there was there on
the mountain side a
great herd of swine
12 feeding. And they
besought him, say-
ing, Send us into the
swine, that we may
enter into them.
13 And he gave them
leave. And the un-
clean spirits came
out, and entered in-
to the swine: and the
herd rushed down the
steep into the sea,
in number about two
thousand; and they
were choked in the
14 sea. And they that
fed them fled, and
told it in the city,
and in the country.
And they came to see
what it was that had
15 come to pass. And
they come to Jesus,
and behold [3]him that
was possessed with
devils sitting, clothed
and in his right mind,
even he that had the
legion: and they were
16 afraid. And they
that saw it declared
unto them how it
befell [3]him that was
possessed with devils,
and concerning the
17 swine. And they be-
gan to beseech them
to depart from their
18 borders. And as he
was entering into the
boat, he that had
been possessed with

Matt. 8:28-34

30 Now there
was afar off from
them a herd of many
31 swine feeding. And
the [2]devils besought
him, saying, If thou
cast us out, send us
away into the herd
32 of swine. And he
said unto them, Go.
And they came out,
and went into the
swine: and behold,
the whole herd rush-
ed down the steep
into the sea, and per-
ished in the waters.
33 And they that fed
them fled, and went
away into the city,
and told everything,
and what was befal-
len to them that
were [1]possessed with
34 devils. And behold,
all the city came out
to meet Jesus: and
when they saw him,
they besought *him*
that he would de-
part from their bor-
ders.

Luke 8:26-39

31 And they intreated
him that he would
not command them
to depart into the
32 abyss. Now there
was there a herd of
swine feeding on the
mountain: and they
intreated him that
he would give them
leave to enter into
them. And he gave
33 them leave. And the
[2]devils came out from
the man, and entered
into the swine: and
the herd rushed down
the steep into the
lake and were choked.
34 And when they that
fed them saw what
had come to pass,
they fled, and told it
in the city and in the
35 country. And they
went out to see what
had come to pass: and
they came to Jesus,
and found the man,
from whom the [2]dev-
ils were gone out, sit-
ting, clothed and in
his right mind, at
the feet of Jesus: and
they were afraid.
36 And they that saw
it told them how he
that was possessed
with [2]devils was
37 [3]made whole. And
all the people of the
country of the [4]Ger-
asenes round about
asked him to depart
from them; for they
were holden with
great fear: and he
entered into a boat,

Mark 5:1-20

[2]devils besought him
that he might be with
19 him. And he suffer-
ed him not, but saith
unto him, Go to thy
house unto thy
friends, and tell them
how great things the
Lord hath done for
thee, and *how* he had
20 mercy on thee. And
he went his way, and
began to publish in
Decapolis how great
things Jesus had done
for him: and all men
did marvel.*

Luke 8:26-39

38 and returned. But
the man from whom
the [2]devils were gone
out prayed him that
he might be with
him: but he sent him
39 away, saying, Return
to thy house, and
declare how great
things God hath
done for thee. And
he went his way, pub-
lishing throughout
the whole city how
great things Jesus had
done for him.

[1] Or, *demoniacs.* [2] Gr. *demons.* [3] Or, *the demoniac.* [4] Many ancient authorities read *Gergesenes;* others *Gadarenes.* [5] Or, *of a long time.* [6] Gr. *demon.* [7] Or, *saved.*

§ 67. THE RETURN AND THE HEALING OF JAIRUS' DAUGHTER AND OF THE WOMAN WHO ONLY TOUCHED CHRIST'S GARMENT

Probably Capernaum

Mark 5:21-43

21 And when Jesus
had crossed over
again in the boat unto
the other side, a great
multitude was gather-
ed unto him: and he
was by the sea.
22 And there cometh
one of the rulers of
the synagogue, Jairus
by name; and seeing
him, he falleth at his
23 feet, and beseecheth
him much, saying,
My little daughter is
at the point of death:
I pray thee, that thou

Matt. 9:18-26

18 While he spake
these things unto
them,† behold, there
came [1]a ruler, and
worshipped him, say-
ing, My daughter is
even now dead: but
come and lay thy

Luke 8:40-56

40 And as Jesus re-
turned, the multi-
tude welcomed him;
for they were all
waiting for him.
41 And behold there
came a man named
Jairus, and he was
a ruler of the syn-
agogue: and he fell
down at Jesus' feet,
and besought him to
come into his house;

* Note in Mark the numerous vivid details and fulness of narrative.

† Broadus felt that the language in Matt. 9:18 compelled him to place 9:18 after 9:17. I do not think so, for "while he spake" may be merely an introductory phrase for a new paragraph. It is best to follow Mark's order, as Luke does, for Matthew is not chronological in this part of his Gospel.

Mark 5:21–43

come and lay thy
hands on her, that
she may be [2]made
24 whole, and live. And
he went with him;
and a great multitude
followed him, and
they thronged him.
25 And a woman,
which had an issue
26 of blood twelve years,
and had suffered
many things of many
physicians, and had
spent all that she
had, and was nothing
bettered, but rather
27 grew worse, having
heard the things concerning
Jesus, came
in the crowd behind,
and touched his gar-
28 ment. For she said,
If I touch but his
garments, I shall be
29 [2]made whole. And
straightway the fountain
of her blood was
dried up; and she felt
in her body that she
was healed of her
30 [5]plague. And straightway
Jesus, perceiving
in himself that the
power *proceeding* from
him had gone forth,
turned him about in
the crowd, and said,
Who touched my gar-
31 ments? And his disciples
said unto him,
Thou seest the multitude
thronging thee,
and sayest thou, Who
32 touched me? And he
looked round about
to see her that had
33 done this thing. But
the woman fearing
and trembling, know-

Matt. 9:18–26

hand upon her, and
19 she shall live. And
Jesus arose, and followed
him, and *so did*
his disciples.

20 And behold, a
woman, who had an
issue of blood twelve
years, came behind
him, and touched the
border of his gar-
21 ment: for she said
within herself, If I do
but touch his garment,
I shall be [2]made
whole.

Luke 8:40–56

42 for he had an only
daughter, about
twelve years of age,
and she lay a dying.
But as he went the
multitudes thronged
him.

43 And a woman having
an issue of blood
twelve years, which
[8]had spent all her
living upon physicians,
and could not
be healed of any,
44 came behind him, and
touched the border of
his garment: and immediately
the issue of
her blood stanched.

45 And Jesus said, Who
is it that touched
me? And when all
denied, Peter said,
[9]and they that were
with him, Master,
the multitudes press
thee and crush *thee.*
46 But Jesus said, Some
one did touch me;
for I perceived that
power had gone forth

Mark 5:21-43

ing what had been
done to her, came
and fell down before
him, and told him
34 all the truth. And
he said unto her,
Daughter, thy faith
hath [3]made thee
whole; go in peace,
and be whole of thy
[5]plague.
35 While he yet spake,
they come from the
ruler of the syna-
gogue's *house*, saying,
Thy daughter is dead:
why troublest thou
the [6]Master any fur-
36 ther? But Jesus,
[7]not heeding the word
spoken, saith unto
the ruler of the syn-
agogue, Fear not,
37 only believe. And he
suffered no man to
follow with him, save
Peter, and James, and
John the brother of
38 James. And they
come to the house
of the ruler of the
synagogue; and he
beholdeth a tumult,
and *many* weeping
and wailing greatly.
39 And when he was
entered in, he saith
unto them, Why
make ye a tumult
and weep? the child
is not dead, but sleep-
40 eth. And they laugh-
ed him to scorn. But
he, having put them
all forth, taketh the
father of the child
and her mother and
them that were with
him, and goeth in
where the child was.

Matt. 9:18-26

22 But
Jesus turning and see-
ing her said, Daugh-
ter, be of good cheer;
thy faith hath [3]made
thee whole. And the
woman was [3]made
whole from that hour.

23 And when Jesus came
into the ruler's house,
and saw the flute-
players, and the
crowd making a tu-
24 mult, he said, Give
place: for the damsel
is not dead, but sleep-
eth. And they laugh-
25 ed him to scorn. But
when the crowd was
put forth, he entered

Luke 8:40-56

47 from me. And when
the woman saw that
she was not hid, she
came trembling, and
falling down before
him declared in the
presence of all the
people for what cause
she touched him, and
how she was healed
48 immediately. And
he said unto her,
Daughter, thy faith
hath [3]made thee
whole; go in peace.

49 While he yet spake,
there cometh one
from the ruler of the
synagogue's *house*,
saying, Thy daughter
is dead; trouble not
50 the [6]Master. But
Jesus hearing it, an-
swered him, Fear not:
only believe, and she
shall be [3]made whole.
51 And when he came
to the house, he suf-
fered not any man to
enter in with him,
save Peter, and John,
and James, and the
father of the maiden
and her mother.
52 And all were weeping,
and bewailing her:
but he said, Weep
not; for she is not
dead, but sleepeth.
53 And they laughed
him to scorn, know-
ing that she was dead.

Mark 5:21–43

41 And taking the child
by the hand, he saith
unto her, Talitha cu-
mi; which is being
interpreted, Damsel,
I say unto thee, Arise.
42 And straightway the
damsel rose up, and
walked; for she was
twelve years old.
And they were amaz-
ed straightway with
a great amazement.
43 And he charged them
much that no man
should know this: and
he commanded that
something should be
given her to eat.

Matt. 9:18–26

in, and took her by
the hand; and the
26 damsel arose. And
[4]the fame hereof went
forth into all that
land.

Luke 8:40–56

54 But he, taking her by
the hand, called, say-
ing, Maiden, arise.
55 And her spirit re-
turned, and she rose
up immediately: and
he commanded that
something be given
56 her to eat. And her
parents were amazed:
but he charged them
to tell no man what
had been done.

[1] Gr. *one ruler.* [2] Or, *saved.* [3] Or, *saved thee.* [4] Gr. *this fame.* [5] Gr. *scourge.* [6] Or, *Teacher.* [7] Or, *overhearing.* [8] Some ancient authorities omit *had spent all her living upon physicians, and.* [9] Some ancient authorities omit *and they that were with him.*

§68. HE HEALS TWO BLIND MEN, AND A DUMB DEMONIAC. A BLASPHEMOUS ACCUSATION

Matt. 9:27–34

27 And as Jesus passed by from thence, two blind men followed him, cry-
28 ing out, and saying, Have mercy on us, thou son of David. And when
he was come into the house, the blind men came to him: and Jesus saith
unto them, Believe ye that I am able to do this? They say unto him,
29 Yea, Lord. Then touched he their eyes, saying, According to your faith
30 be it done unto you. And their eyes were opened. And Jesus [1]strictly
31 charged them, saying, See that no man know it. But they went forth,
and spread abroad his fame in all that land.
32 And as they went forth, behold, there was brought to him a dumb
33 man possessed with a [2]devil. And when the [2]devil was cast out, the
dumb man spake: and the multitudes marvelled, saying, It was never so
34 seen in Israel. But the Pharisees said, [3]By the prince of the [4]devils casteth
he out [4]devils.

[1] Or, *sternly.* [2] Gr. *demon.* [3] Or, *In.* [4] Gr. *demons.*

§69. THE LAST* VISIT TO NAZARETH

Mark 6:1–6

1 And he went out from thence;
and he cometh into his own

Matt. 13:54–58

54 And coming into his own coun-

* There is no sufficient occasion to identify this visit to Nazareth with that described by Luke. That was at the very beginning of the great ministry in Galilee, and this is near its close. The details are quite different. It is perfectly natural that after a long interval he should give the Nazarenes another opportunity to hear his teaching, and to witness miracles, which he would not work for them when demanded, but now voluntarily works in a few cases, so far as their now *wonderful* unbelief left it appropriate.

Mark 6:1–6

country; and his disciples follow
2 him. And when the sabbath
was come, he began to teach in
the synagogue: and [3]many hear-
ing him were astonished, saying,
Whence hath this man these
things? and, What is the wisdom
that is given unto this man, and
what mean such [1]mighty works
3 wrought by his hands? Is not
this the carpenter, the son of
Mary, and brother of James, and
Joses, and Judas, and Simon?
and are not his sisters here with
us? And they were [2]offended in
4 him. And Jesus said unto them,
A prophet is not without honour,
save in his own country, and
among his own kin, and in his
5 own house. And he could there
do no [4]mighty work, save that
he laid his hands upon a few
6 sick folk, and healed them. And
he marvelled because of their
unbelief.

Matt. 13:54–58

try he taught them in their syn-
agogue, insomuch that they were
astonished, and said, Whence
hath this man this wisdom, and
these [1]mighty works?
55 Is not this
the carpenter's son? is not his
mother called Mary? and his
brethren, James, and Joseph, and
56 Simon, and Judas? And his
sisters, are they not all with us?
57 Whence then hath this man all
these things? And they were
[2]offended in him. But Jesus said
unto them, a prophet is not with-
out honour, save in his own
country, and in his own house.
58 And he did not many [1]mighty
works there because of their un-
belief.

[1] Gr. *powers*. [2] Gr. *caused to stumble*. [3] Some ancient authorities insert *the*. [4] Gr. *power*.

In Sections 70 to 71 we have the Third Tour of Galilee (Jesus following the Twelve) and the effect on Herod Antipas.

§ 70. THE THIRD TOUR OF GALILEE AFTER INSTRUCTING THE TWELVE AND SENDING THEM FORTH BY TWOS

Mark 6:6–13

6 And he went round
about the villages
teaching.

Matt. 9:35 to 11:1

35 And Jesus went
about all the cities
and the villages*
teaching in their syn-
agogues, and preach-
ing the gospel of the
kingdom, and healing
all manner of disease
and all manner of
36 sickness. But when

* This is certainly a *second*, and probably a *third* journey about Galilee. Dwell on Matt. 9:35 and 11:1 (end of this section), and try to realize the extent of the Saviour's work in teaching and healing. He "crowded into three short years actions and labours of love that might have adorned a century." (Ro. Hall.)

Mark 6:6–13

7 And he called unto
him the twelve, and
began to send them
forth by two and
two; and he gave
them authority over
the unclean spirits;
8 and he charged them

Matt. 9:35 to 11:1

he saw the multitudes,
he was moved with
compassion for them,
because they were dis-
tressed and scattered,
as sheep not having a
shepherd [*see Num.*
37 *27:17; Ezek. 34:5*].
Then saith he unto his
disciples, the harvest
truly is plenteous, but
the labourers are few.
38 Pray ye therefore the
Lord of the harvest,
that he send forth
labourers into his har-
vest.
1 And he called unto
him his twelve dis-
ciples, and gave them
authority over un-
clean spirits, to cast
them out, and to heal
all manner of disease
and all manner of
sickness.
2 Now the names of
the twelve apostles
are these: The first,
Simon, who is called
Peter, and Andrew
his brother; James
the *son* of Zebedee,
and John his brother;
3 Philip, and Bartholo-
mew; Thomas, and
Matthew the pub-
lican; James the *son*
of Alphæus, and
4 Thaddæus; Simon the
[1]Cananæan, and Ju-
das Iscariot, who also
5 [2]betrayed him. These
twelve Jesus sent
forth, and charged
them, saying, Go not
into *any* way of the
Gentiles, and enter
not into any city of
6 the Samaritans: but

Luke 9:1–6

1 And he called the
twelve together, and
gave them power and
authority over all
[3]devils, and to cure
2 diseases. And he
sent them forth to
preach the kingdom
of God, and to heal
3 [10]the sick. And he
said unto them,

Mark 6:6–13

that they
should take nothing
for *their* journey, save
a staff only; no bread,
no wallet, no [17]money
in their [18]purse; but
9 *to go* shod with sandals:
and, *said he,*
put not on two coats.

10 And he said
unto them, Wheresoever
ye enter into
a house, there abide
till ye depart thence.
11 And whatsoever place

shall not receive
you, and they
hear you not, as ye
go forth thence, shake
off the dust that is
under your feet for a
testimony unto them.

Matt. 9:35 to 11:1

go rather to the lost
sheep of the house of
7 Israel. And as ye go,
preach, saying, The
kingdom of heaven is
8 at hand. Heal the
sick, raise the dead,
cleanse the lepers,
cast out [3]devils: freely
ye received, freely
9 give. Get you no
gold, nor silver, nor
brass in your [4]purses;
10 no wallet for *your*
journey, neither two
coats, nor shoes, nor
staff: for the labourer
is worthy of his food.
11 And into whatsoever
city or village ye
shall enter, search
out who in it is
worthy; and there
abide till ye go forth.
12 And as ye enter into
the house, salute it.
13 And if the house be
worthy, let your
peace come upon it:
but if it be not
worthy, let your
peace return to you.
14 And whosoever shall
not receive you, nor
hear your words, as
ye go forth out of
that house or that
city, shake off the
dust of your feet.
15 Verily, I say unto
you, It shall be more
tolerable for the land
of Sodom and Gomorrah
in the day of
judgement, than for
that city.

Luke 9:1–6

Take nothing
for your journey,
neither staff, nor wallet,
nor bread, nor
money; neither have
two coats.

4 And
into whatsoever
house ye enter, there
abide, and thence de-
5 part. And as many

as receive you not,
when ye depart from
that city,

shake off
the dust from your
feet for a testimony
against them.

16 Behold, I send you forth as sheep in the midst of wolves: be ye there-
17 fore wise as serpents, and [5]harmless as doves. But beware of men:
for they will deliver you up to councils, and in their synagogues they
18 will scourge you; yea and before governors and kings shall ye be brought

Matt. 9:35 to 11:1

19 for my sake, for a testimony to them and to the Gentiles. But when they
deliver you up, be not anxious how or what ye shall speak: for it shall be
20 given you in that hour what ye shall speak. For it is not ye that speak,
21 but the Spirit of your Father that speaketh in you. And brother shall
deliver up brother to death, and the father his child: and children shall
22 rise up against parents, and [6]cause them to be put to death. And ye shall
be hated of all men for my name's sake: but he that endureth to the end,
23 the same shall be saved. But when they persecute you in this city, flee
into the next: for verily I say unto you, Ye shall not have gone through
the cities of Israel, till the Son of man be come.
24 A disciple is not above his [7]master, nor a [8]servant above his lord.
25 It is enough for the disciple that he be as his [7]master, and the [8]servant
as his lord. If they have called the master of the house [9]Beelzebub, how
26 much more *shall they call* them of his household! Fear them not there-
fore: for there is nothing covered, that shall not be revealed; and hid,
27 that shall not be known. What I tell you in the darkness, speak ye in
the light: and what ye hear in the ear, proclaim upon the housetops.
28 And be not afraid of them which kill the body, but are not able to kill
the soul: but rather fear him which is able to destroy both soul and body
29 in [10]hell. Are not two sparrows sold for a farthing? and not one of them
30 shall fall on the ground without your Father: but the very hairs of your
31 head are all numbered. Fear not, therefore; ye are of more value than
32 many sparrows. Every one therefore who shall confess [11]me before men,
33 [12]him will I also confess before my Father which is in heaven. But who-
soever shall deny me before men, him will I also deny before my Father
which is in heaven.
34 Think not that I came to [13]send peace on the earth: I came not to
35 [13]send peace, but a sword. For I came to set a man at variance against
his father, and the daughter against her mother, and the daughter in
36 law against her mother in law: and a man's foes *shall be* they of his own
37 household [*see Micah. 7:6*]. He that loveth father or mother more than me
is not worthy of me: and he that loveth son or daughter more than me is
38 not worthy of me. And he that doth not take his cross and follow after
39 me, is not worthy of me. He that [14]findeth his [15]life shall lose it; and he
that [16]loseth his [15]life for my sake shall find it [*see John 12: 25*].
40 He that receiveth you receiveth me, and he that receiveth me re-
41 ceiveth him that sent me [*see John 13: 20*]. He that receiveth a prophet in
the name of a prophet shall receive a prophet's reward; and he that re-
ceiveth a righteous man in the name of a righteous man shall receive a
42 righteous man's reward. And whosoever shall give to drink unto one of
these little ones a cup of cold water only, in the name of a disciple, verily
I say unto you, he shall in no wise lose his reward.

Mark 6:6–13

12 And they went out,
and preached that
men should repent.
13 And they cast out
many [4]devils, and
anointed with oil

Matt. 9:35 to 11:1

1 And it came to pass,
when Jesus had made
an end of command-
ing his twelve disci-
ples, he departed
thence to teach and

Luke 9:1–6

6 And they departed,
and went throughout
the villages, preach-

Mark 6:6–13

many that were sick,
and healed them.

Matt. 9:35 to 11:1

preach in their
cities.

Luke 9:1–6

ing the gospel, and
healing everywhere.

[1] Or, *Zealot.* See Luke 6:15; Acts 1:13. [2] Or, *delivered him up,* and so always. [3] Gr. *demons.* [4] Gr. *girdles.* [5] Or, *simple.* [6] Or, *put them to death.* [7] Or, *teacher.* [8] Gr. *bond-servant.* [9] Gr. *Beelzebul:* and so elsewhere. [10] Gr. *Gehenna.* [11] Gr. *in me.* [12] Gr. *in him.* [13] Gr. *cast.* [14] Or, *found.* [15] Or, *soul.* [16] Or, *lost.* [17] Gr. *brass.* [18] Gr. *girdle.* [19] Some ancient authorities omit *the sick.*

§71. THE GUILTY FEARS OF HEROD ANTIPAS IN TIBERIAS ABOUT JESUS BECAUSE HE HAD BEHEADED THE BAPTIST IN MACHÆRUS

Mark 6:14–29

14 And king Herod
heard* *thereof;* for his
name had become
known: and [1]he said,
John [2]the Baptist is
risen from the dead,
and therefore do these
powers work in him.
15 But others said, It is
Elijah. And others
said, *It is* a prophet,
even as one of the
16 prophets. But Her-
od, when he heard
thereof, said, John,
whom I beheaded, he
17 is risen. For Herod
himself had sent forth
and laid hold upon
John, and bound him
in prison for the sake
of Herodias, his
brother Philip's wife:
for he had married
18 her. For John said
unto Herod.† It is
not lawful for thee to
have thy brother's
wife [*see Lev. 18:16;*
19 *20:21*]. And Herodias
set herself against

Matt. 14:1–12

1 At that season
Herod the tetrarch
heard the report con-
2 cerning Jesus, and
said unto his serv-
ants, This is John
the Baptist; he is
risen from the dead;
and therefore do these
powers work in him.
3 For Herod had laid
hold on John, and
bound him, and put
him in prison for the
sake of Herodias, his
brother Philip's wife.
4 For John said unto
him, It is not lawful
for thee to have her.
5 And when he would
have put him to
death, he feared the
multitude, because

Luke 9:7–9

7 Now Herod the tet-
rarch heard of all
that was done: and
he was much per-
plexed, because that
it was said by some,
that John was risen
8 from the dead; and
by some, that Elijah
had appeared; and
by others, that one
of the old prophets
was risen again. And
9 Herod said, John I
beheaded: but who is
this, about whom I
hear such things?
And he sought to see
him.

* Mark's connection shows that Herod Antipas was impressed by the account of miracles which the disciples had wrought, as well as by those of Jesus himself.

† Josephus (*Antiquities,* Book XVIII, v., 2) says of John that Herod "thought it best, by putting him to death, to prevent any mischief he might cause, and not bring himself into difficulties, by sparing a man who might make him repent of it when it should be too late." Josephus in no wise controverts the picture in Mark where Herodias appears as the one who prods Antipas to put John out of the way to satisfy her resentment against him for his rebuke of her adulterous marriage. Josephus merely presents the public and political aspects of the imprisonment and death of John.

Mark 6:14–29

him; and desired to
20 kill him; and she
could not; for Herod
feared John, knowing
that he was a right-
eous man and a holy,
and kept him safe.
And when he heard
him, he was much
perplexed; and he
heard him gladly.
21 And when a con-
venient day was
come, that Herod on
his birthday made a
supper to his lords,
and the high cap-
tains, and the chief
22 men of Galilee: and
when the daughter of
Herodias herself came
in and danced, she
pleased Herod and
them that sat at meat
with him; and the
king said unto the
damsel, Ask of me
whatsoever thou wilt,
and I will give it thee.
23 And he sware unto
her, Whatsoever thou
shalt ask of me, I will
give it thee, unto
the half of my king-
24 dom. And she went
out, and said unto
her mother, What
shall I ask? And she
said, The head of
John the Baptist.
25 And she came in
straightway with
haste unto the king,
and asked, saying, I
will that thou forth-
with give me in a
charger the head of
26 John the Baptist. And
the king was exceed-
ing sorry; but for the

Matt. 14:1–12

they counted him as
a prophet.
6 But when Herod's
birthday came, the
daughter of Herodias
danced in the midst,
and pleased Herod.
7 Whereupon he prom-
ised with an oath to
give her whatsoever
8 she should ask. And
she, being put for-
ward by her mother,
saith, Give me here
in a charger the head
of John the Baptist.
9 And the king was
grieved: but for the

Mark 6:14–29

sake of his oaths, and
of them that sat at
meat, he would not
27 reject her. And
straightway the king
sent forth a soldier
of his guard, and com-
manded to bring his
head: and he went
and beheaded him in
28 the prison, and
brought his head in a
charger, and gave it
to the damsel; and
the damsel gave it to
29 her mother. And
when his disciples
heard *thereof*, they
came and took up his
corpse, and laid it in a
tomb.

Matt. 14:1–12

sake of his oaths, and
of them which sat at
meat with him, he
commanded it to be
10 given: and he sent,
and beheaded John
11 in the prison. And
his head was brought
in a charger, and
given to the damsel:
and she brought it to
12 her mother. And
his disciples came,
and took up the
corpse, and buried
him; and they went
and told Jesus.

[1] Some ancient authorities read *they*. [2] Gr. *the Baptizer*. [3] Many ancient authorities read *did many things*. [4] Or, *military tribunes*. Gr. *chiliarch*. [5] Some ancient authorities read *his daughter Herodias*. [6] Or, *it*.

PART VIII

THE SPECIAL TRAINING OF THE TWELVE IN DISTRICTS AROUND GALILEE

Probably Passover in A.D. 29* to near Tabernacles in A.D. 29 or a year earlier (six months from spring to autumn). Just a year from the beginning of this Period till the Crucifixion. Emphasis now on the King of the Kingdom (the Person of the Messiah).

§§ 72–95. Four separate withdrawals† from Galilee are given, in §§ 72, 78, 79, 81. Notice that in every case he keeps out of Herod's territory, and in every case he goes to the mountains.

§ 72. THE FIRST RETIREMENT. THE TWELVE RETURN, AND JESUS RETIRES WITH THEM BEYOND THE LAKE TO REST. FEEDING OF THE FIVE THOUSAND

Mark 6:30–44		Luke 9:10–17	
30 And the apostles gather themselves together unto Jesus; and they told him all things, whatsoever they had done, and whatsoever they had 31 taught. And he saith unto them, Come ye yourselves apart into a desert place, and rest a		10 And the apostles, when they were returned, declared unto him what things they had done.	

* If the ministry of Jesus was three and a half years in length. If there were only three passovers in the ministry, then the year would be A.D. 28. This period begins just before a passover (John 6:4).

† There are five reasons for the withdrawals from Galilee. He withdraws from the jealousy of Herod Antipas (§ 71), from the fanaticism of would-be followers in Galilee (John 6:15), and the hostility of the Jewish rulers; and leaving the hot shores of the Lake of Galilee, he spent the summer in mountain districts around, resting, and *instructing the Twelve.*

Mark 6:30–44

while. For
there were
many coming
and going, and
they had no
leisure so
much as to eat.
32 And they went
away in the
boat to a des-
ert place apart.
33 And *the people*
saw them go-
ing, and many
knew *them*,
and they ran
there together
[1]on foot from
all the cities,
and outwent
34 them. And he
came forth and
saw a great
multitude, and
he had com-
passion on
them, because
they were as
sheep not hav-
ing a shepherd,
and he began
to teach them
many things.
35 And when the
day was now
far spent, his
disciples came
unto him, and
said, The place
is desert, and
the day is now
36 far spent; send
them away
that they may
go into the
country and
villages round

Matt. 14:13–21

13 Now when
Jesus heard *it*,
he withdrew
from thence in
a boat, to a
desert place
apart. And
when the mul-
titudes heard
thereof, they
followed him
[1]on foot from
14 the cities. And
he came forth,
and saw a great
multitude,
and he had
compassion
on them, and
healed their
sick.
15 And when
even was
come, the dis-
ciples came to
him, saying,

The place is
desert, and the
time is already
past; send the
multitudes a-
way, that they
may go into
the villages,
and buy them-

Luke 9:10–17

And he took
them, and
withdrew
apart to a city
called Beth-
saida.*
11 But the multi-
tudes perceiv-
ing it followed
him: and he
welcomed
them, and
spake to them
of the king-
dom of God,
and them that
had need of
healing he
healed.
12 And
the day began
to wear away;
and the twelve
came and said
unto him, Send
the multitude
away, that
they may go
into the vil-
lages and
country round
about, and
lodge, and
get victuals:
for we are here

John 6:1–13

1 After these
things Jesus
went away to
the other side
of the sea of
Galilee, which
is *the sea* of Ti-
berias.
2 And a
great multi-
tude followed
him, because
they beheld
the signs
which he did
on them that
3 were sick. And
Jesus went up
into the moun-
tain, and there
he sat with his
disciples.
4 Now the pass-
over, the feast
of the Jews,
was at hand.
5 Jesus therefore
lifting up his
eyes, and see-
ing that a
great multi-
tude cometh
unto him, saith
unto Philip,
Whence are
we to buy

---

* The Bethsaida of Luke 9:10 was evidently the eastern Bethsaida, which the Tetrarch Philip had named Bethsaida Julias, while that of Mark 6:45 was the western Bethsaida, near Capernaum. The territory belonging to Bethsaida Julias would naturally extend some distance down the lake.

Mark 6:30–44

about, and
buy themselves
somewhat to
37 eat. But he
answered and
said unto them,
Give ye them
to eat. And
they say unto
him, Shall we
go and buy
two hundred
[3]pennyworth
of bread, and
give them to
38 eat? And he
saith unto them,
How many
loaves have
ye? go *and* see.
And when
they knew,
they say, Five,
and two fishes.

39 And
he commanded
them that all
should [2]sit
down by com-
panies upon
the green
40 grass. And
they sat down
in ranks, by
hundreds, and
41 by fifties. And
he took the
five loaves and
the two fishes,
and looking up
to heaven, he
blessed, and
brake the
loaves; and he
gave to the
disciples to set
before them;
and the two
fishes divided

Matt. 14:13–21

selves food.
16 But Jesus said
unto them,
They have no
need to go a-
way; give ye
them to eat.
17 And they say
unto him, We
have here but
five loaves, and
18 two fishes. And
he said, Bring
them hither
19 to me. And
he commanded
the multitudes
to [3]sit down on
the grass;
and
he took the
five loaves, and
the two fishes,
and looking up
to heaven, he
blessed, and
brake and
gave the
loaves to the
disciples, and
the disciples to
the multi-
20 tudes. And

Luke 9:10–17

in a desert
13 place. But he
said unto
them, Give ye
them to eat.
And they said,
We have no
more than five
loaves and two
fishes; except
we should go
and buy food
for all this peo-
14 ple. For they
were about five
thousand. And
he said unto his
disciples, Make
them [2]sit down
in companies,
about fifty
15 each. And they
did so, and
made them all
16 [2]sit down. And
he took the
five loaves and
the two fishes,
and looking up
to heaven, he
blessed them,
and brake; and
gave to the
disciples to set
before the
multitude.
17 And they did
eat, and were

John 6:1–13

[4]bread, that
these may eat?
6 And this he
said to prove
him: for he
himself knew
what he would
7 do. Philip an-
swered him,
Two hundred
[3]pennyworth
of [4]bread is not
sufficient for
them, that
every one may
take a little.
8 One of his dis-
ciples, Andrew,
Simon Peter's
brother, saith
unto him,
9 There is a lad
here, which
hath five bar-
ley loaves, and
two fishes: but
what are these
among so
10 many? Jesus
said, Make the
people sit
down. Now
there was
much grass in
the place. So
the men sat
down, in num-
ber about five
11 thousand. Je-
sus therefore
took the
loaves: and
having given
thanks, dis-
tributed to
them that
were set down;
likewise also of
the fishes as

Mark 6:30–44

he among
42 them all. And
they did all
eat, and were
43 filled. And
they took up
broken pieces,
twelve basketfuls, and also
of the fishes.
44 And they that
ate the loaves
were five thousand men.

Matt. 14:13–21

they did all
eat, and were
filled: and they
took up that
which remained over of the
broken pieces,
twelve baskets
21 full. And they
that did eat
were about
five thousand
men, besides
women and
children.

Luke 9:10–17

all filled: and there was taken up that which remained over to them of broken pieces, twelve baskets.

John 6:1–13

much as they
12 would. And
when they
were filled, he
saith unto his
disciples,
Gather up the
broken pieces
which remain
over, that
nothing be
13 lost. So they
gathered them
up, and filled
twelve baskets
with broken
pieces from
the five barley
loaves, which
remained over
unto them
that had
eaten.*

[1] Or, *by land.* [2] Gr. *recline.* [3] The word in the Greek denotes a coin worth about seventeen cents. [4] Gr. *loaves.*

§73. THE PREVENTION OF THE REVOLUTIONARY PURPOSE TO PROCLAIM JESUS KING (A POLITICAL MESSIAH)

Mark 6:45–46

45 And straightway he
constrained his disciples to enter into
the boat, and to go
before *him* unto the
other side to Bethsaida, while he himself sendeth the mul-
46 titude away. And
after he had taken
leave of them, he
departed into the
mountain to pray.

Matt. 14:22–23

22 And straightway
he constrained the
disciples to enter into the boat, and to
go before him unto
the other side, till
he should send the
multitudes away.
23 And after he had
sent the multitudes
away, he went up
into the mountain
apart to pray:
and
when even was come,
he was there alone.

John 6:14–15

14 When therefore the
people saw the sign
that he did they said,
This is of a truth the
prophet that cometh
unto the world [*see
Deut. 18:15*].
15 Jesus therefore perceiving that they
were about to come
and take him by
force, to make him
king, withdrew again
into the mountain
himself alone.

* Note that here for the first time John runs parallel with all the synoptic gospels. All four report this incident. See Passion Week.

§74. THE PERIL TO THE TWELVE IN THE STORM AT SEA AND CHRIST'S COMING TO THEM ON THE WATER IN THE DARKNESS

Mark 6:47–52

47 And when even was
come, the boat was
in the midst of the
sea, and he alone on
48 the land. And see-
ing them distressed
in rowing, for the
wind was contrary
unto them, about the
fourth watch of the
night he cometh un-
to them, walking on
the sea; and he would
have passed by them:
49 but they, when they
saw him walking on
the sea, supposed that
it was an apparition,
50 and cried out: for they
all saw him, and were
troubled. But he
straightway spake
with them, and saith
unto them, Be of good
cheer: it is I; be not
afraid.

Matt. 14:24–33

24 But the boat [1]was
now in the midst of
the sea, distressed by
the waves; for the
wind was contrary.

25 And in the fourth
watch of the night
he came unto them,
walking upon the sea.

26 And when the
disciples saw him
walking on the sea,
they were troubled,
saying, It is an appa-
rition; and they cried
27 out for fear. But
straightway Jesus
spake unto them,
saying, Be of good
cheer; it is I; be not
28 afraid. And Peter
answered him, and
said, Lord, if it be
thou, bid me come
unto thee upon the
29 waters. And he said,
Come. And Peter
went down from the
boat, and walked up-
on the waters, [2]to
30 come to Jesus. But
when he saw the
[3]wind, he was afraid,
and beginning to sink,
he cried out, saying,
31 Lord, save me. And
immediately Jesus
stretched forth his
hand, and took hold
of him, and saith un-

John 6:16–21

16 And when evening
came, his disciples
went down unto the
17 sea; and they entered
into a boat, and were
going over the sea
unto Capernaum.
And it was now dark,
and Jesus had not
yet come to them.
18 And the sea was ris-
ing by reason of a
great wind that blew.
19 When therefore they
had rowed about five
and twenty or thirty
furlongs, they behold
Jesus walking on the
sea, and drawing nigh
unto the boat: and
they were afraid.

20 But he saith unto
them, It is I; be not
afraid.

Mark 6:47–52

51 And he went up unto
them into the boat;
and the wind ceased:
and they were sore
amazed in themselves
52 for they understood
not concerning the
loaves, but their heart
was hardened.

Matt. 14:24–33

to him, O thou of little faith, wherefore didst thou doubt?
32 And when they were
gone up into the
boat, the wind ceased.
33 And they that were
in the boat worshipped him, saying, Of a truth thou art the Son of God.

John 6:16–21

21 They were willing therefore to receive him into the boat:
and straightway the boat was at the land whither they were going.

[1] Some ancient authorities read *was many furlongs distant from the land.* [2] Some ancient authorities read *and came.* [3] Many ancient authorities add *strong.*

§ 75. THE RECEPTION AT GENNESARET

Mark 6:53–56

53 And when they had [1]crossed
over, they came to the land unto
Gennesaret, and moored to the
54 shore. And when they were come
out of the boat, straightway *the*
55 *people* knew him, and ran about
that whole region, and began to
carry about on their beds those
that were sick, where they heard
56 he was. And wheresoever* he
entered, into villages, or into
cities, or into the country, they
laid the sick in the marketplaces,
and besought him that they might
touch if it were but the border of
his garment: and as many as
touched [2]him were made whole.

Matt. 14:34–36

34 And when they crossed over, they came to the land, unto Gennesaret.

35 And
when the men of that place knew
him, they sent unto all that region
round about, and brought unto
36 him all that were sick; and they
besought him that they might
only touch the border of his garment: and as many as touched were made whole.

[1] Or, *crossed over to the land, they came unto Gennesaret.* [2] Or, *it.*

§ 76. THE COLLAPSE OF THE GALILEAN CAMPAIGN BECAUSE JESUS WILL NOT CONFORM TO POPULAR MESSIANIC EXPECTATIONS

The next day in the Synagogue in Capernaum. The same crowd that had eaten the Loaves and the Fishes leave Christ in disgust on learning that He is the Bread of Life and not a Political Messiah.

John 6:22–71

22 On the morrow the multitude which stood on the other side of the
sea saw that there was none other [1]boat there, save one, and that Jesus

* This general characterization applies to the Galilean work as a whole in Part VII rather than to the precise time at this juncture. But one must allow his imagination to enlarge upon the scope of Christ's work.

John 6:22–71

entered not with his disciples into the boat, but *that* his disciples went
23 away alone (howbeit there came [2]boats from Tiberias nigh unto the place
where they ate the bread after the Lord had given thanks): when the
24 multitude therefore saw that Jesus was not there, neither his disciples,
they themselves got into the [2]boats, and came to Capernaum, seeking
25 Jesus. And when they found him on the other side of the sea, they said
26 unto him, Rabbi, when camest thou hither? Jesus answered them and
said, Verily, verily, I say unto you, Ye seek me, not because ye saw signs,
27 but because ye ate of the loaves and were filled. Work not for the meat
which perished, but for the meat which abideth unto eternal life, which
the Son of man shall give unto you: for him the Father, *even* God, hath
28 sealed. They said therefore unto him, What must we do, that we may
29 work the works of God? Jesus answered and said unto them, This is the
30 work of God, that ye believe on him whom [3]he hath sent. They said
therefore unto him, What then doest thou for a sign, that we may see,
31 and believe thee? what workest thou? Our fathers ate the manna in
32 the wilderness; as it is written, He gave them bread out of heaven to eat
[*see Ex. see 16:4, 15; Ps. 78:24; Neh. 9:15*]. Jesus therefore said unto them,
Verily, verily, I say unto you, It was not Moses that gave you the bread
out of heaven: but my Father giveth you the true bread out of heaven.
33 For the bread of God is that which cometh down out of heaven, and
34 giveth life unto the world. They said therefore unto him, Lord, ever-
35 more give us this bread. Jesus said unto them, I am the bread of life:
he that cometh to me shall not hunger, and he that believeth on me shall
36 never thirst. But I said unto you, that ye have seen me, and yet believe
37 not. All that which the Father giveth me shall come unto me; and him
38 that cometh to me I will in no wise cast out. For I am come down from
39 heaven, not to do mine own will, but the will of him that sent me. And
this is the will of him that sent me, that of all that which he hath given me
40 I should lose nothing, but should raise it up at the last day. For this is
the will of my Father, that every one that beholdeth the Son, and be-
lieveth on him, should have eternal life; [4]I will raise him up at the last day.
41 The Jews therefore murmured concerning him, because he said, I am
42 the bread which came down out of heaven. And they said, Is not this
Jesus, the son of Joseph, whose father and mother we know? how doth
43 he now say, I am come down out of heaven? Jesus answered and said
44 unto them, Murmur not among yourselves. No man can come to me,
except the Father which sent me draw him: and I will raise him up in the
45 last day. It is written in the prophets [*see Isa. 54:13*], And they shall all be
taught of God. Every one that hath heard from the Father, and hath
46 learned, cometh unto me. Not that any man hath seen the Father,
47 save he which is from God, he hath seen the Father. Verily, verily, I
48 say unto you, He that believeth hath eternal life. I am the bread of life.
49 Your fathers did eat the manna in the wilderness, and they died. This
50 is the bread which cometh down out of heaven, that a man may eat
51 thereof, and not die. I am the living bread which came down out of
heaven: if any man eat of this bread, he shall live for ever: yea and the
bread which I will give is my flesh, for the life of the world.
52 The Jews therefore strove one with another, saying, How can this man
53 give us his flesh to eat? Jesus therefore said unto them, Verily, verily,

John 6:22-71

I say unto you, Except ye eat the flesh of the Son of man and drink his
54 blood, ye have not life in yourselves. He that eateth my flesh and
55 drinketh my blood hath eternal life; and I will raise him up at the last
day. For my flesh is [5]meat indeed, and my blood is [6]drink indeed.
56 He that eateth my flesh and drinketh my blood abideth in me, and I in
57 him. As the living Father sent me, and I live because of the Father;
58 so he that eateth me, he also shall live because of me. This is the bread
which came down out of heaven: not as the fathers did eat, and died:
59 he that eateth this bread shall live for ever. These things said he in [7]the
synagogue, as he taught in Capernaum.

60 Many therefore of his disciples, when they heard *this*, said, This is a
61 hard saying; who can hear [8]it? But Jesus knowing in himself that his
disciples murmured at this, said unto them, Doth this cause you to
62 stumble? *What* then if ye should behold the Son of man ascending where
63 he was before? It is the spirit that quickeneth; the flesh profiteth noth-
64 ing: the words that I have spoken unto you are spirit, and are life. But
there are some of you that believe not. For Jesus knew from the be-
ginning who they were that believed not, and who it was that should
65 betray him. And he said, For this cause have I said unto you, that no
man can come unto me, except it be given unto him of the Father.

66 Upon this many of his disciples went back, and walked no more with
67 him. Jesus said therefore unto the twelve, Would ye also go away?
68 Simon Peter answered him, Lord, to whom shall we go? thou [9]hast the
69 words of eternal life. And we have believed and know that thou art the
70 Holy One of God. Jesus answered them, Did not I choose you the
71 twelve, and one of you is a devil? Now he spake of Judas *the son* of
Simon Iscariot, for he it was that should betray him, *being* one of the
twelve.

[1] Gr. *little boat.* [2] Gr. *little boats.* [3] Or, *he sent.* [4] Or, *that I should raise him up.* [5] Gr. *true meat.* [6] Gr. *true drink.* [7] Or, *a synagogue.* [8] Or, *him.* [9] Or, *hast words.*

§ 77. PHARISEES FROM JERUSALEM REPROACH JESUS FOR ALLOWING HIS DISCIPLES TO DISREGARD THEIR TRADITIONS ABOUT CEREMONIAL DEFILEMENT OF THE HANDS. A PUZZLING PARABLE IN REPLY

Probably in Capernaum

Mark 7:1-23

1 And there are gathered together
unto him the Pharisees, and cer-
tain of the scribes, which had come
2 from Jerusalem, and had seen that
some of his disciples ate their
bread with [6]defiled, that is un-
3 washen, hands. For the Phari-
sees, and all the Jews, except
they wash their hands [7]diligently,
eat not, holding the tradition of
4 the elders: and *when they come*

Matt. 15:1-20

1 Then there came to Jesus from Jerusalem Pharisees and scribes,
2 saying, Why do thy disciples

John 7:1

1 And after these things Jesus walked in Galilee: for he would not walk in Judea, because the Jews sought to kill him.

Mark 7:1–23

from the marketplace, except they
[3]wash themselves, they eat not:
and many other things there be,
which they have received to hold,
[4]washings of cups, and pots, and
5 brasen vessels.[10] And the Phari-
sees and the scribes ask him, Why
walk not thy disciples according
to the tradition of the elders, but
eat their bread with [6]defiled
6 hands? And he said unto them,
Well did Isaiah prophesy of you
hypocrites, as it is written,

This people honoureth me with
their lips,
But their heart is far from me.
7 But in vain do they worship me,
Teaching *as their* doctrines the
precepts of men.

8 Ye leave the commandment of
God, and hold fast the tradition
9 of men. And he said unto them,
Full well do ye reject the com-
mandment of God, that ye may
10 keep your tradition. For Moses
[*see Ex. 20:12; Deut. 5:16*] said,
Honour thy father and thy mother;
and, He that speaketh evil of
father or mother, let him [1]die the
11 death; but ye say, If a man shall
say to his father or his mother,
That wherewith thou mightest
have been profited by me is Cor-
ban, that is to say, Given *to God;*
12 [*see Ex. 21:17; Lev. 20:9*]; ye no
longer suffer him to do aught for
his father or his mother; making
void the word of God by your
tradition, which ye have de-
13 livered: and many such like things
14 ye do. And he called to him the
multitude again, and said unto
them, Hear me all of you, and
15 understand: there is nothing from
without the man, that going into
him can defile him: but the things
which proceed out of the man
are those that defile the man.[11]
17 And when he was entered into the
house from the multitude, his

Matt. 15:1–20

transgress the tradition of the
elders? for they wash not their
3 hands when they eat bread. And
he answered and said unto them,
7 Ye hypocrites, well did Isaiah
prophesy of you, saying [*see Isa.
29:13*],

8 This people honoureth me with
their lips;
But their heart is far from me.
9 But in vain do they worship me,
Teaching *as their* doctrines the
precepts of men.

3 Why do ye also transgress the
commandment of God, because
of your tradition?

4 For God
said, Honour thy father and thy
mother: and, He that speaketh
evil of father or mother, let him
5 [1]die the death. But ye say, Who-
soever shall say to his father or
his mother, That wherewith thou
mightest have been profited by
6 me is given *to God;* he shall not
honour his father.[2] And ye have

made void the [3]word of God
because of your tradition.

10 And he
called to him the multitude, and
said unto them, Hear, and under-
11 stand: Not that which entereth

into the mouth defileth the man,
but that which proceedeth out of
the mouth, this defileth the man.

Mark 7:1–23

disciples asked of him the parable.
18 And
he saith unto them, Are ye so
without understanding also? Per-
ceive ye not, that whatsoever
from without goeth into the man,
19 *it* cannot defile him; because it
goeth not into his heart, but into
his belly, and goeth out into the
draught? *This he said*, making
20 all meats clean. And he said,
That which proceedeth out of
the man, that defileth the man.
21 For from within, out of the heart
of men, [12]evil thoughts proceed,
22 fornications, thefts, murders, adul-
teries, covetings, wickednesses,
deceit, lasciviousness, an evil eye,
23 railing, pride, foolishness: all these
evil things proceed from within,
and defile the man.

Matt. 15:1–20

12 Then came the disciples, and said
unto him, Knowest thou that the
Pharisees were [4]offended, when
13 they heard this saying? But he
answered and said, Every [5]plant
which my heavenly Father plant-
14 ed not, shall be rooted up. Let
them alone: they are blind guides.
And if the blind guide the blind,
15 both shall fall into a pit. And
Peter answered and said unto
him, Declare unto us the parable.
16 And he said, Are ye also even yet
17 without understanding? Perceive
ye not, that whatsoever goeth
into the mouth passeth into the
belly, and is cast out into
18 the draught? But the things
which proceed out of the mouth
come forth out of the heart; and
19 they defile the man. For out of
the heart come forth evil thoughts,
murders, adulteries, fornications,
thefts, false witness, railings:
20 these are the things
which defile the man:
but to eat
with unwashen hands defileth
not the man.

[1] Or, *surely die.* [2] Some ancient authorities add *or his mother.* [3] Some ancient authorities read *law.* [4] Gr. *caused to stumble.* [5] Gr. *planting.* [6] Or, *common.* [7] Or, *up to the elbow.* Gr. *with the fist.* [8] Gr. *baptize.* Some ancient authorities read *sprinkle themselves.* [9] Gr. *baptizings.* [10] Many ancient authorities add *and couches.* [11] Many ancient authorities insert ver. 16, *If any man hath ears to hear, let him hear.* [12] Gr. *thoughts that are evil.*

§78. THE SECOND WITHDRAWAL TO THE REGION OF TYRE AND SIDON AND THE HEALING OF THE DAUGHTER OF A SYRO-PHŒNICIAN WOMAN

Mark 7:24–30

24 And from thence he arose, and
went away into the borders of
Tyre [8]and Sidon. And he entered

Matt. 15:21–28

21 And Jesus went out thence,
and withdrew into the parts of
Tyre and Sidon.*

* It used to be questioned whether he actually left the land of Israel. Matthew's expression ought to have settled the question, and the corrected text of Mark 7:31 leaves no doubt.

Mark 7:24–30

into a house, and would have
no man know it: and he could
25 not be hid. But straightway a
woman, whose little daughter
had an unclean spirit, having
heard of him, came and fell down
26 at his feet. Now the woman was
a [4]Greek, a Syrophœnician by
race. And she besought him that
he would cast forth the [1]devil out
of her daughter.

27 And
he said unto her, Let the children
first be filled: for it is not meet
to take the children's [2]bread and
28 cast it to the dogs. But she
answered and saith unto him, Yea,
Lord: even the dogs under the
table eat of the children's crumbs.
29 And he said unto her, For this
saying go thy way; the [1]devil is
30 gone out of thy daughter. And
she went away unto her house,
and found the child laid upon the
bed, and the [1]devil gone out.

Matt. 15:21–28

22 And behold, a
Canaanitish woman came out
from those borders, and cried,
saying, Have mercy on me, O
Lord, thou son of David, my
daughter is grievously vexed with
23 a [1]devil. But he answered her
not a word. And his disciples
came and besought him, saying,
Send her away; for she crieth
24 after us. But he answered
and said, I was not sent but unto
the lost sheep of the house of Is-
25 rael. But she came and wor-
shipped him, saying, Lord, help
26 me. And he answered and said,
It is not meet to take the chil-
dren's [2]bread and cast it to the
27 dogs. But she said, Yea, Lord:
for even the dogs eat of the
crumbs which fall from their
28 masters' table. Then Jesus an-
swered and said unto her, O
woman, great is thy faith; be it
done unto thee even as thou wilt.

And her daughter
was healed from that hour.

[1] Gr. *demon*. [2] Or, *loaf*. [3] Some ancient authorities omit *and Sidon*. [4] Or, *Gentile*.

§ 79. THE THIRD WITHDRAWAL NORTH THROUGH PHŒNICIA AND EAST TOWARDS HERMON AND SOUTH INTO DECAPOLIS (KEEPING OUT OF THE TERRITORY OF HEROD ANTIPAS) WITH THE HEALING OF THE DEAF AND DUMB MAN AND THE FEEDING OF THE FOUR THOUSAND

Mark 7:31–8:9

31 And again he went out from
the borders of Tyre, and came
through Sidon unto the sea of
Galilee, through the midst of the
32 borders of Decapolis.* And they

Matt. 15:29–38

29 And Jesus departed thence,
and came nigh unto the sea of
Galilee; and he went up into the
mountain, and sat there.

* Observe how carefully he keeps away from the territory ruled by Herod Antipas. The tetrarch Philip, who governed the districts east of the Lake of Galilee and of the upper Jordan, was a better man than Antipas, and moreover had no cause to feel uneasy about Jesus.

Mark 7:31–8:9

bring unto him one that was deaf,
and had an impediment in his
speech; and they beseech him to
33 lay his hand upon him. And he
took him aside from the multitude
privately, and put his fingers into
his ears, and he spat, and touched
34 his tongue; and looking up to
heaven, he sighed, and saith unto
him, Ephphatha, that is, Be
35 opened. And his ears were open-
ed, and the bond of his tongue was
36 loosed, and he spake plain. And
he charged them that they should
tell no man: but the more he
charged them, so much the more a
37 great deal they published it. And
they were beyond measure as-
tonished, saying, He hath done
all things well: he maketh even
the deaf to hear, and the dumb
to speak.
1 In those days, when there was
again* a great multitude, and
they had nothing to eat, he called
unto him his disciples, and saith
2 unto them, I have compassion
on the multitude, because they
continue with me now three days,
and have nothing to eat; and
3 if I send them away fasting to
their home, they will faint in
the way; and some of them are
4 come from far. And his disci-
ples answered him, Whence shall
one be able to fill these men
with [1]bread here in a desert place?
5 And he asked them, How many
loaves have ye? And they said,
6 Seven. And he commanded the
multitude to sit down on the
ground: and he took the seven
loaves, and having given thanks,
he brake, and gave to his disciples,
to set before them; and they set
7 them before the multitude. And

Matt. 15:29–38

30 And there came unto him great
multitudes, having with them
the lame, blind, dumb, maimed,
and many others, and they cast
31 them down at his feet; and he
healed them: insomuch that the
multitude wondered, when they
saw the dumb speaking, the
maimed whole, and the lame walk-
ing, and the blind seeing: and they
glorified the God of Israel.
32 And Jesus called unto him his
disciples, and said, I have com-
passion on the multitude, because
they continue with me now three
days and have nothing to eat:
and I would not send them away
fasting, lest haply they faint in
the way.
33 And the disciples say
unto him, Whence should we
have so many loaves in a desert
place, as to fill so great a multi-
34 tude? And Jesus saith unto them,
How many loaves have ye? And
they said, Seven, and a few small
35 fishes. And he commanded the
multitude to sit down on the
36 ground: and he took the seven
loaves and the fishes; and he
gave thanks and brake, and gave
to the disciples, and the disciples
to the multitudes.

* It is to be noted that Mark and Matthew give the feeding of the five thousand and of the four thousand. Mark and Matthew likewise report Jesus as referring to both incidents (Mark 8:19–20 = Matt. 16:9–10). Hence, it is hard to think of a mere confusion in the use of the data. There is no real reason why both incidents could not be true.

Mark 7:31–8:9

they had a few small fishes: and
having blessed them, he commanded to set these also before
8 them. And they did eat, and
were filled: and they took up, of
broken pieces that remained over,
9 seven baskets. And they were
about four thousand: and he sent
them away.

Matt. 15:29–38

37 And
they did all eat, and were filled:
and they took up that which remained over the broken pieces,
38 seven baskets full. And they
that did eat were four thousand
men, beside women and children.

[1] Gr. *loaves*.

§80. THE BRIEF VISIT TO MAGADAN (DALMANUTHA) IN GALILEE AND THE SHARP ATTACK BY THE PHARISEES AND THE SADDUCEES (NOTE THEIR APPEARANCE NOW AGAINST JESUS)

Mark 8:10–12

10 And straightway he entered into
the boat with his disciples, and
came into the parts of Dalmanutha.
11 And the Pharisees came forth,
began to question with him,
seeking of him a sign from heaven,
tempting him.
12 And he
sighed deeply in his spirit, and
saith, Why doth this generation
seek a sign? verily I say unto
you, There shall no sign be given
unto this generation.

Matt. 15:39–16:4

39 And he sent away the multitudes,
and entered into the boat, and
came into the borders of Magadan.*
1 And the Pharisees and Sadducees came, and tempting him†
asked him to shew them a sign
2 from heaven. But he answered
and said unto them, [1]When it is
evening, ye say, *It will be* fair
3 weather: for the heaven is red.
And in the morning, *It will be* foul
weather to-day: for the heaven is
red and lowring. Ye know how
to discern the face of the heaven;
but ye cannot *discern* the signs of
4 the times. An evil and adulterous generation seeketh after a
sign; and there shall no sign be
given unto it, but the sign of
Jonah [*see Jonah 3:4*]. And he
left them, and departed.

[1] The following words, to the end of ver. 3, are omitted by some of the most ancient and other important authorities.

* The situation of Magadan was unknown to some early students or copyists, as it is to us, and so they changed it to the familiar Magdala, found in our common texts.

† The moment he returns to Galilee the Jewish leaders begin to attack him.

§ 81. THE FOURTH RETIREMENT TO BETHSAIDA JULIAS IN THE TETRARCHY OF HEROD PHILIP WITH SHARP REBUKE OF THE DULNESS OF THE DISCIPLES ON THE WAY ACROSS AND THE HEALING OF A BLIND MAN IN BETHSAIDA

Mark 8:13–26

13 And
he left them, and again entering
into *the boat* departed to the other
side.
14 And they forgot to take bread;
and they had not in the boat
with them more than one loaf.
15 And he charged them, saying,
Take heed, beware of the leaven
of the Pharisees and the leaven
16 of Herod. And they reasoned
one with another, [4]saying. [5]We
17 have no bread. And Jesus perceiving
it saith unto them, Why
reason ye, because ye have no
bread? do ye not yet perceive,
neither understand? have ye your
18 heart hardened? having eyes, see
ye not? and having ears, hear
ye not? and do ye not remember
19 [*see Jer. 5:21; Ezek. 12:2*]? When
I brake the five loaves among the
five thousand, how many [6]baskets
full of broken pieces took ye up?
20 They say unto him, Twelve. And
when the seven among the four
thousand, how many [6]basketfuls
of broken pieces took ye up?
21 And they say unto him, Seven.
And he said unto them, Do ye
not yet understand?
22 And they come unto Bethsaida.*
And they bring to him a blind
man, and beseech him to touch
23 him. And he took hold of the
blind man by the hand, and
brought him out of the village;

Matt. 16:5–12

5 And the disciples came to the
other side and forgot to take
6 [1]bread. And Jesus said unto
them, Take heed and beware of
the leaven of the Pharisees and
7 Sadducees. And they reasoned
among themselves, saying, [2]We
8 took no [1]bread. And Jesus perceiving
it said, O ye of little faith,
why reason ye among yourselves
9 because ye have no [1]bread? Do
ye not yet perceive, neither remember
the five loaves of the five
thousand, and how many [3]baskets
10 ye took up? Neither the seven
loaves of the four thousand, and
how many [3]baskets ye took up?
11 How is it that ye do not perceive
that I spake not to you concerning
[1]bread? But beware of the leaven
of the Pharisees and Sadducees.
12 Then they understood how that
he bade them not beware of the
leaven of [1]bread, but of the teaching
of the Pharisees and Sadducees.

* Jesus goes on to the region of Cæsarea Philippi on Mount Hermon, where no hostility had been aroused, and he could quietly instruct the Twelve. He probably remained in that vicinity several months, as this whole period of retirement lasted six months. He was near Bethsaida Julias in the First Retirement and now he stops here again on his way to Cæsarea Philippi. Each of the four retirements is into heathen territory (Ituria twice, Phœnicia, Decapolis), where Greek influence prevails, and where the Greek language is dominant.

Mark 8:13–26

and when he had spit on his eyes,
and laid his hands upon him, he
asked him, Seest thou aught?
24 And he looked up, and said, I see
men; for I behold *them* as trees,
25 walking. Then again he laid his
hands upon his eyes; and he
looked stedfastly, and was re-
stored, and saw all things clearly.
26 And he sent him away to his
home, saying, Do not even enter
into the village.

[1] Gr. *loaves.* [2] Or, It is *because we took no bread.* [3] *Basket* in ver. 9 and 10 represents different Greek words. [4] Some ancient authorities read *because they had no bread.* [5] Or, It is *because we have no bread.* [6] *Basket* in ver. 19 and 20 represents different Greek words.

§82. NEAR CÆSAREA PHILIPPI JESUS TESTS THE FAITH OF THE TWELVE IN HIS MESSIAHSHIP

Mark 8:27–30

27 And Jesus went
forth, and his disci-
ples, into the villages
of Cæsarea Philippi:
and in the way he
asked his disciples,
saying unto them,
Who do men say that
28 I am? And they told
him, saying, John
the Baptist: and
others, Elijah: but
others, One of the
29 prophets. And he
asked them, But who
say ye that I am?
Peter answereth and
saith unto him, Thou
art the Christ.

Matt. 16:13–20

13 Now when Jesus
came into the parts
of Cæsarea Philippi,
he asked his disci-
ples, saying, Who do
men say [1]that the
14 Son of man is? And
they said, Some *say*
John the Baptist;
some, Elijah; and
others, Jeremiah, or
one of the prophets.
15 He saith unto them,
But who say ye that
16 I am? And Simon
Peter answered and
said, Thou art the
Christ,* the Son of
17 the living God. And
Jesus answered and
said unto him, Bless-
ed art thou, Simon
Bar-Jonah: for flesh

Luke 9:18–21

18 And it came to pass,
as he was praying
alone, the disciples
were with him: and
he asked them, say-
ing, Who do the mul-
titudes say that I am?
19 And they answering
said, John the Bap-
tist; but others *say,*
Elijah; and others,
that one of the old
prophets is risen
20 again. And he said
unto them, But who
say ye that I am?
And Peter answering
said, The Christ of
God.

* Some understand ver. 16f. as showing that they had never before believed him to be the Messiah, and so hold that the other Gospels here utterly conflict with John, who represents the first disciples (§§ 28, 35) as believing Jesus to be the Messiah. But it is easy to suppose that their early faith in his Messiahship was shaken by his continued failure to gather armies and set up the expected temporal kingdom, and while still believing him to have a divine mission they had questioned whether he was the Messiah, as John the Baptist did in prison (§ 57). Observe that in Matthew and Luke he long before this time distinctively *implied* that he was the Messiah, in response to the Forerunner's inquiries (§ 57). Besides, at the Baptism and the Temptation, the Synoptic Gospels represent Jesus as the Son of God.

Mark 8:27–30

30 And he
charged them that
they should tell no
man of him.

Matt. 16:13–20

and blood hath not
revealed it unto thee,
but my Father which
18 is in heaven. And I
also say unto thee,
that thou art [2]Peter,
and upon this [3]rock
I will build* my
church [*see Ps. 89:4, 26, 38, 48*]; and the
gates of Hades shall
not prevail against it.
19 I will give unto thee
the keys of the king-
dom of heaven: and
whatsoever thou shalt
bind on earth shall be
bound in heaven: and
whatsoever thou shalt
loose on earth shall
be loosed in heaven.
20 Then charged he the
disciples that they
should tell no man
that he was the
Christ.

Luke 9:18–21

21 But he charged
them, and command-
ed *them* to tell this to
no man;

[1] Many ancient authorities read *that I the Son of man am.* See Mark 8:27; Luke 9:18. [2] Gr. *Petros.* [3] Gr. *petra.*

§83. JESUS DISTINCTLY FORETELLS THAT HE, THE MESSIAH, WILL BE REJECTED AND KILLED, AND WILL RISE THE THIRD DAY

Mark 8:31–37

31 And he began to
teach them, that the
Son of man must suf-
fer many things, and
be rejected by the
elders, and the chief
priests, and the
scribes, and be killed,
and after three days
32 rise again. And he

Matt. 16:21–26

21 From that time be-
gan [1]Jesus to shew
unto his disciples,
how that he must go
unto Jerusalem, and
suffer many things of
the elders and chief
priests and scribes,
and be killed, and
the third day be
raised up.

Luke 9:22–25

22 saying, The Son of
man must suffer
many things, and be
rejected of the elders
and chief priests and
scribes, and be killed,
and the third day be
raised up.

* It is interesting to note that the imagery employed by Jesus here all appears in Ps. 89, a Messianic Psalm built on 1 Sam. 7. Thus note "build" in Ps. 89:4, "rock" in 89:26, "anointed" in 89:38, "the power of Sheol" in 89:48, and the Psalm discusses the perpetuity of the Davidic throne (Kingdom). Jesus applies this imagery to the spiritual Kingdom that He is building.

Mark 8:31-37

spake the saying
openly. And Peter
took him, and began
33 to rebuke him. But
he turning about, and
seeing his disciples,
rebuked Peter, and
saith, Get thee behind
me, Satan: for thou
mindest not the
things of God, but
the things of men.
34 And he called unto
him the multitude
with his disciples, and
said unto them, If
any man would come
after me, let him
deny himself, and
take up his cross,
35 and follow me. For
whosoever would save
his [3]life shall lose it;
and whosoever shall
lose his [3]life for my
sake and the gospel's
36 shall save it. For
what doth it profit a
man, to gain the
whole world, and for-
37 feit his [3]life? For
what should a man
give in exchange for
his [3]life?

Matt. 16:21-26

22 And
Peter took him, and
began to rebuke him,
saying, [2]Be it far
from thee, Lord: this
shall never be unto
23 thee. But he turned,
and said unto Peter,
Get thee behind me,
Satan: thou art a
stumbling-block un-
to me: for thou mind-
est not the things of
God, but the things
24 of men. Then said
Jesus unto his disci-
ples, If any man
would come after me,
let him deny himself,
and take up his cross,
25 and follow me. For
whosoever would save
his [3]life shall lose it:
and whosoever shall
lose his [3]life for my
sake shall find it.
26 For what shall a man
be profited, if he shall
gain the whole world,
and forfeit his [3]life?
or what shall a man
give in exchange for
his [3]life?

Luke 9:22-25

23 And he
said unto all, If any
man would come af-
ter me, let him deny
himself, and take up
his cross daily, and
24 follow me. For who-
soever would save
his [3]life shall lose it;
but whosoever shall
lose his [3]life for my
sake, the same shall
25 save it. For what is
a man profited, if he
gain the whole
world, and lose or
forfeit his own self?

[1] Some ancient authorities read *Jesus Christ*. [2] Or, God *have mercy on thee*. [3] Or, *soul*.

§ 84. THE COMING OF THE SON OF MAN IN THAT GENERATION

Mark 8:38-9:1

38 For whosoever shall
be ashamed of me
and of my words
in this adulterous and
sinful generation, the
Son of man also shall
be ashamed of him,
when he cometh in
the glory of his Father

Matt. 16:27-28

27 For the
Son of man shall
come in the glory of
his Father with his
angels and then shall

Luke 9:26-27

26 For whosoever shall
be ashamed of me and
of my words, of him
shall the Son of man
be ashamed, when he
cometh in his own
glory, and *the glory*
of the Father, and of
27 the holy angels. But

Mark 8:38–9:1

with the holy angels.
1 And he said unto
them, Verily I say
unto you, There be
some here of them
that stand *by*, which
shall in no wise taste
of death, till they
see the kingdom of
God come with power.

Matt. 16:27–28

he render unto every
man according to his
28 [1]deeds [*see Ps. 62:12; Prov. 24:12*]. Verily
I say unto you, There
be some of them that
stand here, which
shall in no wise taste
of death, till they
see the Son of man
coming in his kingdom.

[1] Or, *doings*.

Luke 9:26–27

I tell you of a truth,
There be some of
them that stand here,
which shall in no
wise taste of death,
till they see the kingdom of God.

§85. THE TRANSFIGURATION OF JESUS ON A MOUNTAIN (PROBABLY HERMON*) NEAR CÆSAREA PHILIPPI

Mark 9:2–8

2 And after six days
Jesus taketh with him
Peter, and James, and
John, and bringeth
them up into a high
mountain apart by
themselves: and he
was transfigured be-
3 fore them: and his
garments became
glistering, exceeding
white; so as no fuller
on earth can whiten
4 them. And there
appeared unto them
Elijah with Moses:
and they were talking
with Jesus.

Matt. 17:1–8

1 And after six days
Jesus taketh with him
Peter, and James, and
John his brother, and
bringeth them up into
a high mountain
2 apart: and he was
transfigured before
them; and his face did
shine as the sun, and
his garments became
white as the light.
3 And behold, there
appeared unto them
Moses and Elijah
talking with him.

Luke 9:28–36

28 And it came to pass,
about eight days after these sayings, he
took with him Peter
and John and James,
and went up into the
mountain to pray.
29 And as he was praying, the fashion of
his countenance was
altered, and his raiment *became* white
30 *and* dazzling. And
behold, there talked
with him two men,
which were Moses
31 and Elijah; who appeared in glory, and
spake of his [2]decease
which he was about
to accomplish at
32 Jerusalem. Now
Peter and they that
were with him, were
heavy with sleep: but
[3]when they were fully
awake, they saw his

* The tradition which places the Transfiguration on Mount Tabor is beyond question false.

Mark 9:2-8

5 And Peter answer-
eth and saith unto
Jesus, Rabbi, it is
good for us to be
here: and let us make
three [1]tabernacles,*
one for thee, and one
for Moses, and one for
6 Elijah. For he wist
not what to answer;
for they became sore
7 afraid. And there
came a cloud over-
shadowing them: and
there came a voice
out of the cloud, This
is my beloved Son:
hear ye him [*see
Deut. 18:15; Isa. 42:1;
Ps. 2:7*].†

8 And
suddenly looking
round about, they
saw no one any more,
save Jesus only with
themselves.

Matt. 17:1-8

4 And Peter answer-
ed, and said unto
Jesus, Lord, it is good
for us to be here: if
thou wilt, I will make
here three [1]taberna-
cles; one for thee, and
one for Moses, and
one for Elijah.
5 While he was yet
speaking, behold, a
bright cloud over-
shadowed them: and
behold, a voice out
of the cloud, saying,
This is my beloved
Son, in whom I am
well pleased; hear ye
6 him. And when the
disciples heard it,
they fell on their
face, and were sore
7 afraid. And Jesus
came and touched
them and said, Arise,
and be not afraid.
8 And lifting up their
eyes, they saw no
one, save Jesus only.

Luke 9:28-36

glory, and the two
men that stood with
33 him. And it came
to pass, as they were
parting from him,
Peter said unto Jesus,
Master, it is good for
us to be here: and let
us make three [1]taber-
nacles; one for thee,
and one for Moses,
and one for Elijah:
not knowing what he
34 said. And while he
said these things,
there came a cloud,
and overshadowed
them: and they fear-
ed as they entered
35 into the cloud. And
a voice came out of
the cloud, saying,
This is [4]my Son, my
chosen: hear ye him.

36 And when the voice
[5]came, Jesus was
found alone.

[1] Or, *booths*. [2] Or, *departure*. [3] Or, *having remained awake*. [4] Many ancient authorities read *my beloved Son*. See Matt. 17:5; Mark 9:7. [5] Or, *was past*.

§ 86. THE PUZZLE OF THE THREE DISCIPLES ABOUT THE RESURRECTION AND ABOUT ELIJAH ON THEIR WAY DOWN THE MOUNTAIN

Mark 9:9-13

9 And as they were
coming down from
the mountain, he
charged them that
they should tell no
man what things
they had seen, save
when the Son of man

Matt. 17:9-13

9 And as they were
coming down from
the mountain, Jesus
commanded them,
saying, Tell the vi-
sion to no man, until
the Son of man be
risen from the dead.

Luke 9:36

36 And
they held their peace,
and told no man in
those days any of the
things which they had
seen.

* Probably not long before the feast of tabernacles (near end of September) and Peter may have meant that they celebrate the feast on the mountains instead of going to Jerusalem.
† See § 24 for similar language at the Baptism of Jesus.

Mark 9:9–13

should have risen
again from the dead.
10 And they kept the
saying, questioning
among themselves
what the rising again
from the dead should
11 mean. And they
asked him, saying,
[1]The scribes say that
Elijah must first
12 come. And he said
unto them, Elijah in-
deed cometh first, and
restoreth all things:
and how is it written
of the Son of man,
that he should suffer
many things and be
13 set at naught? But
I say unto you, that
Elijah is come, and
they have also done
unto him whatsoever
they listed, even as it
is written of him.

Matt. 17:9–13

10 And his disciples
asked him, saying,
Why then say the
scribes that Elijah
must first come [*see*
11 [*Mal. 4:5–6*]? And
he answered and said,
Elijah indeed cometh,
and shall restore all
12 things: but I say un-
to you, that Elijah is
come already,* and
they knew him not,
but did unto him
whatsoever they list-
ed [*see 1 Kings 19:2,
10*]. Even so shall the
Son of man also suffer
13 of them. Then
understood the disci-
ples that he spake un-
to them of John the
Baptist.

[1] Or, *How is it that the scribes say . . . come?*

§87. THE DEMONIAC BOY, WHOM THE DISCIPLES COULD NOT HEAL

In the region of Cæsarea Philippi

Mark 9:14–29

14 And when they came
to the disciples, they
saw a great multitude
about them, and
scribes questioning
15 with them. And
straightway all the
multitude, when
they saw him, were
greatly amazed, and
running to him sa-
16 luted him. And he
asked them, What
question ye with

Matt. 17:14–20

14 And when they were
come to the multi-
tude, there came to

Luke 9:37–43

37 And it came to pass,
on the next day,
when they were
come down from the
mountain, a great
multitude met him.

* The Baptist's disclaimer about being Elijah (John 1:21) means only that he was not Elijah in person come back to earth according to popular expectation.

Mark 9:14–29

17 them? And one of
the multitude an-
swered him, [3]Master,
I brought unto thee
my son, which hath
a dumb spirit; and
18 wheresoever it taketh
him, it [4]dasheth him
down: and he foam-
eth, and grindeth his
teeth, and pineth
away: and I spake to
thy disciples that
they should cast it
out; and they were
19 not able. And he an-
swereth them and
saith, O faithless
generation, how long
shall I be with you?
how long shall I bear
with you? bring him
20 unto me. And they
brought him unto
him: and when he
saw him, straightway
the spirit [5]tare him
grievously; and he
fell on the ground,
and wallowed foam-
21 ing. And he asked
his father, How long
time is it since this
hath come unto him?
And he said, From
22 a child. And oft-
times it hath cast
him both into the fire
and into the waters,
to destroy him: but
if thou canst do any-
thing, have compas-
sion on us, and help
23 us. And Jesus said
unto him, If thou
canst! All things are
possible to him that
24 believeth. Straight-
way the father of the
child cried out, and

Matt. 17:14–20

him a man, kneeling
to him, and saying,
15 Lord, have mercy on
my son: for he is ep-
ileptic, and suffereth
grievously: for oft-
times he falleth into
the fire, and oft-
times into the water.
16 And I brought him
to thy disciples, and
they could not cure
him.

17 And Jesus an-
swered and said, O
faithless and perverse
generation, how long
shall I bear with
you? bring him hither
to me.

Luke 9:37–43

38 And behold, a man
from the multitude
cried, saying, [3]Mas-
ter, I beseech thee
to look upon my son;
for he is mine only
39 child: and behold, a
spirit taketh him and
he suddenly crieth
out; and it [9]teareth
him that he foameth,
and it hardly depart-
eth from him, bruis-
40 ing him sorely. And
I besought thy dis-
ciples to cast it out;
and they could not.
41 And Jesus answered
and said, O faithless
and perverse gener-
ation, how long shall
I be with you, and
bear with you? bring
42 hither thy son. And
as he was yet a com-
ing, the [1]devil [10]dashed
him down, and [5]tare
him grievously.

Mark 9:14–29

said[6], I believe; help
thou mine unbelief.
25 And when Jesus saw
that a multitude
came running to-
gether, he rebuked
the unclean spirit,
saying unto him,
Thou dumb and deaf
spirit, I command
thee, come out of
him, and enter no
26 more into him. And
having cried out, and
[9]torn him much, he
came out: and *the
child* became as one
dead; insomuch that
the more part said,
27 He is dead. But Je-
sus took him by the
hand, and raised him
up; and he arose.
28 And when he was
come into the house,
his disciples asked
him privately, [7]*say-
ing,* We could not cast
29 it out. And he said
unto them, This kind
can come out by
nothing, save by
prayer.[8]

Matt. 17:14–20

18 And Jesus rebuked
him; and the [1]devil
went out from him:
and the boy was
cured from that hour.
19 Then came the dis-
ciples to Jesus apart,
and said, Why could
not we cast it out?
20 And he said unto
them, Because of
your little faith: for
verily I say unto you,
If ye have faith as a
grain of mustard seed,
ye shall say unto
this mountain, Re-
move hence to yonder
place; and it shall
remove; and nothing
shall be impossible
unto you.[2]

Luke 9:37–43

But Jesus rebuked
the unclean spirit,
and healed the boy,
and gave him back
43 to his father. And
they were all aston-
ished at the majesty
of God.

[1] Gr. *demon.* [2] Many authorities, some ancient, insert ver. 21 *But this kind goeth not out save by prayer and fasting.* See Mark 9:29. [3] Or, *Teacher.* [4] Or, *rendeth him.* [5] Or, *convulsed.* [6] Many ancient authorities add *with tears.* [7] Or, How is it *that we could not cast it out?* [8] Many ancient authorities add *and fasting.* [9] Or, *convulseth.* [10] Or, *rent him.*

§ 88. RETURNING PRIVATELY THROUGH GALILEE, HE AGAIN FORETELLS HIS DEATH AND RESURRECTION

Mark 9:30–32

30 And they went
forth from thence,
and passed through
Galilee; and he would
not that any man
31 should know it. For
he taught his disciples,
and said unto
them, The Son of
man is delivered up
into the hands of
men, and they shall
kill him; and when
he is killed, after
three days he shall
32 rise again. But they
understood not the
saying,
and
were afraid to ask
him.

Matt. 17:22–23

22 And while they
[1]abode in Galilee, Jesus
said unto them,
The Son of man shall
be delivered up into
the hands of men;
23 and they shall kill
him, and the third
day he shall be raised
up. And they were
exceeding sorry.

Luke 9:43–45

43 But while all were
marvelling at all the
things which he did,
he said unto his dis-
44 ciples, Let these
words sink into your
ears: for the Son of
man shall be delivered
up into the
hands of men.
45 But
they understood not
this saying, and it
was concealed from
them, that they
should not perceive
it: and they were
afraid to ask him
about this saying.

[1] Some ancient authorities read *were gathering themselves together.*

The season of retirement from Galilee is now ended (§§ 72–88). The remaining events at this time (§§ 89–95) probably occupied only a few days.

§ 89. JESUS, THE MESSIAH, PAYS THE HALF-SHEKEL FOR THE TEMPLE

Capernaum

Matt. 17:24–27

24 And when they were come to Capernaum, they that received the
[1]half-shekel came to Peter, and said, Doth not your [2]master pay the
25 [1]half-shekel [*see Ex. 30:11–15*]? He saith, Yea. And when he came into the
house, Jesus spake first to him, saying, What thinkest thou, Simon? the
kings of the earth, from whom do they receive toll or tribute? from their
26 sons, or from strangers? And when he said, From strangers, Jesus said
27 unto him, Therefore the sons are free. But, lest we cause them to stumble,

Matt. 17:24–27

go thou to the sea and cast a hook, and take up the fish that first cometh up; and when thou hast opened his mouth, thou shalt find a [3]shekel: that take, and give unto them for me and thee.

[1] Gr. *didrachma.* [2] Or, *teacher.* [3] Gr. *stater.*

§ 90. THE TWELVE CONTEND AS TO WHO SHALL BE THE GREATEST UNDER THE MESSIAH'S REIGN. HIS SUBJECTS MUST BE CHILDLIKE

Capernaum

Mark 9:33–37

33 And they came to
Capernaum: and
when he was in the
house he asked them,
What were ye reason-
ing in the way?
34 But they held their
peace: for they had
disputed one with an-
other in the way, who
was the [1]greatest.
35 And he sat down, and
called the twelve;
he saith unto them,
If any man would be
first, he shall be last
of all, and minister
36 of all. And he took
a little child, and
set him in the midst
of them: and taking
him in his arms, he
said unto them,
37 Whosoever shall re-
ceive one of such
little children in my
name, receiveth me:
and whosoever re-
ceiveth me, receiv-
eth not me, but him
that sent me.

Matt. 18:1–5

1 In that hour came
the disciples unto Je-
sus, saying, who then
is [1]greatest in the
kingdom of heaven?
2 And he called to him
a little child, and set
him in the midst of
3 them, and said, Ver-
ily I say unto you,
Except ye turn, and
become as little chil-
dren, ye shall in no
wise enter into the
kingdom of heaven.
4 Whosoever therefore
shall humble himself
as this little child,
the same is the
[1]greatest in the king-
5 dom of heaven. And
whoso shall receive
one such little child
in my name receiveth
me:

Luke 9:46–48

46 And there arose a
reasoning among
them, which of them
should be [1]greatest.
47 But when Jesus saw
the reasoning of their
heart, he took a little
child, and set him by
his side, and said
unto them,
48 Whosoever shall re-
ceive this little child
in my name receiveth
me: and whosoever
shall receive me re-
ceiveth him that sent
me: for he that is
[2]least among you all,
the same is great.

[1] Gr. *greater.* [2] Gr. *lesser.*

§91. THE MISTAKEN ZEAL OF THE APOSTLE JOHN REBUKED BY JESUS IN PERTINENT PARABLES

Capernaum

Mark 9:38–50

38 John said unto him,
[7]Master, we saw one
casting out [8]devils
in thy name: and we
forbade him, because
he followed not us.
39 But Jesus said, For-
bid him not: for there
is no man which shall
do a [9]mighty work in
my name, and be able
quickly to speak evil
40 of me. For he that
is not against us is
41 for us. For whoso-
ever shall give you a
cup of water to drink
[10]because ye are
Christ's, verily I say
unto you, he shall in
no wise lose his re-
42 ward. And whosoever
shall cause one of
these little ones that
believe [11]on me to
stumble, it were bet-
ter for him if [2]a great
millstone were hanged
about his neck, and he
were cast into the sea.

43 And if
thy hand cause thee
to stumble, cut it off:
it is good for thee
to enter into life

Matt. 18:6–14

6 but whoso
shall cause one of
these little ones which
believe on me to
stumble, it is profit-
able for him that
[2]a great millstone
should be hanged
about his neck, and
that he should be
sunk in the depth of
7 the sea. Woe unto
the world because of
occasions of stum-
bling! for it must
needs be that the oc-
casions come; but woe
to that man through
whom the occasion
8 cometh! And if thy
hand or thy foot
causeth thee to stum-
ble, cut it off, and
cast it from thee: it

Luke 9:49–50

49 And John answer-
ed and said, Master,
we saw one casting
out [8]devils in thy
name; and we for-
bade him, because he
followeth not with
50 us. But Jesus said
unto him, Forbid *him*
not: for he that is
not against you is for
you.

Mark 9:38–50

maimed, rather than
having thy two hands
to go into [12]hell, into
the unquenchable
45 fire.[13] And if thy
foot cause thee to
stumble, cut it off:
it is good for thee to
enter into life halt,
rather than having
thy two feet to be
47 cast into [12]hell. And
if thine eye cause
thee to stumble, cast
it out: it is good for
thee to enter into the
kingdom of God with
one eye, rather than
having two eyes to
be cast into [12]hell;
48 where their worm
dieth not, and the
fire is not quenched
[*see Isa. 66:24*]. For
49 every one shall be
salted with fire[14] [*see*
50 *Lev. 2:13*]. Salt is good:
but if the salt have
lost its saltness, where-
with will ye season
it? Have salt in
yourselves, and be at
peace one with
another.

Matt. 18:6–14

is good for thee to
enter into life maim-
ed or halt, rather than
having two hands or
two feet to be cast
into the eternal fire.
9 And if thine
eye causeth thee to
stumble, pluck it out,
and cast it from thee:
it is good for thee to
enter into life with
one eye, rather than
having two eyes to
be cast into the [3]hell
of fire.
10 See that ye despise
not one of these little
ones; for I say unto
you, that in heaven
their angels do al-
ways behold the face
of my Father which
12 is in heaven.[4] How
think ye? if any man
have a hundred
sheep,* and one of
them be gone astray,
doth he not leave the
ninety and nine, and
go unto the moun-
tains, and seek that
13 which goeth astray? And if so be that he find it, verily I say unto you,
he rejoiceth over it more than over the ninety and nine which have not
14 gone astray. Even so it is not [5]the will of [6]your Father which is in heaven,
that one of these little ones should perish.

[1] Gr. *greater*. [2] Gr. *a millstone turned by an ass*. [3] Gr. *Gehenna of fire*. [4] Many authorities, some ancient, insert ver. 11 *For the Son of man came to save that which was lost*. See Luke 19:10. [5] Gr. *a thing willed before your father*. [6] Some ancient authorities read *my*. [7] Or, *teacher*. [8] Gr. *demons*. [9] Gr. *power*. [10] Gr. *in name that ye are*. [11] Many ancient authorities omit *on me*. [12] Gr. *Gehenna*. [13] Ver. 44 and 46 (which are identical with ver. 48) are omitted by the best ancient authorities. [14] Many ancient authorities add *and every sacrifice shall be salted with salt*. See Lev. 2:13. [15] Gr. *lesser*.

* Parable of the Lost Sheep.

§ 92. RIGHT TREATMENT OF A BROTHER WHO HAS SINNED AGAINST ONE, AND DUTY OF PATIENTLY FORGIVING A BROTHER (PARABLE OF THE UNMERCIFUL SERVANT)

Matt. 18:15–35

15 And if thy brother sin [1]against thee, go, shew him his fault between
16 thee and him alone: if he hear thee, thou hast gained thy brother. But
if he hear *thee* not, take with thee one or two more, that at the mouth
17 of two witnesses or three every word may be established [*see Deut. 19:15*].
And if he refuse to hear them, tell it unto the [2]church: and if he refuse to
hear the [2]church also, let him be unto thee as the Gentile and the publican.
18 Verily I say unto you, What things soever ye shall bind on earth shall be
bound in heaven: and what things soever ye shall loose on earth shall be
19 loosed in heaven. Again I say unto you, that if two of you shall agree
on earth as touching anything that they shall ask, it shall be done for
20 them of my Father which is in heaven. For where two or three are
gathered together in my name, there am I in the midst of them.
21 Then came Peter, and said to him, Lord, how oft shall my brother sin
22 against me, and I forgive him? until seven times? Jesus saith unto him,
I say not unto thee, Until seven times; but, Until [3]seventy times seven.
23 Therefore is the kingdom of heaven likened* unto a certain king, which
24 would make a reckoning with his [4]servants. And when he had begun
to reckon, one was brought unto him, which owed him ten thousand
25 [5]talents. But forasmuch as he had not *wherewith* to pay, his lord commanded him to be sold, and his wife, and children, and all that he had,
26 and payment to be made. The [6]servant therefore fell down and worshipped him, saying, Lord, have patience with me, and I will pay thee all.
27 And the lord of that [6]servant, being moved with compassion, released him,
28 and forgave him the debt. But that [6]servant went out, and found one
of his fellow-servants, which owed him a hundred [8]pence: and he laid hold
29 on him, and took *him* by the throat, saying, Pay what thou owest. So his
fellow-servant fell down and besought him, saying, Have patience with
30 me, and I will pay thee. And he would not: but went and cast him into
31 prison, till he should pay that which was due. So when his fellow-servants
saw what was done, they were exceedingly sorry, and came and told unto
32 their lord all that was done. Then his lord called him unto him, and
saith unto him, Thou wicked [6]servant, I forgave thee all that debt,[7]
33 because thou besoughtest me: shouldest not thou also have had mercy
34 on thy fellow-servant, even as I had mercy on thee?† And his lord was
wroth, and delivered him to the tormentors, till he should pay all that
35 was due. So shall also my heavenly Father do unto you, if ye forgive
not every one his brother from your hearts.

[1] Some ancient authorities omit *against thee*. [2] Or, *congregation*. [3] Or, *seventy times and seven*. [4] Gr. *bond-servants*. [5] This talent was probably worth about $1200. [6] Gr. *bond-servant*. [7] Or, *loan*. [8] The word in the Greek denotes a coin worth about seventeen cents.

* Parable of the Unforgiving Servant.

† The king forgave the servant $1,200,000; the servant refused to forgive $17. We might say in round numbers, a million, and ten dollars.

§ 93. THE MESSIAH'S FOLLOWERS MUST GIVE UP EVERYTHING FOR HIS SERVICE

Matt. 8:19–22

19 And there came [1]a scribe, and
said unto him, [2]Master, I will
follow thee whithersoever thou
20 goest. And Jesus saith unto him,
the foxes have holes, and the
birds of the heaven *have* [3]nests;
but the Son of man hath not
21 where to lay his head. And an-
other of the disciples saith unto
him, Lord, suffer me first to go
22 and bury my father. But Jesus
saith unto him, Follow me; and
leave the dead to bury their own
dead.

Luke 9:57–62

57 And as they went in the way, a
certain man said unto him, I will
follow thee whithersoever thou
58 goest. And Jesus said unto him,
the foxes have holes, and the
birds of the heaven *have* [3]nests;
but the Son of man hath not
59 where to lay his head. And he
said unto another, Follow me.
But he said, Lord, suffer me first
60 to go and bury my father. But
he said unto him, Leave the
dead to bury their own dead; but
go thou and publish abroad the
61 kingdom of God. And another
also said, I will follow thee, Lord;
but first suffer me to bid farewell
to them that are at my house.
62 But Jesus said unto him, No man,
having put his hand to the plough,
and looking back, is fit for the
kingdom of God

[1] Gr. *one scribe*. [2] Or, *Teacher*. [3] Gr. *lodging-places*.

§ 94. THE UNBELIEVING BROTHERS OF JESUS COUNSEL HIM TO EXHIBIT HIMSELF IN JUDEA, AND HE REJECTS THE ADVICE

John 7:2–9

2 Now the feast of the Jews, the feast of tabernacles, was at hand.
3 His brethren therefore said unto him, Depart hence, and go into Judea,
4 that thy disciples also may behold thy works which thou doest. For no
man doeth anything in secret, [1]and himself seeketh to be known openly.
5 If thou doest these things, manifest thyself to the world. For even his
6 brethren did not believe on him. Jesus therefore saith unto them, My
7 time is not yet come; but your time is always ready. The world cannot
hate you; but me it hateth, because I testify of it, that its works are evil.
8 Go ye up unto the feast: I go not up [2]yet unto this feast; because my
9 time is not yet fulfilled. And having said these things unto them, he
abode *still* in Galilee.

[1] Some ancient authorities read *and seeketh it to be known openly*. [2] Many ancient authorities omit *yet*.

§95. HE GOES PRIVATELY TO JERUSALEM THROUGH SAMARIA

Luke 9:51–56

51 And it came to pass, when the
days [1]were well-nigh come that
he should be received up, he
stedfastly set his face to go to Je-
52 rusalem,* and sent messengers be-
fore his face: and they went, and
entered into a village of the Sa-
maritans, to make ready for him.
53 And they did not receive him,
because his face was as *though he*
54 *were* going to Jerusalem. And
when his disciples James and
John saw *this*, they said, Lord,
wilt thou that we bid fire to come
down from heaven, and consume
55 them [*see 2 Kings 1:10–12*]?[2] But
he turned, and rebuked them.[3]
56 And they went to another village.

John 7:10

10 But when his brethren were
gone up unto the feast, then
went he also up, not publicly,
but as it were in secret.

[1] Gr. *were being fulfilled.* [2] Many ancient authorities add, *even as Elijah did.* [3] Some ancient authorities add, *and said, Ye know not what manner of spirit ye are of.* Some, but fewer, add also *For the Son of man came not to destroy men's lives, but to save them.*

* See note 10 at end of Harmony for the combination of Luke and John and the three journeyings in Luke toward Jerusalem.

PART IX

THE LATER JUDEAN MINISTRY

(Probably Tabernacles to Dedication, about three months, in A.D. 29 or 28 if Ministry only two and a half years in length)

This ministry is given only by John and Luke. John gives the Jerusalem ministry and Luke that in the country of Judea. §§ 96–111.

§ 96. THE COMING OF JESUS TO THE FEAST OF TABERNACLES CREATES INTENSE EXCITEMENT CONCERNING THE MESSIAHSHIP

The attempt of the rulers (the Jews, the chief priests, and Pharisees) to arrest him. Division of sentiment in the Galilean multitude at the feast. Impressions of the Jerusalem populace and the Roman officers and of Nicodemus.

John 7:11–52

11 The Jews therefore sought him at the feast, and said, Where is he?
12 And there was much murmuring among the multitudes concerning him.
Some said, He is a good man; others said, Nay, but he leads the multitude
13 astray. Yet no one spoke openly concerning him, for fear of the Jews.
14 But when it was now the midst of the feast Jesus went up into the
15 temple, and taught. The Jews therefore marvelled, saying, How knoweth
16 this man letters, having never learned? Jesus therefore answered them,
17 and said, My teaching is not mine, but his that sent me. If any man
willeth to do his will, he shall know of the teaching, whether it be of God,
18 or *whether* I speak from myself. He that speaketh from himself seeketh
his own glory: but he that seeketh the glory of him that sent him, the
19 same is true, and no unrighteousness is in him. Did not Moses give you
the law, and *yet* none of you doeth the law? Why seek ye to kill me?
20 The multitude answered, Thou hast a [1]devil: who seeketh to kill thee?
21 Jesus answered and said unto them, I did one work, and ye all [2]marvel.
22 For this cause hath Moses given you circumcision (not that it is of Moses,
but of the fathers); and on the sabbath ye circumcise a man [*see Gen. 17:*
23 *9–14; Lev. 12:1–3*]. If a man receiveth circumcision on the sabbath, that the
law of Moses may not be broken; are ye wroth with me, because I made a
24 man every whit whole on the sabbath? Judge not according to appearance, but judge righteous judgement.
25 Some therefore of them of Jerusalem said, Is not this he whom they
26 seek to kill? And lo, he speaketh openly, and they say nothing unto him.
27 Can it be that the rulers indeed know that this is the Christ? Howbeit
we know this man whence he is: but when the Christ cometh, no one
28 knoweth whence he is. Jesus therefore cried in the temple, teaching
and saying, Ye both know me, and know whence I am; and I am not

John 7:11-52

29 come of myself, but he that sent me is true, whom ye know not. I know
30 him; because I am from him, and he sent me. They sought therefore to
take him: and no man laid his hands on him, because his hour was not yet
31 come. But of the multitude many believed on him; and they said, When
the Christ shall come, will he do more signs than those, which this man
32 hath done? The Pharisees heard the multitude murmuring these things
concerning him; and the chief priests and the Pharisees sent officers to
33 take him. Jesus therefore said, Yet a little while am I with you, and I
34 go unto him that sent me. Ye shall seek me, and shall not find me: and
35 where I am, ye cannot come. The Jews therefore said among themselves,
Whither will this man go that we shall not find him? will he go unto
36 the Dispersion [3]among the Greeks, and teach the Greeks? What is this
word that he said, Ye shall seek me, and shall not find me: and where I
am, ye cannot come?
37 Now on the last day, the great *day* of the feast, Jesus stood and cried,
38 saying, If any man thirst, let him come unto me, and drink. He that be-
lieveth on me, as the scripture hath said, out of his belly shall flow rivers
39 of living water. But this spake he of the Spirit, which they that believed
on him were to receive: [4]for the Spirit was not yet *given;* because Jesus
40 was not yet glorified. *Some* of the multitude therefore, when they heard
41 these words, said, This is of a truth the prophet. Others said, This is the
Christ. But some said, What, doth the Christ come out of Galilee?
42 Hath not the scripture said that the Christ cometh out of the seed of David,
and from Bethlehem [*see 2 Sam. 7:12,17; Mic. 5:2*], the village where David
43 was? So there arose a division in the multitude because of him. And
44 some of them would have taken him; but no man laid hands on him.
45 The officers therefore came to the chief priests* and Pharisees; and
46 they said unto them, Why did ye not bring him? The officers answered,
47 Never man so spake. The Pharisees therefore answered them, Are ye
48 also led astray? Hath any of the rulers believed on him, or of the Phari-
49 sees? But this multitude which knoweth not the law are accursed.
50 Nicodemus saith unto them (he that came to him before, being one of
51 them), Doth our law judge a man, except it first hear from himself and
52 know what he doeth? They answered and said unto him, Art thou also
of Galilee? Search, and [5]see that out of Galilee ariseth no prophet.

[1] Gr. *demon.* [2] Or, *marvel because of this. Moses hath given you circumcision.* [3] Gr. *of.* [4] Some ancient authorities read *for the Holy Spirit was not yet given.* [5] Or, *see; for out of Galilee, etc.*

§97. STORY OF AN ADULTERESS BROUGHT TO JESUS FOR JUDGMENT

John 7:53 to 8:11†

53, 1[[1]And they went every man unto his own house: but Jesus went unto
2 the mount of Olives. And early in the morning he came again into

* The Sanhedrin included both Sadducees (chief priests) and Pharisees. Nicodemus was a member of the Sanhedrin and a Pharisee. Now both parties in the Sanhedrin were united against Jesus and the purpose was to bring Jesus before the Sanhedrin for trial.

† This paragraph can no longer be considered a part of the Gospel of John, but it is in all probability a true story of Jesus, very likely drawn by early students from the collection of Papias, published about A.D. 140. See Hovey on John (American Comm. on N. T.). Observe that without it § 98 goes right on after § 96.

John 7:53 to 8:11

the temple, and all the people came unto him; and he sat down, and
3 taught them. And the scribes and the Pharisees bring a woman taken
4 in adultery; and having set her in the midst, they say unto him, [2]Master,
5 this woman hath been taken in adultery, in the very act. Now in the law
Moses commanded us to stone such [*see Lev. 20:10; Deut. 22:22–24*]: what
6 then sayest thou of her? And this they said, [3]tempting him, that they
might have *whereof* to accuse him. But Jesus stooped down, and with his
7 finger wrote on the ground. But when they continued asking him, he
lifted up himself, and said unto them, He that is without sin among you,
8 let him first cast a stone at her. And again he stooped down, and with
9 his finger wrote on the ground. And they, when they heard it, went
out one by one, beginning from the eldest, *even* unto the last: and Jesus
10 was left alone, and the woman, where she was, in the midst. And Jesus
11 lifted up himself, and said unto her, Woman, where are they? did no man
condemn thee? And she said, No man, Lord. And Jesus said, Neither
do I condemn thee: go thy way; from henceforth sin no more.]

[1] Most of the ancient authorities omit John 7:53–8:11. Those which contain it vary much from each other. [2] Or, *Teacher*. [3] Or, *trying*.

§98. AFTER THE FEAST OF TABERNACLES IN THE TEMPLE JESUS ANGERS THE PHARISEES BY CLAIMING TO BE THE LIGHT OF THE WORLD

John 8:12–20

12 Again therefore Jesus spake unto them, saying, I am the light of the
world: he that followeth me shall not walk in the darkness, but shall
13 have the light of life. The Pharisees therefore said unto him, Thou
14 bearest witness of thyself; thy witness is not true. Jesus answered and
said unto them, Even if I bear witness of myself, my witness is true; for
I know whence I came, and whither I go; but ye know not whence I come,
15 or whither I go. Ye judge after the flesh; I judge no man. Yea and
16 if I judge, my judgement is true; for I am not alone, but I and the Father
17 that sent me. Yea and in your law it is written, that the witness of two
18 men is true [*see Deut. 17:6; 19:15*]. I am he that beareth witness of myself,
19 and the Father that sent me beareth witness of me. They said therefore
unto him, Where is thy Father? Jesus answered, Ye know neither me,
20 nor my Father: if ye knew me, ye would know my Father also. These
words spake he in the treasury, as he taught in the temple: and no man
took him; because his hour was not yet come.

§99. THE PHARISEES ATTEMPT TO STONE JESUS WHEN HE EXPOSES THEIR SINFULNESS

Jerusalem, probably in the Temple

John 8:21–59

21 He said therefore again unto them, I go away, and ye shall seek me,
22 and shall die in your sin: whither I go, ye cannot come. The Jews therefore said, Will he kill himself, that he saith, Whither I go, ye cannot come?

John 8:21-59

23 And he said unto them, Ye are from beneath; I am from above: ye are of
24 this world; I am not of this world. I said therefore unto you, that ye
shall die in your sins: for except ye believe that [1]I am *he*, ye shall die in
25 your sins. They said therefore unto him, Who art thou? Jesus said
unto them, [2]Even that which I have also spoken unto you from the be-
26 ginning. I have many things to speak and to judge concerning you:
howbeit he that sent me is true; and the things which I heard from him,
27 these speak I [3]unto the world. They perceived not that he spake to them
28 of the Father. Jesus therefore said, When ye have lifted up the Son of
man, then shall ye know that [4]I am *he*, and *that* I do nothing of myself,
29 but as the Father taught me, I speak these things. And he that sent me
is with me: he hath not left me alone; for I do always the things that are
30 pleasing to him. As he spake these things, many believed on him.
31 Jesus therefore said to those Jews which had believed him, If ye abide
32 in my word, *then* are ye truly my disciples; and ye shall know the truth,
33 and the truth shall make you free. They answered unto him, We be
Abraham's seed, and have never yet been in bondage to any man: how
34 sayest thou, Ye shall be made free? Jesus answered them, Verily, verily,
I say unto you, Every one that committeth sin is the bondservant of sin.
35 And the bondservant abideth not in the house for ever: the son abideth
36 for ever. If therefore the Son shall make you free, ye shall be free indeed.
37 I know that ye are Abraham's seed; yet ye seek to kill me, because my
38 word [5]hath not free course in you. I speak the things which I have seen
with [6]*my* Father; and ye also do the things which ye heard from *your*
father. They answered and said unto him, Our Father is Abraham.
39 Jesus saith unto them, If ye [7]were Abraham's children, [8]ye would do the
40 works of Abraham. But now ye seek to kill me, a man that hath told
41 you the truth, which I heard from God; this did not Abraham. Ye do the
works of your father. They said unto him, We were not born of fornica-
42 tion; we have one Father, *even* God. Jesus said unto them, If God were
your Father, ye would love me: for I came forth and am come from God;
43 for neither have I come of myself, but he sent me. Why do ye not [9]under-
44 stand my speech? *Even* because ye cannot hear my word. Ye are of
your father, the devil, and the lusts of your father it is your will to do.
He was a murderer from the beginning, [10]and stood not in the truth, be-
cause there is no truth in him. [11]When he speaketh a lie, he speaketh of
45 his own: for he is a liar, and the father thereof. But because I say the
46 truth, ye believe me not. Which of you convicteth me of sin? If I say
47 truth, why do ye not believe me? He that is of God heareth the words
48 of God: for this cause ye hear *them* not, because ye are not of God. The
Jews answered and said unto him, Say we not well that thou art a Samari-
49 tan, and hast a [12]devil? Jesus answered, I have not a [12]devil; but I honour
50 my Father, and ye dishonour me. But I seek not mine own glory: there
51 is one that seeketh and judgeth. Verily, verily, I say unto you, If a man
52 keep my word, he shall never see death. The Jews said unto him, Now
we know that thou hast a [12]devil. Abraham is dead, and the prophets;
and thou sayest, If a man keep my word, he shall never taste of death.
53 Art thou greater than our father Abraham, which is dead? and the prophets
54 are dead: whom makest thou thyself? Jesus answered, If I glorify my-
self, my glory is nothing: it is my Father that glorifieth me: of whom ye

John 8:21:59

55 say, that he is your God; and ye have not known him: but I know him;
and if I should say, I know him not, I shall be like unto you, a liar: but
56 I know him, and keep his word. Your father Abraham rejoiced [13]to see
57 my day; and he saw it, and was glad. The Jews therefore said unto him,
58 Thou art not yet fifty years old, and hast thou seen Abraham? Jesus
said unto them, Verily, verily, I say unto you, Before Abraham [14]was, I
59 am. They took up stones therefore to cast at him: but Jesus [15]hid himself,
and went out of the temple.[16]

[1] Or, *I am.* [2] Or, How is it *that I even speak to you at all?* [3] Gr. *into.* [4] Or, *I am,* or, *I am* he: *and I do.* [5] Or, *hath no place in you.* [6] Or, *the Father: do ye also therefore the things which ye heard from the Father.* [7] Gr. *are.* [8] Some ancient authorities read *ye do the works of Abraham.* [9] Or, *know.* [10] Some ancient authorities read *standeth.* [11] Or, *When one speaketh a lie, he speaketh of his own; for his father also is a liar.* [12] Gr. *demon.* [13] Or, *that he should see.* [14] Gr. *was born.* [15] Or, *was hidden, and went, etc.* [16] Many ancient authorities add *and going through the midst of them went his way, and so passed by.*

§ 100. JESUS HEALS A MAN BORN BLIND WHO OUT-WITS THE PHARISEES. THE RULERS FORBID THE RECOGNITION OF JESUS AS THE MESSIAH. THE CONVERSION OF THE HEALED MAN

Jerusalem

John 9:1–41

1, 2 And as he passed by, he saw a man blind from his birth. And his
disciples asked him, saying, Rabbi, who did sin, this man, or his parents,
3 that he should be born blind? Jesus answered, Neither did this man sin,
nor his parents: but that the works of God should be made manifest in
4 him. We must work the works of him that sent me, while it is day:
5 the night cometh, when no man can work. When I am in the world,
6 I am the light of the world. When he had thus spoken, he spat on the
ground, and made clay of the spittle, and [1]anointed his eyes with the clay,
7 and said unto him, Go, wash in the pool of Siloam (which is by inter-
8 pretation, Sent). He went away therefore, and washed, and came seeing.
The neighbours therefore, and they which saw him aforetime, that he was
9 a beggar, said, Is not this he that sat and begged? Others said, It is he:
10 others said, No, but he is like him. He said, I am *he.* They said there-
11 fore unto him, How then were thine eyes opened? He answered, the man
that is called Jesus made clay, and anointed mine eyes, and said unto
me, Go to Siloam, and wash: so I went away and washed, and I received
12 sight. And they said unto him, Where is he? He saith, I know not.
13, 14 They bring to the Pharisees him that aforetime was blind. Now
it was the sabbath on the day when Jesus made the clay, and opened his
15 eyes. Again therefore the Pharisees also asked him how he received his
sight. And he said unto them, He put clay upon mine eyes, and I washed,
16 and do see. Some therefore of the Pharisees said, This man is not from God,
because he keepeth not the sabbath. But others said, How can a man
17 that is a sinner do such signs? And there was a division among them.
They say therefore unto the blind man again, What sayest thou of him,
18 in that he opened thine eyes? And he said, He is a prophet. The Jews
therefore did not believe concerning him, that he had been blind, and had

John 9:1–41

received his sight, until they called the parents of him that had received
19 his sight, and asked them, saying, Is this your son, who ye say was born
20 blind? how then doth he now see? His parents answered and said, We
21 know that this is our son, and that he was born blind: but how he now
seeth, we know not; or who opened his eyes, we know not; ask him; he is of
22 age; he shall speak for himself. These things said his parents, because
they feared the Jews: for the Jews had agreed already, that if any man
should confess him *to be* Christ, he should be put out of the synagogue.
23 Therefore said his parents, He is of age; ask him. So they called the
24 second time the man that was blind, and said unto him, Give glory to
25 God: we know that this man is a sinner. He therefore answered, Whether
he be a sinner, I know not: one thing I know, that, whereas I was blind,
26 now I see. They said therefore unto him, What did he to thee? how
27 opened he thine eyes? He answered them, I told you even now, and ye
did not hear: wherefore would ye hear it again? would ye also become his
28 disciples? And they reviled him, and said, Thou art his disciple, but we
29 are disciples of Moses. We know that God hath spoken unto Moses:
30 but as for this man, we know not whence he is. The man answered and
said unto them, Why, herein is the marvel, that ye know not whence he is,
31 and *yet* he opened mine eyes. We know that God heareth not sinners:
but if any man be a worshipper of God, and do his will, him he heareth.
32 Since the world began it was never heard that any one opened the eyes of
33 a man born blind. If this man were not from God, he could do nothing.
34 They answered and said unto him, Thou wast altogether born in sins,
and dost thou teach us? And they cast him out.
35 Jesus heard that they had cast him out; and finding him, he said,
36 Dost thou believe on [2]the Son of God? He answered and said, And who
37 is he, Lord, that I may believe on him? Jesus said unto him, Thou hast
38 both seen him, and he it is that speaketh with thee. And he said, Lord,
39 I believe. And he worshipped him. And Jesus said, For judgement came
I into this world, that they which see not may see; and that they which
40 see may become blind. Those of the Pharisees which were with him
41 heard these things, and said unto him, Are we also blind? Jesus said unto
them, If ye were blind, ye would have no sin: but now ye say, We see:
your sin remaineth.

[1] Or, *and with the clay thereof anointed his eyes.* [2] Many ancient authorities read *the Son of man.*

§101. IN THE PARABLE (ALLEGORY) OF THE GOOD SHEPHERD JESUS DRAWS THE PICTURE OF THE HOSTILE PHARISEES AND INTIMATES THAT HE IS GOING TO DIE FOR HIS FLOCK AND COME TO LIFE AGAIN

Jerusalem

John 10:1–21

1 Verily, verily, I say unto you, He that entereth not by the door into the
fold of the sheep, but climbeth up some other way, the same is a thief
2 and a robber. But he that entereth in by the door is [1]the shepherd of the

John 10:1–21

3 sheep. To him the porter openeth; and the sheep hear his voice: and
4 he calleth his own sheep by name, and leadeth them out. When he hath
put forth all his own, he goeth before them, and the sheep follow him:
5 for they know his voice. And a stranger will they not follow, but will
6 flee from him: for they know not the voice of strangers. This [2]parable
spake Jesus unto them: but they understood not what things they were
which he spake unto them.
7 Jesus therefore said unto them again, Verily, verily, I say unto you,
8 I am the door of the sheep. All that came before me are thieves and
9 robbers: but the sheep did not hear them. I am the door: by me if any
man enter in, he shall be saved, and shall go in and go out, and shall
10 find pasture. The thief cometh not, but that he may steal, and kill, and
destroy: I came that they may have life, and may [3]have *it* abundantly.
11 I am the good shepherd: the good shepherd layeth down his life for the
12 sheep. He that is a hireling, and not a shepherd, whose own the sheep
are not, beholdeth the wolf coming, and leaveth the sheep, and fleeth, and
13 the wolf snatcheth them, and scattereth *them: he fleeth* because he is a
14 hireling, and careth not for the sheep. I am the good shepherd; and I
15 know mine own, and mine own know me, even as the Father knoweth
me, and I know the Father; and I lay down my life for the sheep.
16 And other sheep I have, which are not of this fold [*see Ezek. 34:23; 37:24*]:
them also I must [4]bring, and they shall hear my voice; and [5]they shall
17 become one flock, one shepherd. Therefore doth the Father love me, be-
18 cause I lay down my life, that I may take it again. No one [6]taketh it
away from me, but I lay it down of myself. I have [7]power to lay it down,
and I have [7]power to take it again. This commandment received I from
my Father.
19 There arose a division again among the Jews because of these words.
20 And many of them said, He hath a [8]devil, and is mad; why hear ye him?
21 Others said, These are not the sayings of one possessed with a [8]devil.
Can a [8]devil open the eyes of the blind?

[1] Or, *a shepherd.* [2] Or, *proverb.* [3] Or, *have abundance.* [4] Or, *lead.* [5] Or, *there shall be one flock.* [6] Some ancient authorities read *took it away.* [7] Or, *right.* [8] Gr. *demon.*

*In §§100–110 we have matters given by Luke only, which probably occurred in Judea. Several of them are similar to events and discourses of the ministry in Galilee, given by Matthew and Mark.**

§ 102. MISSION OF THE SEVENTY. CHRIST'S JOY IN THEIR WORK ON THEIR RETURN

(Compare Mission of the Twelve in § 69.)

Probably in Judea

Luke 10:1–24

1 Now after these things the Lord appointed seventy[1] others, and sent
them two and two before his face into every city and place, whither he

* Observe that here, as in previous portions of the history, we possess only a few specimens from what must have been the great mass of our Lord's doings and sayings.

Luke 10:1-24

2 himself was about to come. And he said unto them, The harvest is
plenteous, but the labourers are few: pray ye therefore the Lord of the
3 harvest, that he send forth labourers into his harvest. Go your ways:
4 behold, I send you forth as lambs in the midst of wolves. Carry no purse,
5 no wallet, no shoes; and salute no man on the way. And into whatsoever
6 house ye shall [2]enter, first say, Peace *be* to this house. And if a son of
7 peace be there, your peace shall rest upon [3]him: but if not, it shall turn to
you again. And in that same house remain, eating and drinking such
8 things as they give: for the labourer is worthy of his hire. Go not from
house to house. And into whatsoever city ye enter, and they receive
you, eat such things as are set before you: and heal the sick that are
9 therein, and say unto them, The kingdom of God is come nigh unto you.
10 But into whatsoever city ye shall enter, and they receive you not, go out
11 into the streets thereof and say, Even the dust from your city, that
cleaveth to our feet, we do wipe off against you: howbeit know this, that
12 the kingdom of God is come nigh. I say unto you, It shall be more toler-
13 able in that day for Sodom, than for that city [*see Gen. 19:24*]. Woe unto
thee, Chorazin! woe unto thee, Bethsaida! for if the [4]mighty works had
been done in Tyre and Sidon, which were done in you, they would have
14 repented long ago, sitting in sackcloth and ashes. Howbeit it shall be
more tolerable for Tyre and Sidon in the judgement, than for you.
15 And thou, Capernaum, shalt thou be exalted unto heaven? thou shalt
16 be brought down unto Hades [*see Isa. 14:13-15*]. He that heareth you
heareth me; and he that rejecteth you rejecteth me; and he that rejecteth
me rejecteth him that sent me.
17 And the seventy returned with joy, saying, Lord, even the [5]devils are
18 subject unto us in thy name. And he said unto them, I beheld Satan
19 fallen as lightning from heaven. Behold, I have given you authority
to tread upon serpents and scorpions, and over all the power of the
20 enemy: and nothing shall in any wise hurt you. Howbeit in this rejoice
not, that the spirits are subject unto you; but rejoice that your names are
written in heaven.
21 In that same hour he rejoiced [6]in the Holy Spirit, and said, I [7]thank
thee, O Father, Lord of heaven and earth, that thou didst hide these
things from the wise and understanding, and didst reveal them unto
22 babes: yea, Father; [8]for so it was well-pleasing in thy sight. All things
have been delivered unto me of my Father: and no one knoweth who
the Son is, save the Father; and who the Father is, save the Son, and
23 he to whomsoever the Son willeth to reveal *him*. And turning to the
disciples, he said privately, Blessed are the eyes which see the things that
24 ye see: for I say unto you, that many prophets and kings desired to see
the things which ye see, and saw them not: and to hear the things which
ye hear, and heard them not.

[1] Many ancient authorities add *and two;* and so in verse 17. [2] Or, *enter first, say.* [3] Or, *it.* [4] Gr. *powers.* [5] Gr. *demons.* [6] Or, *by.* [7] Or, *praise.* [8] Or, *that.*

§ 103. JESUS ANSWERS A LAWYER'S QUESTION AS TO ETERNAL LIFE, GIVING THE PARABLE OF THE GOOD SAMARITAN

Probably in Judea

Luke 10:25–37

25 And behold, a certain lawyer stood up and tempted him, saying,
26 [1]Master, what shall I do to inherit eternal life? And he said unto him,
27 What is written in the law? how readest thou? And he answering said,
Thou shalt love the Lord thy God [2]with all thy heart, and with all thy
soul, and with all thy strength, and with all thy mind; and thy neighbour
28 as thyself [*see Deut. 6:5; Lev. 19:18*]. And he said unto him, Thou hast
29 answered right: do this, and thou shalt live [*see Lev. 18:5*]. But he, desiring
30 to justify himself, said unto Jesus, And who is my neighbour? Jesus
made answer and said, A certain man was going down from Jerusalem to
Jericho; and he fell among robbers, which both stripped him and beat
31 him, and departed, leaving him half dead. And by chance a certain
priest was going down that way: and when he saw him, he passed by
32 on the other side. And in like manner a Levite also, when he came to
33 the place, and saw him, passed by on the other side. But a certain
Samaritan, as he journeyed, came where he was: and when he saw him,
34 he was moved with compassion, and came to him, and bound up his
wounds, pouring on *them* oil and wine; and he set him on his own beast, and
35 brought him to an inn, and took care of him. And on the morrow he took
out two [3]pence, and gave them to the host, and said, Take care of him;
and whatsoever thou spendest more, I, when I come back again, will
36 repay thee. Which of these three, thinkest thou, proved neighbour to
37 him that fell among the robbers? And he said, He that shewed mercy on
him. And Jesus said unto him, Go, and do thou likewise.

[1] Or, *Teacher*. [2] Gr. *from*. [3] The word in the Greek denotes a coin worth about seventeen cents.

§ 104. JESUS THE GUEST OF MARTHA AND MARY

Bethany, near Jerusalem*

Luke 10:38–42

38 Now as they went on their way, he entered into a certain village:
and a certain woman named Martha received him into her house.
39 And she had a sister called Mary, which also sat at the Lord's feet, and
40 heard his word. But Martha was [1]cumbered about much serving; and
she came up to him, and said, Lord, dost thou not care that my sister
did leave me to serve alone? bid her therefore that she help me.
41 But the Lord answered and said unto her, [2]Martha, Martha, thou art
42 anxious and troubled about many things: [3]but one thing is needful: for
Mary hath chosen the good part, which shall not be taken away from her.

[1] Gr. *distracted*. [2] A few ancient authorities read, *Martha, Martha, thou art troubled; Mary hath chosen, etc.* [3] Many ancient authorities read *but few things are needful, or one*.

* There was another Bethany beyond Jordan (John 1:28, § 26). We shall see Jesus in Bethany near Jerusalem again (John 12:1–8). It was his Jerusalem home in the early days of Passion Week.

§ 105. JESUS AGAIN GIVES A MODEL OF PRAYER (COMP. § 54), AND ENCOURAGES HIS DISCIPLES TO PRAY. PARABLE OF THE IMPORTUNATE FRIEND

Probably in Judea

Luke 11:1–13

1 And it came to pass, as he was praying in a certain place, that when
he ceased, one of his disciples said unto him, Lord, teach us to pray, even
2 as John also taught his disciples. And he said unto them, When ye pray,
3 say, [1]Father, Hallowed be thy Name. Thy kingdom come.[2] Give us
4 day by day [3]our daily bread. And forgive us our sins; for we ourselves
also forgive every one that is indebted to us. And bring us not into
temptation[4].*
5 And he said unto them, Which of you shall have a friend, and shall go
unto him at midnight, and say to him, Friend, lend me three loaves; for
6 a friend of mine is come to me from a journey, and I have nothing to set
7 before him; and he from within shall answer and say, Trouble me not:
the door is now shut, and my children are with me in bed; I cannot rise
8 and give thee? I say unto you, Though he will not rise and give him,
because he is his friend, yet because of his importunity he will arise and
9 give him [5]as many as he needeth. And I say unto you, Ask, and it shall
be given you; seek, and ye shall find; knock, and it shall be opened unto
10 you. For every one that asketh receiveth; and he that seeketh findeth;
11 and to him that knocketh it shall be opened. And of which of you that
is a father shall his son ask a [6]loaf, and he give him a stone? or a fish, and
12 he for a fish give him a serpent? Or *if* he shall ask an egg, will he give
13 him a scorpion? If ye then, being evil, know how to give good gifts unto
your children, how much more shall *your* heavenly Father give the Holy
Spirit to them that ask him?

[1] Many ancient authorities read *Our Father, which art in heaven*. See Matt. 6:9. [2] Many ancient authorities add *Thy will be done, as in heaven, so on earth*. See Matt. 6:10. [3] Gr. *our bread for the coming day*. [4] Many ancient authorities add *but deliver us from the evil* one (or, *from evil*). See Matt. 6:13. [5] Or, *whatsoever things*. [6] Some ancient authorities omit *a loaf, and he gave him a stone? or*.

§ 106. BLASPHEMOUS ACCUSATION OF LEAGUE WITH BEELZEBUB

(Compare § 61) †

Probably in Judea

Luke 11:14–36

14 And he was casting out a [1]devil which was dumb. And it came to pass,
when the [1]devil was gone out, the dumb man spake; and the multitudes

* The language here is different from that in Matt. 6 (§ 54), but the ideas are the same. Evidently the disciples were slow to learn Christ's teaching about prayer.

† It is perfectly natural that the blasphemous accusation made in Galilee (§ 61), and probably more than once (§ 68, Matt. 9:34), should be repeated a year or so afterward in Judea or Perea,

Luke 11:14–36

15 marvelled. But some of them said, [2]By Beelzebub the prince of the
16 [3]devils casteth he out devils. And others, tempting him, sought of him
17 a sign from heaven. But he, knowing their thoughts, said unto them,
Every kingdom divided against itself is brought to desolation; [4]and a
18 house divided against a house falleth. And if Satan also is divided against
himself, how shall his kingdom stand? because ye say that I cast out
19 [3]devils [2]by Beelzebub. And if I [2]by Beelzebub cast out [3]devils, by whom
20 do your sons cast them out? therefore shall they be your judges. But if
I by the finger of God cast out [3]devils, then is the kingdom of God come
21 upon you. When the strong *man* fully armed guardeth his own court,
22 his goods are in peace: but when a stronger than he shall come upon him,
and overcome him, he taketh from him his whole armour wherein he
23 trusted, and divideth his spoils. He that is not with me is against me; and
24 he that gathereth not with me scattereth. The unclean spirit when
[5]he is gone out of the man, passeth through waterless places, seeking
rest; and finding none, [5]he saith, I will turn back unto my house whence
25 I came out. And when he is come, [5]he findeth it swept and garnished.
26 Then goeth [5]he, and taketh *to him* seven other spirits more evil than
[6]himself; and they enter in and dwell there: and the last state of that man
becometh worse than the first.
27 And it came to pass, as he said these things, a certain woman out of
the multitude lifted up her voice, and said unto him, Blessed is the
28 womb that bare thee, and the breasts which thou didst suck. But
he said, Yea rather, blessed are they that hear the word of God, and
keep it.
29 And when the multitudes were gathering together unto him, he began
to say, This generation is an evil generation: it seeketh after a sign; and
there shall no sign be given to it but the sign of Jonah [*see Jonah 3:1–4*].
30 For even as Jonah became a sign unto the Ninevites, so shall also the
31 Son of man be to this generation. The queen of the south shall rise up
in the judgement with the men of this generation, and shall condemn
them: for she came from the ends of the earth to hear the wisdom of
32 Solomon [*see 1 Kings 10:1–3*]; and behold, [7]a greater than Solomon is here.
The men of Nineveh shall stand up in the judgement with this generation
and shall condemn it: for they repented at the preaching of Jonah [*see Jonah
3:5–10*]; and behold, [7]a greater than Jonah is here.
33 No man, when he hath lighted a lamp, putteth it in a cellar, neither
under the bushel, but on the stand, that they which enter in may see
34 the light. The lamp of thy body is thine eye: when thine eye is single,
thy whole body also is full of light; but when it is evil, thy body also is full of
35 darkness. Look therefore whether the light that is in thee be not darkness.
36 If therefore thy whole body be full of light, having no part dark, it shall

---

and that Jesus should make substantially the same argument in reply. This sort of thing occurs to every travelling religious teacher. Our Lord does not here give the solemn warning that such an accusation is really blaspheming against the Holy Spirit, and is unpardonable. (See Luke 12:10.) And the subsequent occurrences are quite different in the two cases. In § 64 he afterwards goes out by the lake-side and gives the great group of parables, presently explaining some of them to the disciples in a house, and then crosses the lake to Gerasa, etc. Here in § 107 he breakfasts with a Pharisee, and utters such solemn woes against the Pharisees as are found only in the closing months of his ministry, and then gives to vast multitudes a series of instructions wholly unlike the great group of parables. So it is quite unsuitable to identify this occurrence with that of § 61.

Luke 11:14-36

be wholly full of light, as when the lamp with its bright shining doth give the light.

[1] Gr. *demon.* [2] Or, *in.* [3] Gr. *demons.* [4] Or, *and house falleth upon house.* [5] Or, *it.* [6] Or, *itself.* [7] Gr. *more than.*

§ 107. WHILE BREAKFASTING WITH A PHARISEE, JESUS SEVERELY DENOUNCES THE PHARISEES AND LAWYERS, AND EXCITES THEIR ENMITY

Probably in Judea

Luke 11:37-54

37 Now as he spake, a Pharisee asketh him to [1]dine with him: and he went
38 in, and sat down to meat. And when the Pharisee saw it, he marvelled
39 that he had not washed before [1]dinner. And the Lord said unto him,
Now do ye Pharisees cleanse the outside of the cup and of the platter;
40 but your inward part is full of extortion and wickedness. Ye foolish ones,
41 did not he that made the outside make the inside also? Howbeit give for
alms those things which [2]are within; and behold, all things are clean
unto you.
42 But woe unto you Pharisees! for ye tithe mint and rue and every herb,
and pass over judgement and the love of God [*see Lev. 27:30; Mic. 6:8*]: but
43 these ought ye to have done, and not to leave the other undone. Woe
unto you Pharisees! for ye love the chief seats in the synagogues, and the
44 salutations in the marketplaces. Woe unto you! for ye are as the tombs
which appear not, and the men that walk over *them* know it not.
45 And one of the lawyers answering saith unto him, [3]Master, in saying
46 this thou reproachest us also. And he said, Woe unto you lawyers also!
for ye lade men with burdens grievous to be borne, and ye yourselves
47 touch not the burdens with one of your fingers. Woe unto you! for ye
48 build the tombs of the prophets, and your fathers killed them. So ye are
witnesses and consent unto the works of your fathers: for they killed them,
49 and ye build *their tombs*. Therefore also said the wisdom of God, I will
50 send unto them prophets and apostles; and *some* of them they shall kill
and persecute; that the blood of all the prophets, which was shed from
51 the foundation of the world, may be required of this generation; from the
blood of Abel unto the blood of Zachariah [*see Gen. 4:8; 2 Chron. 24:20-21*],
who perished between the altar and the [4]sanctuary: yea, I say unto you,
52 it shall be required of this generation. Woe unto you lawyers! for ye
took away the key of knowledge: ye entered not in yourselves, and them
that were entering in ye hindered.
53 And when he was come out from thence, the scribes and the Pharisees
began to [5]press upon *him* vehemently, and to provoke him to speak of
54 [6]many things; laying wait for him, to catch something out of his mouth.

[1] Gr. *breakfast.* [2] Or, *ye can.* [3] Or, *Teacher.* [4] Gr. *house.* [5] Or, *set themselves vehemently against him.* [6] Or, *more.*

§ 108. HE SPEAKS TO HIS DISCIPLES AND A VAST THRONG, ABOUT HYPOCRISY, COVETOUSNESS (PARABLE OF THE RICH FOOL), WORLDLY ANXIETIES, WATCHFULNESS (PARABLE OF THE WAITING SERVANTS, AND OF THE WISE STEWARD), AND HIS OWN APPROACHING PASSION*

Probably in Judea

Luke 12

1 In the mean time, when [1]the many thousands of the multitude were
gathered together, insomuch that they trode one upon another, he began
to [2]say unto his disciples first of all, Beware ye of the leaven of the Phari-
2 sees, which is hypocrisy. But there is nothing covered up; that shall
3 not be revealed: and hid, that shall not be known. Wherefore whatsoever
ye have said in the darkness shall be heard in the light; and what ye have
spoken in the ear in the inner chambers shall be proclaimed upon the
4 housetops. And I say unto you my friends, Be not afraid of them which
5 kill the body, and after that have no more that they can do. But I will
warn you whom ye shall fear: Fear him, which after he hath killed hath
6 [3]power to cast into [4]hell; yea, I say unto you, Fear him. Are not five
sparrows sold for two farthings? and not one of them is forgotten in the
7 sight of God. But the very hairs of your head are all numbered. Fear
8 not: ye are of more value than many sparrows. And I say unto you,
Every one who shall confess [5]me before men, [6]him shall the Son of man also
9 confess before the angels of God: but he that denieth me in the presence
10 of men shall be denied in the presence of the angels of God. And every
one who shall speak a word against the Son of man, it shall be forgiven
him: but unto him that blasphemeth against the Holy Spirit it shall not
11 be forgiven. And when they bring you before the synagogues, and the
rulers, and the authorities, be not anxious how or what ye shall answer,
12 or what ye shall say: for the Holy Spirit shall teach you in that very
hour what ye ought to say.
13 And one out of the multitude said unto him, [7]Master, bid my brother
14 divide the inheritance with me. But he said unto him, Man, who made
15 me a judge or a divider over you? And he said unto them, Take heed,
and keep yourselves from all covetousness: [8]for a man's life consisteth
16 not in the abundance of the things which he possesseth. And he spake
17 a parable unto them, saying, The ground of a certain rich man brought
forth plentifully: and he reasoned within himself, saying, What shall I do,
18 because I have not where to bestow my fruits? And he said, This will
I do: I will pull down my barns, and build greater; and there will I bestow
19 all my corn and my goods. And I will say to my [9]soul, [9]Soul, thou hast
much goods laid up for many years; take thine ease, eat, drink, be merry.
20 But God said unto him, Thou foolish one, this night [10]is thy [9]soul required

* Here we have a series of discourses to the disciples (1–12), to one of the crowd (13–21), to the disciples (22–40), to Peter (41–53), to the multitudes (54–59). The constant interruption is typical of the teaching of Jesus. This address, as often, repeats some of Christ's favorite sayings.

Besides the Parable of the Rich Fool (12:16–21) note those of the Waiting Servants (37–40) and of the Wise Steward (42–48).

Luke 12

21 of thee; and the things which thou hast prepared, whose shall they be?
So is he that layeth up treasure for himself, and is not rich toward God.
22 And he said unto his disciples, Therefore I say unto you, Be not anxious
for *your* [11]life, what ye shall eat; nor yet for your body, what ye shall put
23 on. For the [11]life is more than the food, and the body than the raiment.
24. Consider the ravens, that they sow not, neither reap; which have no
store-chamber nor barn; and God feedeth them: of how much more
25 value are ye than the birds! And which of you by being anxious can
26 add a cubit unto his [12]stature? If then ye are not able to do even that
27 which is least, why are ye anxious concerning the rest? Consider the
lilies, how they grow: they toil not, neither do they spin; yet I say unto
you, Even Solomon in all his glory was not arrayed like one of these.
28 But if God doth so clothe the grass in the field, which to-day is, and to-
morrow is cast into the oven; how much more *shall he clothe* you, O ye
29 of little faith? And seek not ye what ye shall eat, and what ye shall
30 drink, neither be ye of doubtful mind. For all these things do the nations
of the world seek after: but your Father knoweth that ye have need of
31 these things. Howbeit seek ye [13]his kingdom, and these things shall be
added unto you. Fear not, little flock; for it is your Father's good pleas-
33 ure to give you the kingdom. Sell that ye have, and give alms; make
for yourselves purses which wax not old, a treasure in the heavens that
34 faileth not, where no thief draweth near, neither moth destroyeth. For
where your treasure is, there will your heart be also.
35, 36 Let your loins be girded about, and your lamps burning; and be
ye yourselves like unto men looking for their lord, when he shall return
from the marriage feast; that, when he cometh and knocketh, they may
37 straightway open unto him. Blessed are those [14]servants, whom the lord
when he cometh shall find watching: verily I say unto you, that he shall
gird himself, and make them sit down to meat, and shall come and serve
38 them. And if he shall come in the second watch, and if in the third, and
39 find *them* so, blessed are those *servants*. [15]But know this, that if the master
of the house had known in what hour the thief was coming, he would have
40 watched, and not have left his house to be [16]broken through. Be ye also
ready: for in an hour that ye think not the Son of man cometh.
41 And Peter said, Lord, speakest thou this parable unto us, or even unto
42 all? And the Lord said, Who then is [17]the faithful and wise steward,
whom his lord shall set over his household, to give them their portion
43 of food in due season? Blessed is that [18]servant, whom his lord when he
44 cometh shall find so doing. Of a truth I say unto you, that he will set
45 him over all that he hath. But if that [18]servant shall say in his heart,
My lord delayeth his coming; and shall begin to beat the menservants
and the maidservants, and to eat and drink, and to be drunken; the
46 lord of that [18]servant shall come in a day when he expecteth not, and in
an hour when he knoweth not, and shall [19]cut him asunder, and appoint
47 his portion with the unfaithful. And that [18]servant, which knew his
lord's will, and made not ready, nor did according to his will, shall be
48 beaten with many *stripes;* but he that knew not, and did things worthy
of stripes, shall be beaten with few *stripes*. And to whomsoever much
is given, of him shall much be required: and to whom they commit much,
of him will they ask the more.

Luke 12

49 I came to cast fire upon the earth; and what will I, if it is already
50 kindled? But I have a baptism to be baptized with; and how am I
51 straitened till it be accomplished! Think ye that I am come to give
52 peace in the earth? I tell you, Nay; but rather division: for there shall
be from henceforth five in one house divided, three against two, and two
53 against three [*see Mic. 7:6*]. They shall be divided, father against son,
and son against father; mother against daughter, and daughter against
her mother; mother in law against her daughter in law, and daughter in
law against her mother in law.
54 And he said to the multitudes also, When ye see a cloud rising in the
west, straightway ye say, There cometh a shower; and so it cometh to
55 pass. And when *ye see* a south wind blowing, ye say, There will be a
56 [20]scorching heat; and it cometh to pass. Ye hypocrites, ye know how to
[21]interpret the face of the earth and the heaven; but how is it that ye know
57 not how to [21]interpret this time? And why even of yourselves judge ye
58 not what is right? For as thou art going with thine adversary before the
magistrate, on the way give diligence to be quit of him; lest haply he
hale thee unto the judge, and the judge shall deliver thee to the [22]officer,
59 and the [22]officer shall cast thee into prison. I say unto thee, Thou shalt
by no means come out thence, till thou have paid the very last mite.

[1] Gr. *the myriads of.* [2] Or, *say unto his disciples, First of all beware ye.* [3] Or, *authority.* [4] Gr. *Gehenna.* [5] Gr. *in me.* [6] Gr. *in him.* [7] Or, *Teacher.* [8] Gr. *for not in a man's abundance consisteth his life, from the things which he possesseth.* [9] Or, *life.* [10] Gr. *they require thy soul.* [11] Or, *soul.* [12] Or, *age.* [13] Many ancient authorities read *the kingdom of God.* [14] Gr. *bond-servants.* [15] Or, *But this ye know.* [16] Or, *digged through.* [17] Or, *the faithful steward, the wise* man *whom, etc.* [18] Gr. *bond-servant.* [19] Or, *severely scourge him.* [20] Or, *hot wind.* [21] Gr. *prove.* [22] Gr. *exactor.*

§ 109. ALL MUST REPENT OR PERISH (TWO CURRENT TRAGEDIES); PARABLE OF THE BARREN FIG TREE

Probably in Judea

Luke 13:1–9

1 Now there were some present at that very season which told him of
the Galileans, whose blood Pilate had mingled with their sacrifices.
2 And he answered and said unto them, Think ye that these Galileans were
sinners above all the Galileans, because they have suffered these things?
3 I tell you, Nay: but, except ye repent, ye shall all in like manner perish.
4 Or those eighteen, upon whom the tower in Siloam fell, and killed them,
think ye that they were [1]offenders above all the men that dwell in Jeru-
5 salem? I tell you, Nay: but, except ye repent, ye shall all likewise perish.
6 And he spake this parable; A certain man had a fig tree planted in his
7 vineyard; and he came seeking fruit thereon, and found none. And he
said unto the vinedresser, Behold, these three years I come seeking fruit
on this fig tree, and find none: cut it down; why doth it also cumber the
8 ground? And he answering saith unto him, Lord, let it alone this year
9 also, till I shall dig about it, and dung it: and if it bear fruit thenceforth,
well; but if not, thou shalt cut it down.

[1] Gr. *debtors.*

§ 110. JESUS HEALS A CRIPPLED WOMAN ON THE SABBATH AND DEFENDS HIMSELF AGAINST THE RULER OF THE SYNAGOGUE (COMP. §§ 49 TO 51 AND 114). REPETITION OF THE PARABLES OF THE MUSTARD SEED AND OF THE LEAVEN

Luke 13:10–21

10 And he was teaching in one of the synagogues on the sabbath day.
11 And behold, a woman which had a spirit of infirmity eighteen years;
12 and she was bowed together, and could in no wise lift herself up. And
when Jesus saw her, he called her, and said to her, Woman, thou art
13 loosed from thine infirmity. And he laid his hands upon her: and im-
14 mediately she was made straight, and glorified God. And the ruler of
the synagogue, being moved with indignation because Jesus had healed
on the sabbath [*see Ex. 20:8–11; Deut. 5:12–15*], answered and said to
the multitude, There are six days in which men ought to work: in them
15 therefore come and be healed, and not on the day of the sabbath. But the
Lord answered him, and said, Ye hypocrites, doth not each one of you on
the sabbath loose his ox or his ass from the [1]stall, and lead him away to
16 watering? And ought not this woman, being a daughter of Abraham,
whom Satan had bound, lo, *these* eighteen years, to have been loosed from
17 this bond on the day of the sabbath? And as he said these things, all
his adversaries were put to shame: and all the multitude rejoiced for all
the glorious things that were done by him.
18 He said therefore, Unto what is the kingdom of God like? and where-
19 unto shall I liken it? It is like unto a grain of mustard seed, which a
man took, and cast into his own garden; and it grew, and became a tree;
and the birds of the heaven lodged in the branches thereof [*see Dan. 4:*
20 *10–12; 20–22*]. And again he said, Whereunto shall I liken the king-
21 dom of God? It is like unto leaven, which a woman took and hid in three
[2]measures of meal, till it was all leavened.

[1] Gr. *manger*. [2] The word in the Gr. denotes the Hebrew seah, a measure containing nearly a peck and a half (cf. in Matt. 13:33).

Here again the Gospel of John takes us up, and carries us to Jerusalem, and then to Perea.

§ 111. AT THE FEAST OF DEDICATION, JESUS WILL NOT YET OPENLY SAY THAT HE IS THE MESSIAH. THE JEWS TRY TO STONE HIM

Jerusalem

John 10:22–39

22 [1]And it was the feast of the dedication at Jerusalem:* it was winter;
23 and Jesus was walking in the temple in Solomon's porch. The Jews

* Some scholars think that the events in John 9 and 10:1–21 belong to the time of the feast of dedication rather than soon after tabernacles. But the language of John 10:24 seems to call for an interval.

John 10:22–39

24 therefore came round about him, and said unto him, How long dost thou
25 hold us in suspense? If thou art the Christ, tell us plainly. Jesus
answered them, I told you, and ye believe not: the works that I do in my
26 Father's name, these bear witness of me. But ye believe not, because
27 ye are not of my sheep. My sheep hear my voice, and I know them,
28 and they follow me: and I give unto them eternal life; and they shall
29 never perish, and no one shall snatch them out of my hand. [2]My Father,
which hath given *them* unto me, is greater than all; and no one is able to
30, 31 snatch [3]*them* out of the Father's hand. I and the Father are one. The
32 Jews took up stones again to stone him. Jesus answered them, Many
good works have I shewed you from the Father; for which of those works
33 do ye stone me? The Jews answered him, For a good work we stone thee
not, but for blasphemy; and because that thou, being a man, makest
34 thyself God. Jesus answered them, Is it not written in your law, I said,
35 ye are gods [*see Ps. 82:6*]? If he called them gods, unto whom the word
36 of God came (and the scripture cannot be broken), say ye of him, whom
the Father [4]sanctified and sent into the world, Thou blasphemest; because
37 I said, I am *the* Son of God? If I do not the works of my Father, believe
38 me not. But if I do them, though you believe not me, believe the works:
that ye may know and understand that the Father is in me, and I in the
39 Father. They sought again to take him: and he went forth out of their
hand.

[1] Some ancient authorities read *At that time was the feast.* [2] Some ancient authorities read *That which my Father hath given unto me.* [3] Or, *aught.* [4] Or, *consecrated.*

PART X

THE LATER PEREAN MINISTRY

Probably Dedication in A.D. *29 to Last Journey in* A.D. *30 (about three and a half months),* §§ *112–127.*

§ 112. THE WITHDRAWAL FROM JERUSALEM TO BETHANY BEYOND JORDAN

Perea

John 10:40–42

40 And he went away again beyond Jordan into the place where John was
41 at the first baptizing; and there he abode. And many came unto him;
and they said, John indeed did no sign: but all things whatsoever John
42 spake of this man were true. And many believed on him there.

§ 113. TEACHING IN PEREA, ON A JOURNEY* TOWARD JERUSALEM. WARNED AGAINST HEROD ANTIPAS

Luke 13:22–35

22 And he went on his way through cities and villages, teaching, and
23 journeying on unto Jerusalem.† And one said unto him, Lord, are they
24 few that be saved? And he said unto them, Strive to enter in by the
narrow door: for many, I say unto you, shall seek to enter in, and shall
25 not be [1]able. When once the master of the house is risen up, and hath
shut to the door, and ye begin to stand without, and to knock at the door,
saying, Lord, open to us; and he shall answer and say to you, I know
26 you not whence ye are; then shall ye begin to say, We did eat and drink
in thy presence, and thou didst teach in our streets; and he shall say,
27 I tell you, I know not whence ye are; depart from me, all ye workers of
28 iniquity [*see Ps. 6:8*]. There shall be weeping and gnashing of teeth,
when ye shall see Abraham, and Isaac, and Jacob, and all the prophets,
29 in the kingdom of God, and yourselves cast forth without. And they
shall come from the east and west, and from the north and south, and
30 shall [2]sit down in the kingdom of God [*see Ps. 107:3; Isa. 49: 12*]. And

---

* See note 10 at end of Harmony for the combination of Luke and John. After the Feast of the Dedication Jesus retired beyond Jordan (John 10:40), whence he goes to the raising of Lazarus (John 11:17). Luke seems to give incidents that belong to this journey.

† The period of three to four months from the Dedication to the final Passover is divided by another visit to Jerusalem. We cannot tell how many weeks preceded this event. All along here we have only a few specimens of the Saviour's teaching and works.

Luke 13:22–35

behold, there are last which shall be first, and there are first which shall be last.
31 In that very hour there came certain Pharisees, saying to him, Get
32 thee out, and go hence: for Herod would fain kill thee. And he said unto
them, Go and say to that fox, Behold, I cast out [3]devils and perform cures
33 to-day and to-morrow, and the third *day* I am perfected. Howbeit I must
34 go on my way to-day and to-morrow and the *day* following: for it cannot
be that a prophet perish out of Jerusalem. O Jerusalem, Jerusalem,
which killeth the prophets, and stoneth them that are sent unto her! how
often would I have gathered thy children together, even as a hen *gathereth*
35 her own brood under her wings, and ye would not! Behold, your house
is left unto you *desolate:* and I say unto you, Ye shall not see me, until ye
shall say, Blessed *is* he that cometh in the name of the Lord [*see Ps. 118:26; Jer. 12:7; 22:5*].

[1] Or, *able, when once.* [2] Gr. *recline.* [3] Gr. *demons.*

§114. WHILE DINING (BREAKFASTING) WITH A CHIEF PHARISEE, HE AGAIN HEALS ON THE SABBATH, AND DEFENDS HIMSELF (COMP. §§49 TO 51 AND 110). THREE PARABLES SUGGESTED BY THE OCCASION

Probably in Perea

Luke 14:1–24

1 And it came to pass, when he went into the house of one of the rulers
of the Pharisees on a sabbath to eat bread, that they were watching him.
2 And behold, there was before him a certain man which had the dropsy.
3 And Jesus answering spake unto the lawyers and Pharisees, saying, Is
4 it lawful to heal on the sabbath, or not? But they held their peace. And
5 he took him, and healed him, and let him go. And he said unto them,
Which of you shall have [1]an ass or an ox fallen into a well, and will not
6 straightway draw him up on a sabbath day? And they could not answer
again unto these things.
7 And he spake a parable unto those which were bidden, when he marked
8 how they chose out the chief seats; saying unto them, When thou art
bidden of any man to a marriage feast, [2]sit not down in the chief seat;
lest haply a more honourable man than thou be bidden of him, and he
9 that bade thee and him shall come and say to thee, Give this man place;
10 and then thou shalt begin with shame to take the lowest place. But when
thou art bidden, go and sit down in the lowest place; that when he that
hath bidden thee cometh, he may say to thee, Friend, go up higher: then
shalt thou have glory in the presence of all that sit at meat with thee.
11 For every one that exalteth himself shall be humbled; and he that hum-
bleth himself shall be exalted.
12 And he said to him also that had bidden him, When thou makest a

Luke 14:1-24

dinner or a supper,* call not thy friends, nor thy brethren, nor thy kins-
men, nor rich neighbours; lest haply they also bid thee again, and a recom-
13 pense be made thee. But when thou makest a feast, bid the poor, the
maimed, the lame, the blind: and thou shalt be blessed; because they
14 have not *wherewith* to recompense thee: for thou shalt be recompensed in
the resurrection of the just.
15 And when one of them that sat at meat with him heard these things,
he said unto him, Blessed is he that shall eat bread in the kingdom of
16 God. But he said unto him, A certain man made a great supper; and he
17 bade many: and he sent forth his [3]servant at supper time to say to them
18 that were bidden, Come, for *all* things are now ready. And they all
with one *consent* began to make excuse. The first said unto him, I have
bought a field, and I must needs go out and see it: I pray thee have me
19 excused. And another said, I have bought five yoke of oxen, and I go to
20 prove them: I pray thee have me excused. And another said, I have
21 married a wife, and therefore I cannot come. And the [3]servant came,
and told his lord these things. Then the master of the house being angry
said to his [3]servant, Go out quickly into the streets and lanes of the
22 city, and bring in hither the poor and maimed and blind and lame. And
the [3]servant said, Lord, what thou didst command is done, and yet there
23 is room. And the Lord said unto the [3]servant, Go out into the highways
and hedges, and constrain *them* to come in, that my house may be filled.
24 For I say unto you, that none of those men which were bidden shall taste
of my supper.

[1] Many ancient authorities read *a son*. See ch. 13:15. [2] Gr. *recline not*. [3] Gr. *bond-servant*.

§ 115. GREAT CROWDS FOLLOW HIM, AND HE WARNS THEM TO COUNT THE COST OF DISCIPLESHIP TO HIM (COMP. §§ 70 and 83)

Probably in Perea

Luke 14:25-35

25 Now there went with him great multitudes: and he turned, and said
26 unto them, If any man cometh unto me, and hateth not his own father,
and mother, and wife, and children, and brethren, and sisters, yea, and
27 his own life also, he cannot be my disciple. Whosoever doth not bear
28 his own cross, and come after me, cannot be my disciple. For which of
you, desiring to build a tower, doth not first sit down and count the cost,
29 whether he have *wherewith* to complete it? Lest haply, when he hath
laid a foundation, and is not able to finish, all that behold begin to mock
30 him, saying, This man began to build, and was not able to finish. Or
31 what king, as he goeth to encounter another king in war, will not sit
down first and take counsel whether he is able with ten thousand to meet

* More exactly, "a breakfast or a dinner." The two principal meals of the Jews answered to the present English breakfast (in the forenoon and often near noon), and dinner (at or after dark); and so in our cities. In the time of King James, as in many of our country homes now, the meal towards noon answered to dinner, and the night meal to supper. Hence a certain confusion in the older and more recent English versions. In verses 16, 17 the right word would be dinner, according to city usage, and so elsewhere.

Luke 14:25–35

32 him that cometh against him with twenty thousand? Or else, while the
other is yet a great way off, he sendeth an ambassage, and asketh con-
33 ditions of peace. So therefore whosoever he be of you that renounceth
34 not all that he hath, he cannot be my disciple. Salt therefore is good;
35 but if even the salt have lost its savour, wherewith shall it be seasoned? It
is fit neither for the land nor for the dunghill: *men* cast it out. He that hath
ears to hear, let him hear.

§ 116. THE PHARISEES AND THE SCRIBES MURMUR AGAINST JESUS FOR RECEIVING SINNERS. HE DEFENDS HIMSELF BY THREE GREAT PARABLES (THE LOST SHEEP, THE LOST COIN, THE LOST SON)

Probably in Perea

Luke 15:1–32

1 Now all the publicans and sinners were drawing near unto him for to
2 hear him. And both the Pharisees and the scribes murmured, saying,
This man receiveth sinners, and eateth with them.
3, 4 And he spake unto them this parable, saying, What man of you,
having a hundred sheep, and having lost one of them, doth not leave the
ninety and nine in the wilderness, and go after that which is lost, until
5 he find it? And when he hath found it, he layeth it on his shoulders,
6 rejoicing. And when he cometh home, he calleth together his friends and
his neighbours, saying unto them, Rejoice with me, for I have found my
7 sheep which was lost. I say unto you, that even so there shall be joy in
heaven over one sinner that repenteth, *more* than over ninety and nine
righteous persons, which need no repentance.
8 Or what woman having ten [1]pieces of silver, if she lose one piece, doth
not light a lamp, and sweep the house, and seek diligently until she find
9 it? And when she hath found it, she calleth together her friends and
neighbours, saying, Rejoice with me, for I have found the piece which I
10 had lost. Even so, I say unto you, there is joy in the presence of the
angels of God over one sinner that repenteth.
11, 12 And he said, A certain man had two sons: and the younger of them
said to his father, Father, give me the portion of [2]*thy* substance that falleth
13 to me. And he divided unto them his living. And not many days after
the younger son gathered all together, and took his journey into a far
14 country; and there he wasted his substance with riotous living. And
when he had spent all, there arose a mighty famine in that country; and
15 he began to be in want. And he went and joined himself to one of the
citizens of that country; and he sent him into his fields to feed swine.
16 And he would fain have been filled with [3]the husks that the swine did eat:
17 and no man gave unto him. But when he came to himself he said, How
many hired servants of my father's have bread enough and to spare, and
18 I perish here with hunger! I will arise and go to my father, and will say
19 unto him, Father, I have sinned against heaven, and in thy sight: I am no

Luke 15:1-32

more worthy to be called thy son: make me as one of thy hired servants.
20 And he arose, and came to his father. But while he was yet afar off,
his father saw him, and was moved with compassion, and ran, and fell
21 on his neck, and [4]kissed him. And the son said unto him, Father, I have
sinned against heaven, and in thy sight; I am no more worthy to be called
22 thy son.[5] But the father said to his [6]servants, Bring forth quickly the
best robe, and put it on him; and put a ring on his hand, and shoes on his
23 feet: and bring the fatted calf, *and* kill it, and let us eat, and make merry:
24 for this my son was dead, and is alive again; he was lost, and is found.
25 And they began to be merry. Now his elder son was in the field: and as
26 he came and drew nigh to the house, he heard music and dancing. And
he called to him one of the [6]servants, and inquired what these things might
27 be. And he said unto him, Thy brother is come; and thy father hath
killed the fatted calf, because he hath received him safe and sound.
28 But he was angry, and would not go in: and his father came out, and
29 entreated him. But he answered and said to his father, Lo, these many
years do I serve thee, and I never transgressed a commandment of thine:
and *yet* thou never gavest me a kid, that I might make merry with my
30 friends: but when this thy son came, which hath devoured thy living with
31 harlots, thou killedst for him the fatted calf. And he said unto him,
32 [7]Son, thou art ever with me, and all that is mine is thine. But it was meet
to make merry and be glad: for this thy brother was dead, and is alive
again; and *was* lost, and is found.

[1] Gr. *drachma*, a coin worth about sixteen cents. [2] Gr. *the*. [3] Gr. *the pods of the carob-tree*. [4] Gr. *kissed him much*. [5] Some ancient authorities add *make me as one of thy hired servants*. See ver. 19. [6] Gr. *bond-servants*. [7] Gr. *Child*.

§ 117. THREE PARABLES ON STEWARDSHIP (TO THE DISCIPLES, THE PARABLE OF THE UNJUST STEWARD; TO THE PHARISEES, THE PARABLE OF THE RICH MAN AND LAZARUS; TO THE DISCIPLES, THE PARABLE OF THE UNPROFITABLE SERVANTS)

Probably in Perea

Luke 16:1-17:10

16 And he said unto the disciples, There was a certain rich man, which
had a steward; and the same was accused unto him that he was wasting
2 his goods. And he called him, and said unto him, What is this that I
hear of thee? render the account of thy stewardship; for thou canst be no
3 longer steward. And the steward said within himself, What shall I do,
4 seeing that my lord taketh away the stewardship from me? I have
not strength to dig; to beg I am ashamed. I am resolved what to do,
that, when I am put out of the stewardship, they may receive me into their
5 houses. And calling to him each one of his lord's debtors, he said to the
6 first, How much owest thou unto my lord? And he said, A hundred
[1]measures of oil. And he said unto him, Take thy [2]bond, and sit down

Luke 16:1-17:10

7 quickly and write fifty. Then said he to another, And how much owest
thou? And he said, A hundred [3]measures of wheat. He saith unto him,
8 Take thy [4]bond, and write fourscore. And his lord commended [5]the
unrighteous steward because he had done wisely: for the sons of this
[6]world are for their own generation wiser than the sons of the light.
9 And I say unto you, make to yourselves friends [6]by means of the mammon
of unrighteousness; that, when it shall fail, they may receive you into
10 the eternal tabernacles. He that is faithful in a very little is faithful
11 also in much. If therefore ye have not been faithful in the unrighteous
12 mammon, who will commit to your trust the true *riches?* And if ye
have not been faithful in that which is another's, who will give you that
13 which is [7]your own? No [8]servant can serve two masters: for either he
will hate the one, and love the other; or else he will hold to one, and
despise the other. Ye cannot serve God and mammon.
14 And the Pharisees, who were lovers of money, heard all these things;
15 and they scoffed at him. And he said unto them, Ye are they that
justify yourselves in the sight of men; but God knoweth your hearts: for
that which is exalted among men is an abomination in the sight of God.
16 The law and the prophets *were* until John: from that time the gospel of
the kingdom of God is preached, and every man entereth violently into it
17 [*see Matt. 11:12*]. But it is easier for heaven and earth to pass away,
18 than for one tittle of the law to fall. Every one that putteth away his
wife, and marrieth another, committeth adultery: and he that marrieth
one that is put away from a husband committeth adultery.
19 Now there was a certain rich man, and he was clothed in purple and
20 fine linen, [9]faring sumptuously every day: and a certain beggar named
21 Lazarus was laid at his gate, full of sores, and desiring to be fed with the
crumbs that fell from the rich man's table; yea, even the dogs came and
22 licked his sores. And it came to pass, that the beggar died, and that he
was carried away by the angels into Abraham's bosom: and the rich man
23 also died, and was buried. And in Hades he lifted up his eyes, being in
24 torments, and seeth Abraham afar off, and Lazarus in his bosom. And he
cried and said, Father Abraham, have mercy on me, and send Lazarus,
that he may dip the tip of his finger in water, and cool my tongue; for I
25 am in anguish in this flame. But Abraham said, [10]Son, remember that
thou in thy lifetime receivedst thy good things, and Lazarus in like manner
26 evil things: but now here he is comforted, and thou art in anguish. And
[11]beside all this, between us and you there is a great gulf fixed, that they
which would pass from hence to you may not be able, and that none may
27 cross over from thence to us. And he said, I pray thee therefore, father,
28 that thou wouldest send him to my father's house: for I have five brethren;
that he may testify unto them; lest they also come into this place of tor-
29 ment. But Abraham saith, They have Moses and the prophets; let them
30 hear them. And he said, Nay, father Abraham: but if one go to them
31 from the dead, they will repent. And he said unto him, If they hear not
Moses and the prophets, neither will they be persuaded, if one rise from
the dead.
1 And he said unto his disciples, It is impossible but that occasions of
stumbling should come: but woe unto him, through whom they come!
2 It were well for him if a millstone were hanged about his neck, and he

Luke 16:1–17:10

were thrown into the sea, rather than that he should cause one of these
3 little ones to stumble. Take heed to yourselves: if thy brother sin,
4 rebuke him; and if he repent, forgive him. And if he sin against thee
seven times in the day, and seven times turn again to thee, saying, I
repent; thou shalt forgive him.
5, 6 And the apostles said unto the Lord, Increase our faith. And the
Lord said, If ye have faith as a grain of mustard seed, ye would say unto
this sycamine tree, Be thou rooted up, and be thou planted in the sea;
7 and it would have obeyed you. But who is there of you, having a [12]ser-
vant plowing or keeping sheep, that will say unto him, when he is come in
from the field, Come straightway and sit down to meat; and will not
8 rather say unto him, Make ready wherewith I may sup, and gird thyself,
and serve me, till I have eaten and drunken; and afterward thou shalt
9 eat and drink? Doth he thank the [12]servant because he did the things
10 that were commanded? Even so ye also, when ye shall have done all
the things that are commanded you, say, We are unprofitable [13]servants;
we have done that which it was our duty to do.

[1] Or, baths, the bath being a Hebrew measure. See Ezek. 45:10, 11, 14. [2] Gr. *writings*. [3] Gr. *cors*, the cor being a Hebrew measure. See Ezek. 45:14. [4] Gr. *the steward of unrighteousness*. [5] Or, *age*. [6] Gr. *out of*. [7] Some ancient authorities read, *our own*. [8] Gr. *household servant*. [9] Or, *living in mirth and splendor every day*. [10] Gr. *Child*. [11] Or, *in all these things*. [12] Gr. *bond-servant*. [13] Gr. *bond-servants*.

§ 118. JESUS RAISES LAZARUS FROM THE DEAD

From Perea* to Bethany near Jerusalem

John 11:1–44

1 Now a certain man was sick, Lazarus of Bethany, of the village of
2 Mary and her sister Martha. And it was that Mary, which anointed
the Lord with ointment, and wiped his feet with her hair, whose brother
3 Lazarus was sick. The sisters therefore sent unto him, saying, Lord,
4 behold, he whom thou lovest is sick. But when Jesus heard it, he said,
this sickness is not unto death, but for the glory of God, that the Son of
5 God may be glorified thereby. Now Jesus loved Martha, and her sister,
6 and Lazarus. When therefore he heard that he was sick, he abode at
7 that time two days in the place where he was. Then after this he saith
8 to the disciples, Let us go into Judea again. The disciples say unto him,
Rabbi, the Jews were but now seeking to stone thee; and goest thou thither
9 again? Jesus answered, Are there not twelve hours in the day? If a
man walk in the day, he stumbleth not, because he seeth the light of this
10 world. But if a man walk in the night, he stumbleth, because the light
11 is not in him. These things spake he: and after this he saith unto them,
Our friend Lazarus is fallen asleep; but I go, that I may awake him out of
12 sleep. The disciples therefore said unto him, Lord, if he is fallen asleep,
13 he will [1]recover. Now Jesus had spoken of his death: but they thought

* Our Lord was apparently at a distance of two or three days' journey (verses 6, 17) from Bethany; and he was probably in Perea. This visit to Bethany, a suburb of Jerusalem, may be that to which Luke pointed in 13:22.

John 11:1–44

14 that he spake of taking rest in sleep. Then Jesus therefore said unto
15 them plainly, Lazarus is dead. And I am glad for your sakes that I was
not there, to the intent ye may believe; nevertheless let us go unto him.
16 Thomas therefore, who is called [2]Didymus, said unto his fellow-disciples,
Let us also go, that we may die with him.
17 So when Jesus came, he found that he had been in the tomb four days
18 already. Now Bethany was nigh unto Jerusalem, about fifteen furlongs
19 off; and many of the Jews had come to Martha and Mary, to console
20 them concerning their brother. Martha therefore, when she heard
that Jesus was coming, went and met him: but Mary still sat in the house.
21 Martha therefore said unto Jesus, Lord, if thou hadst been here, my
22 brother had not died. And even now I know that whatsoever thou shalt
23 ask of God, God will give thee. Jesus saith unto her, Thy brother shall
24 rise again. Martha saith unto him, I know that he shall rise again in
25 the resurrection at the last day. Jesus said unto her, I am the resur-
26 rection, and the life: he that believeth on me, though he die, yet shall he
27 live: and whosoever liveth and believeth on me shall never die. Believest
thou this? She saith unto him, Yea, Lord: I have believed that thou art
28 the Christ, the Son of God, *even* he that cometh into the world. And when
she had said this, she went away, and called Mary [3]her sister secretly,
29 saying, The [4]Master is here, and calleth thee. And she, when she heard
30 it, arose quickly, and went unto him. (Now Jesus was not yet come into the
31 village, but was still in the place where Martha met him.) The Jews then
which were with her in the house, and were comforting her, when they
saw Mary, that she rose up quickly and went out, followed her, supposing
32 that she was going unto the tomb to [5]weep there. Mary therefore, when
she came where Jesus was, and saw him, fell down at his feet, saying unto
33 him, Lord, if thou hadst been here, my brother had not died. When
Jesus therefore saw her [6]weeping, and the Jews *also* [6]weeping, which
34 came with her, he [7]groaned in the spirit, and [8]was troubled, and said, Where
35 have ye laid him? They say unto him, Lord, come and see. Jesus wept.
36, 37 The Jews therefore said, Behold how he loved him! But some of
them said, Could not this man, which opened the eyes of him that was
38 blind, have caused that this man also should not die? Jesus therefore
again [9]groaning in himself cometh to the tomb. Now it was a cave, and
39 a stone lay [10]against it. Jesus saith, Take ye away the stone. Martha,
the sister of him that was dead, saith unto him, Lord, by this time he
40 stinketh: for he hath been *dead* four days. Jesus saith unto her,
Said I not unto thee, that, if thou believedst, thou shouldest
41 see the glory of God? So they took away the stone. And Jesus lifted
up his eyes, and said, Father, I thank thee that thou heardest me.
42 And I knew that thou hearest me always: but because of the multitude
which standeth around I said it, that they may believe that thou didst
43 send me. And when he had thus spoken, he cried with a loud voice,
44 Lazarus, come forth. He that was dead came forth, bound hand and
foot with [11]grave-clothes; and his face was bound about with a napkin.
Jesus saith unto them, Loose him, and let him go.

[1] Gr. *be saved.* [2] That is, *Twin.* [3] Or, *her sister, saying secretly.* [4] Or, *Teacher.* [5] Gr. *wail.* [6] Gr. *wailing.* [7] Or, *was moved with indignation in the spirit.* [8] Gr. *troubled himself.* [9] Or, *being moved with indignation in himself.* [10] Or, *upon.* [11] Or, *grave-bands.*

§119. THE EFFECT OF THE RAISING OF LAZARUS (ON THE PEOPLE, ON THE SANHEDRIN, ON THE MOVEMENTS OF JESUS)

Jerusalem and Ephraim in Judea

John 11:45–54

45 Many therefore of the Jews, which came to Mary and beheld [1]that
46 which he did, believed on him. But some of them went away to the
Pharisees, and told them the thing which Jesus had done.
47 The chief priests therefore and the Pharisees gathered a council, and
48 said, What do we? for this man doeth many signs. If we let him thus
alone, all men will believe on him: and the Romans will come and take
49 away both our place and our nation. But a certain one of them, Caiaphas,
being high priest that year, said unto them, Ye know nothing at all,
50 nor do ye take account that it is expedient for you that one man should
51 die for the people, and that the whole nation perish not. Now this he
52 said not of himself: but being high priest that year, he prophesied that
Jesus should die for the nation; and not for the nation only, but that he
might also gather together into one the children of God that are scattered
53 abroad. So from that day forth they took counsel that they might put
him to death.
54 Jesus therefore walked no more openly among the Jews, but departed
thence into the country near to the wilderness, into a city called Ephraim;
and there he tarried with the disciples.

[1] Many ancient authorities read *the things which he did.*

§120. JESUS STARTS ON THE LAST JOURNEY TO JERUSALEM BY WAY OF SAMARIA AND GALILEE

He heals the Ten Lepers and explains the Nature of the Kingdom of God to the Pharisees and the Disciples.

In Samaria or Galilee

Luke 17:11–37

11 And it came to pass, [1]as they were on the way to Jerusalem, that he
12 was passing [2]through the midst of Samaria and Galilee.* And as he
entered into a certain village, there met him ten men that were lepers,
13 which stood afar off [*see Lev. 13:45–46*]: and they lifted up their voices,
14 saying, Jesus, Master, have mercy on us. And when he saw them, he

* As Ephraim (§ 119) was pretty certainly in the northern part of Judea, it has been reasonably supposed (Wieseler, Clark, and others) that, when the Passover was approaching, Jesus went from that region northward through Samaria into the southern or southeastern part of Galilee, so as to fall in with the pilgrims going from Galilee through Perea to Jerusalem. We thus again combine Luke's account with that of John in easy agreement. And this explains Luke's mention of Samaria first, which would be strange in describing a journey from Galilee through Samaria to Jerusalem, while the marginal translation, "between Samaria and Galilee," would be obscure and hard to account for. From this point he is making his final journey to Jerusalem, for the Passover of the crucifixion.

Luke 17:11–37

said unto them, Go and shew yourselves unto the priests [*see Lev. 13:49;*
15 *14:1–3*]. And it came to pass, as they went, they were cleansed. And
one of them, when he saw that he was healed, turned back, with a loud
16 voice glorifying God; and he fell upon his face at his feet, giving him
17 thanks: and he was a Samaritan. And Jesus answering said, Were not
18 the ten cleansed? but where are the nine? [3]Were there none found that
19 returned to give glory to God, save this [4]stranger? And he said unto
him, Arise, and go thy way: thy faith hath [5]made thee whole.
20 And being asked by the Pharisees, when the kingdom of God cometh,
he answered them and said, the kingdom of God cometh not with obser-
21 vation: neither shall they say, Lo, here! or, There! for lo, the kingdom of
God is [6]within you.
22 And he said unto the disciples, The days will come, when ye shall
desire to see one of the days of the Son of man, and ye shall not see it.
23 And they shall say to you, Lo, there! Lo, here! go not away, nor follow
24 after *them:* for as the lightning, when it lighteneth out of the one part
under the heaven, shineth unto the other part under heaven; so shall
25 the Son of man be [7]in his day. But first must he suffer many things and
26 be rejected of this generation. And as it came to pass in the days of Noah,
even so shall it be also in the days of the Son of man [*see Gen. 6:11–13;*
27 *7, 21–23*]. They ate, they drank, they married, they were given in mar-
riage, until the day that Noah entered the ark, and the flood came, and
28 destroyed them all. Likewise even as it came to pass in the days of Lot;
they ate, they drank, they bought, they sold, they planted, they builded
29 [*see Gen 18:20–22*]: but in the day that Lot went out from Sodom [*see Gen.*
30 *19:24–25*] it rained fire and brimstone from heaven, and destroyed them
all: after the same manner shall it be in the day that the Son of
31 man is revealed. In that day, he which shall be on the housetop, and his
goods in the house, let him not go down to take them away: and let him
32, 33 that is in the field likewise not return back. Remember Lot's wife [*see*
Gen. 19:26]. Whosoever shall seek to gain his [8]life shall lose it: but who-
34 soever shall lose *his life* shall [9]preserve it. I say unto you, In that night
there shall be two men on one bed; the one shall be taken and the other
35 shall be left. There shall be two women grinding together; the one shall
37 be taken, and the other shall be left [10]. And they answering say unto
him, Where, Lord? And he said unto them, Where the body *is*, thither
will the [11]eagles also be gathered together.

[1] Or, *as he was.* [2] Or, *between.* [3] Or, *There were none found . . . save this stranger.* [4] Or, *alien.* [5] Or, *saved thee.* [6] Or, *in the midst of you.* [7] Some ancient authorities omit *in his day.* [8] Or, *soul.* [9] Or, *save it alive.* [10] Some ancient authorities add ver. 36 *There shall be two men in the field: the one shall be taken, and the other shall be left.* [11] Or, *vultures.*

§121. TWO PARABLES ON PRAYER (THE IMPORTUNATE WIDOW, THE PHARISEE, AND THE PUBLICAN)

Luke 18:1–14

1 And he spake a parable unto them to the end that they ought always
2 to pray, and not to faint; saying, There was in a city a judge, which
3 feared not God, and regarded not man: and there was a widow in that

Luke 18:1-14

city; and she came oft unto him, saying, [1]Avenge me of mine adversary.
4 And he would not for a while: but afterward he said within himself,
5 Though I fear not God, nor regard man; yet because this widow troubleth
me, I will avenge her, lest she [2]wear me out by her continual coming.
6 And the Lord said, Hear what [3]the unrighteous judge saith. And shall
7 not God avenge his elect, which cry to him day and night, and he is long-
8 suffering over them? I say unto you, that he will avenge them speedily.
Howbeit when the Son of man cometh, shall he find [4]faith on the earth?
9 And he spake also this parable unto certain which trusted in them-
10 selves that they were righteous, and set [5]all others at nought: Two men
went up into the temple to pray; the one a Pharisee, and the other a
11 publican. The Pharisee stood and prayed thus with himself, God, I
thank thee, that I am not as the rest of men, extortioners, unjust, adulter-
12 ers, or even as this publican. I fast twice in the week; I give tithes of all
13 that I get. But the publican, standing afar off, would not lift up so much
as his eyes unto heaven, but smote his breast, saying, God, [6]be merciful
14 to me [7]a sinner. I say unto you, This man went down to his house
justified rather than the other: for every one that exalteth himself shall be
humbled; but he that humbleth himself shall be exalted.

[1] Or, *Do me justice of;* and so in verses 5, 7, 8. [2] Gr. *bruise.* [3] Gr. *the judge of unrighteousness.* [4] Or, *the faith.* [5] Gr. *the rest.* [6] Or, *be propitiated.* [7] Or, *the sinner.*

§ 122. GOING FROM GALILEE THROUGH PEREA,* HE TEACHES CONCERNING DIVORCE

Perea

Mark 10:1-12

1 And he arose from thence, and
cometh into the borders of Judea
and beyond Jordan: and mul-
titudes come together unto him
again; and, as he was wont, he
taught them again.

2 And there came unto him
Pharisees, and asked him, Is it
lawful for a man to put away *his*
3 wife? tempting him. And he
answered and said unto them,
What did Moses command you
4 [*see Deut. 24:1*]? And they said,

Matt. 19:1-12

1 And it came to pass, when Jesus
had finished these words, he de-
parted from Galilee, and came
into the borders of Judea beyond
2 Jordan; and great multitudes fol-
lowed him; and he healed them
there.

3 And there came unto him
[1]Pharisees, tempting him, and
saying, Is it lawful *for a man* to
put away his wife for every cause?
4 And he answered and said, Have

* Matthew expressly states that he went from Galilee through Perea, and soon afterwards carries him forward to Jericho and Jerusalem. (Comp. Mark also.) Yet he says that Jesus did this when he had finished the parable of the unforgiving servant, which we have placed nearly six months earlier (§ 92). Luke here presently agrees with Matthew and Mark, and they go on together to the end, while heretofore Matthew and Mark have given us nothing since Jesus went to the Feast of Tabernacles. In one way or another we must suppose quite a break in their narrative. See Broadus' commentary on Matthew 19:1, and compare note 10 at end of Harmony.

Mark 10:1-12

Moses suffered to write a bill
of divorcement, and to put her
5 away. But Jesus said unto them,
For your hardness of heart he
wrote you this commandment.
6 But from the beginning of the
creation, Male and female made
7 he them [*see Gen. 1:27*]. For
this cause shall a man leave his
father and mother, [5]and shall
8 cleave to his wife; and the twain
shall become one flesh [*see Gen.
2:24*]: so that they are no more
9 twain, but one flesh. What there-
fore God hath joined together, let
10 not man put asunder. And in the
house the disciples asked him
again of this matter.

11 And he saith unto them, Who-
soever shall put away his wife,
and marry another, committeth
12 adultery against her: and if she
herself shall put away her hus-
band, and marry another, she
committeth adultery.

Matt. 19:1-12

ye not read, that he which [2]made
them from the beginning made
5 them male and female, and said,
For this cause shall a man leave
his father and mother, and shall
cleave to his wife; and the twain
6 shall become one flesh? So that
they are no more twain, but one
flesh. What therefore God hath
joined together, let not man put
asunder.
7 They say unto
him, Why then did Moses com-
mand to give a bill of divorce-
8 ment, and to put *her* away? He
saith unto them, Moses for your
hardness of heart suffered you
to put away your wives: but from
the beginning it hath not been
9 so. And I say unto you, Whoso-
ever shall put away his wife, [3]ex-
cept for fornication, and shall
marry another, committeth adul-
tery: [4]and he that marrieth her
when she is put away committeth
10 adultery. The disciples say unto
him, If the case of the man is so
with his wife, it is not expedient
11 to marry. But he said unto them,
All men cannot receive this saying,
but they to whom it is given.
12 For there are eunuchs which were
so born from their mother's womb:
and there are eunuchs, which were
made eunuchs by men: and there
are eunuchs, which made them-
selves eunuchs for the kingdom of
heaven's sake. He that is able to
receive it, let him receive it.

[1] Many authorities, some ancient, insert *the*. [2] Some ancient authorities read *created*. [3] Some ancient authorities read *saving for the cause of fornication, maketh her an adulteress;* as in ch. 5:32, § 43. [4] The following words, to the end of the verse, are omitted by some ancient authorities. [5] Some ancient authorities omit *and shall cleave to his wife*.

§ 123. CHRIST AND CHILDREN AND THE FAILURE OF THE DISCIPLES TO UNDERSTAND THE ATTITUDE OF JESUS

Perea

Mark 10:13–16	Matt. 19:13–15	Luke 18:15–17*
13 And they brought unto him little children, that he should touch them: and the disciples rebuked	13 Then were there brought unto him little children, that he should lay his hands on them, and pray: and the disciples rebuked them.	15 And they brought unto him also their babes, that he should touch them: but when the disciples saw it, they rebuked them.
14 them. But when Jesus saw it, he was moved with indignation, and said unto them, Suffer the little children to come unto me; forbid them not: for of such is the kingdom of God.	14 But Jesus said, Suffer the little children, and forbid them not, to come unto me: for of such is the kingdom of heaven.	16 But Jesus called them unto him, saying, Suffer the little children to come unto me, and forbid them not: for of such is the kingdom of
15 Verily I say unto you, Whosoever shall not receive the kingdom of God as a little child, he shall in no wise enter therein.		17 God. Verily I say unto you, Whosoever shall not receive the kingdom of God as a little child, he shall in no wise enter therein.
16 And he took them in his arms, and blessed them, laying his hands upon them.	15 And he laid his hands on them, and departed thence.	

§ 124. THE RICH YOUNG RULER, THE PERILS OF RICHES, AND AMAZEMENT OF THE DISCIPLES. THE REWARDS OF FORSAKING ALL TO FOLLOW THE MESSIAH WILL BE GREAT, BUT WILL BE SOVEREIGN (PARABLE OF THE LABORERS IN THE VINEYARD)

In Perea

Mark 10:17–31	Matt. 19:16 to 20:16	Luke 18:18–30
17 And as he was going forth [3]into the way, there ran one to him, and kneeled to him, and asked him, Good [2]Master,	16 And behold, one came to him and said, [1]Master,[2] what good	18 And a certain ruler asked him, saying, Good [2]Master, what

* From this point Matthew, Mark and Luke will be parallel more frequently than they were even during the great ministry in Galilee.

Mark 10:17–31

what shall I do that
I may inherit eternal
18 life? And Jesus said
unto him, Why callest
thou me good? none
is good save one,
even God.

19 Thou knowest the
commandments [*see
Ex. 20:12–16; Deut.
5:16–20*],

Do
not kill, Do not com-
mit adultery

Do not
steal, Do not bear
false witness, Do not
defraud, Honour thy
father and mother.
20 And he
said unto him, [2]Mas-
ter, all these things
have I observed from
21 my youth. And Je-
sus looking upon him
loved him, and said
unto him, One thing
thou lackest: go, sell
whatsoever thou
hast, and give to the
poor, and thou shalt
have treasure in
heaven: and come,
22 follow me. But his
countenance fell at
the saying, and he
went away sorrowful:
for he was one that
had great possessions.
23 And Jesus looked
round about, and
saith unto his disci-
ples, How hardly
shall they that have
riches enter into the
kingdom of God!

Matt. 19:16 to 20:16

thing shall I do that
I may have eternal
17 life? And he said
unto him, [3]Why ask-
est thou me concern-
ing that which is
good? One there is
who is good: but if
thou wouldest enter
into life, keep the
18 commandments. He
saith unto him,
Which? And Jesus
said, Thou shalt not
kill, Thou shalt not
commit adultery,

Thou shalt not steal,
Thou shalt not bear
19 false witness, Honour
thy father and thy
mother: and, Thou
shalt love thy neigh-
20 bour as thyself. The
young man saith un-
to him, All these
things have I ob-
served: what lack I
21 yet? Jesus said unto
him, If thou wouldest
be perfect, go, sell
that thou hast, and
give to the poor, and
thou shalt have treas-
ure in heaven: and
come, follow me.

22 But
when the young man
heard the saying, he
went away sorrowful:
for he was one that
had great possessions.
23 And Jesus said un-
to his disciples, Ver-
ily I say unto you, It
is hard for a rich
man to enter into the
kingdom of heaven.

Luke 18:18–30

shall I do to inherit
19 eternal life? And
Jesus said unto him,
Why callest thou me
good? none is good
save one, *even* God.

20 Thou knowest
the commandments,

Do not commit adul-
tery, Do not kill,

Do not steal, Do not
bear false witness,
Honour thy father
and mother.

21 And he said,
All these things have
I observed from my
22 youth up. And when
Jesus heard it, he
said unto him, One
thing thou lackest
yet: sell all that thou
hast, and distribute
unto the poor, and
thou shalt have treas-
ure in heaven: and
come, follow me.
23 But when he heard
these things, he be-
came exceeding sor-
rowful; for he was
very rich.

24 And Jesus
seeing him said, How
hardly shall they that
have riches enter into
the kingdom of God!

Mark 10:17–31

24 And the disciples
were amazed at his
words. But Jesus an-
swereth again, and
saith unto them,
Children, how hard
is it [9]for them that
trust in riches to en-
ter into the kingdom
25 of God! It is easier
for a camel to go
through a needle's
eye, than for a rich
man to enter into
the kingdom of God.
26 And they were as-
tonished exceedingly,
saying [10]unto him,
Then who can be
27 saved? Jesus look-
ing upon them saith,
With men it is im-
possible, but not with
God for all things
are possible with
God [*see Gen. 18:24;*
28 *Job, 42:2*]. Peter be-
gan to say unto him,
Lo, we have left all,
and followed thee.
29 Jesus
said, Verily I say
unto you,

There is
no man that hath
left house, or breth-
ren, or sisters, or
mother, or father, or
children, or lands,
for my sake, and for
30 the gospel's sake, but
he shall receive a
hundredfold now in
this time, houses, and

Matt. 19:16 to 20:16

24 And again I say unto
you, It is easier for a
camel to go through
a needle's eye, than
for a rich man to en-
ter into the kingdom
25 of God. And when
the disciples heard
it, they were aston-
ished exceedingly,
saying, Who then can
26 be saved? And Jesus
looking upon *them*
said to them, With
men this is im-
possible; but with
God all things are
27 possible. Then an-
swered Peter and said
unto him, Lo, we have
left all, and followed
thee; what then shall
28 we have? And Jesus
said unto them, Ver-
ily I say unto you,
that ye which have
followed me, in the
regeneration when
the Son of man shall
sit on the throne of
his glory, ye also
shall sit upon twelve
thrones, judging the
twelve tribes of Isra-
29 el. And every one
that hath left houses,
or brethren, or sis-
ters, or father, or
mother, [4]or children,
or lands, for my
name's sake, shall

Luke 18:18–30

25 For it is
easier for a camel to
enter in through a
needle's eye, than for
a rich man to enter
into the kingdom of
God.
26 And they
that heard it said,
Then who can be
saved?

27 But he said,
The things that are
impossible with men
are possible with God.
28 And Peter said, Lo,
we have left [12]our
own, and followed
thee.
29 And
he said unto them,
Verily I say unto you,

There is no man
that hath left house,
or wife, or brethren,
or parents, or chil-
dren, for the king-
dom of God's sake,

Mark 10:17–31	Matt. 19:16 to 20:16	Luke 18:18–30
brethren, and sisters, and mothers, and children, and lands, with persecutions; and in the [11]world to come eternal life.	receive [5]a hundred fold, and shall inherit eternal life.	30 who shall not receive manifold more in this time, and in the [11]world to come eternal life.
31 But many *that are* first shall be last; and the last first.	30 But many shall be last *that are* first; and first *that are* last.	

1 For the kingdom of heaven is like unto a man that is a householder,
which went out early in the morning to hire labourers into his vine-
2 yard. And when he had agreed with the labourers for a [6]penny a day,
3 he sent them into his vineyard. And he went out about the third hour
4 and saw others standing in the marketplace idle; and to them he said,
Go ye also into the vineyard, and whatsoever is right I will give you.
5 And they went their way. Again he went out about the sixth and the
6 ninth hour, and did likewise. And about the eleventh *hour* he went out,
7 and found others standing; and he saith unto them, Why stand ye here
all the day idle? They say unto him, Because no man hath hired us.
8 He saith unto them, Go ye also into the vineyard. And when even was
come, the lord of the vineyard saith unto his steward, Call the labourers,
9 and pay them their hire, beginning from the last unto the first. And when
they came that *were hired* about the eleventh hour, they received every
10 man a [6]penny. And when the first came, they supposed that they would
11 receive more; and they likewise received every man a [6]penny. And
when they received it, they murmured against the householder, saying,
12 These last have spent *but* one hour, and thou hast made them equal unto
us, which have borne the burden of the day and the [7]scorching heat.
13 But he answered and said to one of them, Friend, I do thee no wrong:
14 didst not thou agree with me for a [6]penny? Take up that which is thine,
and go thy way; it is my will to give unto this last, even as unto thee.
15 Is it not lawful for me to do what I will with mine own? or is thine eye
16 evil, because I am good? So the last shall be first, and the first last.

[1] Some ancient authorities read *Good Master*. See Mark 10:17; Luke 18:18. [2] Or, *Teacher*. [3] Some ancient authorities read *Why callest thou me good? None is good save one, even God*. See Mark 10:18; Luke 18:19. [4] Many ancient authorities add *or wife;* as in Luke 18:29. [5] Some ancient authorities read *manifold*. [6] The Roman denarius, about seventeen cents of our money. [7] Or, *hot wind*. [8] Or, *on his way*. [9] Some ancient authorities omit *for them that trust in riches*. [10] Many ancient authorities read *among themselves*. [11] Or, *age*. [12] Or, *our own* homes.

§ 125. JESUS AGAIN FORETELLS TO THE DISCIPLES HIS DEATH AND RESURRECTION (COMP. §§ 83, 85, 86, 88), AND REBUKES THE SELFISH AMBITION OF JAMES AND JOHN

Probably in Perea

Mark 10:32–45	Matt. 20:17–28
32 And they were in the way, going up	17 And as Jesus was going up to Jerusalem,

Mark 10:32–45

to Jerusalem*; and
Jesus was going be-
fore them: and they
were amazed; [a]and
they that followed
were afraid. And he
took again the
twelve, and began to
tell them the things
that were to happen
unto him, *saying,*
33 Behold, we go up to
Jerusalem; and the
Son of man shall be
delivered unto the
chief priests and the
scribes; and they
shall condemn him to
death, and shall
deliver him unto the
34 Gentiles: and they
shall mock him,
and shall spit
upon him, and shall
scourge him, and shall
kill him; and after
three days he shall
rise again.

35 And there come near
unto him James and
John, the sons of
Zebedee, saying unto
him, [c]Master, we
would that thou
shouldest do for us
whatsoever we shall
ask of thee. And he
36 said unto them, What
would ye that I should
37 do for you? And they
said unto him, Grant

Matt. 20:17–28

he took the
twelve disciples
apart, and in the way
he said unto them,
18 Behold, we go up to
Jerusalem; and the
Son of man shall be
delivered unto the
chief priests and
scribes; and they
shall condemn him
19 to death, and shall
deliver him unto the
Gentiles to mock,
and to scourge, and
to crucify; and the
third day he shall
be raised up.

20 Then came to him
the mother of the sons
of Zebedee with her
sons, worshipping
him, and asking a
certain thing of him.
21 And he
said unto her, What wouldest thou? She
said unto him, Command that these my two
sons may sit, one on thy right hand, and one
on thy left hand, in thy kingdom.

Luke 18:31–34

31 And he took unto
him the twelve, and
said unto them, Be-
hold, we go up to Je-
rusalem, and all the
things that are writ-
ten [b]by the prophets
shall be accomplished
unto the Son of man.
32 For he shall be
delivered up unto the
Gentiles, and shall
be mocked, and
shamefully entreated,
and spit upon: and
33 they shall scourge and
kill him: and the
third day he shall
34 rise again. And they
understood none of
these things; and this
saying was hid from
them, and they per-
ceived not the things
that were said.

* He left Galilee in § 122, crossing the Jordan into Perea, probably in company with many Jews from Galilee (who regularly went this way to Jerusalem), and will now soon cross the river again and reach Jericho (§ 126).

Mark 10:32–45

unto us that we may sit, one
on thy right hand, and one on
38 *thy* left hand, in thy glory. But
Jesus said unto them, Ye know
not what ye ask. Are ye able
to drink the cup that I drink?
or to be baptized with the baptism
39 that I am baptized with? And
they said unto him, We are able.
And Jesus said unto them, The cup
that I drink ye shall drink; and
with the baptism that I am bap-
tized withal shall ye be baptized:
40 but to sit on my right hand or on
my left hand is not mine to give:
but *it is for them* for whom it hath
41 been prepared. And when the ten
heard it, they began to be moved
with indignation concerning
42 James and John. And Jesus called
them to him, and saith unto them,
Ye know that they which are
accounted to rule over the Gentiles
lord it over them: and their great
ones exercise authority over them.
43 But it is not so among you: but
whosoever would become great
among you, shall be your [1]minister:
44 and whosoever would be first
among you, shall be [2]servant of
45 all. For verily the Son of man
came not to be ministered unto,
but to minister, and to give his life
a ransom for many.

Matt. 20:17–28

22 But Jesus answered and said, Ye
know not what ye ask. Are ye
able to drink the cup that I am
about to drink?
They say
unto him, We are able.
23 He saith
unto them, My cup indeed ye shall
drink:
but to sit on my right
hand, and on *my* left hand, is not
mine to give, but *it is for them*
for whom it hath been prepared of
24 my Father. And when the ten
heard it, they were moved with in-
dignation concerning the two
25 brethren. But Jesus called them
unto him, and said, Ye know that
the rulers of the Gentiles lord it
over them, and their great ones
26 exercise authority over them. Not
so shall it be among you; but who-
soever would become great among
27 you shall be your [1]minister; and
whosoever would be first among
28 you shall be your [2]servant: even
as the Son of man came not to
be ministered unto, but to min-
ister, and to give his life a ransom
for many.

[1] Or, *servant.* [2] Gr. *bond-servant.* [3] Or, *but some as they followed were afraid.* [4] Or, *Teacher.* [5] Or, *through.*

§ 126. BLIND BARTIMÆUS AND HIS COMPANION HEALED

At Jericho

Mark 10:46–52

46 And they come to
Jericho: and as he
went out from Jeri-
cho, with his disci-
ples and a great mul-
titude, the son of
Timæus, Bartimæus,

Matt. 20:29–34

29 And as they went
out from Jericho, a
great multitude fol-
lowed him.
30 And be-

Luke 18:35–43

35 And it came to
pass, as he drew nigh
unto Jericho,
a cer-

Mark 10:46–52

a blind beggar, was
sitting by the way
side.

47 And when he
heard that it was Je-
sus of Nazareth, he
began to cry out, and
say, Jesus, thou son
of David, have mercy
48 on me. And many
rebuked him, that he
should hold his peace:
but he cried out the
more a great deal,
Thou son of David,
have mercy on me.
49 And Jesus
stood still, and said,
Call ye him. And
they call the blind
man, saying unto him,
Be of good cheer: rise,
50 he calleth thee. And
he, casting away his
garment, sprang up,
and came to Jesus.
51 And Jesus answered
him, and said, What
wilt thou that I
should do unto thee?
And the blind man
said unto him, [1]Rab-
boni, that I may re-
52 ceive my sight. And
Jesus said unto him,
Go thy way; thy
faith hath [2]made thee
whole. And straight-
way he received his
sight, and followed
him in the way.

Matt. 20:29–34

hold, two *blind men
sitting by the way
side,

when they heard
that Jesus was pass-
ing by, cried out,
saying, Lord, have
mercy on us, thou
31 Son of David. And
the multitude rebuked
them, that they should
hold their peace:
but they cried out
the more, saying,
Lord, have mercy on
us, thou son of David.
32 And Jesus stood still,
and called them,

and said,
What will ye that I
should do unto you?
33 They say unto him,
Lord, that our eyes
34 may be opened. And
Jesus being moved
with compassion,
touched their eyes:
and straightway they
received their sight,
and followed him.

Luke 18:35–43

tain blind man sat by
the way side begging:
36 and hearing a multi-
tude going by, he
inquired what this
37 meant. And they
told him, that Jesus
of Nazareth passeth
38 by. And he cried,
saying, Jesus, thou
son of David, have
39 mercy on me. And
they that went before
rebuked him, that he
should hold his peace:
but he cried out the
more a great deal,
Thou son of David,
have mercy on me.
40 And Jesus stood, and
commanded him to
be brought unto him:

and when
he was come near, he
41 asked him, What wilt
thou that I should do
unto thee? And he
said, Lord, that I
may receive my sight.
42 And Jesus said unto
him, Receive thy
sight: thy faith hath
[2]made thee whole.
43 And immediately he
received his sight, and
followed him, glorify-
ing God: and all the
people, when they
saw it, gave praise
unto God.

[1] See John 20:16. [2] Or, *saved thee*.

* Matthew mentions two blind men, while Mark and Luke describe one, probably the more conspicuous one.—The discrepancy as to place, "as he went out from Jericho," "as he drew nigh unto Jericho," is best explained by the recent suggestion that the healing occurred after he left the old Jericho, and as he was approaching the new Jericho which Herod the Great had built at some distance away. An older, and also possible explanation was that the blind men made application when he was approaching the city, but were not then healed, and only when he had left the city were they healed. (Comp. Matt. 15:23 ff., and Mark 8:22 f.)

§127. JESUS VISITS ZACCHÆUS, AND SPEAKS THE PARABLE OF THE POUNDS,* AND SETS OUT FOR JERUSALEM

Jericho

Luke 19:1–28

1, 2 And he entered and was passing through Jericho. And behold, a
man called by name Zacchæus; and he was a chief publican, and he was
3 rich. And he sought to see Jesus who he was; and could not for the crowd,
4 because he was little of stature. And he ran on before, and climbed up
5 into a sycamore tree to see him: for he was to pass that way. And when
Jesus came to the place, he looked up, and said unto him, Zacchæus, make
6 haste, and come down; for to-day I must abide at thy house. And he
7 made haste, and came down, and received him joyfully. And when they
saw it, they all murmured, saying, He is gone in to lodge with a man that
8 is a sinner. And Zacchæus stood, and said unto the Lord, Behold, Lord,
the half of my goods I give to the poor; and if I have wrongfully exacted
9 aught of any man, I restore fourfold [*see Ex. 22:1; Num. 5:6–7*]. And
Jesus said unto him, To-day is salvation come to this house, forasmuch
10 as he also is a son of Abraham. For the Son of man came to seek and to
save that which was lost [*Ezek. 34:16*].

11 And as they heard these things, he added and spake a parable, be-
cause he was nigh to Jerusalem, and *because* they supposed that the
12 kingdom of God was immediately to appear. He said therefore, A
certain nobleman went into a far country, to receive for himself a king-
13 dom, and to return. And he called ten [1]servants of his, and gave them
14 ten [2]pounds, and said unto them, Trade ye *herewith* till I come. But his
citizens hated him, and sent an ambassage after him, saying, We will not
15 that this man reign over us. And it came to pass, when he was come back
again, having received the kingdom, that he commanded these [1]servants,
unto whom he had given the money, to be called to him, that he might
16 know what they had gained by trading. And the first came before him,
17 saying, Lord, thy pound hath made ten pounds more. And he said unto
him, Well done, thou good [3]servant: because thou wast found faithful in
18 a very little, have thou authority over ten cities. And the second came,
19 saying, Thy pound, Lord, hath made five pounds. And he said unto him
20 also, Be thou also over five cities. And [4]another came, saying, Lord,
21 behold, *here is* thy pound, which I kept laid up in a napkin: for I feared thee,
because thou art an austere man: thou takest up that thou layedst not
22 down, and reapest that thou didst not sow. He saith unto him, Out of
thine own mouth will I judge thee, thou wicked [3]servant. Thou knewest
that I am an austere man, taking up that I laid not down, and reaping
23 that I did not sow; then wherefore gavest thou not my money into the
bank, and [5]I at my coming should have required it with interest?
24 And he said unto them that stood by, Take away from him the pound,
25 and give it unto him that hath the ten pounds. And they said unto

* The similar parable of the Talents was given several days later. See § 139. On this first occasion the illustration has a specific design (ver. 11 f.), which will not appear on the second, *viz.*, to check the wild enthusiasm of the multitude to make Jesus King in Jerusalem as they had once planned a year ago (John 6:15, § 73).

Luke 19:1-28

26 him, Lord, he hath ten pounds. I say unto you, that unto every one that
hath shall be given; but from him that hath not, even that which he hath
27 shall be taken away from him. Howbeit these mine enemies, which would
not that I should reign over them, bring hither, and slay them before me.
28 And when he had thus spoken, he went on before, going up to Jerusalem.

[1] Gr. *bond-servants*. [2] *Mina*, here translated a pound, is equal to one hundred drachmas. See ch. 15:8. [3] Gr. *bond-servant*. [4] Gr. *the other*. [5] Or, *I should have gone and required*.

PART XI

THE LAST PUBLIC MINISTRY IN JERUSALEM

Friday before to Tuesday of Passion Week, Spring of A.D. *30* (*or* A.D. *29*).* *Just before Passover.* §§ *128a–138.*

§ 128a. JESUS ARRIVES AT BETHANY,† NEAR JERUSALEM

Friday afternoon

John 11:55 to 12:1, 9–11

55 Now the passover of the Jews was at hand: and many went up to
Jerusalem out of the country before the passover, to purify themselves.
56 They sought therefore for Jesus, and spake one with another, as they
stood in the temple, What think ye? That he will not come to the
57 feast? Now the chief priests and the Pharisees had given commandment,
that, if any man knew where he was, he should shew it, that they might
take him.
1 Jesus therefore six days before the passover came to Bethany, where
Lazarus was, whom Jesus raised from the dead.‡
9 The common people therefore of the Jews learned that he was there:
and they came, not for Jesus' sake only, but that they might see Lazarus
10 also, whom he raised from the dead. But the chief priests took counsel
11 that they might put Lazarus also to death; because that by reason of him
many of the Jews went away, and believed on Jesus.

In §§ 128b–138 we have the Saviour's movements and teachings on Sunday, Monday and Tuesday—the close of his public ministry, except the little that he said during the Jewish and Roman trial. All of his teaching thereafter will be given to his disciples.

§ 128b. HIS TRIUMPHAL ENTRY INTO JERUSALEM AS THE MESSIAH§

From Bethany to Jerusalem and back (*Sunday*). A Day of Messianic Demonstration

Mark 11:1–11	Matt. 21:1–11, 14–17	Luke 19:29–44
1 And when they draw nigh	1 And when they drew nigh	29 And it came to pass, when

* If the feast of John 5:1 was a Passover, and so his ministry lasted over three years, then his death was pretty certainly in A.D. 30; otherwise in A.D. 29.

† Compare former visits to this Bethany, §§ 104, 118, and see also below, § 141.

‡ John (12:2–8) gives the supper in the house of Simon the leper at this stage, probably because it is the last mention of Bethany in his Gospel. It seems better to follow the order of Mark here in the location of the anointing of Jesus by Mary of Bethany.

§ Jesus now makes a formal challenge to the Jerusalem leaders who have so long opposed his claims. This was a Day of Triumph that seemed to the excited crowds to mean the establishment of a political Messianic Kingdom.

Mark 11:1–11

unto Jerusa-
lem, unto
Bethphage and
Bethany, at
the mount of
Olives, he send-
eth two of his
2 disciples, and
saith unto
them, Go your
way into the
village that is
over against
you, and
straightway as
ye enter into
it, ye shall find
a colt tied,
whereon no
man ever yet
sat; loose him,
and bring him.
3 And if any one
say unto you,
Why do ye
this? say ye,
The Lord hath
need of him;
and straight-
way [2]he will
send him [3]back
4 hither. And
they went a-
way, and found
a colt tied at
the door with-
out in the open
street; and
they loose
5 him. And cer-
tain of them
that stood
there said unto
them, What do
ye, loosing the
6 colt? And they
said unto them
even as Jesus
had said: and

Matt. 21:1–11, 14–17

unto Jerusa-
lem, and came
unto Beth-
phage, unto
the mount of
Olives, then
Jesus sent two
2 disciples, say-
ing unto them,
Go into the
village that is
over against
you, and
straightway ye
shall find an
ass tied, and a
colt with her:
loose *them*, and
bring *them* un-
to me.

3 And if
any one say
aught unto
you, ye shall
say, The Lord
hath need of
them; and
straightway he
will send them.
6 And the disci-
ples went, and
did even as Je-
sus appointed
them,

Luke 19:29–44

he drew nigh
unto Beth-
phage and
Bethany, at
the mount
that is called
the mount of
Olives, he sent
two of the dis-
ciples, saying,
30 Go your way
into the village
over against
you; in the
which as ye
enter ye shall
find a colt tied,
whereon no
man ever yet
sat: loose him,
and bring him.
31 And if any one
ask you, Why
do ye loose
him? thus shall
ye say, The
Lord hath
need of him.
32 And they that
were sent went
away, and
found even as
he had said un-
33 to them. And
as they were
loosing the
colt, the own-
ers thereof said
unto them,
Why loose ye
34 the colt? And
they said, The
Lord hath
need of him.
35 And they
brought him

John 12:12–19

12 On the mor-
row [8]a great
multitude that
had come to
the feast, when
they heard
that Jesus was
coming to Je-
rusalem, took
13 the branches
of the palm
trees, and went
forth to meet

Mark 11:1–11

they let them
7 go. And they
bring the colt
unto Jesus,and
cast on him
their gar-
ments; and he
sat upon him.

8 And many
spread their
garments upon
the way; and
others branch-
es, which they
had cut from
9 the fields. And
they that went
before, and
they that fol-
lowed, cried,
Hosanna, Bles-
sed *is* he that
cometh in the
name of the
Lord [*see Ps.
118: 25–26*]:

Matt. 21:1–11, 14 to 17

7 and
brought the
ass and the
colt, and put
on them their
garments, and
he sat thereon.
4 Now this is
come to pass,
that it might
be fulfilled
which was spo-
ken [1]by the
prophet [*see
Isa. 62:11;
Zech. 9:9*], say-
ing:
5 Tell ye the
daughter
of Zion,
Behold, thy
King,
cometh
unto thee
Meek, and
riding up-
on an ass
And upon a
colt the
foal of an
ass.
8 And the most
part of the
multitude
spread their
garments in
the way; and
others cut
branches from
the trees, and
spread them
in the way.
9 And the mul-
titudes that
went before
him, and that
followed, cried,
saying, Ho-
sanna to the

Luke 19:29–44

to Jesus: and
they threw
their garments
upon the colt,
and set Jesus
thereon.

36 And as he
went, they
spread their
garments in
37 the way. And
as he was now
drawing nigh,
even at the de-
scent of the
mount of
Olives the
whole multi-
tude of the dis-
ciples began to
rejoice and
praise God
with a loud
voice for all

John 12:12–19

him, and cried
out, Hosanna:
Blessed *is* he
that cometh in
the name of
the Lord, even
the King of
14 Israel. And
Jesus, having
found a young
ass, sat there-
on; as it is
15 written, Fear
not, daughter
of Zion:behold
thy King com-
eth, sitting on
an ass's colt.
16 These things
understood not
his disciples at
the first: but
when Jesus
was glorified,
then remem-
bered they
that these
things were
written of him,
and that they
had done these
things unto
17 him. The mul-
titude there-
fore that was
with him when
he called Laz-
arus out of the
tomb, and
raised him
from the dead
bare witness.
18 For this cause
also the multi-
tude went and
met him, for
thattheyheard
that he had
done this sign.

Mark 11:1-11

10 Blessed *is* the
kingdom that
cometh, *the
kingdom* of our
father David:
Hosanna in
the highest.

Matt. 21:1-11, 14-17

son of David:
Blessed *is* he
that cometh in
the name of
the Lord; Ho-
sanna in the
highest.

Luke 19:29-44

the [5]mighty
works which
they had seen;
38 saying, Bles-
sed *is* the King
that cometh in
the name of
the Lord:
peace in heav-
en, and glory
in the highest.
39 And some of the Pharisees from
the multitude said unto him,
40 [6]Master, rebuke thy disciples. And
he answered and said, I tell you
that, if these shall hold their peace,
the stones will cry out.
41 And when he drew nigh, he
saw the city and wept over it,
42 saying, [7]If thou hadst known in
this day, even thou, the things
which belong unto peace! but now
43 they are hid from thine eyes. For
the days shall come upon thee,
when thine enemies shall cast up
a [8]bank about thee, and compass
44 thee round, and keep thee in on
every side, and shall dash thee to
the ground, and thy children
within thee; and they shall not
leave in thee one stone upon
another; because thou knewest
not the time of thy visitation [*see
Ps. 139:9*].

John 12:12-19

19 The Phar-
isees therefore
said among
themselves,
[10]Behold how
ye prevail
nothing: lo, the
world is gone
after him.

Mark 11:1-11

11 And he entered into Jerusalem,

into the temple;

Matt. 21:1-11, 14-17

10 And when he was come into Je-
rusalem, all the city was stirred,
11 saying, Who is this? And the
multitudes said, This is the
prophet, Jesus, from Nazareth
14 of Galilee. And the blind and
the lame came to him in the
temple: and he healed them.
15 But when the chief priests and
the scribes saw the wonderful
things that he did, and the chil-
dren that were crying in the
temple and saying, Hosanna to

Mark 11:1–11

and when
he had looked round about upon
all things, it being now eventide,
he went out unto Bethany with
the twelve.

Matt. 21:1–11,14–17

the son of David; they were
16 moved with indignation, and
said unto him, Hearest thou
what these are saying? And
Jesus saith unto them, Yea: did
ye never read [*see Ps. 8:2*], Out of the
mouth of babes and sucklings thou
17 hast perfected praise? And he
left them, and went forth out of
the city to Bethany, and lodged
there.

[1] Or, *through*. [2] Gr. *sendeth*. [3] Or, *again*. [4] Gr. *layers of leaves*. [5] Gr. *powers*. [6] Or, *Teacher*. [7] Or, *O that thou hadst known*. [8] Gr. *palisade*. [9] Some ancient authorities read *the common people*. [10] Or, *Ye behold*.

§ 129. THE BARREN FIG TREE CURSED, AND THE SECOND * CLEANSING OF THE TEMPLE. (COMP. § 31)

Bethany and Jerusalem (*Monday*). A Day of Messianic Power

Mark 11:12–18

12 And on the morrow, when they were
come out from Bethany, he hungered.
13 And seeing a fig tree
afar off having leaves,
he came, if haply he
might find anything
thereon: and when
he came to it, he
found nothing but
leaves; for it was not
the season of figs.
14 And he answered and
said unto it, No man
eat fruit from thee
henceforward for
ever. And his disciples heard it.
15 And they come to
Jerusalem: and he
entered into the temple, and began to

Matt. 21:18, 19, 12, 13

18 Now in the morning as he returned to
the city, he hungered.
19 And seeing a [1]fig tree
by the way side,

he came to it
and found nothing
thereon, but leaves
only;
and he saith
unto it, Let there be
no fruit from thee
henceforward for
ever.
12 And Jesus entered
into the temple [2]of
God, and cast out all
them that sold and

Luke 19:45–48

45 And he entered into the temple, and
began to cast out
them that sold,

* Once more at the close of the Ministry in Jerusalem, as at the beginning, Jesus asserts his authority over the Temple as the Messiah. In both instances his authority is sharply challenged by the Jewish rulers.

Mark 11:12–18

cast out them that
sold and them that
bought in the temple,
and overthrew the
tables of the money-
changers, and the
seats of them that
16 sold the doves; and
he would not suffer
that any man should
carry a vessel through
17 the temple. And he
taught, and said un-
to them, Is it not
written, My house
shall be called a house
of prayer for all the
nations? but ye have
made it a den of
18 robbers. And the
chief priests and the
scribes heard it, and
sought how they
might destroy him:
for they feared him,
for all the multitude
was astonished at his
teaching.

Matt. 21:18, 19, 12, 13

bought in the temple,
and overthrew the
tables of the money-
changers, and the
seats of them that
sold the doves;
13 and he saith unto
them, It is written,
My house shall be
called a house of
prayer: but ye make
it a den of robbers.

Luke 19:45–48

46 say-
ing unto them, It is
written [*see Isa. 56:7; Jer. 7:11*], And my
house shall be a house
of prayer: but ye
have made it a den
of robbers.
47 And he was teach-
ing daily in the tem-
ple. But the chief
priests and the
scribes and the prin-
cipal men of the peo-
ple sought to destroy
48 him: and they could
not find what they
might do; for the
people all hung upon
him, listening.

[1] Or, *a single*. [2] Some ancient authorities omit *of God*.

§ 130. THE DESIRE OF SOME GREEKS TO SEE JESUS PUZZLES THE DISCIPLES AND LEADS JESUS IN AGITATION OF SOUL TO INTERPRET LIFE AND DEATH AS SACRIFICE AND TO SHOW HOW BY BEING "LIFTED UP" HE WILL DRAW ALL MEN TO HIM

Jerusalem (*Monday*)

John 12:20–50

20 Now there were certain Greeks among those that went up to worship
21 at the feast: these therefore came to Philip, which was of Bethsaida of
22 Galilee, and asked him saying, Sir, we would see Jesus. Philip cometh
and telleth Andrew: Andrew cometh, and Philip, and they tell Jesus.

John 12:20-50

23 And Jesus answereth them, saying, The hour is come, that the Son of
24 man should be glorified. Verily, verily, I say unto you, Except a grain
of wheat fall into the earth and die, it abideth by itself alone; but if it
25 die, it beareth much fruit. He that loveth his [1]life loseth it; and he that
26 hateth his [1]life in this world shall keep it unto life eternal. If any man
serve me, let him follow me; and where I am, there shall also my servant
27 be: if any man serve me, him will the Father honour. Now is my soul
troubled; and what shall I say [*see Ps. 42:6*]? Father, save me from this
[2]hour. But for this cause came I unto this hour. Father, glorify thy
28 name. There came therefore a voice out of heaven, *saying*, I have both
29 glorified it, and will glorify it again. The multitude therefore, that stood
by, and heard it, said that it had thundered: others said, An angel hath
30 spoken to him. Jesus answered and said, This voice hath not come for
31 my sake, but for your sakes. Now is [3]the judgement of this world: now
32 shall the prince of this world be cast out. And I, If I be lifted up [4]from
33 the earth, will draw all men unto myself. But this he said, signifying by
34 what manner of death he should die. The multitude therefore answered
him, We have heard out of the law that the Christ abideth for ever: and
how sayest thou, The Son of man must be lifted up? who is this Son of
35 man? Jesus therefore said unto them, Yet a little while is the light
[5]among you. Walk while ye have the light, that darkness overtake you
not: and he that walketh in the darkness knoweth not whither he goeth.
36 While ye have the light, believe on the light, that ye may become sons of
light.

These things spake Jesus, and he departed and [6]hid himself from them.
37 But though he had done so many signs before them, yet they believed
38 not* on him: that the word of Isaiah the prophet might be fulfilled [*see
Isa. 53:1*], which he spake,

Lord, who hath believed our report?
And to whom hath the arm of the Lord been revealed?

39 For this cause they could not believe, for that Isaiah said again,
40 He hath blinded their eyes, and he hardened their heart;
Lest they should see with their eyes, and perceive with their heart,
And should turn,
And I should heal them.

41 These things said Isaiah [*see Isa. 6: 1, 10*], because he saw his glory: and he
42 spake of him. Nevertheless even of the rulers many believed on him;
but because of the Pharisees they did not confess [7]*it*, lest they should be
43 put out of the synagogue; for they loved the glory of men more than the
glory of God.

44 And Jesus cried and said, He that believeth on me, believeth not on
45 me, but on him that sent me. And he that beholdeth me beholdeth
46 him that sent me. I am come a light into the world, that whosoever
47 believeth on me may not abide in the darkness. And if any man hear
my sayings, and keep them not, I judge him not: for I came not to judge
48 the world, but to save the world. He that rejecteth me, and receiveth
not my sayings, hath one that judgeth him: the word that I spake, the
49 same shall judge him in the last day. For I spake not from myself; but

* The rejection of Jesus by the Jews is clearly set forth by John's Gospel The Pharisees made many timid and afraid.

John 12:20–50

the Father which sent me, he hath given me a commandment, what I
50 should say, and what I should speak. And I know that his commandment is life eternal: the things therefore which I speak, even as the Father hath said unto me, so I speak.

[1] Or, *soul.* [2] Or, *hour?* [3] Or, *a judgement.* [4] Or, *out of.* [5] Or, *in.* [6] Or, *was hidden from them.* [7] Or, *him.*

§ 131. THE BARREN FIG TREE FOUND TO HAVE WITHERED

On the way from Bethany to Jerusalem. (*Tuesday**)

Mark 11:19–25

19 And [1]every evening [2]he went forth
20 out of the city. And as they passed by in the morning, they saw the fig tree withered away from
21 the roots. And Peter calling to remembrance saith unto him, Rabbi, behold, the fig tree which thou cursedst is with-
22 ered away. And Jesus answering saith unto them, Have
23 faith in God. Verily I say unto you, Whosoever shall say unto this mountain, Be thou taken up and cast into the sea; and shall not doubt in his heart, but shall believe that what he saith cometh to pass; he shall have it.
24 Therefore I say unto you, All things whatsoever ye pray and ask for, believe that ye have received them, and ye shall have them.
25 And whensoever ye stand praying, forgive, if ye have aught against any one; that your Father also which is in heaven may forgive you your trespasses.[3]

Matt. 21:19–22

19 And immediately the fig tree withered
20 away. And when the disciples saw it, they marvelled, saying, How did the fig tree immediately
21 wither away? And Jesus answered and said unto them, Verily I say unto you, If ye have faith, and doubt not, ye shall not only do what is done to the fig tree, but even if ye shall say unto this mountain, Be thou taken up and cast into the sea, it shall be done.
22 And all things, whatsoever ye shall ask in prayer, believing, ye shall receive.

Luke 21:37, 38

37 And every day he was teaching in the temple; and every night he went out, and lodged in the mount that is called *the mount* of Olives.
38 And all the people came early in the morning to him in the temple, to hear him.

[1] Gr. *whenever evening came.* [2] Some ancient authorities read *they.* [3] Many ancient authorities add ver. 26 *But if ye do not forgive, neither will your Father which is in heaven forgive your trespasses.*

* The Synoptic Gospels give more details of the teaching of Jesus on this Tuesday in the Temple and on the Mount of Olives than for any other single day. We had another Busy Day in Galilee (§§ 61–66).

§ 132. THE RULERS (SANHEDRIN) FORMALLY CHALLENGE* THE AUTHORITY OF JESUS AS AN ACCREDITED TEACHER (RABBI)

Jesus bases His human authority on John the Baptist, His Forerunner who baptized him, and demands the Sanhedrin's opinion of the Baptism of John. This pertinent counter-question paralyzes the Jewish leaders and Jesus drives His argument home by three parables. (a) Parable of the Two Sons. (b) Parable of the Wicked Husbandmen. (c) Parable of the Marriage Feast of the King's Son.

In the court of the Temple. (*Tuesday*†) A Day of Controversy

Mark 11:27–12:12	Matt. 21:23–22:14	Luke 20:1–19
27 And they come		1 And it came to
again to Jerusalem:		pass, on one of the
and as he was walking	23 And when he was	days, as he was teach-
in the temple, there	come into the temple,	ing the people in the
come to him the	the chief priests and	temple, and preaching
chief priests, and the	the elders of the peo-	the gospel, there came
scribes, and the	ple came unto him	upon him the chief
28 elders; and they said	as he was teaching,	priests and the scribes
unto him,	and said,	2 with the elders; and
		they spake, saying
	By	unto him, Tell us: By
By what authority	what authority doest	what authority doest
doest thou these	thou these things?	thou these things? or
things? or who gave	and who gave thee	who is he that gave
thee this authority	24 this authority? And	thee this authority?
to do these things?	Jesus answered and	3 And he answered and
29 And Jesus said unto	said unto them, I	said unto them, I also
them, I will ask of	also will ask you one	will ask you a [1]ques-
you one [1]question,	[1]question, which if	tion; and tell me:
and answer me, and	ye tell me, I likewise	4 The baptism of John,
I will tell you by	will tell you by what	was it from heaven,
what authority I do	authority I do these	or from men?
30 these things. The	25 things. The baptism	
baptism of John, was	of John, whence was	
it from heaven, or	it? from heaven or	
from men? answer me.	from men? And they	5 And they rea-
31 And they reasoned	reasoned with them-	soned with them-

* It was very common to test a Rabbi with hard questions. See this continued in the following sections. In like manner the Fourth Gospel gave us much animated dialogue between Jesus and the Jews at Jerusalem in chap. 5, and chap. 7–10. The Sanhedrin were within their rights in challenging the ecclesiastical and scholastic (scribal) standing of Jesus. He did not dodge in his answer.

† On this last day of Christ's public ministry the Sanhedrin seek to break the power of Jesus with the people whose hero he is since the Triumphal Entry. The first attempt fails miserably, but it is followed by a series of other efforts to entrap Jesus and so turn the crowd against him. The three parables leave the rulers exposed by Jesus and they keenly feel the denunciation of the reply of Jesus.

Mark 11:27–12:12

with themselves, say-
ing, If we shall say,
From heaven; he will
say, Why then did
ye not believe him?
32 [7]But should we say,
From men—they
feared the people: [8]for
all verily held John
33 to be a prophet. And
they answered Jesus
and said, We know
not. And Jesus saith
unto them, Neither
tell I you by what
authority I do these
things.

Matt. 21:23–22:14

selves, saying, If we
shall say, From heav-
en; he will say unto
us, Why then did ye
26 not believe him? But
if we shall say, From
men; we fear the
multitude; for all hold
John as a prophet.
27 And they answered
Jesus, and said, We
know not.
He also said unto
them, Neither tell I
you by what author-
ity I do these things.
28 But what think ye?
A man had two sons;
And he came to the
first, and said, [9]Son,
go work to-day in the
29 vineyard. And he
answered and said, I
will not: but after-
ward he repented
himself, and went.
30 And he came to the
second, and said like-
wise. And he an-
swered and said, I *go*,
sir: and went not.
31 Whether of the twain
did the will of his
father? They say,
The first. Jesus saith
unto them, Verily I
say unto you, that
the publicans and the
harlots go into the
kingdom of God be-
32 fore you. For John
came unto you in the
way of righteousness,
and ye believed him
not: but the publicans
and the harlots be-
lieved him: and ye,
when ye saw it, did
not even repent your-

Luke 20:1–19

selves, saying, If we
shall say, From
heaven; he will say,
Why did ye not be-
6 lieve him? But if
we shall say, From
men; all the people
will stone us: for
they be persuaded
that John was a
7 prophet. And they
answered, that they
knew not whence *it*
8 *was*. And Jesus said
unto them, Neither
tell I you by what
authority I do these
things.

Mark 11:27–12:12

1 And he began to
speak unto them in
parables. A man
planted a vineyard,
and set a hedge
about it, and digged
a pit for the wine-
press, and built a
tower, and let it out
to husbandmen, and
went into another
country.
2 And at
the season he sent
to the husbandmen
a [9]servant, that he
might receive from
the husbandmen of
the fruits of the vine-
3 yard. And they took
him, and beat him,
and sent him away
4 empty. And again
he sent unto them
another [9]servant: and
him they wounded in
the head, and handled
5 shamefully. And he
sent another; and him
they killed: and many
others; beating some,
6 and killing some. He
had yet one, a beloved
son: he sent him last
unto them, saying,
they will reverence
7 my son. But those
husbandmen said a-
mong themselves,
This is the heir; come,
let us kill him, and
the inheritance shall
be ours.
8 And
they took him, and
killed him, and cast
him forth out of the
9 vineyard. What

Matt. 21:23–22:14

selves afterward, that
ye might believe him.
33 Hear another par-
able: There was a
man that was a
householder, which
planted a vineyard,
and set a hedge about
it, and digged a wine-
press in it, and built
a tower, and let it
out to husbandmen,
and went into another
country.
34 And when
the season of the
fruits drew near, he
sent his [3]servants to
the husbandmen, to
receive [4]his fruits.
35 And the husbandmen
took his [3]servants,
and beat one, and
killed another, and
stoned another.
36 Again, he sent other
[3]servants more than
the first: and they did
unto them in like
manner.
37 But
afterward he sent
unto them his son,
saying, They will
reverence my son.
38 But the husbandmen,
when they saw the
son, said among
themselves, This is
the heir; come, let us
kill him and take his
inheritance.
39 And
they took him, and
cast him forth out of
the vineyard, and

Luke 20:1–19

9 And he began to
speak unto the people
this parable [*see Isa. 5:1–2*]: A man plant-
ed a vineyard,
and let it
out to husbandmen,
and went into another
country for a long
10 time. And at the
season he sent unto
the husbandmen a
[9]servant, that they
should give him of the
fruit of the vineyard:
but the husbandmen
beat him, and sent
him away empty.
11 And he sent yet an-
other [9]servant: and
him also they beat,
and handled him
shamefully, and sent
him away empty.
12 And he sent yet a
third: and him also
they wounded, and
13 cast him forth. And
the Lord of the vine-
yard said, What shall
I do? I will send my
beloved son: it may
be they will reverence
him.
14 But when
the husbandmen saw
him, they reasoned
one with another, say-
ing, This is the heir:
let us kill him, that
the inheritance may
15 be ours. And they
cast him forth out of
the vineyard, and
killed him. What

Mark 11:27–12:12	Matt. 21:23–22:14	Luke 20:1–19
therefore will the lord of the vineyard do?	40 killed him. When therefore the lord of the vineyard shall come, what will he do unto those hus-	therefore will the lord of the vineyard do unto them?
he will come and destroy the hus- bandmen, and will give the vineyard unto others.	41 bandmen? They say unto him, He will miserably destroy those miserable men, and will let out the vineyard unto other husbandmen, which shall render him the fruits in their sea-	16 He will come and de- stroy these husband- men, and will give the vineyard unto others. And when they heard it, they said, [10]God forbid.
10 Have ye not read even this scripture; The stone which the builders re- jected, The same was made the head of the corner: 11 This was from the Lord, And it is marvellous in our eyes?	42 sons. Jesus saith unto them, Did ye never read in the scriptures [*see Ps. 118: 22–23*], The stone which the builders re- jected, The same was made the head of the corner: This was from the Lord, And it is marvel- lous in our eyes?	17 But he looked upon them, and said, What then is this that is written [*see Ps. 118: 22*], The stone which the builders re- jected, The same was made the head of the corner?
	43 Therefore say I unto you, the kingdom of God shall be taken away from you, and shall be given to a nation bringing forth the fruits thereof.	
	44 [5]And he that falleth on this stone shall be broken to pieces; but on whomsoever it shall fall, it will scat- 45 ter him as dust. And when the chief priests and the Pharisees heard his parables, they perceived that he spake of them.	18 Every one that falleth on that stone shall be broken to pieces; but on whomsoever it shall fall, it will scat- ter him as dust [*see Isa. 8:14–15*]. 19 And the scribes and the chief priests
12 And they sought to lay hold on him; and they feared the multi-	46 And when they sought to lay hold on him, they feared the	sought to lay hands on him in that very

Mark 11:27–12:12	Matt. 21:23–22:14	Luke 20:1–19
tude; for they perceived that he spake the parable against them: and they left him and went away.	multitudes, because they took him for a prophet.	hour; and they feared the people: for they perceived that he spake this parable against them.

1 And Jesus answered and spake again in parables unto them, saying,
2 The kingdom of heaven is likened unto a certain king, which made a
3 marriage feast for his son, and sent forth his [3]servants to call them that
4 were bidden to the marriage feast: and they would not come. Again he
sent forth other [3]servants, saying, tell them that are bidden, Behold, I
have made ready my dinner: my oxen and my fatlings are killed, and all
5 things are ready; come to the marriage feast. But they made light of it,
and went their ways, one to his own farm, another to his merchandise:
6 and the rest laid hold on his [3]servants, and entreated them shamefully,
7 and killed them. But the king was wroth; and he sent his armies, and
8 destroyed those murderers, and burned their city. Then saith he to his
[3]servants, The wedding is ready, but they that were bidden were not
9 worthy. Go ye therefore unto the partings of the highways, and as many
10 as ye shall find, bid to the marriage feast. And those [3]servants went out
into the highways, and gathered together all as many as they found, both
11 bad and good: and the wedding was filled with guests. But when the king
came in to behold the guests, he saw there a man which had not on a
12 wedding-garment; and he saith unto him, Friend, how camest thou in
hither not having a wedding-garment? And he was speechless. Then
13 the king said to the [6]servants, Bind him hand and foot, and cast him out
into the outer darkness; there shall be the weeping and gnashing of teeth.
14 For many are called, but few chosen.

[1] Gr. *word.* [2] Gr. *Child.* [3] Gr. *bond-servants.* [4] Or, *the fruits of it.* [5] Some ancient authorities omit ver. 44. [6] Or, *ministers.* [7] Or, *But shall we say, From men?* [8] Or, *for all held John to be a prophet indeed.* [9] Gr. *bond-servant.* [10] Gr. *Be it not so.*

§133. THE PHARISEES AND THE HERODIANS TRY TO ENSNARE JESUS ABOUT PAYING TRIBUTE TO CÆSAR

Mark 12:13–17	Matt. 22:15–22	Luke 20:20–26
13 And they send unto him certain of the Pharisees and of the Herodians, that they might catch him in talk. 14 And when they were come, they say	15 Then went the Pharisees, and took counsel how they might ensnare him in *his* 16 talk. And they send to him their disciples*, with the Hero-	20 And they watched him, and sent forth spies, which feigned themselves to be righteous, that they might take hold of his speech, so as to deliver him up to the rule and to the au-

* The Pharisees send a group of their keenest students to go with the Herodians to catch Jesus with the dilemma about paying tribute to Cæsar, a live question in current politics and theology. They offered Jesus the alternative of popular disfavor or of disloyalty to the Roman government.

Mark 12:13–17

unto him, [1]Master,
we know that thou
art true, and carest
not for any one; for
thou regardest not
the person of men,
but of a truth teach-
est the way of God:
Is it lawful to give
tribute unto Cæsar,
or not? Shall we
give, or shall we not
15 give? But he, know-
ing their hypocrisy,
said unto them, Why
tempt ye me? bring
me a [2]penny, that I
16 may see it. And
they brought it. And
he saith unto them,
Whose is this image
and superscription?
And they said unto
17 him, Cæsar's. And
Jesus said unto them,
Render unto Cæsar
the things that are
Cæsar's, and unto
God the things that
are God's.
And
they marvelled great-
ly at him.

Matt. 22:15–22

dians, saying, [1]Mas-
ter, we know that
thou art true, and
teachest the way of
God in truth, and
carest not for any
one: for thou regard-
est not the person of
17 men. Tell us there-
fore, What thinkest
thou? Is it lawful to
give tribute unto
18 Cæsar, or not? But
Jesus perceived their
wickedness, and said,
Why tempt ye me,
19 ye hypocrites? Shew
me the tribute
money. And they
brought unto him a
20 [2]penny. And he saith
unto them, Whose is
this image and super-
21 scription? They say
unto him, Cæsar's.
Then saith he unto
them, Render there-
fore unto Cæsar the
things that are
Cæsar's; and unto God
the things that are
God's.
22 And
when they heard it,
they marvelled, and
left him, and went
their way.

Luke 20:20–26

thority of the gov-
21 ernor. And they
asked him, saying,
[1]Master, we know
that thou sayest and
teachest rightly, and
acceptest not the per-
son *of any*, but of a
truth teachest the
22 way of God [*see John 3:2*]: Is it lawful for
us to give tribute
unto Cæsar, or not?
23 But he per-
ceived their crafti-
ness, and said unto
24 them, Shew me a
[2]penny.
Whose image
and superscription
hath it? And they
25 said, Cæsar's. And
he said unto them,
Then render unto
Cæsar the things that
are Cæsar's, and unto
God the things that
26 are God's. And they
were not able to take
hold of the saying be-
fore the people: and
they marvelled at his
answer, and held their
peace.

[1] Or, *Teacher*. [2] See marginal note on Matt. 18:28.

§ 134. THE SADDUCEES ASK HIM A PUZZLING QUESTION* ABOUT THE RESURRECTION

In the Court of the Temple. (*Tuesday*)

Mark 12:18–27

18 And there come
unto him Sadducees,
which say that there

Matt. 22:23–33

23 On that day there
came to him Saddu-
cees, [1]which say that

Luke 20:27–40

27 And there came to
him certain of the
Sadducees, they

* Probably a stock conundrum that the Sadducees had often propounded to the discomfort of the Pharisees.

Mark 12:18–27

is no resurrection;
and they asked him,
19 saying, [2]Master,
Moses wrote unto us,
If a man's brother
die, and leave a wife
behind him, and
leave no child, that
his brother should
take his wife, and
raise up seed unto
20 his brother. There
were seven brethren:
and the first took a
wife, and dying left
21 no seed; and the sec-
ond took her, and
died, leaving no seed
behind him; and the
22 third likewise: and
the seven left no
seed. Last of all the
woman also died.
23 In the resurrection
whose wife shall she
be of them? for the
seven had her to
24 wife. Jesus said un-
to them, Is it not for
this cause that ye
err, that ye know
not the [4]scriptures,
nor the power of
God?
25 For when they
shall rise from the
dead, they neither
marry, nor are given
in marriage; but are
as angels in heaven.

Matt. 22:23–33

there is no resurrec-
24 tion: and they asked
him, saying, [2]Master,
Moses said, If a man
die, having no chil-
dren, his brother
[3]shall marry his wife,
and raise up seed un-
to his brother.
25 Now
there were with us
seven brethren: and
the first married and
deceased, and having
no seed left his wife
26 unto his brother: in
like manner the sec-
ond also, and the
third, unto the [4]sev-
27 enth. And after them
all the woman died.
28 In the resurrection
therefore whose wife
shall she be of the
seven? for they all
29 had her. But Jesus
answered and said
unto them, Ye do
err, not knowing the
scriptures, nor the
power of God.
30 For in the resurrec-
tion they neither
marry, nor are given
in marriage, but are
as angels [5]in heaven.

Luke 20:27–40

which say that there
is no resurrection;
and they asked him,
28 saying, [2]Master,
Moses wrote unto us
[*see Gen. 38:8; Deut. 25:5–6*], that if a
man's brother die,
having a wife, and
he be childless, his
brother should take
the wife, and raise
up seed unto his
29 brother. There were
therefore seven breth-
ren; and the first
30 took a wife, and died
childless, and the
31 second; and the third
took her; and like-
wise the seven also
left no children; and
died.
32 Afterward
the woman also died.
33 In the resurrection
therefore whose wife
of them shall she be?
for the seven had her
34 to wife. And Jesus
said unto them,
The
sons of this [6]world
marry, and are given
35 in marriage: but they
that are accounted
worthy to attain to
that [6]world, and the
resurrection from the
dead, neither marry,
nor are given in mar-
36 riage: for neither can
they die any more:
for they are equal un-
to the angels; and
are sons of God, being
sons of the resurrec-

Mark 12:18–27

26 But as touching the dead, that they are raised; have ye not read in the book of Moses, in *the place concerning* the Bush, how God spake unto him, saying, I *am* the God of Abraham, and the God of Isaac, and the God of Jacob?
27 He is not the God of the dead, but of the living: ye do greatly err.

Matt. 22:23–33

31 But as touching the resurrection of the dead, have ye not read that which was spoken unto you by God, saying,
32 I am the God of Abraham, and the God of Isaac, and the God of Jacob? God is not *the God* of the dead, but of the
33 living. And when the multitudes heard it, they were astonished at his teaching.

Luke 20:27–40

37 tion. But that the dead are raised, even Moses showed in *the place concerning* the Bush, when he calleth the Lord the God of Abraham, and the God of Isaac, and the
38 God of Jacob [*see Ex. 3:6*]. Now he is not the God of the dead, but of the living: for all live unto him.
39 And certain of the scribes answering said, [2]Master, thou
40 hast well said. For they durst not any more ask him any question.

[1] Gr. *saying*. [2] Or, *Teacher*. [3] Gr. *shall perform the duty of a husband's brother to his wife*. Compare Deut. 25:5. [4] Gr. *seven*. [5] Many ancient authorities add *of God*. [6] Or, *age*.

§ 135. THE PHARISEES REJOICE OVER THE ROUT OF THE SADDUCEES AND A PHARISAIC LAWYER ASKS JESUS A LEGAL QUESTION

In the Court of the Temple. (*Tuesday*)

Mark 12:28–34

28 And one of the scribes came, and heard them questioning together, and knowing that he had answered them well, asked him, What commandment is the first of all
29 [*see Deut. 6:4*]? Jesus answered, The first is, Hear, O Israel; [3]The Lord our God [*see Deut. 6:4*], the
30 Lord is one: and thou shalt love the Lord thy God [4]with all thy heart, and [4]with all thy soul, and [4]with all thy mind, and [4]with all
31 thy strength [*see Deut. 6:5*]. The second is this, Thou shalt love thy neighbour as thyself [*see Lev.*

Matt. 22:34–40

34 But the Pharisees, when they heard that he had put the Sadducees to silence, gathered them-
35 selves together. And one of them, a lawyer, asked him a question,
36 tempting him, [1]Master, which is the great commandment in the law? And he said unto him,
37 Thou shalt love the Lord thy God with all thy heart, and with all thy soul,
38 and with all thy mind. This is the great and first commandment.
39 [2]And a second like *unto it* is this, Thou shalt love thy neighbour as

Mark 12:28–34

19:18]. There is none other com-
mandment greater than these.
32 And the scribe said unto him,
Of a truth, [1]Master, thou hast
well said that he is one; and there
is none other but he: and to
33 love him with all the heart, and
with all the understanding, and
with all the strength, and to love
his neighbour as himself, is much
more than all whole burnt offer-
ings and sacrifices [*see 1 Sam. 15:*
34 *22*]. And when Jesus saw that
he answered discreetly, he said
unto him, Thou art not far from
the kingdom of God. And no
man after that durst ask him any
question.

Matt. 22:34–40

40 thyself. On these two command-
ments hangeth the whole law,
and the prophets.

[1] Or, *Teacher.* [2] Or, *And a second is like unto it, Thou shalt love, etc.* [3] Or, *The Lord is our God: the Lord is one.* [4] Gr. *from.*

§ 136. JESUS, TO THE JOY OF THE MULTITUDE, SILENCES HIS ENEMIES BY THE PERTINENT QUESTION OF THE MESSIAH'S DESCENT FROM DAVID AND LORDSHIP OVER DAVID

In the Court of the Temple. (*Tuesday*)

Mark 12:35–37

35 And Jesus answer-
ed and said, as he
taught in the temple,
How say the scribes
that the Christ is
the son of David?
36 David himself said
in the Holy Spirit,
[*see Ps. 110:1*],
The Lord said unto
my Lord,
Sit thou on my
right hand,
Till I make thine
enemies [1]the foot-
stool of thy feet.

Matt. 22:41–46

41 Now while the
Pharisees were gath-
ered together, Jesus
asked them a ques-
42 tion, saying, What
think ye of the
Christ? whose son is
he? They say unto
him, *The son* of David.
43 He saith unto them,
How then doth David
in the Spirit call him
Lord, saying,
44 The Lord said unto
my Lord,
Sit thou on my
right hand,
Till I put thine
enemies under-
neath thy feet?

Luke 20:41–44

41 And he said unto
them,
How say they
that the Christ is
David's son?
42 For Da-
vid himself saith in
the book of Psalms,
The Lord said unto
my Lord,
Sit thou on my
right hand,
43 Till I make thine
enemies the foot-
stool of thy feet.

Mark 12:35–37

37 David himself calleth him Lord; and whence is he his son?
And [2]the common people heard him gladly.

Matt. 22:41–46

45 If David then calleth him Lord, how is he
46 his son? And no one was able to answer him a word, neither durst any man from that day forth ask him any more questions.

Luke 20:41–44

44 David therefore calleth him Lord, and how is he his son?

[1] Some ancient authorities read, *underneath thy feet*. [2] Or, *the great multitude*.

§ 137. IN HIS LAST PUBLIC DISCOURSE, JESUS SOLEMNLY DENOUNCES* THE SCRIBES AND PHARISEES (COMP. § 107)

In the Court of the Temple. (*Tuesday*)

Mark 12:38–40

38 And in his teaching he said, Beware of the scribes,

which desire to walk in long

Matt. 23:1–39

1 Then spake Jesus to the multitudes and to his disciples,
2 saying, The scribes and the Pharisees sit on Moses' seat: all
3 things therefore whatsoever they bid you, *these* do and observe: but do not ye after their works; for they say, and do not.
4 Yea, they bind heavy burdens [1]and grievous to be borne, and lay them on men's shoulders; but they themselves will not move them with their finger.
5 But all their works they do for to be seen of men [*see Ex. 13: 9; Num. 13; 38–39; Deut. 6:8; 11:18*]: for they make broad their phylacteries, and enlarge the borders *of their garments*,

Luke 20:45–47

45 And in the hearing of all the people he said unto his disci-
46 ples, Beware of the scribes,

which desire to walk in long robes,

* Jesus has been criticized for lack of self-control in this exposure of the hypocrisy of the Pharisees. One must bear in mind the tremendous sins of which the Pharisees are guilty. The very teachers of righteousness are now in the act of rejecting and finally crucifying the Son of God. See my book, *The Pharisees and Jesus*, for full discussion.

Mark 12:38–40

robes, and *to have*
salutations in the
39 marketplaces, and
chief seats in the
synagogues, and chief
places at feasts:

40 they which devour
widows' houses, [12]and
for a pretence make
long prayers; these
shall receive greater
condemnation.

Matt. 23:1–39

6 and love the chief
place at feasts, and
the chief seats in the
7 synagogues, and the
salutations in the
marketplaces, and to
be called of men,
8 Rabbi. But be not
ye called Rabbi: for
one is your teacher,
and all ye are breth-
9 ren. And call no
man your father on
the earth: for one is
your Father, [2]which
10 is in heaven. Neither
be ye called masters:
for one is your
master, *even* the
11 Christ. But he that
is [3]greatest among
you shall be your
12 [4]servant. And who-
soever shall exalt
himself shall be hum-
bled; and whosoever
shall humble himself
shall be exalted.
13 But woe unto you,
scribes and Pharisees,
hypocrites! because
ye shut the king-
dom of heaven
[5]against men: for ye
enter not in your-
selves, neither suffer
ye them that are en-
tering in to enter.[6]

Luke 20:45–47

and love salutations
in the marketplaces,
and chief seats in the
synagogues, and chief
places at feasts;

47 which de-
vour widows' houses,
and for a pretence
make long prayers:
these shall receive
greater condemna-
tion.

15 Woe unto you, scribes and Pharisees, hypo-
crites! for ye compass sea and land to make one
proselyte; and when he is become so, ye make
him twofold more a son of [7]hell than yourselves.

Matt. 23:1–39

16 Woe unto you, ye blind guides, which say, Whosoever shall swear by
the [8]temple, it is nothing; but whosoever shall swear by the gold of the
17 [8]temple he is [9]a debtor. Ye fools and blind: for whether is greater, the
18 gold, or the [8]temple that hath sanctified the gold? And, Whosoever
shall swear by the altar, it is nothing; but whosoever shall swear by the
19 gift that is upon it, he is [9]a debtor. Ye blind: for whether is greater, the
20 gift, or the altar that sanctified the gift? He therefore that sweareth
21 by the altar, sweareth by it, and by all things thereon. And he that
sweareth by the [8]temple, sweareth by it, and by him that dwelleth therein.
22 And he that sweareth by the heaven, sweareth by the throne of God, and
by him that sitteth thereon.
23 Woe unto you, scribes and Pharisees, hypocrites! for ye tithe mint and
[10]anise and cummin [*see Lev. 27:30; Mic. 6:8*], and have left undone the
weightier matters of the law, judgement, and mercy, and faith: but these
24 ye ought to have done, and not to have left the other undone. Ye blind
guides, which strain out the gnat, and swallow the camel.
25 Woe unto you, scribes and Pharisees, hypocrites! for ye cleanse the
outside of the cup and of the platter, but within they are full from ex-
26 tortion and excess. Thou blind Pharisee, cleanse first the inside of the
cup and of the platter, that the outside thereof may become clean also.
27 Woe unto you, scribes and Pharisees, hypocrites! for ye are like unto
whited sepulchres, which outwardly appear beautiful, but inwardly are
28 full of dead men's bones, and of all uncleanness. Even so ye also out-
wardly appear righteous unto men, but inwardly ye are full of hypocrisy
and iniquity.
29 Woe unto you, scribes and Pharisees, hypocrites! for ye build the
sepulchres of the prophets, and garnish the tombs of the righteous, and
30 say, If we had been in the days of our fathers, we should not have been
31 partakers with them in the blood of the prophets. Wherefore ye witness
32, 33 to yourselves, that ye are sons of them that slew the prophets. Fill ye
up then the measure of your fathers. Ye serpents, ye offspring of vipers,
34 how shall ye escape the judgement of [7]hell? Therefore, behold, I send
unto you prophets, and wise men, and scribes: some of them shall ye kill
and crucify: and some of them shall ye scourge in your synagogues, and
35 persecute from city to city: that upon you may come all the righteous
blood shed on the earth, from the blood of Abel the righteous unto the
blood of Zachariah son of Barachiah, whom ye slew between the sanctuary
36 and the altar [*see Gen. 4:8; 2 Chron. 24: 20–21*]. Verily I say unto you, All
these things shall come upon this generation.
37 O Jerusalem, Jerusalem, which killeth the prophets, and stoneth them
that are sent unto her! how often would I have gathered thy children
together, even as a hen gathereth her chickens under her wings, and ye
38 would not! Behold, your house is left unto you [11]desolate [*see Jer. 12:7;*
39 *22:5*]. For I say unto you, Ye shall not see me henceforth, till ye shall
say, blessed *is* he that cometh in the name of the Lord [*see Ps. 118:26*].

[1] Many ancient authorities omit *and grievous to be borne.* [2] Gr. *the heavenly.* [3] Gr. *greater.* [4] Or, *minister.* [5] Gr. *before.* [6] Some authorities insert here or after ver. 12, ver. 14, *Woe unto you, scribes and Pharisees, hypocrites! for ye devour widows' houses, even while for a pretence ye make long prayers; therefore ye shall receive greater condemnation.* See Mark 12:40: Luke 20:47, above. [7] Gr. *Gehenna.* [8] Or, *sanctuary;* as in ver. 35. [9] Or, *bound* by his oath. [10] Or, *dill.* [11] Some ancient authorities omit *desolate.* [12] Or, *even while for a pretence they make.*

§ 138. JESUS CLOSELY OBSERVES* THE CONTRIBUTIONS IN THE TEMPLE, AND COMMENDS THE POOR WIDOW'S GIFT

(*Tuesday*)

Mark 12:41–44

41 And he sat down over against
the treasury, and beheld how the
multitude cast [1]money into the
treasury: and many that were
42 rich cast in much. And there
came [2]a poor widow, and she cast
in two mites, which make a
43 farthing. And he called unto
him his disciples, and said unto
them, Verily I say unto you, This
poor widow cast in more than all
they which are casting into the
44 treasury: for they all did cast in
of their superfluity; but she of
her want did cast in all that she
had, *even* all her living.

Luke 21:1–4

1 And he looked up, [3]and saw the
rich men that were casting their
2 gifts into the treasury. And he
saw a certain poor widow casting
in thither two mites.
3 And he
said, Of a truth I say unto you,
This poor widow cast in more
4 than they all: for all these did
of their superfluity cast in unto
the gifts: but she of her want did
cast in all the living that she had.

[1] Gr. *brass.* [2] Gr. *one.* [3] Or, *and saw them that . . . treasury, and they were rich.*

* Notice that this was the last occurrence in the Saviour's public ministry, except the trial and the crucifixion. This is the last appearance of Jesus in the Temple. His public teaching is over save the words of defence in his trial and the seven sayings on the Cross. The Pharisees and Sadducees had withdrawn in terror at the explosion of the wrath of Jesus and even the disciples were at some distance as Jesus sat alone by the treasury. It is useless further to plead with his enemies. The task now remains to get the disciples prepared for the Master's death and the time is short and they as yet have completely failed to grasp the fact or the significance of his death and the promise of his resurrection on the third day.

PART XII

IN THE SHADOW WITH JESUS

Tuesday afternoon to Thursday night of Passion Week, A.D. *30 (or 29). Jerusalem.*

§§ 139–152. Jesus now seeks to prepare the disciples for the tragedy of His death and for carrying on His work after His departure.

§ 139. SITTING ON THE MOUNT OF OLIVES, JESUS SPEAKS TO HIS DISCIPLES ABOUT THE DESTRUCTION OF JERUSALEM, AND HIS OWN SECOND COMING, IN APOCALYPTIC LANGUAGE. THE GREAT ESCHATOLOGICAL DISCOURSE*

(Tuesday Afternoon)

	Mark 13:1–37	Matt. 24 and 25	Luke 21:5–36
1 Occasion of the Prophecy about the Destruction of the Temple.	1 And as he went forth out of the temple, one of his disciples saith unto him, [18]Master, behold, what manner of stones and what manner of buildings!	1 And Jesus went out from the temple, and was going on his way; and his disciples came to him to shew him the buildings of the temple.	5 And as some spake of the temple, how it was adorned with goodly stones and of-
		2 But he answered and	6 ferings, he said, As for these things which ye behold,
	2 And Jesus said unto him, Seest thou these great build-	said unto them, See ye not all these things? verily	the days will come, in which there shall not be

* This great discourse has as its background the death of Christ. Further on as part punishment for this crime lies the destruction of Jerusalem. This catastrophe is itself a symbol of the end of the world and in one sense a coming of Christ in power and judgment. But Christ boldly predicts his own personal return to earth, though the time is not revealed. But he does exhort an expectant attitude toward the promises of his coming and readiness for his return which will be at an unexpected hour. Jesus employs the common Jewish apocalyptic imagery to portray this most difficult subject. Some scholars insist that Jesus was himself merely a wild enthusiast who was carried away by the Messianic hopes of his people, but that is a one-sided and distorted view of Christ's life and ignores the great mass of his ethical teaching. It forgets also that Jesus has a world program of conquest and of power. The various aspects of the discourse are not kept distinct. Some think that the Gospels have misunderstood or misrepresented Jesus in this discourse. But we can catch the general drift of the teaching and leave alone minute details of time and place against which Jesus himself warned us.

2 Inquiry for Further Light from Peter and James and John and Andrew on Christ's Second Coming and the End of the World.

Mark 13:1–37

ings? there shall not be left here one stone upon another, which shall not be thrown down.
3 And as he sat on the mount of Olives over against the temple, Peter and James and John and Andrew asked him privately,
4 Tell us, when shall these things be? and what *shall be* the sign when these things are all about to be accom-
5 plished? And Jesus began to say unto them, Take heed that no man lead you astray.
6 Many shall come in my name, saying, I am *he;* and shall lead many astray.
7 And when ye shall hear of wars and rumours of wars, be not troubled: *these things* must needs come to pass; but the end is not yet.
8 For nation shall rise against nation,

Matt. 24 and 25

I say unto you, There shall not be left here one stone upon another, that shall not be thrown down.
3 And as he sat on the mount of Olives, the disciples came unto him privately, saying,
Tell us, when shall these things be? and what *shall be* the sign of thy [1]coming, and of [2]the end of the world?
4 And Jesus answered and said unto them, Take heed that no man lead you
5 astray. For many shall come in my name, saying, I am the Christ; and shall lead many astray.
6 And ye shall hear of wars and rumours of wars: see that ye be not troubled: for *these things* must needs come to pass; but the end is not yet.
7 For nation

Luke 21:5–36

left here one stone upon another, that shall not be thrown down.
7 And they asked him, saying, [18]Master, when therefore shall these things be? and what *shall be* the sign when these things are about to come to pass?
8 And he said, Take heed that ye be not led astray: for many shall come in my name, saying, I am *he;* and, The time is at hand: go ye not after them.
9 And when ye shall hear of wars and tumults, be not terrified: for these things must needs come to pass first; but the end is not immediately.
10 Then said he unto them, Nation shall

Mark 13:1–37	Matt. 24 and 25	Luke 21:5–36
and kingdom against kingdom: there shall be earthquakes in divers places; there shall be famines:	shall rise against nation, and kingdom against kingdom: and there shall be famines and earthquakes in divers places.	rise against nation, and kingdom against kingdom: 11 and there shall be great earthquakes, and in divers places famines and pestilences; and there shall be terrors and great signs from heaven.
these things are the beginning of travail [*see Isa. 19:2*].	8 But all these things are the beginning of travail.	12 But before all these things, they shall lay their hands on you, and shall persecute you, delivering you up to the synagogues and prisons, bringing you before kings and governors for my name's 13 sake. It shall turn unto you for a testimony.
9 But take ye heed to yourselves: for they shall deliver you up to councils; and in synagogues shall ye be beaten; and before governors and kings shall ye stand for my sake, for a testimony unto them.	9 Then shall they deliver you up unto tribulation, and shall kill you: and ye shall be hated of all the nations for my name's sake.	
10 And the gospel must first be preached unto all the nations. 11 And when they lead you *to judgement*, and deliver you up, be not anxious beforehand what ye shall speak: but whatsoever		14 Settle it therefore in your hearts, not to meditate beforehand how to 15 answer: for I

Mark 13:1–37

shall be given
you in that
hour, that
speak ye: for
it is not ye
that speak,
but the Holy
12 Ghost. And
brother shall
deliver up
brother to
death, and the
father his
child: and chil-
dren shall rise
up against par-
ents, and
[19]cause them
to be put to
death [*see Mi-*
13 *cah 7:6*]. And
ye shall be
hated of all
men for my
name's sake:

but he that
endureth to
the end, the
same shall be
saved.

Matt. 24 and 25

10 And then
shall many
stumble, and
shall deliver
up one an-
another, and
shall hate one
another.

11 And many
false prophets
shall arise, and
shall lead
many astray.
12 And because
iniquity shall
be multiplied,
the love of the
many shall wax
13 cold. But he
that endureth
to the end, the
same shall be
14 saved. And
[25]this gospel of
the kingdom
shall be
preached in
the whole

Luke 21:5–36

will give you
a mouth and
wisdom, which
all your ad-
versaries shall
not be able to
withstand or
to gainsay.
16 But ye shall
be delivered
up even by
parents, and
brethren, and
kinsfolk, and
friends; and
some of you
[23]shall they
cause to be put
17 to death. And
ye shall be
hated of all
men for my
name's sake.
18 And not a hair
of your head
shall perish.
19 In your pa-
tience ye shall
win your
[24]souls.

	Mark 13:1–37	Matt. 24 and 25	Luke 21:5–36
		[4]world for a testimony unto all the nations; and then shall the end come.	
3 *Sign of the Destruction of Jerusalem.*	14 But when ye see the abomination of desolation standing where he ought not	15 When therefore ye see the abomination of desolation, which was spoken of [5]by Daniel the prophet [*see Dan. 9:27; 11:31; 12:11*], standing in [6]the holy place	
	(let him that readeth understand),	(let him that readeth understand),	
	then let them that are in Judea flee unto the mountains: 15 and let him that is on the housetop not go down, nor enter in, to take anything out of his 16 house: and let him that is in the field return not back to take his cloke.	16 then let them that are in Judea flee unto the moun- 17 tains: let him that is on the housetop not go down to take out the things that are in his 18 house: and let him that is in the field not return back to take his cloke.	20 But when ye see Jerusalem compassed with armies, then know that her desolation is at 21 hand. Then let them that are in Judea flee unto the mountains; and let them that are in the midst of her depart out; and let not them that are in the country enter therein.
			22 For these are days of vengeance, that all things which are written may be

Mark 13:1–37

17 But woe unto
them that are
with child and
to them that
give suck in
those days!
18 And pray ye
that it be not
in the winter.
19 For those days
shall be trib-
ulation, such
as there hath
not been the
like from the
beginning of
the creation
which God
created until
now, and never
20 shall be. And
except the
Lord had
shortened the
days no flesh
would have
been saved:
but for the
elect's sake,
whom he
chose, he
shortened the
days.

Matt. 24 and 25

19 But
woe unto them
that are with
child and to
them that give
suck in those
20 days! And
pray ye that
your flight be
not in the
winter, neither
on a sabbath:
21 for then shall
be great tribu-
lation, such as
hath not been
from the begin-
ning of the
world until
now, no, nor
ever shall be
[*see Dan.12:1*].
22 And except
those days had
been short-
ened, no flesh
would have
been saved:
but for the
elect's sake
those days
shall be short-
ened.

Luke 21:5–36

23 fulfilled. Woe
unto them
that are with
child and to
them that give
suck in those
days!

for there
shall be great
distress upon
the [25]land, and
wrath unto
this people.
24 And they shall
fall by the
edge of the
sword, and
shall be led
captive into all
nations: and
Jerusalem
shall be trod-
den down of
the Gentiles,

Luke 21:5–36

until the times
of the Gentiles
be fulfilled.

4 False Christs and the Second Coming.

Mark 13:1–37

21 And then if
any man shall
say unto you,
Lo, here is the
Christ; or, Lo,
there; believe
22 [h]*it* not: for
there shall
arise false
Christs and
false prophets,
and shall shew
signs and wonders,
that they
may lead astray,
if possible,
the elect.

23 But take ye
heed: behold,
I have told
you all things
beforehand.

24 But in those

Matt. 24 and 25

23 Then if
any man shall
say unto you,
Lo, here is the
Christ, or,
Here; believe
24 [h]*it* not. For
there shall
arise false
Christs, and
false prophets,
and shall shew
great signs and
wonders; so as
to lead astray,
if possible,
even the elect
[*see Deut. 13:*
25 *1*]. Behold, I
have told you
26 beforehand. If
therefore they
shall say unto
you, Behold,
he is in the
wilderness; go
not forth: Behold,
he is in
the inner
chambers; believe
[s]*it* not.
27 For as the
lightning cometh
forth from
the east, and
is seen even
unto the west;
so shall be the
[l]coming of the
Son of man.
28 Wheresoever
the carcase is,
there will the
[s]eagles be
gathered together.
29 But immedi-

Mark 13:1–37	Matt. 24 and 25	Luke 21:5–36
days, after that tribulation, the sun shall be darkened, and the moon shall not give her light, 25 and the stars shall be falling from heaven,	ately, after the tribulation of those days the sun shall be darkened, and the moon shall not give her light, and the stars shall fall from heaven	25 And there shall be signs in sun and moon and stars; and upon the earth distress of nations, in perplexity for the roaring of the sea and the 26 billows; men [26]fainting for fear, and for expectation of the things which are coming on [27]the
and the powers that are in the heavens shall be shaken.	and the powers of the heavens shall be shaken: 30 and then shall appear the sign of the Son of man in heaven [*see Zech. 12:12*]: and then shall all the tribes of the earth mourn, and	world: for the powers of the heavens shall be shaken [*see Isa. 13:9–10; Ezek. 32:7–8; Joel 2:1–2, 10–11, 30–31; Amos 8:9; Zeph. 1:14–16*].
26 And then shall they see the Son of man coming in clouds with great power 27 and glory. And then shall he send forth the angels, and shall gather together his elect from the four winds, from the uttermost part of the earth to the	they shall see the Son of man coming on the clouds of heaven with power and great 31 glory. And he shall send forth his angels [10]with [11]a great sound of a trumpet, and they shall gather together his elect from the four winds, from	27 And then shall they see the Son of man coming in a cloud with power and great glory [*see Dan. 7:13–14 (Septuagint)*].

Mark 13:1–37

uttermost part
of heaven.

Parable of the Fig Tree.

28 Now from
the fig tree
learn her para-
ble: when her
branch is now
become tender,
and putteth
forth its
leaves, ye know
that the sum-
29 mer is nigh;
even so ye
also, when ye
see those
things coming
to pass, know
ye that [12]he is
nigh, *even* at
30 the doors. Ver-
ily I say unto
you, This gen-
eration shall
not pass away,
until all these
things be ac-
complished.
31 Heaven and
earth shall
pass away: but
my words shall
not pass away.
32 But of that
day or that

Matt. 24 and 25

one end of
heaven to the
other.

32 Now from
the fig tree
learn her para-
ble: when her
branch is now
become ten-
der, and put-
teth forth its
leaves, ye
know that the
summer is
33 nigh; even so
ye also, when
ye see all these
things, know
ye that [12]he is
nigh, *even* at
34 the doors. Ver-
ily I say unto
you, This gen-
eration shall
not pass away,
till all these
things be ac-
complished.
35 Heaven and
earth shall
pass away, but
my words shall
not pass away.
36 But of that
day and hour
knoweth no

Luke 21:5–36

28 But
when these
things begin to
come to pass,
look up, and
lift up your
heads; because
your redemp-
tion draweth
nigh [*see Deut.
30:4* (*Septua-
gint*); *Isa. 27:
12–13; Zech. 2:
6* (*Septuagint*).
29 And he
spake to them
a parable: Be-
hold the fig
tree, and all
30 trees: when
they now
shoot forth,
ye see it and
know of your
own selves
that the sum-
mer is now
31 nigh. Even
so ye also,
when ye see
these things
coming to
pass, know ye
that the king-
dom of God
32 is nigh. Ver-
ily I say unto
you, this gen-
eration shall
not pass away,
till all things
be accomplish-
33 ed. Heaven
and earth shall
pass away: but
my words shall
not pass away.

Mark 13:1-37

hour knoweth no one, not even the angels in heaven, neither the Son, but the Father.

Matt. 24 and 25

one, not even the angels of heaven, [13]neither the Son, but the Father only.
37 And as *were* the days of Noah, so shall be the [1]coming of the Son of man [*see Gen. 6:11-13; 7:7,*
38 *21-23*]. For as in those days which were before the flood they were eating and drinking, marrying and giving in marriage, until the day that Noah entered into
39 the ark, and they knew not until the flood came, and took them all away; so shall be the [1]coming of the Son of man.
40 Then shall two men be in the field; one is taken, and one is left:
41 two women *shall be* grinding at the mill; one is taken, and one is left

Luke 21:5-36

5 Readiness urged by Series of Parables.

Mark:

33 Take ye heed, watch [20]and pray: for ye know not when the time
34 is. *It is* as *when* a man,

Luke:

34 But take heed to yourselves, lest haply your hearts be overcharged with surfeiting and

Parable of the Porter

Mark 13:1–37

sojourning in another country, having left his house, and given authority to his [21]servants, to each one his work, commanded also the porter to
35 watch. Watch therefore: for ye know not when the lord of the house cometh, whether at even, or at midnight, or at cockcrowing, or in the morn-
36 ing; lest coming suddenly he find you
37 sleeping. And what I say unto you I say unto all, Watch.

Matt. 24 and 25

42 Watch therefore: for ye know not on what day your Lord cometh.

Luke 21:5–36

drunkenness, and cares of this life, and that day come on you suddenly as a
35 snare: for *so* shall it come upon all them that dwell on the face of all the earth.
36 But watch ye at every season, making supplication, that ye may prevail to escape all these things that shall come to pass, and to stand before the Son of man.

Matt. 24 and 25

Parable of the Master of the House.

43 [14]But know this, that if the master of the house had
known in what watch the thief was coming, he would
have watched and would not have suffered his house
44 to be [15]broken through. Therefore be ye also ready:
45 for in an hour that ye think not the Son of man
cometh. Who then is the faithful and wise [16]servant,
whom his lord hath set over his household, to give
46 them their food in due season? Blessed is that

Parable of the Faithful Servant and of the Evil Servant.

[16]servant, whom his lord when he cometh shall find
47 so doing. Verily I say unto you, that he will set him
48 over all that he hath. But if that evil [16]servant shall
say in his heart, My lord tarrieth; and shall begin to
49 beat his fellow-servants, and shall eat and drink with
50 the drunken; the lord of that [16]servant shall come in
51 a day when he expecteth not, and in an hour when he
knoweth not, and shall [17]cut him asunder, and ap-

Matt. 24 and 25

point his portion with the hypocrites: there shall be the weeping and gnashing of teeth.

[1] Gr. *presence.* [2] Or, *the consummation of the age.* [3] Or, *these good tidings.* [4] Gr. *inhabited earth.* [5] Or, *through.* [6] Or, *a holy place.* [7] Or, *him.* [8] Or, *them.* [9] Or, *vultures.* [10] Many ancient authorities read *with a great trumpet, and they shall gather, &c.* [11] Or, *a trumpet of great sound.* [12] Or, *it.* [13] Many authorities, some ancient, omit *neither the Son.* [14] Or, *But this ye know.* [15] Gr. *digged through.* [16] Gr. *bond-servant.* [17] Or, *severely scourge him.* [18] Or, *Teacher.* [19] Or, *put them to death.* [20] Some ancient authorities omit *and pray.* [21] Gr. *bond-servants.* [22] Gr. *you being brought.* [23] Or, *shall they put to death.* [24] Or, *lives.* [25] Or, *earth.* [26] Or, *expiring.* [27] Gr. *the inhabited earth.*

Matt. chap. 25

Parable of the Ten Virgins.

1 Then shall the kingdom of heaven be likened unto
ten virgins, which took their [1]lamps, and went forth
2 to meet the bridegroom. And five of them were
3 foolish, and five were wise. For the foolish, when
4 they took their [1]lamps, took no oil with them: but the
5 wise took oil in their vessels with their [1]lamps. Now
while the bridegroom tarried, they all slumbered and
6 slept. But at midnight there is a cry, Behold, the
7 bridegroom! Come ye forth to meet him. Then all
those virgins arose, and trimmed their [1]lamps.
8 And the foolish said unto the wise, Give us of your
9 oil; for our [1]lamps are going out. But the wise answered, saying, Peradventure there will not be enough
10 for us and you: go ye rather to them that sell, and buy
for yourselves. And while they went away to buy,
the bridegroom came; and they that were ready went
in with him to the marriage feast: and the door was
11 shut. Afterward, come also the other virgins, saying,
12 Lord, Lord, open to us. But he answered and said,
13 Verily I say unto you, I know you not. Watch
therefore, for ye know not the day nor the hour.

Parable of the Talents

14 For *it is as when* a man, going into another country,
called his own [2]servants, and delivered unto them his
15 goods. And unto one he gave five talents, to another
two, to another one; to each according to his several
16 ability; and he went on his journey. Straightway he
that received the five talents went and traded with
17 them, and made other five talents. In like manner
18 he also that *received* the two gained other two. But
he that received the one went away and digged in the
19 earth, and hid his lord's money. Now after a long
time the lord of those [2]servants cometh and maketh
20 a reckoning with them. And he that received the
five talents came and brought other five talents, saying, Lord, thou deliveredst unto me five talents: lo,
21 I have gained other five talents. His lord said unto
him, Well done, good and faithful [3]servant: thou hast
been faithful over a few things, I will set thee over
22 many things; enter thou into the joy of thy lord. And
he also that *received* the two talents came and said,
Lord, thou deliveredst unto me two talents: lo, I have

Matt. chap. 25

23 gained other two talents. His lord said unto him,
Well done, good and faithful [3]servant; thou hast been
faithful over a few things, I will set thee over many
24 things: enter thou into the joy of thy lord. And he
also that had received the one talent came and said,
Lord, I knew thee that thou art a hard man, reaping
where thou didst not sow, and gathering where thou
25 didst not scatter: and I was afraid, and went away
and hid thy talent in the earth: lo, thou hast thine
26 own. But his lord answered and said unto him,
Thou wicked and slothful [3]servant, thou knowest that
I reap where I sowed not, and gather where I did not
27 scatter; thou oughtest therefore to have put my money
to the bankers, and at my coming I should have re-
28 ceived back mine own with interest. Take ye away
therefore the talent from him, and give it unto him
29 that hath the ten talents. For unto every one that
hath shall be given, and he shall have abundance:
but from him that hath not, even that which he hath
30 shall be taken away. And cast ye out the unprofit-
able [3]servant into the outer darkness: there shall be
the weeping and gnashing of teeth.

6 Picture of the Judgment with Parable of the Sheep and the Goats.

31 But when the Son of man shall come in his glory,
and all the angels with him [*see Zech. 14:5*], then
32 shall he sit on the throne of his glory: and before him
shall be gathered all the nations: and he shall separate
them one from another, as the shepherd separateth
33 the sheep from the [4]goats; and he shall set the sheep
34 on his right hand, but the [4]goats on the left. Then
shall the King say unto them on his right hand, Come,
ye blessed of my Father, inherit the kingdom pre-
pared for you from the foundation of the world:
35 for I was an hungred, and ye gave me meat: I was
thirsty, and ye gave me drink: I was a stranger, and
36 ye took me in; naked, and ye clothed me: I was sick,
and ye visited me: I was in prison, and ye came unto
37 me. Then shall the righteous answer him, saying,
Lord, when saw we thee an hungred, and fed thee?
38 or athirst, and gave thee drink? And when saw we
thee a stranger, and took thee in? or naked, and
39 clothed thee? And when saw we thee sick, or in
40 prison, and came unto thee? And the King shall
answer and say unto them, Verily I say unto you,
Inasmuch as ye did it unto one of these my brethren,
41 *even* these least, ye did it unto me. Then shall he
say also unto them on the left hand, [5]Depart from me,
ye cursed, into the eternal fire which is prepared for
42 the devil and his angels: for I was an hungred, and
ye gave me no meat: I was thirsty, and ye gave me
43 no drink: I was a stranger, and ye took me not in;

Matt. chap. 25

44 naked, and ye clothed me not; sick, and in prison, and
ye visited me not. Then shall they also answer,
saying, Lord, when saw we thee an hungred, or athirst,
or a stranger, or naked, or sick, or in prison, and did
45 not minister unto thee? Then shall he answer them,
saying, Verily, I say unto you, Inasmuch as ye did
it not unto one of these least, ye did it not unto me.
46 And these shall go away into eternal punishment:
but the righteous into eternal life [*see Dan. 12:2*].

[1] Or, *torches*. [2] Gr. *bond-servants*. [3] Gr. *bond-servant*. [4] Gr. *kids*. [5] Or, *Depart from me under a curse*.

§ 140. JESUS PREDICTS HIS CRUCIFIXION TWO DAYS HENCE (JEWISH FRIDAY)

Probably at Bethany on Tuesday evening (beginning of Jewish Wednesday). The Rulers in Jerusalem plot His death

Mark 14:1–2	Matt. 26:1–5	Luke 22:1–2
1 Now after two days was *the feast of* the passover and the unleavened bread:	1 And it came to pass, when Jesus had finished all these words, he said unto 2 his disciples, Ye know that after two days the passover cometh, and the Son of man is delivered up to be 3 crucified. Then were	1 Now the feast of unleavened bread drew nigh, which is called the Passover.
and the chief priests and the scribes	gathered together the chief priests, and the elders of the people, unto the court of the high priest, who was called Caiaphas: and	2 And the chief priests and the
sought how they might take him with subtilty, 2 and kill him: for they said, Not during the feast, lest haply there shall be a tumult of the people.	4 they took counsel together that they might take Jesus by subtilty, and kill him. 5 But they said, Not during the feast, lest a tumult arise among the people.	scribes sought how they might put him to death; for they feared the people.

§141. AT THE FEAST IN THE HOUSE OF SIMON THE LEPER MARY OF BETHANY ANOINTS JESUS FOR HIS BURIAL

At Bethany (Tuesday evening, Jewish Wednesday)

Mark 14:3–9

3 And while he was
in Bethany in the
house of Simon the
leper, as he sat at
meat, there came a
woman having [1]an
alabaster cruse of
ointment of [2]spike-
nard very costly, *and*
she brake the cruse,
and poured it over
4 his head. But there
were some that had
indignation among
themselves, *saying*,
To what purpose hath
this waste of the oint-
ment been made?
5 For this ointment
might have been sold
for above three hun-
dred [3]pence, and
given to the poor.
And they murmured
6 against her. But
Jesus said, Let her
alone, why trouble ye
her? she hath wrought
a good work on me.
7 For ye have the poor
always with you, and
whensoever ye will
ye can do them good:
but me ye have not
8 always. She hath

Matt. 26:6–13

6 Now when Jesus
was in Bethany, in
the house of Simon
7 the leper, there came
unto him a woman
having an alabaster
cruse of exceeding
precious ointment,
and she poured it
upon his head as he
8 sat at meat. But
when the disciples
saw it, they had in-
dignation, saying,

To what
purpose is this waste?
9 For this ointment
might have been sold
for much, and given
to the poor.

10 But Jesus perceiving
it said unto them,
Why trouble ye the
woman? for she hath
wrought a good work
11 upon me. For ye
have the poor always
with you; but me you
have not always.
12 For in that she poured
this ointment upon

John 12:2–8

2 So they made him
a supper there: and
Martha served; but
Lazarus was one of
them that sat at meat
3 with him. Mary*
therefore took a
pound of ointment
of [2]spikenard, very
precious, and anoint-
ed the feet of Jesus,
and wiped his feet
with her hair: and the
house was filled with
the odour of the oint-
4 ment. But Judas
Iscariot, one of his
disciples, which
should betray him,
5 saith, Why was not
this ointment sold for
three hundred [3]pence,
and given to the
6 poor? Now this he
said, not because he
cared for the poor;
but because he was a
thief, and having the
[4]bag [5]took away what
was put therein.
7 Jesus therefore said,
[6]Suffer her to keep
it against the day of
8 my burying. For
the poor ye have al-

* This anointing has nothing in common with that given by Luke (§ 59), except the fact of a woman anointing the Saviour's feet, and the name Simon, which was common. The former was in Galilee, this is at Bethany near Jerusalem. There the host despised the woman who anointed, here her brother is one of the guests, and her sister an active attendant. There the woman was "a sinner," a notoriously bad woman, here it is the devout Mary who "sat at the Lord's feet and heard his word" months before (§ 104). There the host thought strange that Jesus allowed her to touch him, here the disciples complain of the waste. There the Saviour gave assurance of forgiveness, here of perpetual and world-wide honor. Especially notice that here the woman who anoints is anticipating his speedy death and burial, of which at the former time he had never distinctly spoken. In view of all these differences it is absurd to represent the two anointings as the same, and outrageous on such slender ground to cast reproach on Mary of Bethany.

Mark 14:3–9	Matt. 26:6–13	John 12:2–8
done what she could: she hath anointed my body aforehand for 9 the burying. And verily I say unto you, Wheresoever the gospel shall be preached throughout the whole world, that also which this woman hath done shall be spoken of for a memorial of her.	my body, she did it to prepare me for burial. 13 Verily I say unto you, Wheresoever this gospel shall be preached in the whole world, that also which this woman hath done shall be spoken of for a memorial of her.	**ways with you; but me ye have not always.**

[1] Or, *a flask.* [2] Gr. *pistic nard,* pistic being perhaps a local name. Some take it to mean *genuine:* others, *liquid.* [3] The word in the Greek denotes a coin worth about seventeen cents. [4] Or, *box.* [5] Or, *carried what was put therein.* [6] Or, *let her alone: it was that she might keep it.*

§ 142. JUDAS, STUNG BY THE REBUKE OF JESUS AT THE FEAST, BARGAINS WITH THE RULERS TO BETRAY JESUS

Tuesday Night in Jerusalem

Mark 14:10–11	Matt. 26:14–16	Luke 22:3–6
10 And Judas Iscariot, [1]he that was one of the twelve, went away	14 Then one of the twelve, who was called Judas Iscariot,	3 And Satan entered into Judas who was called Iscariot, being of the number of the 4 twelve. And he went
unto the chief priests,	went unto the chief priests, and said,	away, and communed with the chief priests and captains, how he
that he might deliver him unto them.		might deliver him unto them.
	15 What are ye willing to give me, and I will deliver him unto you?	
11 And they, when they heard it, were glad, and promised to give him money.	And they weighed unto him thirty pieces 16 of silver [*see Zech. 11:12*]. And from that time he sought opportunity to deliver him *unto them.*	5 And they were glad, and covenanted to give him 6 money. And he consented,
And he sought how he might conveniently deliver him *unto them.*		and sought opportunity to deliver him unto them [2]in the absence of the multitude.

[1] Gr., *the one of the twelve.* [2] Or, *without tumult.*

§ 143. THE PREPARATION FOR THE PASCHAL MEAL AT THE HOME OF A FRIEND (POSSIBLY THAT OF JOHN MARK'S FATHER AND MOTHER)

Jerusalem, Thursday* afternoon. (A Day of Preparation)

Mark 14:12–16

12 And on the first
day of unleavened
bread, when they
sacrificed the pass-
over, his disciples say
unto him, Where wilt
thou that we go and
make ready that thou
mayest eat the pass-
over [*see Ex. 12:18–*
13 *20*]? And he sendeth
two of his disciples,
and saith unto them,
Go into
the city, and there
shall meet you a man
bearing a pitcher of
water: follow him;
14 and wheresoever he
shall enter in, say to
the goodman of the
house, The [1]Master
saith, Where is my
guest-chamber, where
I shall eat the pass-
over with my dis-
15 ciples? And he will
himself shew you a
large upper room fur-
nished *and* ready: and
there make ready for
16 us. And the disciples
went forth, and came

Matt. 26:17–19

17 Now on the first
day of unleavened
bread the disciples
came to Jesus, say-
ing,
Where wilt thou
that we make ready
for thee to eat the
18 passover? And he
said,
Go into the city
to such a man, and
say unto him,
The
[1]Master saith, My
time is at hand; I
keep the passover at
thy house with my
disciples.
19 And
the disciples did as

Luke 22:7–13

7 And the day of un-
leavened bread came,
on which the pass-
over must be sacri-
ficed.
8 And he sent
Peter and John, say-
ing, Go and make
ready for us the pass-
over, that we may
9 eat. And they said
unto him, Where wilt
thou that we make
10 ready? And he said
unto them, Behold,
when ye are entered
into the city, there
shall meet you a man
bearing a pitcher of
water; follow him
into the house where-
11 into he goeth. And
ye shall say unto the
goodman of the
house, The [1]Master
saith unto thee,
Where is the guest-
chamber, where I
shall eat the passover
with my disciples?
12 And he will shew you
a large upper room
furnished: there make
ready.
13 And they went,

* Wednesday (A Day of Rest) was apparently spent with the disciples in retirement in Bethany. Thursday was spent wholly with the disciples till the arrest in Gethsemane after midnight.

Mark 14:12–16	Matt. 26:17–19	Luke 22:7–13
into the city, and found as he had said unto them: and they made ready the passover.	Jesus appointed them; and they made ready the passover.	and found as he had said unto them: and they made ready the passover.

[1] Or, *Teacher*.

§ 144. JESUS PARTAKES OF THE PASCHAL MEAL WITH THE TWELVE APOSTLES AND REBUKES THEIR JEALOUSY

Jerusalem, Thursday evening after sunset (beginning of Jewish Friday)

Mark 14:17	Matt. 26:20	Luke 22:14–16, 24–30
17 And when it was evening he cometh with the twelve.	20 Now when even was come he was sitting at meat with the twelve [1]disciples;	14 And when the hour was come, he sat down, and the apos-

15 tles with him. And he said unto them, With desire I have desired to eat
16 this passover* with you before I suffer: for I say unto you, I will not eat
it, until it be fulfilled in the kingdom of God.
24 And there arose also a contention among them, which of them is ac-
25 counted to be [2]greatest. And he said unto them, The kings of the Gen-
tiles have lordship over them; and they that have authority over them
26 are called Benefactors. But ye *shall* not *be* so: but he that is the greater
among you, let him become as the younger; and he that is chief, as he
27 that doth serve. For whether is greater, he that [3]sitteth at meat, or he
that serveth? is not he that [3]sitteth at meat? but I am in the midst of you
28 as he that serveth. But ye are they which have continued with me in
29 my temptations; and [4]I appoint unto you a kingdom, even as my Father
appointed unto me, that ye may eat and drink at my table in my king-
30 dom; and ye shall sit on thrones judging the twelve tribes of Israel.

[1] Many authorities, some ancient, omit *disciples*. [2] Gr. *greater*. [3] Gr. *reclineth*. [4] Or, *I appoint unto you, even as my Father appointed unto me a kingdom, that ye may eat and drink, etc.*

§ 145. DURING THE PASCHAL MEAL, JESUS WASHES THE FEET OF HIS DISCIPLES

Evening before the Crucifixion (our Thursday, Jewish Friday)

John 13:1–20

1 Now before† the feast of the passover, Jesus knowing that his hour
was come that he should depart out of this world unto the Father, having

* Some regard certain expressions in the Gospel of John as showing that Jesus did not eat the Paschal meal, thus hopelessly contradicting the other Gospels. But no one of John's expressions shows what is supposed, and one of them really indicates the contrary. See note at end of volume. Matthew, Mark, and Luke clearly show that he did eat the regular Passover meal.

† It is needlessly inferred that John by this expression means that it was a full day before the passover meal. In fact, the words in verse 2 "during supper" rather imply that "before passover" was just before the meal began.

John 13:1–20

loved his own which were in the world, he loved them [1]unto the end.
2 And during supper, the devil having already put into the heart of Judas
3 Iscariot, Simon's *son*, to betray him, *Jesus*, knowing that the Father had
given all things into his hands, and that he came forth from God and
4 goeth unto God, riseth from supper, and layeth aside his garments; and
5 he took a towel and girded himself. Then he poured water into the
bason, and began to wash the disciples' feet, and to wipe them with the
6 towel wherewith he was girded. So he cometh to Simon Peter. He saith
7 unto him, Lord, dost thou wash my feet? Jesus answered and said unto
him, What I do thou knowest not now; but thou shalt understand here-
8 after. Peter saith unto him, Thou shalt never wash my feet. Jesus
9 answered him, If I wash thee not, thou hast no part with me. Simon
Peter saith unto him, Lord, not my feet only, but also my hands and my
10 head. Jesus saith to him, He that is bathed needeth not [2]save to wash
11 his feet, but is clean every whit: and ye are clean, but not all. For he
knew him that should betray him; therefore said he, Ye are not all clean.
12 So when he had washed their feet, and taken his garments, and [3]sat
13 down again, he said unto them, Know ye what I have done to you? Ye
14 call me, [4]Master, and, Lord: and ye say well; for so I am. If I then, the
Lord and the [4]Master, have washed your feet, ye also ought to wash one
15 another's feet. For I have given you an example, that ye also should
16 do as I have done to you. Verily, verily, I say unto you, A [5]servant is
not greater than his lord; neither [6]one that is sent greater than he that
17 sent him. If ye know these things, blessed are ye if ye do them. I
18 speak not of you all: I know whom I [7]have chosen: but that the scripture
may be fulfilled, He that eateth [8]my bread lifted up his heel against me
19 [*see Ps. 41:9*]. From henceforth I tell you before it come to pass, that,
20 when it is come to pass, ye may believe that [9]I am *he*. Verily, verily, I
say unto you, He that receiveth whomsoever I send receiveth me; and
he that receiveth me receiveth him that sent me.

[1] Or, *to the uttermost.* [2] Some ancient authorities omit *save*, and *his feet.* [3] Gr. *reclined.* [4] Or, *Teacher.* [5] Gr. *bond-servant.* [6] Gr. *an apostle.* [7] Or, *chose.* [8] Many ancient authorities read *his bread with me.* [9] Or, *I am.*

§ 146. AT THE PASCHAL MEAL JESUS POINTS OUT JUDAS AS THE BETRAYER

Thursday evening (Jewish Friday)

Mark 14:18–21

18 And as they [1]sat and were eating, Jesus said, Verily I say unto you, One of you shall betray me, *even* he that eateth with me [*see Ps. 41:9*].

Matt. 26:21–25

21 and as they were eating, he said, Verily I say unto you, that one of you shall betray me.

Luke 22:21–23

21 But behold, the hand of him that betrayeth me is with me on the
22 table. For the Son of man indeed goeth, as it hath been determined: but woe unto

John 13:21–30

21 When Jesus had thus said, he was troubled in the spirit and testified, and said, Verily, verily, I say unto you, that one of you shall betray me.

Mark 14:18–21	Matt. 26:21–25	Luke 22:21–23	John 13:21–30
		that man through whom he is betrayed!	
19 They began to be sorrowful, and to say unto him one by one, Is it I?	22 And they were exceeding sorrowful, and began to say unto him every one, Is it I, Lord?	23 And they began to question among themselves, which of them it was that should do this thing.	22 The disciples looked one on another, doubting of whom he spake.
20 And he said unto them, *It is* one of the twelve, he that dippeth with me in the dish.	23 And he answered and said, He that dipped his hand with me in the dish, the same shall betray me.		
21 For the Son of man goeth, even as it is written of him: but woe unto that man through whom the Son of man is betrayed! good were it for that man if he had not been born.	24 The Son of man goeth, even as it is written of him: but woe unto that man through whom the Son of man is betrayed! good were it for that man if he had not been born.		
			23 There was at the table reclining in Jesus' bosom one of his disci- 24 ples, whom Jesus loved. Simon Peter therefore beckoneth to him, and saith unto him, Tell *us* who 25 it is of whom he speaketh. He leaning back, as he was, on Jesus' breast saith unto him, 26 Lord, who is it? Jesus therefore answereth, He it is, for whom I shall dip the sop, and give it him. So when he had dipped the sop, he taketh and giveth it to Judas, *the son* of Simon Iscariot.
	25 And Judas, which betrayed him,		

Matt. 26:21–25	John 13:21–30
answered and said, Is it I, Rabbi? He saith unto him, Thou hast said.	
	27 And after the sop, then entered Satan into him. Jesus therefore saith unto him, That thou doest,

28 do quickly. Now no man at the table knew for what intent he spake
29 this unto them. For some thought, because Judas had the [2]bag, that
Jesus said unto him, Buy what things we have need of for the feast: or,
30 that he should give something to the poor. He then having received
the sop went out straightway: and it was night.

[1] Gr. *him if that man.* [2] Or, *box.*

§ 147. AFTER THE DEPARTURE OF JUDAS JESUS WARNS THE DISCIPLES (PETER IN PARTICULAR) AGAINST DESERTION, WHILE ALL PROTEST THEIR LOYALTY

		John 13:31–38
		31 When therefore he was gone out, Jesus saith, Now [1]is the Son of man glorified, and God [1]is glorified in him; 32 and God shall glorify him in himself, and straightway shall he glorify 33 him. Little children, yet a little while I am with you. Ye shall seek me: and as I said unto the Jews, Whither I go, ye cannot come; so now I say unto you. 34 A new commandment I

Mark 14:27–31

27 And Jesus
saith unto
them, All ye
shall be [3]of-
fended: for it
is written [*see
Zech. 13:7*], I
will smite the
shepherd, and
the sheep shall
be scattered
28 abroad. How-
beit, after I
am raised up,
I will go before
you into Gali-
lee.
29 But Peter
said unto
him, Although
all shall be [3]of-
fended, yet
will not I.
30 And Jesus
saith unto
him, Verily I
say unto thee,
that thou to-
day, even this
night, before
the cock crow
twice shalt de-
ny me thrice.
31 But he spake
exceeding ve-
hemently, If I

Matt. 26:31–35

31 Then saith
Jesus unto
them, All ye
shall be [3]of-
fended in me
this night: for
it is written,
I will smite
the shepherd,
and the sheep
of the flock
shall be scat-
tered abroad.
32 But after I am
raised up, I
will go before
you into Gali-
33 lee. But Peter
answered and
said unto him,
If all shall be
[3]offended in
thee, I will
never be [3]of-
34 fended. Jesus
said unto him,
Verily I say
unto thee, that
this night, be-
fore the cock
crow, thou
shalt deny me
35 thrice. Peter
saith unto
him, Even if I
must die with

Luke 22:31–38

31 Simon, Si-
mon, behold,
Satan [4]asked
to have you,
that he might
sift you as
32 wheat: but I
made supplica-
tion for thee,
that thy faith
fail not: and
do thou, when
once thou hast
turned again,
stablish thy
brethren.

33 And he
said unto him,
Lord, with thee
I am ready to
go both to
prison and to
34 death. And he
said, I tell thee,
Peter, the cock
shall not crow
this day, until
thou shalt
thrice deny
that thou
knowest me.

John 13:31–38

give unto you,
that ye love
one another
[2]even as I have
loved you,
that ye also
love one an-
35 other. By this
shall all men
know that ye
are my disci-
ples, if ye have
love one to an-
other.
36 Simon Peter
saith unto
him, Lord,
whither goest
thou? Jesus
answered,
Whither I go,
thou canst not
follow me now;
but thou shalt
follow after-
wards.

37 Peter
saith unto
him, Lord, why
cannot I follow
thee even
now? I will
lay down my
life for thee.
38 Jesus answer-
eth, Wilt thou
lay down thy
life for me?
Verily, verily,
I say unto
thee, The cock
shall not crow,
till thou hast
denied me
thrice.

Mark 14:27–31

must die with
thee, I will not
deny thee. And
in like manner
also said they
all.

Matt. 26:31–35

thee, *yet* will
I not deny
thee. Likewise
also said all
the disciples.

Luke 22:31–38

35 And he said unto them, When
I sent you forth without purse,
and wallet, and shoes, lacked ye
anything? And they said, Noth-
36 ing. And he said unto them, But
now, he that hath a purse, let him
take it, and likewise a wallet: [5]and
he that hath none, let him sell his
37 cloke, and buy a sword. For I
say unto you, that this which is
written must be fulfilled in me [*see
Isa. 53:12*], And he was reckoned
with transgressors: for that which
38 concerneth me hath [6]fulfilment.
And they said, Lord, behold, here
are two swords. And he said unto
them, It is enough.

[1] Or, *was.* [2] Or, *even as I loved you, that ye also may love one another.* [3] Or, *caused to stumble.* [4] Or, *obtained you by asking.* [5] Or, *and he that hath no sword, let him sell his cloak and buy one.* [6] Gr, *end.*

§148. JESUS INSTITUTES THE MEMORIAL OF EATING BREAD AND DRINKING WINE

Jerusalem. Evening before the Crucifixion

Luke* 22:17–20

17 And he re-
ceived a cup,
and when he
had given
thanks he said,
Take this, and
divide it a-
mong your-
18 selves: for I
say unto you,
I will not
drink from
henceforth of

* Luke here (see § 144) departs from the order of Mark (and Matthew) and mentions the institution of the supper earlier in the evening. It seems best to follow the chronology of Mark, who places it after the departure of Judas.

Mark 14:22–25

22 And as they were eating, he took [1]bread, and when he had blessed, he brake it, and gave to them, and said, Take ye: this is my body.

23 And he took a cup, and when he had given thanks, he gave to them, and they all drank of it.

24 And he said unto them, This is my blood of [3]the [4]covenant which is shed for many [*see Ex. 24:8; Lev. 4:18–20; Jer. 31:31; Zech. 9:*

25 *11*]. Verily I say unto you, I will no more drink of the fruit of the vine, until that day when I drink it new in the kingdom of God.

Matt. 26:26–29

26 And as they were eating, Jesus took [1]bread, and blessed, and brake it; and he gave to the disciples, and said, Take, eat; this is my body.

27 And he took [2]a cup, and gave thanks, and gave to them, saying, Drink ye all of it;

28 for this is my blood of [3]the [4]covenant, which is shed for many unto remission of

29 sins. But I say unto you, I will not drink henceforth of this fruit of the vine, until that day when I drink it new with you in my Father's kingdom.

Luke 22:17–20

the fruit of the vine until the kingdom of God shall come.

19 And he took [1]bread, and when he had given thanks, he brake it, and gave to them, saying, This is my body [5]which is given for you: this do in remembrance of

20 me. And the cup in like manner after supper, saying, This cup is the new [6]covenant in my blood, *even* that which is poured out for you.

1 Cor.* 11–23:26

23 For I received of the Lord that which also I delivered unto you, how that the Lord Jesus in the night in which he was betrayed took

24 bread; and when he had given thanks, he brake it, and said, This is my body, which [7]is for you: this do in remembrance of me.

25 In like manner also the cup, after supper, saying, This cup is the new [6]covenant in my blood: this do, as oft as ye drink *it*, in remembrance of

26 me. For as often as ye eat this bread, and drink the cup, ye proclaim the Lord's death till he come.

[1] Or, *a loaf*. [2] Some ancient authorities read *the cup*. [3] Or, *the testament*. [4] Many ancient authorities insert *new*. [5] Some ancient authorities omit *which is given for you...which is poured out for you*. [6] Or, *testament*. [7] Many ancient authorities read *is broken for you*.

* These are two parallel reports of the institution of the supper. Mark is followed by Matthew and 1 Corinthians (about A.D. 56) by Luke (not earlier than A.D. 58).

§ 149. THE FAREWELL DISCOURSE TO HIS DISCIPLES IN THE UPPER ROOM

Jerusalem

John 14*

1 Let not your heart be troubled: [1]ye believe in God, believe also in me.
2 In my Father's house are many [2]mansions; if it were not so, I would have
3 told you; for I go to prepare a place for you. And if I go and prepare a
4 place for you, I come again, and will receive you unto myself; that where
5 I am *there* ye may be also. [3]And whither I go, ye know the way. Thomas
saith unto him, Lord, we know not whither thou goest; how know we the
6 way? Jesus saith unto him, I am the way, and the truth, and the life:
7 no one cometh unto the Father, but [4]by me. If ye had known me, ye would
have known my Father also: from henceforth ye know him, and have seen
8 him. Philip saith unto him, Lord, shew us the Father, and it sufficeth us.
9 Jesus saith unto him, Have I been so long time with you, and dost thou
not know me, Philip? he that hath seen me hath seen the Father; how sayest
10 thou, Shew us the Father? Believest thou not that I am in the Father, and
the Father in me? the words that I say unto you I speak not from myself:
11 but the Father abiding in me doeth his works. Believe me that I am in
the Father and the Father in me: or else believe me for the very works'
12 sake. Verily, verily, I say unto you, he that believeth on me, the works
that I do shall he do also; and greater *works* than these shall he do; because
13 I go unto the Father. And whatsoever ye shall ask in my name, that
14 will I do, that the Father may be glorified in the Son. If ye shall ask [5]me
15 anything in my name, that will I do. If ye love me, ye will keep my com-
16 mandments. And I will [6]pray the Father, and he shall give you another
[7]Comforter, that he may be with you for ever, *even* the Spirit of truth:
17 whom the world cannot receive; for it beholdeth him not, neither knoweth
18 him: ye know him; for he abideth with you, and shall be in you. I will
19 not leave you [8]desolate: I come unto you. Yet a little while, and the
world beholdeth me no more; but ye behold me: because I live, [9]ye shall
20 live also. In that day ye shall know that I am in my Father, and ye in
21 me, and I in you. He that hath my commandments, and keepeth them,
he it is that loveth me: and he that loveth me shall be loved of my Father,
22 and I will love him, and will manifest myself unto him. Judas (not Is-
cariot) saith unto him, Lord, what is come to pass that thou wilt manifest
23 thyself unto us, and not unto the world? And Jesus answered and said
unto him, If a man love me, he will keep my word: and my Father will
love him, and we will come unto him, and make our abode with him.
24 He that loveth me not keepeth not my words: and the word which ye
hear is not mine, but the Father's who sent me.
25 These things have I spoken unto you, while *yet* abiding with you.
26 But the [7]Comforter, *even* the Holy Spirit, whom the Father will send in
my name, he shall teach you all things, and bring to your remembrance
27 all that I said unto you. Peace I leave with you; my peace I give unto

* Chapters 13 to 17 in John really belong together. There is first the effort of Jesus to stop the bickerings of the Twelve, then his warning and their reply. Jesus continues to address them with repeated interruption (dialogue), but finally they fear to ask him further (monologue). The discourse concludes with the wonderful prayer (the real Lord's Prayer) in chapter 17.

John 14

you: not as the world giveth, give I unto you. Let not your heart be
28 troubled, neither let it be fearful. Ye heard how I said to you, I go away,
and I come unto you. If ye loved me, ye would have rejoiced, because
29 I go unto the Father: for the Father is greater than I. And now I have
told you before it come to pass, that, when it is come to pass, ye may
30 believe. I will no more speak much with you, for the prince of the world
31 cometh: and he hath nothing in me; but that the world may know that
I love the Father, and as the Father gave me commandment, even so I
do. Arise, let us go hence.*

[1] Or, *believe in God.* [2] Or, *abiding-places.* [3] Many ancient authorities read *And whither I go, ye know, and the way ye know.* [4] Or, *through.* [5] Many ancient authorities omit *me.* [6] Gr. *make request of.* [7] Or, *Advocate.* Or, *Helper.* Gr. *Paraclete.* [8] Or, *orphans.* [9] Or, *and ye shall live.*

§150. THE DISCOURSE ON THE WAY TO GETHSEMANE

Possibly on the Street

John 15 and 16†

1 I am the true vine, and my Father is the husbandman. Every branch
2 in me that beareth not fruit, he taketh it away: and every *branch* that
3 beareth fruit, he cleanseth it, that it may bear more fruit. Already ye
4 are clean because of the word which I have spoken unto you. Abide in
me, and I in you. As the branch cannot bear fruit of itself, except it
5 abide in the vine; so neither can ye, except ye abide in me. I am the vine,
ye are the branches: He that abideth in me, and I in him, the same beareth
6 much fruit: for apart from me ye can do nothing. If a man abide not in
me, he is cast forth as a branch, and is withered; and they gather them,
7 and cast them into the fire, and they are burned. If ye abide in me, and
my words abide in you, ask whatsoever ye will, and it shall be done unto
8 you. Herein [1]is my Father glorified, [2]that ye bear much fruit: and *so*
9 shall ye be my disciples. Even as the Father hath loved me, I also have
10 loved you: abide ye in my love. If ye keep my commandments, ye shall
abide in my love; even as I have kept my Father's commandments, and
11 abide in his love. These things have I spoken unto you, that my joy
12 may be in you, and *that* your joy may be fulfilled. This is my command-
13 ment, that ye love one another, even as I have loved you. Greater love
14 hath no man than this, that a man lay down his life for his friends. Ye
15 are my friends, if ye do the things which I command you. No longer do
I call you [3]servants; for the [4]servant knoweth not what his lord doeth:
but I have called you friends; for all things that I heard from my Father
16 I have made known unto you. Ye did not choose me, but I chose you,
and appointed you, that ye should go and bear fruit, and *that* your fruit
should abide: that whatsoever ye shall ask of the Father in my name,
17, 18 he may give it you. These things I command you, that ye may love
one another. If the world hateth you, [5]ye know that it hath hated me
19 before *it hated* you. If ye were of the world, the world would love its own;
but because ye are not of the world, but I chose you out of the world,

* Apparently they leave the Upper Room.

† Chapters 14–17 are called the Heart of Christ. Nowhere does the Master lay bare his very soul more completely than here in chapters 15 and 16, with the allegory of the Vine and the teaching concerning the Holy Spirit.

John 15 and 16

20 therefore the world hateth you. Remember the word that I said unto
you, A [4]servant is not greater than his lord. If they persecuted me, they
will also persecute you; if they keep my word, they will keep yours also.
21 But all these things will they do unto you for my name's sake, because
22 they know not him that sent me. If I had not come and spoken unto
them, they had not had sin: but now they have no excuse for their sin.
23, 24 He that hateth me hateth my Father also. If I had not done among
them the works which none other did, they had not had sin: but now
25 have they both seen and hated both me and my Father. But *this cometh
to pass*, that the word may be fulfilled that is written in their law, They
26 hated me without a cause [*see Ps. 35:19; 69:4*]. But when the [6]Comforter
is come, whom I will send unto you from the Father, *even* the Spirit of
truth, which [7]proceedeth from the Father, he shall bear witness of me:
27 [8]and ye also bear witness, because ye have been with me from the be-
ginning.

1 These things have I spoken unto you that ye should not be made to
2 stumble. They shall put you out of the synagogues: yea, the hour cometh,
that whosoever killeth you shall think that he offereth service unto God.
3 And these things will they do, because they have not known the Father,
4 nor me. But these things have I spoken unto you, that when their hour
is come, ye may remember them, how that I told you. And these things
5 I said not unto you from the beginning, because I was with you. But now
I go unto him that sent me; and none of you asketh me, Whither goest
6 thou? But because I have spoken these things unto you, sorrow hath
7 filled your heart. Nevertheless I tell you the truth; It is expedient for
you that I go away: for if I go not away, the [6]Comforter will not come
8 unto you; but if I go, I will send him unto you. And he, when he is come,
9 will convict the world in respect of sin, and of righteousness, and of judge-
10 ment: of sin, because they believe not on me: of righteousness, because I
11 go to the Father, and ye behold me no more; of judgement, because the
12 prince of this world hath been judged. I have yet many things to say
13 unto you, but ye cannot bear them now. Howbeit when he, the Spirit
of truth, is come, he shall guide you into all the truth: for he shall not
speak from himself; but what things soever he shall hear, *these* shall he
speak: and he shall declare unto you the things that are to come.
14 He shall glorify me: for he shall take of mine, and shall declare *it* unto
15 you. All things whatsoever the Father hath are mine: therefore said I,
16 that he taketh of mine, and shall declare *it* unto you. A little while, and
ye behold me no more; and again a little while, and ye shall see me.
17 *Some* of his disciples therefore said one to another, What is this that he
saith unto us, A little while, and ye behold me not; and again a little
18 while, and ye shall see me: and, Because I go to the Father? They said
19 therefore, What is this that he saith, A little while? We know not what
he saith. Jesus perceived that they were desirous to ask him, and he
said unto them, Do ye inquire among yourselves concerning this, that I
said, A little while, and ye behold me not, and again a little while, and ye
20 shall see me? Verily, verily, I say unto you, that ye shall weep and
lament, but the world shall rejoice: ye shall be sorrowful, but your sorrow
21 shall be turned into joy. A woman when she is in travail hath sorrow

John 15 and 16

because her hour is come: but when she is delivered of the child, she
remembereth no more the anguish, for the joy that a man is born into the
22 world. And ye therefore now have sorrow: but I will see you again,
and your heart shall rejoice, and your joy no one taketh away from you
23 [*see Isa. 66:14*]. And in that day ye shall [9]ask me nothing. Verily,
verily, I say unto you, If ye shall ask anything of the Father, he will give
24 it you in my name. Hitherto have ye asked nothing in my name: ask
and ye shall receive, that your joy may be fulfilled.
25 These things have I spoken unto you in [10]proverbs: the hour cometh,
when I shall no more speak unto you in [10]proverbs, but shall tell you
26 plainly of the Father. In that day ye shall ask in my name: and I say
27 not unto you, that I will [11]pray the Father for you; for the Father him-
self loveth you, because ye have loved me, and have believed that I came
28 forth from the Father. I came out from the Father, and am come into
29 the world: again, I leave the world, and go unto the Father. His disciples
30 say, Lo, now speakest thou plainly, and speakest no [12]proverb. Now know
we that thou knowest all things, and needest not that any man should
31, 32 ask thee: by this we believe that thou camest forth from God. Jesus
answered them, Do ye now believe? Behold, the hour cometh, yea, is
come, that ye shall be scattered, every man to his own, and shall leave
33 me alone: and *yet* I am not alone, because the Father is with me. These
things have I spoken unto you, that in me ye may have peace. In the
world ye have tribulation: but be of good cheer; I have overcome the world.

[1] Or, *was.* [2] Many ancient authorities read *that ye bear much fruit, and be my disciples.* [3] Gr. *bond-servants.* [4] Gr. *bond-servant.* [5] Or, *know ye.* [6] Or, *Advocate.* Or, *Helper.* Gr. *Paraclete.* [7] Or, *goeth forth from.* [8] Or, *and bear ye also witness.* [9] Or, *ask me no question.* [10] Or, *parables.* [11] Gr. *make request of.* [12] Or, *parable.*

§151. CHRIST'S INTERCESSORY PRAYER

Possibly near Gethsemane

John 17

1 These things spake Jesus; and lifting up his eyes to heaven, he said,
2 Father, the hour is come; glorify thy Son, that the Son may glorify thee:
even as thou gavest him authority over all flesh, that whatsoever thou
3 hast given him, to them he should give eternal life. And this is life eternal,
that they should know thee the only true God, and him whom thou didst
4 send, *even* Jesus Christ. I glorified thee on the earth, having accomplished
5 the work which thou hast given me to do. And now, O Father, glorify
thou me with thine own self with the glory which I had with thee before
6 the world was. I manifested thy name unto the men whom thou gavest
me out of the world: thine they were, and thou gavest them to me; and
7 they have kept thy word. Now they know that all things whatsoever
8 thou hast given me are from thee: for the words which thou hast given me
I have given unto them; and they received *them*, and knew of a truth that
I came forth from thee, and they believed that thou didst send me.
9 I [1]pray for them: I [1]pray not for the world, but for those whom thou
10 hast given me; for they are thine: and all things that are mine are thine,
11 and I am glorified in them. And I am no more in the world, and these are

John 17

in the world, and I come to thee. Holy Father, keep them in thy name
12 which thou hast given me, that they may be one, even as we *are*. While
I was with them, I kept them in thy name which thou hast given me: and
I guarded them, and not one of them perished, but the son of perdition;
13 that the scripture might be fulfilled [*see Ps. 41:9*]. But now I come to thee:
and these things I speak in the world, that they may have my joy fulfilled
14 in themselves. I have given them my word; and the world hated them,
15 because they are not of the world, even as I am of the world. I [1]pray
not that thou shouldest take them [2]from the world, but that thou shouldest
16 keep them [2]from [3]the evil *one*. They are not of the world, even as I am
17 not of the world. [4]Sanctify them in the truth: thy word is truth. As
18 thou didst send me into the world, even so sent I them into the world.
19 And for their sakes I [4]sanctify myself, that they themselves also may be
20 sanctified in truth. Neither for these only do I [1]pray, but for them also
21 that believe on me through their word; that they may all be one; even as
thou, Father, *art* in me, and I in thee, that they also may be in us: that
22 the world may believe that thou didst send me. And the glory which
thou hast given me I have given unto them; that they may be one, even
23 as we *are* one; I in them, and thou in me, that they may be perfected into
one; that the world may know that thou didst send me, and lovedst them,
24 even as thou lovedst me. Father, [5]that which thou hast given me, I will
that, where I am, they also may be with me; that they may behold my
glory, which thou hast given me: for thou lovedst me before the foundation
25 of the world. O righteous Father, the world knew thee not, but I knew
26 thee; and these knew that thou didst send me; and I made known unto
them thy name, and will make it known; that the love wherewith thou
lovedst me may be in them, and I in them.

[1] Gr. *make request.* [2] Gr. *out of.* [3] Or, *evil.* [4] Or, *Consecrate.* [5] Many ancient authorities read *those whom.*

§ 152. GOING FORTH TO GETHSEMANE, JESUS SUFFERS LONG IN AGONY

In an Open Garden, between the Brook Kedron and the Foot of the Mount of Olives

Late in the night introducing Friday

Mark 14:26, 32–42	Matt. 26:30, 36–46	Luke 22:39–46	John 18:1
[*]26 And when they had sung a hymn, they went out unto the Mount of Olives.	30 And when they had sung a hymn, they went out unto the Mount of Olives.	39 And he came out, and went, as his custom was, unto the Mount of Ol-ives; and the	1 When Jesus had spoken these words, he went forth with his disci-ples over the

[*] The Synoptic Gospels do not give the great discourse of Jesus in John 14 to 17. Hence they represent Jesus as going forth to Gethsemane after the institution of the supper (§ 148). The time was probably not long and they apparently sang the hymn (probably one of the Psalms) as they rose to leave the Upper Room (John 14:31). Hence the passage in John 15 to 17 comes in between singing the hymn and reaching Gethsemane.

Mark 14:26, 32–42

32 And they
come unto [1]a
place which
was named
Gethsemane:
and he saith
unto his dis-
ciples, Sit ye
here, while I
pray.
33 And he taketh
with him Pe-
ter and James
and John, and
began to be
greatly amaz-
ed, and sore
34 troubled. And
he saith unto
them, My soul
is exceeding
sorrowful even
unto death
[*see Ps. 42:6*]:
abide ye here,
and watch.
35 And he went
forward a
little, and fell
on the ground,
and prayed
that, if it were
possible, the
hour might
pass away
36 from him. And
he said, Abba,
Father, all
things are
possible unto
thee; remove
this cup from
me: howbeit
not what I
will, but what
thou wilt.

Matt. 26:30, 36–46

36 Then cometh
Jesus with
them unto [1]a
place called
Gethsemane,
and saith unto
his disciples,
Sit ye here,
while I go
yonder and
37 pray. And he
took with him
Peter and the
two sons of
Zebedee, and
began to be
sorrowful and
sore troubled.
38 Then saith he
unto them, My
soul is exceed-
ing sorrowful,
even unto
death: abide
ye here, and
watch with
39 me. And he
went forward
a little, and
fell on his face,
and prayed,
saying, O my
Father, if it be
possible, let
this cup pass
away from
me: neverthe-
less, not as I
will, but as
thou wilt.

Luke 22:39–46

disciples also
followed him.
40 And when he
was at the
place, he said
unto them,
Pray that ye
enter not into
temptation.
41 And
he was parted
from them
about a stone's
cast: and he
kneeled down
and prayed,
42 saying,
Father,
if thou be will-
ing, remove
this cup from
me: neverthe-
less not my
will, but thine,
be done.
43 [3]And
there appeared

John 18:1

[4]brook [5]Kid-
ron, where was
a garden, into
the which he
entered, him-
self and his
disciples.

Mark 14:26, 32–42

37 And
he cometh,
and findeth
them sleeping,
and saith unto
Peter, Simon,
sleepest thou?
couldest thou
not watch one
hour?
38 [2]Watch
and pray, that
ye enter not
into tempta-
tion: the spirit
indeed is will-
ing, but the
flesh is weak.
39 And again he
went away,
and prayed,
saying the
same words.

40 And
again he came,
and found
them sleeping,
for their eyes
were very

Matt. 26:30, 36–46

40 And
he cometh un-
to the disci-
ples, and find-
eth them
sleeping, and
saith unto Pe-
ter, What,
could ye not
watch with me
one hour?
41 [2]Watch and
pray, that ye
enter not into
temptation:
the spirit in-
deed is willing,
but the flesh
42 is weak. Again
a second time
he went away,
and prayed,
saying, O my
Father, if this
cannot pass
away, except
I drink it, thy
will be done.
43 And he came
again and
found them
sleeping, for
their eyes were

Luke 22:39–46.

unto him an an-
gel from heav-
en strength-
ening him.
44 And being in
an agony he
prayed more
earnestly: and
his sweat be-
came as it were
great drops of
blood falling
down upon the
45 ground. And
when he rose
up from his
prayer, he
came unto the
disciples, and
found them
sleeping for
46 sorrow, and
said unto
them, Why
sleep ye? rise
and pray, that
ye enter not
into tempta-
tion.

Mark 14:26, 32–42.	Matt. 26:30, 36–46.		
heavy; and they wist not what to answer him.	44 heavy. And he left them again, and went away, and prayed a third time, saying again the same words.		
41 And he cometh the third time, and saith unto them, Sleep on now, and take your rest: it is enough; the hour is come; behold, the Son of man is betrayed into the hands of	45 Then cometh he to the disciples, and saith unto them, Sleep on now, and take your rest: behold, the hour is at hand, and the Son of man is betrayed unto the hands of sinners.		
42 sinners. Arise, let us be going: behold, he that betrayeth me is at hand.	46 Arise, let us be going: behold, he is at hand that betrayeth me.		

[1] Gr. *an enclosed piece of ground.* [2] Or, *Watch ye, and pray that ye enter not.* [3] Many ancient authorities omit verses 43, 44. [4] Or, *ravine.* Gr. *winter-torrent.* [5] Or, *of the Cedars.*

PART XIII

THE ARREST, TRIAL, CRUCIFIXION AND BURIAL OF JESUS

Thursday Night, Friday, and Saturday of Passion Week (Days of Darkness for the Kingdom of God). §§ 153–168.*

§ 153. JESUS IS BETRAYED, ARRESTED AND FORSAKEN

Garden of Gethsemane. Friday, long before dawn

Mark 14:43–52	Matt. 26:47–56	Luke 22:47–53	John 18:2–12
			2 Now Judas also, which betrayed him, knew the place: for Jesus ofttimes resorted thither with his disciples.
43 And straightway, while he yet spake, cometh Judas, one of the twelve, and with him a multitude with swords and staves, from the chief priests and the scribes and the elders.	47 And while he yet spake, lo, Judas, one of the twelve, came, and with him a great multitude with swords and staves, from the chief priests and elders of the people.	47 While he yet spake, behold, a multitude, and he that was called Judas, one of the twelve, went before them;	3 Judas then, having received the [a]band *of soldiers*, and officers from the chief priests and the Pharisees, cometh thither with lanterns and torches and weapons. 4 Jesus therefore, knowing all the things that were coming upon him, went forth, and saith unto them, Whom

* "Your hour and the power of darkness" (Luke 22:53). Friday, the Day of Suffering, has become for Christians the Day of the Cross and of Glory.

Mark 14:43–52

44 Now he
that betrayed
him had given
them a token,
saying, Whom-
soever I shall
kiss, that is he:
take him, and
lead him away
45 safely. And
when he was
come, straight-

Matt. 26:47–56

48 Now he
that betrayed
him gave them
a sign, saying,
Whomsoever I
shall kiss, that
is he; take
him.

49 And

John 18:2–12

5 seek ye? They
answered him,
Jesus of Naza-
reth. Jesus
saith unto
them, I am *he.*
And Judas al-
so, which be-
trayed him,
was standing
with them.
6 When there-
fore he said
unto them,
I am *he*, they
went back-
ward, and fell
to the ground.
7 Again there-
fore he asked
them, Whom
seek ye? And
they said,
Jesus of Naza-
8 reth. Jesus an-
swered, I told
you that I am
he: if therefore
ye seek me, let
these go their
9 way: that the
word might be
fulfilled which
he spake, Of
those whom
thou hast
given me I lost
not one.

Mark 14:43–52

way he came
to him, and
saith, Rabbi;
and [1]kissed
him.

46 And they
laid hands on
him, and took
him.
47 But a cer-
tain one of
them that
stood by drew
his sword, and
smote the [2]ser-
vant of the
high priest,
and struck off
his ear.

Matt. 26:47–56

straightway he
came to Jesus,
and said, Hail,
Rabbi; and
[1]kissed him.

50 And Jesus said
unto him,
Friend, do that
for which thou
art come. Then
they came and
laid hands on
Jesus, and took
51 him. And be-
hold, one of
them that
were with
Jesus stretch-
ed out his
hand, and drew
his sword, and
smote the [2]ser-
vant of the
high priest,
and struck off
52 his ear. Then
saith Jesus un-
to him, Put up
again thy
sword into its
place: for all
they that take
the sword shall
perish with
53 the sword. Or
thinkest thou
that I cannot
beseech my
Father, and he
shall even now
send me more
than twelve le-
gions of an-
54 gels? How
then should
the scriptures

Luke 22:47–53

and he drew
near unto Je-
sus, to kiss
48 him. But Je-
sus said unto
him, Judas, be-
trayest thou
the Son of man
with a kiss?
49 And when they
that were about
him saw what
would follow,
they said,
Lord, shall we
smite with the
sword?
50 And a
certain one of
them smote
the [2]servant of
the high priest,
and struck off
his right ear.

51 But
Jesus answer-
ed and said,
Suffer ye thus
far. And he
touched his
ear, and heal-
ed him.

John 18:2–12

10 Simon Peter
therefore hav-
ing a sword
drew it, and
struck the
high priest's
[2]servant, and
cut off his right
ear. Now the
[2]servant's name
was Malchus.
11 Jesus there-
fore said unto
Peter, Put up
the sword into
the sheath: the
cup which the
Father hath
given me, shall
I not drink it?

12 So the [3]band
and the [4]chief
captain, and
the officers of
the Jews, seiz-
ed Jesus and
bound him.

Mark 14:43–52

48 And
Jesus answer-
ed and said un-
to them,

Are
ye come out as
against a rob-
ber, with
swords and
staves to seize
49 me? I was
daily with you
in the temple
teaching, and
ye took me
not: but *this
is done* that
the scriptures
might be ful-
50 filled. And
they all left
him, and fled.

51 And a cer-
tain young
man followed
with him, hav-
ing a linen
cloth cast
about him,
over *his* naked
body: and they
lay hold on
52 him; but he
left the linen
cloth, and fled
naked.

Matt. 26:47–56

be fulfilled,
that thus it
55 must be? In
that hour said
Jesus to the
multitudes,

Are
ye come out
as against a
robber with
swords and
staves to seize
me? I sat daily
in the temple
teaching, and
ye took me
56 not. But all
this is come to
pass, that the
scriptures of
the prophets
might be ful-
filled. Then
all the disci-
ples left him
and fled.

Luke 22:47–53

52 And Jesus
said unto the
chief priests,
and captains
of the temple,
and elders,
which were
come against
him, Are ye
come out, as
against a rob-
ber, with
swords and
53 staves? When
I was daily
with you in the
temple, ye
stretched not
forth your
hands against
me: but this is
your hour, and
the power of
darkness.

[1] Gr. *kissed him much.* [2] Gr. *bond-servant.* [3] Or, *cohort.* [4] Or, *military tribune.* Gr. *chiliarch.*

§ 154. JESUS FIRST* EXAMINED BY ANNAS, THE EX-HIGH-PRIEST

The Jewish Trial and related occurrences, §§ *154–162.*

Friday before dawn

John 18:12–14, 19–23

12 So the [1]band and the [2]chief captain, and the officers of the Jews, seized
13 Jesus and bound him, and led him to Annas first; for he was father in
14 law to Caiaphas, which was high priest that year. Now Caiaphas was
he which gave counsel to the Jews, that it was expedient that one man
should die for the people.
19 The high priest therefore asked Jesus of his disciples, and of his teach-
20 ing. Jesus answered him, I have spoken openly to the world; I ever taught
in [3]synagogues, and in the temple, where all the Jews come together;
21 and in secret spake I nothing. Why askest thou me? ask them that have
22 heard *me*, what I spake unto them: behold, these know the things which
I said. And when he had said this one of the officers standing by struck
23 Jesus [4]with his hand, saying, Answerest thou the high priest so? Jesus
answered him, If I have spoken evil, bear witness of the evil; but if well,
why smitest thou me?

[1] Or, *cohort.* [2] Or, *military tribune.* Gr. *chiliarch.* [3] Gr. *synagogue.* [4] Or, *with a rod.*

§ 155. JESUS HURRIEDLY TRIED AND CONDEMNED BY CAIAPHAS AND THE SANHEDRIN, WHO MOCK AND BUFFET HIM

Residence of the High-priest Caiaphas. Before dawn on Friday

Mark 14:53,55–65	Matt.26:57,59–68	Luke 22:54, 63–65	John 18:24
53 And they led Jesus away to the high priest: and there come together with him all the chief priests and the elders and the scribes.	57 And they that had taken Jesus led him away to *the house of* Caiaphas the high priest, where the scribes and the elders were gathered together.	54 And they seized him, and led him away, and brought him into the high priest's house.	24 Annas therefore sent him bound unto Caiaphas the high priest.
55 Now the chief priests and the whole council sought	59 Now the chief priests and the whole council sought		

* The *Jewish trial* comprised three stages, the preliminary examination by Annas (§ 154), the informal trial by the Sanhedrin, probably before dawn, and the formal trial after dawn. With these are narrated two related matters, the denial by Peter and the suicide of Judas.

Mark 14:53, 55–65

witness against
Jesus to put
him to death;
and found it
56 not. For many
bare false wit-
ness against
him, and their
witness agreed
not together.
57 And there
stood up cer-
tain, and bare
false witness
against him,
58 saying, We
heard him say,
I will destroy
this [1]temple
that is made
with hands,
and in three
days I will
build another
made without
59 hands. And
not even so did
their witness
agree togeth-
60 er. And the
high priest
stood up in the
midst, and
asked Jesus,
saying, An-
swerest thou
nothing? what
is it which
these witness
against thee?
61 But he held
his peace, and
answered no-
thing. Again
the high priest
asked him, and
saith unto
him,

Matt. 26:57, 59–68

false witness
against Jesus,
that they
might put him
60 to death; and
they found it
not, though
many false
witnesses
came.
61 But afterward
came two, and
said,
This man
said, I am able
to destroy the
[1]temple of
God, and to
build it in
three days [*see
John 2:19*].
62 And the high
priest stood
up, and said
unto him, An-
swerest thou
nothing? what
is it which
these witness
against thee?
63 But Jesus held
his peace.
And
the high priest
said unto him,
I adjure thee
by the living
God, that thou
tell us whether

Mark 14:53, 55–65

Art thou the
Christ, the Son
of the Blessed?
62 And Jesus
said, I am: and
ye shall see
the Son of
man sitting at
the right hand
of power, and
coming with
the clouds of
63 heaven [*see Ps.
110:1; Dan. 7:
13*]. And the
high priest
rent his
clothes, and
saith,

What
further need
have we of wit-
64 nesses? Ye
have heard
the blasphe-
my [*see Lev.
24:16*]: what
think ye? And
they all con-
demned him
to be [2]worthy
65 of death. And
some began to
spit on him,
and to cover
his face, and
to buffet him,
and to say un-
to him, Proph-
esy: and the
officers receiv-
ed him with
[4]blows of their
hands.

Matt. 26:57, 59–68

thou be the
Christ, the Son
of God.
64 Jesus
saith unto
him, Thou
hast said:
nevertheless I
say unto you,
Henceforth
ye shall see the
Son of man
sitting at the
right hand of
power, and
coming on the
clouds of heav-
65 en. Then the
high priest
rent his gar-
ments, saying,
He hath spok-
en blasphemy:
what further
need have we
of witnesses?
behold, now ye
have heard
the blasphe-
66 my: what think
ye? They an-
swered and
said, He is
[2]worthy of
death.
67 Then
did they spit
in his face and
buffet him: and
some smote
him [3]with the
palms of their
68 hands, saying,
Prophesy unto
us, thou Christ,
who is he that
struck thee?

Luke 22:54, 63–65

63 And the men
that held [5]*Je-
sus* mocked
him and beat
64 him. And they
blindfolded
him, and asked
him, saying,
Prophesy:
who is he that
struck thee?
65 And many
other things
spake they
against him,
reviling him.

[1] Or, *sanctuary;* as in Matt. 23:35; and chap. 27:5. [2] Gr. *liable to.* [3] Or, *with rods.* [4] Or, *strokes of rods.* [5] Gr. *him.*

§ 156. PETER THRICE* DENIES HIS LORD

COURT OF THE HIGH-PRIEST'S RESIDENCE, DURING THE SERIES OF TRIALS

Friday before and about dawn

Mark 14:54, 66–72	Matt. 26:58, 69–75	Luke 22:54–62	John 18:15–18, 25–27
54 And Peter had followed him afar off,	58 But Peter followed him afar off,	54 But Peter followed afar off.	15 And Simon Peter followed Jesus, and *so did* another disciple. Now that disciple was known unto the high priest, and entered in with Jesus into the court of the high priest; but Peter was 16 standing at the door without. So the other disciple,
even within, into the court of the high priest;	unto the court of the high priest, and entered in,		which was known unto the high priest, went out and spake unto her that kept the door, and brought in Pe- 17 ter. The maid therefore that kept the door saith unto Peter, Art thou also *one* of this man's disciples? He saith, I am

* Each of the four Gospels records three denials; but the details differ considerably, as must always be the case where in each narrative a few facts are selected out of many sayings and doings. We have seen (footnote on § 154) that there were *three stages* of the Jewish trial, (1) before Annas, (2) before Caiaphas and the Sanhedrin for informal examination, (3) before them in a formal trial. Now John gives only the first of the three stages, Luke only the last, Matthew and Mark give the second stage fully, and the third in brief mention. If Peter's denials ran through all three (and Luke says in ver. 59 that there was an hour between his second and third denials), then no one of the four Gospels could give each of the denials precisely at the time of its occurrence; and so each Gospel merely throws them together, as in another way we here bring them together in one section. There is no difficulty about the substantial fact of the denials; and we must be content with our inability to arrange all the circumstances into a complete programme.

Mark 14:54, 66–72	Matt. 26:58, 69–75	Luke 22:54–62	John 18:15–18, 25–27
and he was sitting with the officers, and warming himself in the light *of the fire*.	and sat with the officers, to see the end.	55 And when they had kindled a fire in the midst of the court, and had sat down together, Peter sat in the midst of them.	18 not. Now the [5]servants and the officers were standing *there*, having made [6]a fire of coals; for it was cold; and they were warming themselves: and Peter also was with them, standing and warming himself.
66 And as Peter was beneath in the court, there cometh one of the maids of the high priest; 67 and seeing Peter warming himself, she looked upon him, and saith, Thou also wast with the Nazarene, *even* Jesus.	69 Now Peter was sitting without in the court: and a maid came unto him, saying, Thou also wast with Jesus the Galilæan.	56 And a certain maid seing him as he sat in the light *of the fire*, and looking stedfastly upon him, said, This man also was with him.	25 Now Simon Peter was standing and warming himself. They said therefore unto him, Art thou also one of his disciples?
68 But he denied, saying, [1]I neither know, nor understand what thou sayest: and he went out into the [2]porch; [3]and the cock crew.	70 But he denied before them all, saying, I know not what thou sayest.	57 But he denied, saying, Woman, I know him not.	He denied and said, I am not.
69 And the maid saw him, and began again to say to them that stood by, This is *one* of them.	71 And when he was gone out into the proch, another *maid* saw him, and saith unto them that were there, This man also was with Jesus the	58 And after a little while another saw him, and said, Thou also art *one* of them. But Peter said, Man, I am not.	

Mark 14:54, 66–72	Matt. 26:58, 69–75	Luke 22:54–62	John 18:15–18, 25–27
70 But he again denied it.	Nazarene. 72 And again he denied with an oath, I know not the man.		
And after a little while again they that stood by said to Peter, Of a truth thou art *one* of them; for thou art a 71 Galilæan. But he began to curse, and to swear, I know not this man of whom ye 72 speak.	73 And after a little while they that stood by came and said to Peter, Of a truth thou also art *one* of them; for thy speech bewrayeth thee. 74 Then began he to curse and to swear, I know not the man.	59 And after the space of about one hour another confidently affirmed, saying, Of a truth this man also was with him: for he is a Gali- 60 læan. But Peter said, Man, I know not what thou sayest.	26 One of the [5]servants of the high priest being a kinsman of him whose ear Peter cut off, saith, Did not I see thee in the garden 27 with him? Peter therefore denied again:
And straightway the second time the cock crew.	And straightway the cock crew.	And immediately, while he yet spake, the cock crew. 61 And the Lord turned, and looked upon Peter.	and straightway the cock crew.
And Peter called to mind the word, how that Jesus said unto him, Before the cock crow twice, thou shalt deny me thrice. [4]And when he thought thereon, he wept.	75 And Peter remembered the word which Jesus had said, Before the cock crow, thou shalt deny me thrice. And he went out, and wept bitterly.	And Peter remembered the word of the Lord, how that he said unto him, Before the cock crow this day, thou shalt deny me 62 thrice. And he went out, and wept bitterly.	

[1] Or, *I neither know, nor understand: thou, what sayest thou?* [2] Gr. *forecourt.* [3] Many ancient authorities omit *and the cock crew.* [4] Or, *And he began to weep.* [5] Gr. *bond-servants.* [6] Gr. *a fire of charcoal.*

§ 157. AFTER DAWN, JESUS IS FORMALLY* CONDEMNED BY THE SANHEDRIN

Friday

Mark 15:1

1 And straightway in the morning the chief priests with the elders and scribes, and the whole council, held a consultation,

Matt. 27:1

1 Now when morning was come, all the chief priests and the elders of the people took counsel against Jesus to put him to death:

Luke 22:66–71

66 And as soon as it
was day, the assembly of the elders
of the people was
gathered together,
both chief priests and
scribes, and they led
him away into their
67 council, saying, If
thou art the Christ,
tell us. But he said
unto them, If I tell
you, ye will not be-
68 lieve: and if I ask *you*,
ye will not answer.
69 But from henceforth
shall the Son of man
be seated on the right
hand of the power of
God [*see Ps. 110:1;*
70 *Dan. 7:13*]. And they
all said, Art thou then
the Son of God? And
he said unto them,
[1]Ye say that I am.
71 And they said, What
further need have we
of witness? for we
ourselves have heard
from his own mouth.

[1] Or, *Ye say it, because I am.*

§ 158. REMORSE AND SUICIDE OF JUDAS THE BETRAYER

IN THE TEMPLE AND IN A PLACE WITHOUT THE WALLS OF JERUSALEM

Friday morning

Matt. 27:3–10

3 Then Judas, which betrayed him, when he saw that he was con-

Acts 1:18, 19

18 (Now this man obtained a field with the reward of his iniquity;

* This ratification of the condemnation after dawn was an effort to make the action legal. But no ratification of a wrong can make it right. Some modern Jewish writers admit the illegalities and argue the unhistorical character of the narrative. But the hate of the Sanhedrin for Jesus made them violate their own rules of legal procedure. See my book, *The Pharisees and Jesus.*

Matt. 27:3–10

demned, repented himself, and
brought back the thirty pieces of
silver to the chief priests and
4 elders, saying, I have sinned in
that I betrayed [1]innocent blood.
5 But they said, What is that to us?
see thou *to it*. And he cast down
the pieces of silver into the sanctu-
ary, and departed; and he went
6 away and hanged himself. And
the chief priests took the pieces of
silver, and said, It is not lawful to
put them into the [2]treasury, since
it is the price of blood [*see Deut.*
7 *23:18*]. And they took counsel,
and bought with them the potter's
8 field, to bury strangers in. Where-
fore that field was called, The
field of blood, unto this day.
9 Then was fulfilled that which was
spoken [3]by Jeremiah the prophet,
saying, And [4]they took the thirty
pieces of silver, the price of him
that was priced, [5]whom *certain* of
10 the children of Israel did price;
and [6]they gave them for the pot-
ter's field, as the Lord appointed
me [*see Zech. 11:13; Jer. 18:2;*
19:2; 32:6–15].

Acts 1:18, 19

and falling headlong, he burst
asunder in the midst, and all his
19 bowels gushed out. And it be-
came known to all the dwellers at
Jerusalem; insomuch that in their
language that field was called
Akeldama, that is, The field of
blood.)

[1] Many ancient authorities read *righteous*. [2] Gr. *corbanas*, that is, *sacred treasury*. Comp. Mark 7:11. [3] Or, *through*. [4] Or, *I took*. [5] Or, *whom they priced on the part of the sons of Israel*. [6] Some ancient authorities read *I gave*.

§159. JESUS BEFORE PILATE THE FIRST* TIME

Jerusalem. Friday, early morning

Mark 15:1–5

1 and bound Jesus, and carried him away, and delivered him up to Pilate.

Matt. 27:2, 11–14

2 and they bound him, and led him away, and delivered him up to Pilate the governor.

Luke 23:1–5

1 And the whole company of them rose up, and brought him before Pilate.

John 18:28–38

28 They lead Jesus therefore from Caiaphas into the [1]palace: and it was early;
and they themselves entered not into

* The Roman Trial also comprised three stages, (1) the first appearance before the Roman procurator Pilate (§ 159), (2) the appearance before Herod Antipas, the native ruler of Galilee appointed by the Romans (§ 160), and (3) the final appearance before Pilate (§ 161).

Mark 15:1–5	Matt. 27:2, 11–14	Luke 23:1–5	John 18:28–38
		2 And they began to accuse him, saying, We found this man perverting our nation, and forbidding to give tribute to Cæsar, and saying that he himself is [1]Christ a king.	the [2]palace, that they might not be defiled, but might eat the 29 passover. Pilate therefore went out unto them, and saith, What accusation bring ye against this 30 man? They answered and said unto him, If this man were not an evil-doer we should not have delivered him up unto 31 thee. Pilate therefore said unto them, Take him yourselves, and judge him according to your law. The Jews said unto him, It is not lawful for us to put any man to death: 32 that the word of Jesus might be fulfilled, which he spake signifying by what manner of death he should die.
2 And Pilate asked him,	11 Now Jesus stood before the governor:	3 And Pilate asked him, saying,	33 Pilate therefore entered again into the [2]palace, and called Jesus, and said unto him,

Mark 15:1–5

Art thou the King of the Jews? And he answering saith unto him, Thou sayest.

Matt. 27:2, 11–14

and the governor asked him, saying, Art thou the King of the Jews? And Jesus said unto him, Thou sayest.

Luke 23:1–5

Art thou the King of the Jews? And he answered him and said, Thou sayest.

John 18:28–38

Art thou
the King of the
34 Jews? Jesus
answered, Say-
est thou this of
thyself, or did
others tell it
thee concern-
35 ing me? Pilate
answered, Am
I a Jew? Thine
own nation
and the chief
priests deliver-
ed thee unto
me: what hast
thou done?
36 Jesus answer-
ed, My king-
dom is not of
this world: if
my kingdom
were of this
world, then
would my
[3]servants fight,
that I should
not be deliver-
ed to the Jews:
but now is my
kingdom not
from hence.
37 Pilate there-
fore said unto
him, Art thou
a king then?
Jesus answer-
ed, [4]Thou say-
est that I am
a king. To
this end have
I been born,
and to this end
am I come into
the world, that
I should bear
witness unto

Mark 15:1–5

3 And the chief priests accused him of many things.
4 And Pilate again asked him, saying, Answerest thou nothing? behold how many things they accuse
5 thee of. But Jesus no more answered anything; insomuch that Pilate marvelled.

Matt. 27:2, 11–14

12 And when he was accused by the chief priests and elders, he answered noth-
13 ing. Then saith Pilate unto him, Hearest thou not how many things they witness against
14 thee? And he gave him no answer, not even to one word: insomuch that the governor marvelled greatly.

Luke 23:1–5

4 And Pilate said unto the chief priests and the multitudes, I find no fault in this man.

5 But they were the more urgent, saying, He stirreth up the people, teaching throughout all Judea, and beginning from Galilee even unto this place.

John 18:28–38

the truth. Every one that is of the truth heareth my
38 voice. Pilate saith unto him, What is truth? And when he had said this, he went out again unto the Jews, and saith unto them, I find no crime in him.

[1] Or, *an anointed king.* [2] Gr. *Prætorium.* [3] Or, *officers;* as in verses 3, 12, 18, 22. [4] Or, *Thou sayest it, because I am a king.*

§ 160. JESUS BEFORE HEROD ANTIPAS THE TETRARCH

Jerusalem. Friday, early morning

Luke 23:6–12

6 But when Pilate heard it, he asked whether the man were a Galilæan.
7 And when he knew that he was of Herod's jurisdiction, he sent him unto
Herod, who himself also was at Jerusalem in these days.
8 Now when Herod saw Jesus, he was exceeding glad: for he was of a
long time desirous to see him, because he had heard concerning him;*
9 and he hoped to see some [1]miracle done by him. And he questioned
10 him in many words; but he answered him nothing. And the chief priests
11 and the scribes stood, vehemently accusing him. And Herod with his
soldiers set him at nought, and mocked him, and arraying him in gor-
12 geous apparel sent him back to Pilate. And Herod and Pilate became
friends with each other that very day: for before they were at enmity
between themselves.

[1] Gr. *sign*.

§ 161. JESUS THE SECOND TIME BEFORE PILATE

Pilate slowly and reluctantly and in fear surrenders to the demand of the Sanhedrin for the crucifixion of Christ.

Friday toward sunrise (John 19:14)

Mark 15:6–15	Matt. 27:15–26		
6 Now at [1]the feast he used to release unto them one prisoner, whom they asked of 7 him. And there was one called Barabbas, *lying* bound with them that had made insurrection, men who in the insurrection had committed mur- 8 der. And the multitude went up and began to ask	15 Now at [1]the feast the governor was wont to release unto the multitude one prisoner, whom they 16 would. And they had then a notable prisoner, called Barabbas.		

* See § 71.

Mark 15:6–15	Matt. 27:15–26	Luke 23:13–25	John 18:39–19:16
him *to do* as he was wont to do unto them.			
		13 And Pilate called together the chief priests and the rulers and the 14 people, and said unto them, Ye brought unto me this man, as one that perverteth the people: and behold, I, having examined him before you, found no fault in this man touching those things whereof ye accuse him: 15 no, nor yet Herod: for he sent him back unto us; and behold, nothing worthy of death hath been done by him.	
			39 But ye have a custom, that I should release unto you one at the passover: will ye therefore that I release unto you the King of the Jews?
9 And Pilate answered them, saying, Will ye that I release unto you the King of the Jews? 10 For he perceived that for envy the chief priests	17 When therefore they were gathered together, Pilate said unto them, Whom will ye that I release unto you? Barabbas, or Jesus which is called 18 Christ? For he knew that for envy they had delivered	16 I will therefore chastise him, and release him.[5]	

Mark 15:6–15	Matt. 27:15–26	Luke 23:13–25	John 18:39–19:16
had delivered him up.	19 him up. And while he was sitting on the judgement seat, his wife sent unto him, saying, Have thou nothing to do with that righteous man: for I have suffered many things this day in a dream because of		
11 But the chief priests stirred up the multitude that he should rather release Barabbas unto them.	20 him. Now the chief priests and the elders persuaded the multitudes that they should ask for Barabbas, and destroy Jesus. 21 But the governor answered and said unto them, Whether of the twain will ye that I release unto you? And they said, Barabbas.		
		18 But they cried out all together, saying, Away with this man, and release unto us 19 Barabbas: one who for a certain insurrection made in the city, and for murder, was cast into prison.	40 They cried out therefore again, saying, Not this man, but Barabbas. Now Barabbas was a robber.
			1 Then Pilate therefore took Jesus, and

Mark 15:6–15

12 And Pilate
again answer-
ed and said un-
to them, What
then shall I do
unto him
whom ye call
the King of
13 the Jews? And
they cried out
again, Crucify
14 him. And Pi-
late said unto
them, Why,
what evil hath
he done?

Matt. 27:15–26

22 Pilate saith
unto them,
What then
shall I do unto
Jesus which is
called Christ?
They all say,
Let him be
crucified.
23 And
he said, Why,
what evil hath
he done?

Luke 23:13–25

20 And Pilate
spake unto
them again,
desiring to re-
lease Jesus;
21 but they
shouted, say-
ing,
Cru-
cify, crucify
22 him. And he
said unto them
the third time,
Why, what evil
hath this man
done? I have
found no cause

John 18:39–19:16

scourged him.
2 And the sol-
diers plaited
a crown of
thorns, and put
it on his head,
and arrayed
him in a purple
3 garment; and
they came un-
to him, and
said, Hail,
King of the
Jews! and they
struck him
with their
4 hands. And
Pilate went
out again, and
saith unto
them, Behold,
I bring him
out to you,
that ye may
know that I
find no crime
5 in him. Jesus
therefore came
out, wearing
the crown of
thorns and the
purple gar-
ment. And
Pilate saith un-
to them, Be-
hold, the man!
6 When there-
fore the chief
priests and the
officers saw
him, they cried
out, saying,
Crucify *him*,
crucify *him*.
Pilate saith
unto them,
Take him
yourselves,
and crucify
him, for I find

Mark 15:6–15	Matt. 27:15–26	Luke 23:13–25	John 18:39–19:16
		of death in him I will therefore chastise him and release him.	no crime in 7 him. The Jews answered him, We have a law, and by that law he ought to die, because he made himself the Son of 8 God. When Pilate therefore heard this
But they cried out exceedingly, Crucify him.	But they cried out exceedingly, saying, Let him be crucified.		

9 saying, he was the more afraid; and he entered into the [3]palace again,
10 and saith unto Jesus, Whence art thou? But Jesus gave him no answer.
Pilate therefore saith unto him, Speakest thou not unto me? knowest
thou not that I have [7]power to release thee, and have [7]power to crucify
11 thee? Jesus answered him, Thou wouldest have no [7]power against me,
except it were given thee from above: therefore he that delivered me unto
thee hath greater sin.
12 Upon this Pilate sought to release him: but the Jews cried out, saying,
If thou release this man, thou art not Cæsar's friend: every one that
13 maketh himself a king [8]speaketh against Cæsar. When Pilate therefore
heard these words, he brought Jesus out, and sat down on the judgement
14 seat at a place called The Pavement, but in Hebrew, Gabbatha. Now it
was the Preparation of the passover: it was about the sixth hour.* And
he saith unto the Jews, Behold, your King!

		23 But they were instant with loud voices, asking that he might be crucified.	15 They therefore cried out, away with *him*, away with *him*, crucify him. Pilate saith unto them, Shall I crucify your King? The chief priests answered, We have no king but Cæsar.
	24 So when Pilate saw that	And their voices	

* It appears that John, who wrote in Asia Minor, long after the destruction of Jerusalem, makes the day begin at midnight, as the Greeks and Romans did. We seem compelled so to understand him in 20:19 (comp. Luke 24:29–39); and in no passage of his Gospel is that view unsuitable. Here then we understand that Pilate passed the sentence about sunrise, which at the Passover, near the vernal equinox, would be 6 o'clock. The intervening three hours might be occupied in preparations, and the Crucifixion occurred at 9 o'clock, viz. the third hour as counted by the Jews (Mark 15:25).

Mark 15:6–15	Matt. 27:15–26	Luke 23:13–25	John 18:39–19:16
	he prevailed nothing, but rather that a tumult was arising, he took water, and washed his hands before the multitude [*see Deut. 21: 6-9*], saying, I am innocent [2]of the blood of this righteous man: see	prevailed.	
	25 ye *to it*. And all the people answered and said, His blood *be* on us, and on our children.*		
15 And Pilate, wishing to content the multitude,		24 And Pilate gave sentence that what they asked for should	
released unto them Barabbas,	26 Then released he unto them Barabbas:	25 be done. And he released him that for insurrection and murder had been cast into prison, whom they asked for;	
and delivered Jesus, when he had scourged him, to be crucified.	but Jesus he scourged and delivered to be crucified.	but Jesus he delivered up to their will.	16 Then therefore he delivered him unto them to be crucified.

[1] Or, *a feast*. [2] Some ancient authorities read *of this blood; see ye, etc.* [3] Gr. *Prætorium*. See Mark 15:16. [4] Or, *palace*. [5] Many ancient authorities insert ver. 17 *Now he must needs release unto them at the feast one prisoner*. Others add the same words after ver. 19. [6] Or, *with rods*. [7] Or, *authority*. [8] Or, *opposeth Cæsar*.

* Pilate, of course, could not escape full legal and moral responsibility for his cowardly surrender to the Sanhedrin to keep his own office. The guilt of the Sanhedrin (both Pharisees and Sadducees unite in the demand for the blood of Jesus) is beyond dispute. It is impossible to make a mere political issue out of it and to lay all the blame on the Sadducees, who feared a revolution. The Pharisees began the attacks against Jesus on theological and ecclesiastical grounds. The Sadducees later joined the conspiracy against Christ. Judas was a mere tool of the Sanhedrin, who had his resentments and grievances to avenge. There is guilt enough for all the plotters in the greatest wrong of the ages.

§ 162. THE ROMAN SOLDIERS MOCK* JESUS

Friday, between 6 and 9 A.M.

Mark 15:16–19

16 And the soldiers led him away
within the court, which is the
[4]Prætorium; and they call together
17 the whole [2]band. And they clothe
him with purple, and plaiting a
crown of thorns, they put it on
18 him; and they began to salute
him, Hail, King of the Jews!
19 And they smote his head with a
reed, and did spit upon him, and
bowing their knees worshipped
him.

Matt. 27:27–30

27 Then the soldiers of the governor
took Jesus into the [1]palace,
and gathered unto him the whole
28 [2]band. And they [3]stripped him,
and put on him a scarlet robe.
29 And they plaited a crown of thorns
and put it upon his head, and a
reed in his right hand; and they
kneeled down before him, and
mocked him, saying, Hail, King
30 of the Jews! And they spat upon
him, and took the reed and smote
him on the head.

[1] Gr. *Prætorium.* [2] Or, *cohort.* [3] Some ancient authorities read *clothed him.* [4] Or, *palace.*

§ 163. JESUS ON THE WAY TO THE CROSS (*VIA DOLOROSA*) ON GOLGOTHA†

Before 9 A.M. Friday

Mark 15:20–23

20 And when they
had mocked
him, they took
off from him
the purple, and
put on him his
garments. And
they lead him
out to crucify
him.
21 And they
[2]compel one
passing by, Simon
of Cyrene,
coming from
the country,
the father of
Alexander and
Rufus, to go
with them, that

Matt. 27:31–34

31 And when they
had mocked
him, they took
off from him
the robe, and
put on him his
garments, and
led him away
to crucify him.
32 And as they
came out, they
found a man
of Cyrene, Simon
by name:
him they [1]compelled
to go
with them, that
he might bear
his cross.

Luke 23:26–33

26 And when
they led him
away, they laid
hold upon one
Simon of Cyrene,
coming
from the country,
and laid
on him the
cross, to bear

John 19:16–17

16 They took Jesus
therefore;
17 and he went
out bearing the
cross for himself,

* The Sanhedrin likewise had mocked Jesus when they had condemned him to death (§ 155).

† Golgotha is the Aramaic word for "skull," and Calvary is the Latin word. The place cannot have been where the so-called "Church of the Holy Sepulchre" stands, far within the walls. There is of late a rapidly growing agreement that it was the northern end of the Temple hill, whose rounded summit (without the city wall), and southern face with holes in the rock, looks at a little distance much like a skull. This place fulfils all the conditions.

Mark 15:20-23

he might bear
his cross.

Luke 23:26-33

it after Jesus.

27 And there
followed him a
great multi-
tude of the
people, and of
women who
bewailed and
lamented him.
28 But Jesus turn-
ing unto them
said, Daugh-
ters of Jerusa-
lem, weep not
for me, but
weep for your-
selves, and for
your children.
29 For behold, the
days are com-
ing, in which
they shall say,
Blessed are the
barren, and the
wombs that
never bare, and
the breasts that
never gave
30 suck. Then
shall they be-
gin to say to
the moun-
tains, Fall on
us; and to the
hills, Cover us
31 [*see Hos. 10:
8*]. For if they
do these things
in the green
tree, what shall
be done in the
dry?
32 And there
were also two
others, male-
factors, led
with him to be
put to death.

Mark 15:20–23	Matt. 27:31–34	Luke 23:26–33	John 19:16–17
22 And they bring him unto the place Golgotha, which is, being interpreted, The place of a 23 skull. And they offered him wine mingled with myrrh: but he received it not.	33 And when they were come unto a place called Golgotha, that is to say, The place of a 34 skull, they gave him wine to drink mingled with gall [*see Ps. 69:21*] and when he had tasted it, he would not drink	33 And when they came unto the place which is called [3]The skull,	unto the place called The place of a skull, which is called in Hebrew Golgotha:

[1] Gr. *impressed.* [2] Gr. *impress.* [3] According to the Latin, *Calvary*, which has the same meaning.

§ 164. THE FIRST THREE HOURS ON THE CROSS

From nine A.M. *till noon on Friday (three sayings of Jesus; the soldiers gambling for the garment of Jesus; the inscription on the Cross; the scoffing of Jesus by the multitude, the Sanhedrin, the soldiers, and even by the two robbers on each side of Christ)**

Mark 15:24–32	Matt. 27:35–44	Luke 23:33–43	John 19:18–27
24 And they crucify him, and part his garments among them, casting lots upon them, what each should take [*see Ps. 22:18*].	35 And when they had crucified him, they parted his garments among them, casting lots: 36 and they sat and watched him there.	33 there they crucified him, and the malefactors, one on the right hand and the other on 34 the left. [4]And Jesus said, Father, forgive them: for they know not what they do.	18 where they crucified him, and with him two others, on either side one, and Jesus in the midst.
		And parting his garments a-	23 The soldiers therefore, when they had crucified Jesus, took his garments,

* It is not easy to tell the precise order of the events during this period of three hours, since the Gospels do not present them in the same detail or order. On the whole it has seemed best simply to follow Mark's arrangement as we have done uniformly in the Harmony. Thus the apparent order of the sayings is (1) The Prayer of Christ's enemies in Luke 23:34. (2) The Promise to the Repentant Robber in Luke 23:43. (3) The Charge to the Mother of Jesus and to the Beloved Disciple in John 19:26, 27. These three sayings are with reference to others.

Mark 15:24–32

25 And it was
the third hour,
and they cruci-
fied him.
26 And the super-
scription of his
accusation was
written over,
THE KING OF
THE JEWS.

27 And
with him they
crucify two
robbers; one
on his right
hand, and one
on his left[3].

Matt. 27:35–44

37 And
they set up
over his head
his accusation
written, THIS
IS JESUS THE
KING OF THE
JEWS.

38 Then are
there crucified
with him two
robbers, one on
the right hand,
and one on the
left.

Luke 23:33–43

mong them,
they cast lots.

38 And there was
also a super-
scription over
him, THIS IS
THE KING OF
THE JEWS.

John 19:18–27

and made four
parts, to every
soldier a part;
and also the
[5]coat: now the
[5]coat was with-
out seam, wov-
en from the
top through-
24 out. They said
therefore one
to another, Let
us not rend it,
but cast lots
for it, whose it
shall be: that
the scripture
might be fulfill-
ed, which saith,
They parted
my gar-
ments
among
them,
And upon my
vesture did
they cast
lots. [*Ps.
22:18*].
These things
therefore the
soldiers did.
19 And Pilate
wrote a title al-
so, and put it
on the cross.
And there was
written, JESUS
OF NAZARETH,
THE KING OF
20 THE JEWS. This
title therefore
read many of
the Jews: [7]for
the place where
Jesus was cru-
cified was nigh
to the city: and
it was written
in Hebrew, *and*

Mark 15:24–32	Matt. 27:35–44	Luke 23:33–43	John 19:18–27
			in Latin, *and* in 21 Greek. The chief priests of the Jews there- fore said to Pi- late, Write not, The King of the Jews; but, that he said, I am King of 22 the Jews. Pi- late answered, What I have written I have written.
29 And they that passed by rail- ed on him, wagging their heads [*see Ps.* *22:7*], and say- ing, Ha! thou that destroyest the [1]temple, and buildest it in three days 30 save thyself, and come down from the cross.	39 And they that passed by rail- ed on him, wagging their 40 heads, and say- ing, Thou that destroyest the [1]temple, and buildest it in three days, save thyself: if thou art the Son of God come down from the cross.	35 And the peo- ple stood be- holding.	
31 In like manner also the chief priests mock- ing *him* a- mong them- selves with the scribes said, He saved oth- ers; [2]himself he cannot save. 32 Let the Christ, the King of Is- rael, now come down from the cross, that we may see and believe.	41 In like manner also the chief priests mock- ing *him*, with the scribes and 42 elders, said, He saved others; [2]himself he cannot save. He is the King of Israel; let him now come down from the cross, and we will believe on 43 him. He trust- eth on God [*see* *Ps. 22:8*]; let him deliver him now if he	And the rulers also scoffed at him, saying, He saved others: let him save himself, if this is the Christ of God, his 36 chosen. And the soldiers also mocked him, coming to him, offering 37 him vinegar, and saying, If thou art the King of the Jews, save thy- self.	

Mark 15:24–32

And
they that were
crucified with
him reproach-
ed him.

Matt. 27:35–44

desireth him:
for he said, I
am the Son of
44 God. And the
robbers also
that were cru-
cified with him
cast upon him
the same re-
proach.

Luke 23:33–43

39 And one of
the malefac-
tors which
were hanged
railed on him,
saying, Art not
thou the
Christ? save
thyself and us.
40 But the other
answered, and
rebuking him
said, Dost thou
not even fear
God, seeing
thou art in the
same condem-
41 nation? And we
indeed justly;
for we receive
the due reward
of our deeds:
but this man
hath done no-
thing amiss.
42 And he said,
Jesus, remem-
ber me when
thou comest[6] in
thy kingdom.
43 And he said
unto him, Ver-
ily I say unto
thee, To-day
shalt thou be
with me in
Paradise.

John 19:18–27

25 But there were
standing by the
cross of Jesus

John 19:18–27

his mother, and
his mother's
sister, Mary
the *wife* of
Cleopas, and
Mary Magda-
26 lene. When
Jesus therefore
saw his mother
and the dis-
ciple standing
by, whom he
loved, he saith
27 unto his moth-
er, Woman, be-
hold, thy son!
Then saith
he to the dis-
ciple, Behold,
thy mother!
And from that
hour the dis-
ciple took her
unto his own
home.

[1] Or, *sanctuary.* [2] Or, *can he not save himself?* [3] Many ancient authorities insert ver. 28 *And the scripture was fulfilled which saith, And he was reckoned with transgressors.* See Luke 22:37. [4] Some ancient authorities omit *And Jesus said, Father, forgive them: for they know not what they do.* [5] Or, *tunic.* [6] Some ancient authorities read *into thy kingdom.* [7] Or, *for the place of the city where Jesus was crucified was nigh at hand.*

§ 165. THE THREE HOURS OF DARKNESS FROM NOON TO THREE P.M.

(Four More Sayings at the Close of the Darkness and the Death of Christ.)*

Mark 15:33–37

33 And when the
sixth hour was
come, there
was darkness
over the whole
[1]land until the
ninth hour.
34 And at the
ninth hour Je-

Matt. 27:45–50

45 Now from the
sixth hour
there was
darkness over
all the [1]land
until the ninth
46 hour. And a-
bout the ninth
hour Jesus

Luke 23:44–46

44 And it was
now about the
sixth hour, and
a darkness
came over the
whole [1]land un-
til the ninth
45 hour,[4] the sun's
light failing.

* The probable order of these four sayings coming just before the death of Jesus in (1) The Cry of Desolation, Mark 15:34 = Matt. 27:46. (2) The Cry of Physical Anguish, John 19:28. (3) The Cry of Victory, John 19:30. (4) The Cry of Resignation, Luke 23:46. These four sayings of Jesus are with reference to himself.

Mark 15:33–37	Matt. 27:45–50	Luke 23:44–46	John 19:28–30
sus cried with a loud voice, Eloi, Eloi, lama sabachthani? which is, being interpreted, My God, my God, [2]why hast thou forsaken me?	cried with a loud voice, saying Eli, Eli, lama, sabachthani? that is, My God, my God, [2]why hast thou forsaken me[*Ps. 22:1*]?		
35 And some of them that stood by, when they heard it, said, Behold, he calleth Elijah.	47 And some of them that stood there, when they heard it, said, This man calleth Elijah.		
			28 After this Jesus, knowing that all things are now finished, that the scripture might be accomplished, saith, I 29 thirst. There was set there a vessel full of vinegar: so they put a sponge full of the vinegar upon hyssop, and brought it to his mouth [*see Ps. 69:21*].
36 And one ran, and filling a sponge full of vinegar, put it on a reed, and gave him to drink, saying, Let be; let us see whether Elijah cometh to take him down.	48 And straightway one of them ran, and took a sponge, and filled it with vinegar, and put it on a reed, and gave him to drink. 49 And the rest said, Let be; let us see whether Elijah cometh to save him.[3]		
			30 When Jesus therefore had received the vinegar,
37 And Jesus uttered a loud voice,	50 And Jesus cried again with a loud voice,	46 [5]And when Jesus had cried with a loud voice, he said,	he said, It is finished:
		Father, into thy hands I commend my spirit [*see Ps. 31:5*]; and hav-	

Mark 15:33–37	Matt. 27:45–50	Luke 23:44–46	John 19:28–30
		ing said this,	and he bowed his head,
and gave up the ghost.	and yielded up his spirit.	he gave up the ghost.	and gave up his spirit.

[1] Or, *earth.* [2] Or, *why didst thou forsake me?* [3] Many ancient authorities add *And another took a spear and pierced his side, and there came out water and blood.* See John 19:34. [4] Gr. *the sun failing.* [5] Or, *And Jesus, crying with a loud voice, said.*

§ 166. THE PHENOMENA ACCOMPANYING THE DEATH OF CHRIST

Mark 15:38–41	Matt. 27:51–56	Luke 23:45, 47–49
38 And the veil of the [2]temple was rent in twain from the top to the bottom.	51 And behold, the veil of the [2]temple was rent in twain from the top to the bottom; and the earth did quake; and the rocks were rent; and 52 the tombs were opened; and many bodies of the saints that had fallen asleep were 53 raised; and coming forth out of the tombs after his resurrection they entered into the holy city and appeared unto many.	45 And the veil of the [2]temple was rent in the midst.
39 And when the centurion, which stood by over against him, saw that he [1]so gave up the ghost, he said, Truly this man was [3]the Son of 40 God.	54 Now the centurion, and they that were with him watching Jesus, when they saw the earthquake, and the things that were done, feared exceedingly, saying, Truly this was [3]the Son of 55 God.	47 And when the centurion saw what was done, he glorified God, saying, Certainly this was a righteous man.
And there were also women beholding from afar: among whom *were* both Mary Magdalene, and Mary the mother of James the [4]less and of	And many women were there beholding from afar, which had followed Jesus from Galilee, ministering unto him: 56 among whom was Mary Magdalene, and Mary the mother of James and Joses, and	48 And all the multitudes that came together to this sight, when they beheld the things that were done, returned smiting their 49 breasts. And all his acquaintance, and the women that followed with him from Gal-

Mark 15:38–41	Matt. 27:51–56	Luke 23:45, 47–49
Joses, and Salome; 41 who, when he was in Galilee, followed him, and ministered unto him: and many other women which came up with him unto Jerusalem.	the mother of the sons of Zebedee.	ilee, stood afar off, seeing these things.

[1] Many ancient authorities read, *so cried out and gave up the ghost.* [2] Or, *sanctuary.* [3] Or, *a Son of God.* [4] Gr. *little.*

§ 167. THE BURIAL OF THE BODY OF JESUS IN THE TOMB OF JOSEPH OF ARIMATHEA AFTER PROOF OF HIS DEATH

Friday afternoon before 6 P.M.

Mark 15:42–46	Matt. 27:57–60	Luke 23:50–54	John 19:31–42
			31 The Jews, therefore, because it was

the Preparation, that the bodies should not remain on the cross upon
the sabbath (for the day of that sabbath was a high *day*), asked of Pilate
that their legs might be broken, and *that* they might be taken away.
32 The soldiers therefore came, and brake the legs of the first, and of the
33 other which was crucified with him: but when they came to Jesus, and
saw that he was dead already, they brake not his legs: howbeit one of
34 the soldiers with a spear pierced his side, and straightway there came out
35 blood and water. And he that hath seen hath borne witness, and his
witness is true: and he knoweth that he saith true, that ye also may
36 believe. For these things came to pass, that the scripture might be
fulfilled [*see Ex. 12:46; Num. 9:12; Ps. 34:20*], A bone of him shall not
37 be [3]broken. And again another scripture saith [*see Zech. 12:10. Deut.
21:22–23; Ex. 34:24*], They shall look on him whom they pierced.

Mark	Matt.	Luke	John
42 And when even was now come, because it was the Preparation, that is, the day before the sabbath,	57 And when even was come,		
43 there came Joseph of Arimathæa, a councillor of honourable estate,	there came a rich man from Arimathæa, named Joseph,	50 And behold, a man named Joseph, who was a councillor, a good man and a 51 righteous (he	38 And after these things Joseph of Arimathæa,

Mark 15:42–46	Matt. 27:57–60	Luke 23:50–54	John 19:31–42
		had not consented to their counsel and deed), *a man* of Arimathæa, a city of the Jews,	
who also himself was looking for the kingdom of God;	who also himself was Jesus' disciple:	who was looking for the kingdom of God:	being a disciple of Jesus, but secretly for fear of the Jews,
and he boldly went in unto Pilate, and asked for the body of Je- 44 sus. And Pilate marvelled if he were already dead: and calling unto him the centurion, he asked him whether he [1]had been any while dead. 45 And when he learned it of the centurion, he granted the corpse to Joseph.	58 this man went to Pilate, and asked for the body of Jesus. Then Pilate commanded it to be given up.	52 this man went to Pilate, and asked for the body of Jesus.	asked of Pilate that he might take away the body of Jesus: and Pilate gave *him* leave. He came therefore, and took away 39 his body. And there came also Nicodemus, he who at the first came to him by night, bringing a [4]mixture of myrrh and aloes, about a hundred pound 40 *weight.* So they took the body of Jesus, and bound it in linen cloths with
46 And he bought a linen cloth, and taking him down, wound him in the linen cloth,	59 And Joseph took the body, and wrapped it in a clean linen cloth,	53 And he took it down, and wrapped it in a linen cloth,	

Mark 15:42–46	Matt. 27:57–60	Luke 23:50–54	John 19:31–42
			the spices, as the custom of the Jews is to 41 bury. Now in the place where he was crucified there was a garden; and in the garden a new tomb wherein was never man yet 42 laid [*see Deut. 21:22–23*]. There then because of the Jews' Preparation (for the tomb was nigh at hand) they laid Jesus.
and laid him in a tomb which had been hewn out of a rock; and he rolled a stone against the door of the tomb.	60 and laid it in his own new tomb, which he had hewn out in the rock: and he rolled a great stone to the door of the tomb and departed.	and laid him in a tomb that was hewn in stone, where never man had 54 yet lain. And it was the day of the Preparation, and the sabbath [2]drew on.	

[1] Many ancient authorities read, *were already dead*. [2] Gr. *began to dawn*. [3] Or, *crushed*. [4] Some ancient authorities read *roll*.

§ 168. THE WATCH OF THE WOMEN BY THE TOMB OF JESUS

The women maintain their watch and rest on the Sabbath (beginning 6 P.M.) while the Pharisees have a guard of Roman soldiers to keep watch over the Roman seal on the tomb.

Friday afternoon till Saturday afternoon

Mark 15:47	Matt. 27:61–66	Luke 23:55–56
47 And Mary Magdalene and Mary the *mother* of Joses beheld where he was laid.	61 And Mary Magdalene was there, and the other Mary, sitting over against the sepulchre.	55 And the women, which had come with him out of Galilee, followed after, and beheld the tomb, and how his body was laid. 56 And they returned, and prepared spices and ointments. And on the sabbath* they rested

* Luke (23:54) notes that "the Sabbath drew on" after the burial on Friday afternoon. The Sabbath began at 6 P.M. Then Luke notes that the women rested during the Sabbath (our Friday night and Saturday).

Matt. 27:61–66	Luke 23:55–56
	according to the commandment [*see Ex. 12:16; 20:8–11; Deut. 5:12–15*].
62 Now on the morrow, which is *the day* after the Preparation,	

the chief priests and the Pharisees were gathered
together unto Pilate, saying, Sir, we remem-
63 ber that that deceiver said, while he was yet
alive, After three days I rise again. Com-
64 mand therefore that the sepulchre be made
sure until the third day, lest haply his disciples
come and steal him away, and say unto the
people, He is risen from the dead: and the last
65 error will be worse than the first. Pilate said
unto them, [1]Ye have a guard: go your way,
66 [2]make it *as* sure as ye can. So they went, and
made the sepulchre sure, sealing the stone, the
guard being with them.

[1] Or, *take a guard.* [2] Gr. *make it sure, as ye know.*

PART XIV

THE RESURRECTION, APPEARANCES, AND ASCENSION OF CHRIST

During forty days beginning with Sunday after the death of Christ. Spring of A.D. *30 (or 29). Judea and Galilee**. §§ *169–184.*

§ 169. THE VISIT OF THE WOMEN TO THE TOMB OF JESUS

They watch the tomb late on the Sabbath (our Saturday afternoon); and the purchase of spices by them after the Sabbath (after 6 P.M. *Saturday) on the first day of the week.*

GOLGOTHA AND BETHANY

Our late Saturday afternoon and early evening

Mark 16:1

1 And when the sabbath was past, Mary Magdalene, and Mary the *mother* of James, and Salome, bought spices, that they might come and anoint him.

Matt. 28:1

1 Now late †on the sabbath day, as it began to dawn toward the first *day* of the week, came Mary Magdalene and the other Mary to see the sepulchre.

---

* Of this period we see that he remained at or near Jerusalem for a week. Then he probably left at once for Galilee (Matt. 28:7; Mark 16:7). In the month that followed we cannot fix the exact time of the events that occurred in Galilee, but just at the end of the forty days we find him again in Jerusalem.

† This phrase once gave much trouble, but the usage of the vernacular *Koiné* Greek amply justifies the translation. The visit of the women to inspect the tomb was thus made before the sabbath was over (before 6 P.M. on Saturday). But the same Greek idiom was occasionally used in the sense of "after." See Robertson, Grammar of the Greek New Testament in the Light of Historical Research, p. 645. The distance from Bethany to Golgotha was not more than a sabbath day's journey. The spices could be purchased after sundown either in Bethany or Jerusalem. It must be borne in mind that the Jewish First Day of the Week began at 6 P.M. on our Saturday.

§ 170. THE EARTHQUAKE, THE ROLLING AWAY OF THE STONE BY AN ANGEL, AND THE FRIGHT OF THE ROMAN WATCHERS

Sunday before sunrise

Matt. 28:2-4

2 And behold, there was a great earthquake; for an angel of the Lord
descended from heaven, and came and rolled away the stone, and sat upon
3 it. His appearance was as lightning, and his raiment white as snow:
4 and for fear of him the watchers did quake, and became as dead men.

§ 171. THE VISIT OF THE WOMEN TO THE TOMB OF JESUS ABOUT SUNRISE SUNDAY MORNING AND THE MESSAGE OF THE ANGELS ABOUT THE EMPTY TOMB

Golgotha. Early Sunday morning

Mark 16:2-8

2 And very early
on the first
day of the
week they
come to the
tomb when the
sun was risen.
3 And they were
saying among
themselves,
Who shall roll
us away the
stone from the
door of the
4 tomb? and
looking up

Luke 24:1-8

1 But on the
first day of the
week, at early
dawn,* they
came unto the
tomb, bringing
the spices
which they
had prepared.
2 And they found
the stone roll-
ed away from
3 the tomb. And
they entered
in, and found
not the body

John 20:1

1 Now on the
first *day* of the
week cometh
Mary Magda-
lene early while
it was yet dark
unto the tomb,
and seeth
the stone taken
away from the
tomb.

* So he had already risen at early dawn on the first day of the week. He was buried (§ 167) shortly before sunset on Friday, and at sunset the sabbath began. So he lay in the tomb a small part of Friday, all of Saturday, and 10 or 11 hours of Sunday. This corresponds exactly with the seven times repeated statement that he would or did rise "on the third day," which *could not possibly* mean after 72 hours. The phrase two or three times given, "after three days," naturally denoted for Jews, as for Greeks and Romans, a whole central day and any part of a first and third, thus agreeing with "on the third day." Even the "three days and three nights" of Matt. 12:40 need not, according to known Jewish usage, mean more than we have described. So these expressions *can* be reconciled with "on the third day," and with the facts as recorded, while "on the third day" *cannot* mean after 72 hours. See Note 13 at end of the Harmony for full discussion of the question. There is no real appeal from the testimony of Luke, who gives the whole period. Luke states that Jesus was buried just before the sabbath "drew on" (our Friday evening); that the women rested during the sabbath (our Saturday), and that Jesus was already risen early Sunday morning when the women came to the tomb.

Mark 16:2–8

they see that
the stone is
rolled back: for
it was exceed-
5 ing great. And
entering into
the tomb, they
saw a young
man sitting on
the right side,
arrayed in a
white robe;
and they were
6 amazed. And
he saith unto
them, Be not
amazed: ye
seek Jesus the
Nazarene,
which hath
been crucified:
he is risen; he
is not here: be-
hold, the place
where they
7 laid him! But
go, tell his dis-
ciples and
Peter, He go-
eth before you
into Galilee:
there shall ye
see him, as he
said unto you.
8 And they went
out, and fled
from the tomb;
for trembling
and astonish-
ment had come
upon them; and
they said noth-
ing to any one;
for they were
afraid.

Matt. 28:5–8

5 And
the angel an-
swered and
said unto the
women, Fear
not ye: for I
know that ye
seek Jesus,
which hath
been crucified.
6 He is not here;
for he is risen,
even as he
said. Come,
see the place
[1]where the
7 Lord lay. And
go quickly, and
tell his disci-
ples, He is ris-
en from the
dead; and lo,
he goeth be-
fore you into
Galilee; there
shall ye see
him: lo, I have
8 told you. And
they departed
quickly from
the tomb with
fear and great
joy, and ran to
bring his dis-
ciples word.

Luke 24:1–8

[2]of the Lord
Jesus.
4 And it
came to pass,
while they
were perplex-
ed thereabout,
behold, two
men stood by
them in daz-
zling apparel:
5 and as they
were affright-
ed, and bowed
down their
faces to the
earth, they
said unto
them, Why
seek ye [3]the
living among
6 the dead? [4]He
is not here,
but is risen:
remember how
he spake unto
you when he
was yet in Gal-
7 ilee, saying
that the Son
of man must
be delivered
up into the
hands of sinful
men, and be
crucified, and
the third day
8 rise again. And
they remem-
bered his
words.

[1] Many ancient authorities read *where he lay*. [2] Some ancient authorities omit *of the Lord Jesus*.
[3] Gr. *him that liveth*. [4] Some ancient authorities omit *He is not here, but is risen*.

§ 172. MARY MAGDALENE AND THE OTHER WOMEN REPORT TO THE APOSTLES AND PETER AND JOHN VISIT THE EMPTY TOMB

Luke 24:9–12

9 and returned [1]from the tomb, and
told all these things to the eleven,
10 and to all the rest. Now they
were Mary Magdalene, and Joanna, and Mary the *mother* of James:
and the other women with them
told these things unto the apostles.
11 And these words appeared in their
sight as idle talk; and they disbelieved them.
12 [2]But Peter arose, and ran into the
tomb; and stooping and looking
in, he seeth the linen clothes by
themselves; and he [3]departed to
his home, wondering at that which
was come to pass.

John 20:2–10

2 She runneth therefore, and cometh to Simon Peter, and to the
other disciple, whom Jesus loved,
and saith unto them, They have
taken away the Lord out of the
tomb, and we know not where
3 they have laid him. Peter therefore went forth, and the other
disciple, and they went toward the
4 tomb. And they ran both together;
and the other disciple outran
Peter, and came first to the tomb;
5 and stooping and looking in, he
seeth the linen cloths lying; yet
6 entered he not in. Simon Peter
therefore also cometh, following
him, and entered into the tomb;
and he beholdeth the linen cloths
7 lying, and the napkin, that was
upon his head, not lying with the
linen cloths, but rolled up in a
8 place by itself. Then entered in
therefore the other disciple also,
which came first to the tomb, and
9 he saw, and believed. For as yet
they knew not the scripture, that
he must rise again from the dead.
10 So the disciples went away again
unto their own home.

[1] Some ancient authorities omit *from the tomb*. [2] Some ancient authorities omit verse 12. [3] Or, *departed, wondering with himself.*

Five appearances are given as occurring on the day of his resurrection, and five subsequently during the forty days. The five appearances on this day were (1) to Mary Magdalene (John and Mark); (2) to other women (Matthew); (3) to the two going to Emmaus; (4) to Simon Peter (Luke 24:34); (5) to ten apostles and others.

§ 173. THE APPEARANCE OF JESUS TO MARY MAGDALENE AND THE MESSAGE TO THE DISCIPLES

Jerusalem. The first day of the week (Sunday)

John 20:11–18

11 But Mary was standing without
at the tomb weeping: so, as she

Mark 16:9–11	John 20:11–18
	wept, she stooped and looked into 12 the tomb; and she beholdeth two angels in white sitting, one at the head, and one at the feet, where 13 the body of Jesus had lain. And they say unto her, Woman, why weepest thou? She saith unto them, Because they have taken away my Lord, and I know not
9 [1]Now when he was risen early on the first day of the week, he ap- peared first to Mary Magdalene, from whom he had cast out seven [2]devils.	14 where they have laid him. When she had thus said, she turned her- self back, and beholdeth Jesus standing, and knew not that it 15 was Jesus. Jesus saith unto her, Woman, why weepest thou? whom seekest thou? She, supposing him to be the gardener, saith unto him, Sir, if thou hast borne him hence, tell me where thou hast laid him, 16 and I will take him away. Jesus saith unto her, Mary. She turneth herself, and saith unto him in He- brew, Rabboni; which is to say, 17 [3]Master. Jesus saith to her, [4]Touch me not; for I am not yet ascended unto the Father: but go unto my brethren, and say to them, I ascend unto my Father and your Father, 18 and my God and your God. Mary
10 She went and told them that had been with him, as they mourned and wept.	Magdalene cometh and telleth the disciples, I have seen the Lord; and *how that* he had said these things unto her.
11 And they, when they heard that he was alive, and had been seen of her, disbelieved.	

[1] The two oldest manuscripts, and some other authorities, omit from ver. 9 to the end. Some other authorities have a different ending to the Gospel. [2] Gr. *demons*. [3] Or, *Teacher*. [4] Or, *Take hold not on me.*

§ 174. THE APPEARANCE OF JESUS TO THE OTHER WOMEN

Jerusalem. Sunday the first day of the week

Matt. 28:9–10

9 And behold, Jesus met them, saying, All hail. And they came and
10 took hold of his feet, and worshipped him. Then saith Jesus unto them,
Fear not: go tell my brethren that they depart into Galilee, and there
shall they see me.

§ 175. SOME OF THE GUARD REPORT TO THE JEWISH RULERS

Matt 28:11–15

11 Now while they were going, behold, some of the guard came into the
city, and told unto the chief priests all the things that were come to pass.
12 And when they were assembled with the elders, and had taken counsel,
13 they gave large money unto the soldiers, saying, Say ye, His disciples
14 came by night, and stole him away while we slept. And if this [1]come to
15 the governor's ears, we will persuade him, and rid you of care. So they
took the money, and did as they were taught: and this saying was spread
abroad among the Jews, *and continueth* until this day.

[1] Or, *come to a hearing before the governor.*

§ 176. THE APPEARANCE TO TWO DISCIPLES (CLEOPHAS AND ANOTHER) ON THE WAY TO EMMAUS

Sunday afternoon

Mark 16:12, 13

12 And after these things he was
manifested in another form unto
two of them, as they walked on
13 their way into the country. And
they went away and told it unto
the rest: neither believed they
them.

Luke 24:13–32

13 And behold, two of them were
going that very day to a village
named Emmaus, which was three-
score furlongs from Jerusalem.
14 And they communed with each
other of all these things which
15 had happened. And it came to
pass, while they communed and
questioned together,
16 that Jesus himself drew near, and went with them. But their eyes
17 were holden that they should not know him. And he said unto them,
[1]What communications are these that ye have one with another, as
18 ye walk? And they stood still, looking sad. And one of them, named
Cleopas, answering said unto him, [2]Dost thou alone sojourn in Jeru-
salem and not know the things which are come to pass there in
19 these days? And he said unto them, What things? And they said
unto him, The things concerning Jesus of Nazareth, which was a
prophet mighty in deed and word before God and all the people: and
20 how the chief priests and our rulers delivered him up to be condemned to
21 death, and crucified him. But we hoped that it was he which should
redeem Israel. Yea and beside all this, it is now the third day since
22 these things came to pass. Moreover certain women of our company
23 amazed us, having been early at the tomb; and when they found not his
body, they came, saying, that they had also seen a vision of angels, which
24 said that he was alive. And certain of them that were with us went to
the tomb, and found it even so as the women had said: but him they saw
25 not. And he said unto them, O foolish men, and slow of heart to believe
26 [3]in all that the prophets have spoken! Behoved it not the Christ to suffer
27 these things, and to enter into his glory? And beginning from Moses
and from all the prophets, he interpreted to them in all the scriptures

Luke 24:13-32

28 the things concerning himself. And they drew nigh unto the village,
whither they were going: and he made as though he would go further.
29 And they constrained him, saying, Abide with us: for it is toward evening,
and the day is now far spent. And he went in to abide with them.
30 And it came to pass, when he had sat down with them to meat, he took
31 the [4]bread, and blessed it, and brake, and gave to them. And their eyes
were opened, and they knew him; and he vanished out of their sight.
32 And they said one to another, Was not our heart burning within us,
while he spake to us in the way, while he opened to us the scriptures?

[1] Gr. *What words are these that ye exchange one with another?* [2] Or, *Dost thou sojourn alone in Jerusalem, and knowest thou not the things.* [3] Or, *after.* [4] Or, *loaf.*

§ 177. THE REPORT OF THE TWO DISCIPLES AND THE NEWS OF THE APPEARANCE TO SIMON PETER

Jerusalem. Sunday evening

Luke 24:33-35

33 And they rose up that very hour, and returned
to Jerusalem, and found the eleven gathered
together, and them that were with them,
34 saying, The Lord is risen indeed, and hath ap-
35 peared to Simon. And they rehearsed the
things *that happened* in the way, and how he
was known of them in the breaking of the
bread.

1 Cor. 15:5

5 and that he appeared to Cephas.

§ 178. THE APPEARANCE TO THE ASTONISHED DISCIPLES (THOMAS ABSENT) WITH A COMMISSION AND THEIR FAILURE TO CONVINCE THOMAS

Jerusalem. Sunday evening

Mark 16:14

14 And afterward he was manifested unto the eleven themselves as they sat at meat;

Luke 24:36-43

36 And as they spake
these things, he him-
self stood in the midst
of them, [1]and saith
unto them, Peace *be*
37 unto you. But they
were terrified and affrighted, and supposed that they beheld a spirit.

John 20:19-25

19 When therefore it was evening, on that day, the first *day* of the week, and when the doors were shut where the disciples were, for fear of the Jews, Jesus came and stood in the midst, and saith unto them, Peace *be* unto you.

Mark 16:14

and he up-
braided them with
their unbelief and
hardness of heart, be-
cause they believed
not them which had
seen him after he was
risen.

Luke 24:36–43

38 And he said unto
them, Why are ye
troubled? and where-
fore do reasonings
arise in your heart?
39 See my hands and
my feet, that it is I
myself; handle me,
and see; for a spirit
hath not flesh and
bones, as ye behold
40 me having. [2]And
when he had said
this, he shewed them
his hands and his feet.
41 And while they still
disbelieved for joy,
and wondered, he said
unto them, Have ye
here anything to eat?
42 And they gave him a
piece of a broiled fish[3].
43 And he took it, and
did eat before them.

John 20:19–25

20 And when he had
said this, he shewed
unto them his hands
and his side.
The dis-
ciples therefore were
glad, when they saw
21 the Lord. Jesus therefore said to them again, Peace *be* unto you: as
22 the Father hath sent me, even so send I you. And when he had said
this, he breathed on them, and saith unto them, Receive ye the [4]Holy
23 Ghost: whosoever sins ye forgive, they are forgiven unto them; whosoever
sins ye retain, they are retained.*
24 But Thomas, one of the twelve, called [5]Didymus, was not with them
25 when Jesus came. The other disciples therefore said unto him, We
have seen the Lord. But he said unto them, Except I shall see in his
hands the print of the nails, and put my finger into the print of the nails
and put my hand into his side, I will not believe.

[1] Some ancient authorities omit *and saith unto them, Peace be unto you.* [2] Some ancient authorities omit ver. 40. [3] Many ancient authorities add *and a honeycomb.* [4] Or, *Holy Spirit.* [5] That is, *Twin.*

* Of our Lord's final commissions to the apostles and others (Luke 24:33), this is the first. See a second in § 181, and a third in § 183.

§ 179. THE APPEARANCE TO THE DISCIPLES THE NEXT SUNDAY NIGHT AND THE CONVINCING OF THOMAS

Jerusalem

John 20:26–31

26 And after eight days again his
disciples were within, and Thomas
with them. Jesus cometh, the
doors being shut, and stood in the
midst, and said, Peace *be* unto you.
27 Then saith he to Thomas, Reach
hither thy finger, and see my
hands; and reach *hither* thy hand,
and put it into my side: and be not
28 faithless, but believing. Thomas
answered and said unto him, My
29 Lord and my God. Jesus saith
unto him, Because thou hast seen
me, [1]thou hast believed: blessed
are they that have not seen, and
yet have believed.
30 Many other signs therefore did
Jesus in the presence of the disciples, which are not written in
31 this book: but these are written,
that ye may believe that Jesus is
the Christ, the Son of God; and
that believing ye may have life
in his name.

1 Cor. 15:5.

5 [and that he appeared to Cephas;]
then to the twelve;

[1] Or, *hast thou believed?*

§ 180. THE APPEARANCE TO SEVEN DISCIPLES BESIDE THE SEA OF GALILEE.* THE MIRACULOUS DRAUGHT OF FISHES

John 21

1 After these things Jesus manifested himself again to the disciples at the
2 sea of Tiberias; and he manifested *himself* on this wise. There were
together Simon Peter, and Thomas called [1]Didymus, and Nathanael of
Cana in Galilee, and the *sons* of Zebedee, and two other of his disciples.
3 Simon Peter saith unto them, I go a fishing. They say unto him, We also
come with thee. They went forth, and entered into the boat; and that
4 night they took nothing. But when day was now breaking, Jesus stood
5 on the beach; howbeit the disciples knew not that it was Jesus. Jesus

* The precise date of this sixth appearance is not known except that it was after that on the Resurrection Day and before the Ascension.

John 21

6 therefore said unto them, Children, have ye aught to eat? They answered
him, No. And he said unto them, Cast the net on the right side of the
boat, and ye shall find. They cast therefore, and now they were not
7 able to draw it for the multitude of fishes. That disciple therefore whom
Jesus loved saith unto Peter, It is the Lord. So when Simon Peter heard
that it was the Lord, he girt his coat about him (for he was naked), and
8 cast himself into the sea. But the other disciples came in the little boat
(for they were not far from the land, but about two hundred cubits off),
9 dragging the net *full* of fishes. So when they got out upon the land, they
10 see [2]a fire of coals there, and [3]fish laid thereon, and [4]bread. Jesus saith
11 unto them, Bring of the fish which ye have now taken. Simon Peter
therefore went [5]up, and drew the net to land, full of great fishes, a hundred
and fifty and three: and for all there were so many, the net was not rent.
12 Jesus saith unto them, Come *and* break your fast. And none of the disciples
durst inquire of him, Who art thou? knowing that it was the Lord.
13 Jesus cometh, and taketh the [6]bread, and giveth them, and the fish like-
14 wise. This is now the third time that Jesus was manifested to the disciples,
after he was risen from the dead.
15 So when they had broken their fast, Jesus saith to Simon Peter, Simon,
son of [7]John, [8]lovest thou me more than these? He saith unto him,
Yea, Lord; thou knowest that I [9]love thee. He saith unto him, Feed my
16 lambs. He saith to him again a second time, Simon, *son* of [7]John, [8]lovest
thou me? He saith unto him, Yea, Lord; thou knowest that I [9]love thee.
17 He saith unto him, Tend my sheep. He saith unto him the third time,
Simon, *son* of [7]John, [9]lovest thou me? Peter was grieved because he said
unto him the third time, [9]Lovest thou me? And he said unto him, Lord,
thou knowest all things; thou [10]knowest that I [9]love thee. Jesus saith
18 unto him, Feed my sheep. Verily, verily, I say unto thee, When thou
wast young, thou girdedst thyself, and walkedst whither thou wouldest:
but when thou shalt be old, thou shalt stretch forth thy hands, and another
19 shall gird thee, and carry thee whither thou wouldest not. Now this he
spake, signifying by what manner of death he should glorify God. And
20 when he had spoken this, he saith unto him, Follow me. Peter, turning
about, seeth the disciple whom Jesus loved following; which also leaned
back on his breast at the supper, and said, Lord, who is he that betrayeth
21 thee? Peter therefore seeing him saith to Jesus, Lord, [11]and what shall
22 this man do? Jesus saith unto him, If I will that he tarry till I come,
23 what *is that* to thee? follow thou me. This saying therefore went forth
among the brethren, that that disciple should not die: yet Jesus said not
unto him, that he should not die; but, If I will that he tarry till I come,
what *is that* to thee?
24 This is the disciple which beareth witness of these things, and wrote
these things: and we know that his witness is true.
25 And there are also many other things which Jesus did, the which if
they should be written every one, I suppose that even the word itself
would not contain the books that should be written.

[1] That is, *Twin*. [2] Gr. *a fire of charcoal*. [3] Or, *a fish*. [4] Or, *a loaf*. [5] Or, *aboard*. [6] Or, *loaf*. [7] Gr. *Joanes*. See ch. 1:42. [8], [9] *Love* in these places represents two different Greek words. [10] Or, *perceivest*. [11] Gr. *and this man, what?*

§ 181. THE APPEARANCE TO ABOVE FIVE HUNDRED* ON AN APPOINTED MOUNTAIN IN GALILEE, AND A COMMISSION GIVEN

Mark 16:15–18

15 And he said unto
them, Go ye into all
the world, and preach
the gospel to the
whole creation.

16 He that
believed and is bap-
tized shall be saved:
but he that disbe-
lieveth shall be con-
17 demned. And these
signs shall follow
them that believe:
in my name shall
they cast out [3]devils;
they shall speak with
18 [4]new tongues; they
shall take up ser-
pents, and if they
drink any deadly
thing, it shall in no

Matt. 28:16–20

16 But the eleven dis-
ciples went into Gali-
lee, unto the moun-
tain, where Jesus had
17 appointed them. And
when they saw him,
they worshipped *him:*
but some doubted.
18 And Jesus came to
them and spake unto
them, saying, All au-
thority hath been
given unto me in
heaven and on earth.

19 Go ye therefore, and
make disciples of all
the nations, baptizing
them into the name
of the Father and of
the Son and of the
Holy Ghost: teaching
20 them to observe all
things whatsoever I
commanded you:

1 Cor. 15:6

6 then he appeared to
above five hundred
brethren at once, of
whom the greater
part remain until
now, but some are
fallen asleep:

---

* The meeting attended by so large a number as stated by Paul was most probably that which Jesus had appointed (Matt. 28:16), and it could be held on an appointed mountain without attracting the attention of unbelievers. — The Commission in Mark may perhaps be reckoned the same as Matthew's here. A third Commission is given by Luke in § 183. This is what is called by many the Great Commission.

Mark 16:15–18

wise hurt them; they
shall lay hands on
the sick, and they
shall recover.

Matt. 28:16–20

and lo, I am
with you [1]alway, even
unto [2]the end of the
world.

[1] Gr. *all the days.* [2] Or, *the consummation of the age.* [3] Gr. *demons.* [4] Some ancient authorities omit *new.*

§ 182. THE APPEARANCE TO JAMES THE BROTHER OF JESUS

1 Cor. 15:7

7 Then he appeared
to James; then to all
the apostles.

§ 183. THE APPEARANCE TO THE DISCIPLES WITH ANOTHER COMMISSION

Jerusalem

Luke 24:44–49

44 And he said unto them, These
are my words which I spake unto
you, while I was yet with you,
how that all things must needs be
fulfilled, which are written in the
law of Moses, and the prophets,
and the psalms, concerning me.
45 Then opened he their mind, that
they might understand the scrip-
46 tures; and he said unto them,
Thus it is written [*see Hos. 6:2*],
that the Christ should suffer, and
rise again from the dead the third
47 day; and that repentance [1]and re-
mission of sins should be preached
in his name unto all [2]nations, be-
48 ginning from Jerusalem. Ye are
49 witnesses of these things. And
behold, I send forth the promise
of my Father upon you: but tarry
ye in the city, until ye be clothed
with power from on high.

Acts 1:3–8

3 to whom he also [3]shewed himself
alive after his passion by many
proofs, appearing unto them by
the space of forty days, and speak-
ing the things concerning the
4 kingdom of God: and [4]being as-
sembled together with them he
charged them not to depart from
Jerusalem, but to wait for the
promise of the Father, which,
said he, ye heard from me: for
5 John indeed baptized with water;
but ye shall be baptized [5]with the
Holy Ghost not many days hence.
6 They therefore, when they were
come together, asked him, saying,
Lord, dost thou at this time re-
store the kingdom to Israel?
7 And he said unto them, It is not
for you to know times or seasons,
which the Father hath [6]set within
8 his own authority. But ye shall
receive power, when the Holy

Acts 1:3-8

Ghost is come upon you: and ye shall be my witnesses both in Jerusalem, and in all Judea and Samaria, and unto the uttermost part of the earth.

[1] Some ancient authorities read *unto*. [2] Or, *nations. Beginning from Jerusalem, ye are witnesses*. [3] Gr. *presented*. [4] Or, *eating with them*. [5] Or, *in*. [6] Or, *appointed by*.

§ 184. THE LAST APPEARANCE AND THE ASCENSION

On Olivet between Jerusalem and Bethany

Mark 16:19, 20

19 So then the Lord Jesus, after he had spoken unto them, was received up into heaven,

and sat down at the right hand of God.

Luke 24:50-53

50 And he led them out until *they were* over against Bethany, and he lifted up his hands, and blessed
51 them. And it came to pass, while he blessed them, he parted from them, [1]and was carried up into heaven.

52 And they [2]worshipped him, and returned to Jerusalem with great joy: and
53 were continually in

Acts 1:9-12

9 And when he had said these things, as they were looking, he was taken up;

and a cloud received him out of their sight.

10 And while they were looking stedfastly into heaven as he went, behold two men stood by them in
11 white apparel; which also said, Ye men of Galilee, why stand ye looking into heaven? this Jesus, which was received up from you into heaven, shall so come in like manner as ye beheld him going into heaven.

12 Then returned they unto Jerusalem.

Mark 16:19–20	Luke 24:50–53	
20 And they went forth, and preached everywhere, the Lord working with them, and confirming the word by the signs that followed. Amen.	the temple, blessing God.	

[1] Some ancient authorities omit *and was carried up into heaven.* [2] Some ancient authorities omit *worshipped him, and.*

EXPLANATORY NOTES ON POINTS OF SPECIAL DIFFICULTY IN THE HARMONY

1. *About Harmonies of the Gospels*

We do not know how soon an effort was made to combine in one book the several portrayals of the life of Jesus. Luke in his Gospel (1:1–4) makes a selection of the material and incorporates data from different sources, but with the stamp of his own arrangement and style. He followed, in the main, the order of Mark's Gospel, as is easily seen. But this method is not what is meant by a harmony of the Gospels, for the result is a selection from all sorts of material (oral and written), monographs and longer treatises.

The first known harmony is Tatian's Diatessaron (*dia tessaron*, by four) in the second century (about 160 A.D.) in the Syriac tongue. It was long lost, but an Arabic translation has been found and an English rendering appeared in 1894 by J. Hamlyn Hill. It is plain that Tatian has blended into one narrative our Four Gospels with a certain amount of freedom as is shown by Hobson's *The Diatessaron of Tatian and the Synoptic Problem* (1904). There have been modern attempts also to combine into one story the records of the Four Gospels. There is a superficial advantage in such an effort in the freedom from variations in the accounts, but the loss is too great for such an arbitrary gain. The word harmony calls for such an arrangement, but it is not the method of the best modern harmonies which preserve the differences in material and style just as they are in the Four Gospels.

In the third century Ammonius arranged the Gospels in four parallel columns (the *Sections* of Ammonius). This was an attempt to give a conspectus of the material in the Gospels side by side. In the fourth century Eusebius with his *Canons* and *Sections* enabled the reader to see at a glance the parallel passages in the Gospels. The ancients took a keen interest in this form of study of the Gospels, as Augustine shows.

Of modern harmonies that by Edward Robinson has had the most influence. The edition in English appeared in 1845, that in Greek in 1846. Riddle revised Robinson's Harmony in 1889. There were many others that employed the Authorized Version, like Clark's, and that divided the life of Christ according to the feasts.

Broadus (June, 1893) followed Waddy (1887) in the use of the Canterbury Revision, but was the first to break away from the division by feasts and to show the historical development in the life of Jesus. Stevens and Burton followed (December, 1893) Broadus within six months and, like him, used the Canterbury Revision and had an independent division of the life of Christ to show the historical unfolding of the events. These two harmonies have held the field for nearly thirty years for students of the English Gospels. In 1903 Kerr issued one in the American Standard Version and James one in the Canterbury Revision (1901).

Harmonies of the Gospels in the Greek continued to appear, like Tischendorf's (1851, new edition 1891), Wright's *A Synopsis of the Gospels in Greek* (1903), Huck's *Synopse der drei ersten Evangelien* (1892, English translation in 1907), Campbell's *First Three Gospels in Greek* (1899), *A Harmony of the Synoptic Gospels in Greek* by Burton and Goodspeed (1920).

The progress in synoptic criticism emphasized the difference in subject matter and style between the Synoptic Gospels and the Fourth Gospel as appears in the works of Huck, Campbell, and Burton and Goodspeed that give only the Synoptic Gospels. Burton and Goodspeed have also an English work, *A Harmony of the Synoptic Gospels for Historical and Critical Study* (1917). In 1917 Sharman (*Records of the Life of Jesus*) gives first a harmony of the Synoptic Gospels with references to the Fourth Gospel and then an outline of the Fourth Gospel with references to the Synoptic Gospels.

Once more in 1919 Van Kirk produced *The Source Book of the Life of Christ* which is only a partial harmony, for the parables and speeches of Jesus are only referred to, not quoted. But he endeavored to show the results of Gospel criticism in the text of the book. There is much useful material here for a harmony, but it is not a real harmony that can be used for the full story of the life of Jesus. Van Kirk, however, is the first writer to place Mark in the first column instead of Matthew. I had already done it in my outline before I saw Van Kirk's book, but his was published first. It is an immense improvement to put Mark first. The student thus see sthat the arrangement of the material is not arbitrary and whimsical, but orderly and natural. Both Matthew and Luke follow Mark's order except in the first part of Matthew where he is topical in the main. John supplements the Synoptic Gospels, particularly in the Judean (Jerusalem) Ministry.

Slowly, therefore, progress has been made in the harmonies of the Gospels. But the modern student is able to reproduce the life and words of Jesus as has not been possible since the first century. It is a fourfold portrait of Christ that we get, but the whole is infinitely richer than the picture given by any one of the Four Gospels. The present Harmony aims to put the student in touch with the results of modern scholarly research and to focus attention on the actual story in the Gospels themselves. One may have his own opinion of the Fourth Gospel, but it is needed in a harmony for completeness.

2. *Synoptic Criticism*

The criticism of the synoptic gospels has been able to reach a broad general conclusion that is likely to stand the test of time. The reason for this happy solution lies in the fact that the processes and results can be tested. It is not mere subjective speculation. Any one who knows how to weigh evidence can compare Mark, Matthew, and Luke in the English, and still better in the Greek. The pages of the present harmony offer proof enough. It is plain as a pikestaff that both our Matthew and Luke used practically all of Mark and followed his general order of events. For this reason Mark has been placed first on the pages where this Gospel appears at all. But another thing is equally clear and that is that both Matthew and Luke had another source in common because they each give practically identical matter for much that is not in Mark at all. This second common source for Matthew and Luke has been called Logia because it is chiefly discourses. It is sometimes referred to as "Q", the first letter of the German word *Quelle* (source). Unfortunately we do not have the whole of the Logia (Q) before us as in the case of Mark, though we probably do not possess the original ending of Mark in 16:9–20. But we can at least reproduce what is preserved. Still, just as sometimes either Matthew or Luke made use of Mark, so in the case of the Logia that is probably true. Hence we cannot tell the precise limits of the Logia. Besides, a small part of Mark is not employed by either Matthew or Luke and that may be true of the Logia. But the fact of these two sources for Matthew and Luke seems to be proven.

But there are various other points to be observed. One is that both Matthew and Luke may have had various other sources. Luke tells us (Luke 1:1–4) that he made use of "many" such sources, both oral and written. And a large part of Luke does not appear in the other gospels or at least similar events and sayings occur in different environments and times. Hence our solid conclusion must allow freedom and flexibility to the writers in various ways. We can see for ourselves how Matthew and Luke handled both Mark and the Logia, each in his own way and with individual touches of style and purpose.

One other matter calls for attention. Papias is quoted by Eusebius as saying that Matthew wrote in Hebrew (or Aramaic) whereas our present Matthew is in Greek. It is now commonly held that the real Matthew (Levi) wrote the Logia first in Aramaic and that either he or some one else used that with Mark and other sources for our present Gospel of Matthew.

It should be added also that there is a considerable body of evidence for the view that Mark wrote under the influence of Simon Peter and preserves the vividness and freshness of Peter's own style as an eyewitness.

One other result has come. It is increasingly admitted that the Logia was very early, before 50 A.D., and Mark likewise if Luke wrote the Acts while Paul was still alive. Luke's Gospel comes (Acts 1:1) before the Acts. The date of Acts is still in dispute, but the early date (about A.D. 63) is gaining support constantly. The upshot of these centuries of synoptic criticism has brought into sharp outline the facts that now stand out with reasonable clearness. There are many points in dispute still, but we at least know how the synoptic gospels were written, and are reasonably certain of the dates and the authors.

There are many good books on the subject, like Hawkin's *Horae Synopticae* (second edition), Sanday's *Oxford Studies in the Synoptic Problem*, Harnack's *Sayings of Jesus* and his *Date of the Synoptic Gospels and Acts.* My own views appear in my *Commentary on Matthew* (Bible for Home and School), *Studies in Mark's Gospel*, and *Luke the Historian in the Light of Research.*

3. *The Authorship of the Fourth Gospel*

It has come to pass that one has to defend the use of the Fourth Gospel on a par with the Synoptic Gospels. The Johannine problem is an old one and a difficult one. It cannot be said that modern scholarship has come to a clear result here, as is true of the Synoptic Gospels. As a matter of fact, the battle still rages vigorously. There are powerful arguments on both sides. A mere sketch of the real situation is all that can be attempted here.

The Gospel and the Epistles are in the same style and can be confidently affirmed to be by the same author. The Apocalypse has some striking peculiarities of its own. There are likenesses in vocabulary and idiom beyond a doubt of a subtle nature, but the grammatical irregularities in the Book of Revelation have long been a puzzle to those who hold to the Johannine authorship. A full discussion of these grammatical details can be found in the leading commentaries on the Apocalypse. A brief survey is given in my *Grammar of the Greek New Testament in the Light of Historical Research.* The facts are undisputed and have a most interesting parallel in the papyri fragments of some of the less educated writers of the *Koiné* as one can see for himself in Milligan's *Greek Papyri* or in any other collection.

There are two solutions of the problem with two alternatives in each instance. There are those who roundly assert that the same man could not have written both the Gospel and the Apocalypse. Some of these affirm that the Apostle John wrote the Apocalypse but not the Gospel. Certainly a "John" wrote the Revelation or claimed it at any rate. Others of this group hold that an inferential Presbyter John (not "the elder" in 2 and 3 John) supposed to be meant by Papias wrote the Apocalypse while some one else wrote the Gospel whether the Apostle John or not.

But a considerabe body of scholars still hold that the same man wrote both the Gospel and the Apocalypse, but a different explanation is offered by two groups. One class of writers affirm that John wrote the Apocalypse first before he had come to be at home in the Greek idiom as we see it in the Gospel and the Epistles. We know that John and Peter were fishermen and were not considered men of literary training by the Sanhedrin (Acts 4:14). This explanation is sufficient but for the further fact that the early date of the Apocalypse (about 70 A.D.) is not now so generally held to be true. The later or Domitianic date as given by Irenæus seems pretty clearly to be correct. So the other group suggest that the books may belong substantially to the same period (the Domitianic date) and that the explanation of the grammatical infelicities in the Apocalypse may be due to the fact that John being on the Isle of Patmos when he wrote did not have the benefit of friends in Ephesus who apparently read the Gospel (John 21:24–25). Besides, the excited state of John's mind because of the visions may have added to the number of the solecisms in the Apocalypse. This view I personally hold as probable. The unity of both Gospel and Apocalypse is denied by some.

So the matter stands as between the Gospel and the Apocalypse. But the Fourth Gospel has difficulties of its own. These relate in part to the book in itself. It is true there is a great similarity in language and style between the narrative parts of the book and the discourses of Jesus. It is affirmed that the writer has colored the speeches of Jesus with his own style or even made up the dialogues so that they are without historical value or at least on a much lower plane than the Synoptic Gospels as objective history. There is something in this point, but one must remember that the Synoptic Gospels vary in their manner of reporting the speeches of Jesus and aim to give the substance rather than the precise words of the Master in all instances. It is at most a matter of degree. There is a Johannine type of thought and phrase beyond a doubt, but curiously enough we have a paragraph in Matthew 11:24–31 and Luke 10:21–23 that is precisely like the Johannine specimens, written long before the Fourth Gospel. One must remember the versatility of Jesus, who could not be retained in any one style or mold. But there are those who admit the Johannine authorship of the Gospel and yet who refuse to put it on the same plane as the Synoptic Gospels. Every one must decide for himself on this point. For myself I see too much of Christ in the Fourth Gospel in the most realistic and dramatic form to be mere invention. We can enlarge our conception of Christ to make room for the Fourth Gospel.

But even so it is urged that the Beloved Disciple cannot be the Apostle John. If not, then the Fourth Gospel ignores the Apostle John,—a very curious situation. It is a long story for which one must go to the able books in defense of the Johannine authorship by Ezra Abbott, James Drummond, W. Sanday, Luthardt, Watkins and many others. The ablest modern attacks are made by Bacon and Wendt and Schmiedel. My own view is given in my *The Divinity of Christ in the Gospel of John.*

4. *The Jesus of History*

It is not long since the cry of "Back to Christ" was raised and away from Paul and John. Soon this cry was changed to an appeal to the Jesus of History in opposition to the Christ of Theology. So we had the "Jesus or Christ" controversy (see the Hibbert Journal Supplement for 1909). It was gravely affirmed by some that Paul had created the Christ of Christianity and had permanently altered the simple program of Jesus for a social Kingdom and had turned it into a great ecclesiastical system with speculative Christological interpretations quite beyond the range of the vision of the Jesus of the Synoptic Gospels. It was admitted that the Fourth Gospel, the Apocalypse, and the Epistles all gave the Pauline view.

To the Synoptic Gospels, therefore, we all went. But the Christ of Paul and of John is in the Synoptic Gospels. In all essentials the picture is the same in Luke as in John and Paul. The shading is different, but Jesus in Luke is the Son of God as well as the Son of Man (see my *Luke the Historian in the Light of Research*). It was admitted that Matthew gives the picture of Jesus as the Jewish Messiah. Mark reflects Peter's conception of Jesus and gives Jesus as Lord and Christ (see my *Studies in Mark's Gospel*). And Q (the Logia), the earliest document that we have for the life of Christ and almost contemporary with the time of Christ, gives the same essential features of Jesus as the Son of Man and Son of God (see my article *The Christ of the Logia* in the Contemporary Review for August, 1919). The sober results of modern critical research show the same figure in the very earliest documents that we possess (Q and Mark's Gospel). The Christ of Paul and of John walks as the Jesus of History in the Synoptic Gospels. We do know the earthly life of Jesus much more distinctly and the research of centuries has had a blessed outcome in the enrichment of our knowledge. Matthew and Luke are the first critics of the sources for the life of Jesus. We see how they made use of Mark, the Logia, and other documents. The Fourth Gospel comes last with knowledge of the Synoptic Gospels.

There are, to be sure, a few men who even deny that Jesus ever lived at all. That was the next step; but this absurdity has met complete refutation. The Christ of faith is the Christ of fact. There is no getting away from the fact of Christ, the chief fact of all the ages, the centre of all history, the hope of the ages. Jesus Christ we can still call him, our Lord and Saviour, and he never made such an appeal to men as he does today in the full blaze of modern historical research. Men are just beginning to take his words to heart in all the spheres of human life. The one hope of a new world of righteousness lies precisely in the program of Jesus Christ for the life of the individual in his private affairs, in his family relations, in his business and social dealings, in his political ideals and conduct. And nations must also follow the leadership of Jesus the supreme Teacher of the race.

The purpose of a harmony is not to teach theology, but to make available for men of any faith the facts in the Gospels concerning Jesus of Nazareth. Each interprets these facts and teachings as he sees the light. We can all acknowledge our debt to modern scholarship for the tremendous contributions made to a richer understanding of the environment into which Jesus came and to a juster appreciation of the real significance of his person and his message. The Gospels are still the most fascinating books in the world for sheer simplicity and beauty. One can first trace the picture of Jesus in the Logia, then in Mark, in Matthew, in Luke, in John. To these he can add the pictures of Christ in the Acts, the Epistles, the Apocalypse.

5. *The Two Genealogies of Christ*

Sceptics of all ages, from Porphyry and Celsus to Strauss, have urged the impossibility of reconciling the difficulties in the two accounts of the descent of Jesus. Even Alford says it is impossible to reconcile them. But certainly several possible explanations have been suggested. The chief difficulties will be discussed.

1. In Matthew's list several discrepancies are pointed out.

(*a*) It is objected that Matthew is mistaken in making three sets of fourteen each. There are only forty-one names, and this would leave one set with only thirteen. But does Matthew say he has mentioned forty-two names? He does say (1:17) that there are three sets of fourteen and divides them for us himself: "So all the generations from Abraham unto David are fourteen generations; and from David unto the carrying away to Babylon fourteen generations; and from the carrying away to Babylon unto the Christ fourteen generations." The points of division are David and the captivity; in the one case a man, in the other an event. He counts David in each of the first two sets, although Jechoniah is counted only once. David was the connecting link between the patriarchal line and the royal line. But he does not say "from David to Jechoniah," but "from David to the carrying away unto Babylon," and Josiah is the last name he counts before that event. And so the first name after this same event is Jechoniah. Thus Matthew deliberately counts David in two places to give symmetry to the division, which made an easy help to the memory.

(*b*) The omissions in Matthew's list have occasioned some trouble. These omissions are after Joram, the names of Ahaziah, Joash, Amaziah, and after Josiah, these of Jehoiakim and Eliakim (2 Kings 8:24; 1 Chron. 3:11; 2 Chron. 22:1, 11; 24:27; 2 Kings 23:34; 24:6). But such omissions were very common in the Old Testament genealogies. See 2 Chron. 22:9. Here "son of Jehoshaphat" means "grandson of Jehoshaphat." So in Matt. 1:1 Jesus is called the son of David, the son of Abraham. A direct line of descent is all that it is designed to express. This is all that the term "begat" necessarily means here. It is a real descent. Whatever omissions were made for various reasons, would not invalidate the line. The fact that Ahaziah, Joash, and Amaziah were the sons of Ahab and Jezebel would be sufficient ground for omitting them.

(*c*) Matthew mentions four women in his list, which is contrary to Jewish custom, viz. Tamar, Rahab, Ruth, and the wife of Uriah. But neither one is counted in the lists of fourteen, and each one has something remarkable in her case (Broadus, Comm. on Matt. *in loco*). Three were guilty of gross sin, and one, Ruth, was of Gentile origin and deserved mention for that reason. This circumstance would seem to indicate that Matthew did not simply copy the genealogical history of Joseph. He did this, omitting what suited his purpose and adding likewise remarks of his own. His record is thus reliable and yet made a part of his own story.

2. A comparison of the lists of Matthew and Luke.

If no list had been given by Luke, no further explanations would be necessary. But Luke not only gives a list, but one radically different from Matthew's, and in inverse order. Matthew begins with Abraham and comes to Jesus; Luke begins with Jesus and concludes with Adam [the son of God]. Several explanations are offered to remove the apparent contradiction.

(*a*) As early as Julius Africanus it was suggested that the two lines had united in accordance with the law of Levirate marriage. By this theory, Heli and Jacob being stepbrothers, Jacob married Heli's widow and was the real father of Joseph. Thus both genealogies would be the descent of Joseph, one the real, the other the legal. This theory is ably advocated by McClellan, pp. 416 ff., and Waddy, p. xvii. It is argued that Jechoniah's children were born in captivity and so, being slaves, lost both his royal dignity and his legal status. Stress is laid upon the word "begat" to show that Matthew's descent must be the natural pedigree of Joseph, and upon the use of the expression "son (as was supposed) of Joseph." Hence both Joseph's real and legal standing are shown, for by Luke's account he had an undisputed legal title to descend from David. This is certainly possible, although it rests on the hypothesis of the Levirate marriage.

(*b*) Lord Arthur Hervey, in his volume on the Genealogies of Our Lord, and in Smith's Dictionary, argues that Matthew gives Joseph's legal descent as successor to the throne of David. According to this theory Solomon's line failed in Jechoniah (Jer. 22:30) and Shealtiel of Matthew's line took his place. Luke's account, on the other hand, gives Joseph's real parentage. Matthew's Matthan and Luke's Mattathias are identified as one, and the law of Levirate marriage comes into service with Jacob and Heli. This explanation has received favor with such writers as Mill, Alford, Wordsworth, Ellicott, Westcott, Fairbairn. McNeile (on Matthew) considers this the "only possible" view. The chief objection seems to be the most natural meaning of "begat," implying direct descent, and the necessity for two suppositions, one about Shealtiel and another about Jacob and Heli. It is even fairly probable that the Shealtiel and Zerubbabel of Matthew and Luke are different persons.

(*c*) The third and most plausible solution yets uggested makes Matthew give the real descent of Joseph, and Luke the real descent of Mary. Several arguments of more or less weight can be adduced for this hypothesis.

(1) The most natural meaning of "begat" in Matthew is preserved. Jesus goes through David's royal line and so fulfils prophecy. It is not elsewhere stated that Mary was of Davidic descent, although presumptive evidence exists in the language of the angel (Luke 1:32) and the enrollment of Mary (Luke 2:5). So Robinson (Revised edition).

(2) The use of Joseph without the article, while it is used with every other name in the list. "The absence of the article puts the name outside of the genealogical series properly so-called."—Godet. This would seem to indicate that Joseph belonged to the parenthesis, "as was supposed." It would read thus, "being son (as was supposed of Joseph) of Heli." Luke had already clearly stated the manner of Christ's birth, so that no one would think he was the son of Joseph. Jesus would thus be Heli's grandson, an allowable meaning of "son." See Andrews' (new edition) *Life of Our Lord*, p. 63.

(3) It would seem proper that Matthew should give the *legal* descent of Jesus, since he wrote chiefly for Jews. This, of course, could only be through Joseph.

(4) And it would seem equally fitting that Luke should give the *real* genealogy of Jesus, since he was writing for all. And this could come only through Mary. If it is objected that a woman's genealogy is never given, it may be replied that women are mentioned for special reasons in Matthew's list, though not counted, and that Mary's name is not mentioned in this list. The genealogy goes back to her father either by skipping her as suggested above and making son mean the grandson of Heli, or by allowing Joseph to stand in her place in the list, as he would have to do anyhow. On the whole, then, this theory seems the most plausible and pleasing. So practically Luther, Bengel, Olshausen, Lightfoot, Wieseler, Robinson, Alexander, Godet, Weiss, Andrews (new edition, p. 65), Broadus, and many recent writers.

But Bacon (Genealogy of Jesus Christ, Hastings D. B. and Am. J. of Theol. Jan., 1911) says that nearly all writers of authority abandon any effort to reconcile the two pedigrees of Jesus save as the effort of Christians to give "His Davidic sonship rather than His actual descent." See Machen's survey of negative criticism, on the subject in Princeton Theol. Review (Jan., 1906). Barnard (Hastings D.C.G.) admits two independent accounts, but sees no solution, but Sweet (Int. St. Bible Encyl.) accepts the view that Matthew gives the real genealogy of Joseph and Luke that of Mary. Plummer

(Comm. on Luke) thinks it incredible that Mary's genealogy should be given by Luke.

6. *The Probable Time of the Saviour's Birth*

Every one now understands that the accepted date of our Lord's birth is wrong by several years. The estimates of the true date vary all the way from one to seven years B.C. There are various data that fix the year with more or less certainty, but none of them with absolute precision. They do, however, agree in marking pretty clearly a narrow limit for this notable occurrence, B.C. 6 or 5.

1. The death of Herod the Great is relied on with most certainty to fix the year of Christ's birth. The rule of Archelaus and Antipas demands B.C. 4. Josephus mentions an eclipse of the moon which occurred shortly before he died. Ant. XVII, 6, 4. This eclipse is the only one alluded to by Josephus, and fixes with absolute certainty the time after which the birth of Jesus could not have occurred, since, according to Matt. 2:1–6, Jesus was born while Herod was still living. The question to be determined would be the year of this eclipse. Astronomical calculations name an eclipse of the moon March 12 and 13, in the year of Rome 750, and no eclipse occurred the following year that was visible in Palestine. Josephus (Ant. XVII, 8, 1), says that Herod died thirty-seven years after he was declared king by the Romans. In 714 he was proclaimed king, and this would bring his death counting from Nisan to Nisan, as Josephus usually does, "in the year from 1st Nisan 750 to 1st Nisan 751, according to Jewish computation, at the age of seventy" (Andrews). Herod died shortly before the Passover of 750, then, according to the eclipse and the length of his reign. Caspari contends for January 24, 753, as the date of Herod's death, because there was a total eclipse of the moon January 10. So he puts his death fourteen days later. Mr. Page (*New Light from Old Eclipses*) argues for the eclipse that occurred July 17, 752, as the one preceding Herod's death. He thinks that this makes unnecessary the subtraction of two years from the reign of Tiberius on the theory that Tiberius was contemporary ruler with Augustus for two years. But he finds difficulty in lengthening Herod's reign so long, and his theory has gained no great acceptance as yet. Our present era makes the birth of Christ in the year of Rome 754, and is due to the Abbot Dionysius Exiguus in the Sixth Century. Hence it is clear that if Herod died in the early spring of 750, Jesus must have been born *at least* four years before 754, the common era, and likely in the year 749.

2. It has been inferred by some that Jesus was at least two or three years old when Herod slaughtered the infants in Bethlehem, Matt. 2:16. Thus the year would be put two years further back to the end of 747 or beginning of 748. But this is not demanded by the "two years" of Matthew, for Herod

would naturally extend the limit so as to be sure to include the child in the number slain, and a child just entering the second year would be called "two years" old by Jewish custom. No more definite note of time comes from this circumstance, save that the massacre probably took place some months before Herod's death, which fact would bring the Saviour's birth back some time into the year 749.

3. The appearance of the "star in the east" (Matt. 2:2). This, of course, was before Herod's death, and would agree in time with the slaughter of the children, if the star be looked upon as a supernatural phenomenon, and not the wise men's interpretation of a natural conjunction of planets. Kepler first suggested that, as there was a conjunction of Jupiter and Saturn in 747, to which Mars was added in 748, this conjunction might have been the bright star that led on the wise men. See Wieseler, *Synopsis*, p. 57. Kepler had also suggested that a periodical star or a comet might have joined the constellation. The Chinese records preserve the account of the appearance of a comet in the spring of 749. Either of these theories is fascinating in itself, especially to those minds that prefer a natural explanation of anything that looks miraculous. Both phenomena are possible in themselves, but they hardly meet the requirements of the record in Matthew. (1) The word used is *aster*, star, and not *astron*, a group of stars. (2) Rev. C. Pritchard, whose calculations have been verified at Greenwich (Smith's Dic.), has shown that those "planets could never have appeared as one star, for they never approached each other within double the apparent diameter of the moon." So Ideler's hypothesis that the wise men all had weak eyes seems rather feeble. (3) The year 747 would conflict slightly with other evidence for Christ's birth that favors 749, although Wieseler, p. 53, note 4, contends that the star first appeared to the wise men two years before their visit, and a second time on their visit to Bethlehem. (4) Besides, the star is said to have stood over "where the young child was," v. 9. If it were a natural star it would have kept going as they went, and would not have stopped till they stopped. Even then it would appear as far away as ever from Bethlehem. It seems best, therefore, to admit the existence of a miracle here, and hence gain nothing from the visit of the Magi to establish the date of the Saviour's birth, save that it was not long before the slaughter of the infants, and would at least agree with the date 749. See Broadus, Comm. *in loco*.

4. The language of the heavenly host in Luke 2:14 is urged by some as fixing the birth at a time when there was universal peace throughout the world. The closing of the temple of Janus in the time of Augustus is also adduced, but it is not certainly known when it was closed apart from 725 and 729. It was intended to be closed at the end of 744, but was delayed on account of trouble among the Daci and Dalmatæ. See Greswell i. 469. Nothing specific can be obtained from this fact, save that there was a time

of comparative quiet in the Roman world from 746 to 752. There was a hush in the clangor of war when Jesus was born.

5. The entrance of John the Baptist upon his ministry gives us another note of time. See Luke 3:1 f. John emerged from the wilderness seclusion in the fifteenth year of the reign of Tiberius. Augustus died August 29, 767. Adding fifteen years to this, the fifteenth year of Tiberius would begin August 29, 781. John was of a priestly family and so could naturally enter upon his work when thirty years of age. Thirty years subtracted from this gives 751, as the date of John's birth. But that is too late by two years to agree with the other date. Here, however, the Roman histories come to our help. Tacitus, Ann. 1, 3: "Tiberius is adopted by Augustus as his son, and *colleague in empire.*" Vell. Pat. 2, 121; "At the request of Augustus, Tiberius was invested with equal authority in all the provinces." So Suetonius Aug. 97 and Tib. 21. It is clear, then, that Tiberius reigned jointly with Augustus about two years before he assumed full control of the empire at the death of Augustus. Luke could have used either date, but Tiberius' power was already equal to that of Augustus in the provinces two years before his death. Luke would naturally use the provincial point of view. Taking off the two years from the joint reign of Augustus, we again come to the year 749, as John was born six months before Jesus. So if John was born in the early part of the spring, Jesus would have been born in the summer or fall of 749.

6. The age of Jesus at his entrance upon his ministry, Luke 3:23. "And Jesus himself, when he began to teach, was about thirty years of age." So most modern scholars, taking the language in the obvious sense. Origen refers it to the beginning of a new life, by the second birth of baptism, after his spiritualizing fashion. The Authorized Version has it: "And Jesus himself began to be about thirty years of age," applying the "beginning" to the period of thirty years. McClellan argues that it means "about thirty years, beginning"; that is, a little the rise of thirty years. The Revised Version seems to be preferable and the only doubt would be as to what is included in the phrase "about thirty years." It has been variously argued that Jesus was from one to three years younger or older than thirty. It seems more reasonable to give the words the meaning that he was just about thirty, a few months under or over. Apparently this fact explains the idiom. The argument that Jesus had to be exactly thirty years old because the priest had to be so, when he entered upon his work, has no great force. For Jesus was not a priest save in a spiritual sense. John had been preaching no great while when Jesus was baptized by him and so entered upon his public ministry. If John began his ministry when he was thirty years old in the fifteenth year of Tiberius, then Jesus's ministry would begin about six months later. His birth would then come in the latter part of 749,

unless John was born in the latter part of 748, when it would be earlier in the year.

7. The building of the temple of Herod gives a further clue to the date of Christ's birth. In John 2:20, the Jews say, "Forty and six years was this temple in building." Josephus tells us in one place that Herod began rebuilding the temple in the fifteenth year of his reign, War. I, 21, 1, and in another that he did so in the eighteenth year of his reign, Ant. XV, 11, 1. In the account of Herod's death, Ant. XVII, 8, 1, he used two dates for his reign, according as he counted from his declaration as king by the Romans 714, or the death of Antigonus 717. Eighteen and fifteen would both be correct, according as he reckoned from the one date or the other. Eighteen added to forty-six and both to 714 would make 778. It was at the first Passover in his ministry that this expression is used. It has been probably six months since his baptism. If thirty and a half years be taken from 778, his birth would be thrown back to the year 747, unless the forty-six years be taken as completed, when it would be 748. So Robinson. But this does not quite agree with the other notes of time we have. Many modern harmonists count the eighteen years from 717, and so bring the whole number, adding forty-six, down to 780, or, if the years are complete, 781. Thirty and a half from this would give the autumn of 749 or 750. This is done because Josephus usually reckons Herod's reign from the death of Antigonus, 717. On the whole it seems clear that Josephus is wrong in the War. It is common enough to find Josephus in one passage contradicting what he has said elsewhere. The temple was begun the year that the Emperor came to Syria, as is plain from Josephus. According to Dio Cassius, LIV, 7, this visit was made in B.C. 20 or 19. Correcting Josephus by himself and by Dio Cassius we thus again get B.C. 5 as the probable year of the birth of Christ. See Schuerer, *History of the Jewish People in the Time of Jesus Christ*, Div. I., Vol. I., p. 410.

8. The census of Augustus Cæsar mentioned in Luke 2:1 f., furnishes the last note of time for this event. This subject is involved in a great many difficulties, and for a full discussion, the reader is referred to Ramsay's *Was Christ Born at Bethlehem*, and his *Bearing of Recent Discovery on the Trustworthiness of the New Testament* (Chap. XX) and to my *Luke the Historian in the Light of Research*. Every statement made by Luke in 2:1–7 was once challenged. Every one is now shown to be correct.

(1) It used to be said that no census was ever taken by Augustus, but heathen writers mention three, in 726, 746, 767. One of these, 746, may be the one here mentioned, which was delayed for various reasons, or which was executed slowly in the distant provinces. But it is not necessary that the phrase "all the world" should be pressed to its literal meaning, though this is more natural. Nor does the argument from silence prove that no

other general census was taken by Augustus. But Ramsay has triumphantly vindicated Luke and the general census under Augustus by proof from the papyri that Augustus inaugurated a periodical census under fourteen years from B.C. 8 on. The second occurred A.D. 6 (Acts 5:37). See Ramsay's *Was Christ Born at Bethlehem, and Bearing of Recent Discovery on Trustworthiness of the New Testament* (Chap. XX) and my *Luke the Historian* (Chap. XX). We have only to think that there was delay in the carrying out of the census in Palestine to bring this date down to B.C. 6 (or even 5).

(2) It is not a "taxing," but an "enrollment" (Rev. Ver.) that was taken. There was a taxing later (Acts 5:37). And if it were done while Herod was king, Augustus could not have taxed Judea without Herod's consent. But Herod was not now in good form with Augustus.

(3) This helps to explain another objection that the enrollment would not have included Judea anyhow, because it was not yet a province, but a kingdom. But it is not likely that Herod would have displeased Augustus by refusing such information if it was desired. Tacitus asserts that the *regna*, the dependent kingdoms, were included in the census taken by Augustus.

(4) Hence, also, it is natural that the enrollment should have taken place according to the Jewish and not according to the usual Roman method, because Herod would wish it to be in accordance with the customs of his kingdom. So every one went to his own city. We now know from numerous papyri that in Egypt the family went to the home city. The Jews were used to enrollment by tribes and that was allowed. See Deissmann's *Light from the Ancient East*, p. 268, and Ramsay's *Was Christ Born at Bethlehem*, p. 108.

(5) We now have to meet the objection that Quirinius was not governor till ten years later, A.D. 6, when a taxing did occur. (See Acts 5:37.)

It is now possible to give a real solution of this problem. Luke is now shown to be wholly correct in his statement that Quirinius was twice governor, and that the first census took place during the first period. A series of inscriptions in Asia Minor show that Quirinius was governor of Syria B.C. 10–7 and so twice governor of Syria (second time A.D. 6; Josephus, Ant. XVIII, 1:1). See Ramsay, *Bearing of Recent Discovery*, pp. 273–300, and my *Luke the Historian*, pp. 127–9. Tertullian (*adv. marc.* iv, 19) says that Sentius Saturninus was governor of Syria B.C. 9–6. But we now know that Varus was controlling the internal affairs of Syria while Quirinius was leader of the army. Luke is therefore quite accurate in his statement about Quirinius being twice governor of Syria. The *Lapis Tiburtinus* has *iterum Syriam* about Quirinius. Ramsay has cleared up this famous historical puzzle and has completly vindicated Luke.

Few subjects have excited as much interest, even needless curiosity, as the date of the birth of the Saviour. But it is noticeable that by the masses of Christians more interest is taken in the day of Christ's birth than in the year. The Christmas festivities and the natural desire to make that the birthday of Jesus cause this widespread interest in December 25. Not only is it impossible to determine with any degree of certainty the day of the month, but the time of the year also is equally uncertain. The chief thing that appears proved is that December 25 is not the time, since the shepherds would hardly be in the fields at night with the flocks, which were usually taken into the folds in November and kept in till March. The nights of December would scarcely allow watching in the mountain fields even as far south as Bethlehem. And besides, the long journey from Nazareth to Bethlehem would hardly be made by Joseph and Mary in winter, the rainy season. McClellan argues for December 25, but his arguments are not convincing. The ancients had various days for Christ's birth: May 20 (Clement of Alexandria), April 20, December 25, January 5. Tertullian and others even say that the day of his birth (December 25) was kept in the register at Rome. But chronologists attach little weight to this testimony, since the same tradition puts the birth of John, June 24; the annunciation of Mary, March 25, and Elizabeth's conception, September 25—the four cardinal points of the year. If one might hazard an opinion, it would be that the birth of Jesus occurred in the summer or early in the fall of 749 or of 748, that is B.C. 6 or 5. Turner (Chronology, Hastings D B) reaches B.C. 6 as the probable year of the birth of Jesus though he did not have the new light on the census and on Quirinius which confirms it. Hitchcock (Hastings D C G) saw the bearing of the periodical census that called for B.C. 7–5, but did not yet know the discovery about Quirinius. Armstrong (Chronology New Testament, Int. St. Bible Encycl.) is less certain about the precise year.

7. *The Feast of John 5:1, and the Duration of Our Lord's Ministry*

It seems almost impossible to decide with certainty what feast is alluded to in John 5:1. One can only speak with moderation where everything is so doubtful. Various feasts have been suggested as solving the problem.

1. The Feast of Dedication has been proposed by Kepler and Petavius. But this view has met with no great amount of favor, for there is too short an interval between the first Passover and December, when it occurred. It might be a later Feast of Dedication, but this feast was not one of the great feasts and would hardly have drawn Jesus all the way from Galilee to attend it. He did attend this feast once (John 10:22), but he was already in Judea at this time, having come up to attend the Feast of Tabernacles (John 7:2, 14). So Robinson, Clark, etc. So this feast seems to be ruled out of the question.

2. The Feast of Tabernacles is advocated by Ebrard, Ewald, Patritius.

It is very unlikely that the Feast of Tabernacles after the first Passover could be meant, as the Saviour did not return to Galilee for some time afterwards. He could hardly have come back so soon to Jerusalem. But the Feast of Tabernacles after the Passover of John 6:4 is mentioned later, John 7:2 f., which Jesus attended, it seems, because he was hindered from going up to the previous Passover by the murderous designs of the Jews. It is possible that the feast of John 5:1 may have been the Feast of Tabernacles after a Passover not mentioned, and so would come after the second Passover of his public ministry. But we do not know that Jesus attended any other Feast of Tabernacles save the one in John 7:2, which he may have done because he missed the preceding Passover.

3. The Feast of Purim, first suggested by Kepler, has had great favor with modern harmonists, but apparently more on sentimental than on scholarly grounds. Meyer says, "Without doubt it was Purim." But it is by no means so certain as Meyer would have us believe. (*a*) Meyer relies on John 4:35 and 6:4 to show that this was the Feast of Purim just before John 6:4. But the expression, "Say not ye, There are yet four months and then cometh the harvest?" may be, and probably is a proverbial saying indicating the usual length of time between sowing and reaping, which, as a matter of fact, was about four months. Hence nothing can be determined by this note of time. And, besides, the four months could precede the Passover just as well as Purim, because the sowing lasted a month or so. (*b*) The Feast of Purim occurred a month before the Passover. Is it at all likely that two circuits of all Galilee were made in the meantime, besides much work of other kinds? See Luke 8:1 and Matt. 9:25–38. The three general circuits throughout Galilee, besides the mission of the twelve and a large part of their training, the general statements about the Master's work of preaching and healing, require an expansion rather than a contraction of the time for this period of his ministry. It seems then quite unreasonable, when once the mind takes in this enlarged conception of the missionary work of Jesus, as recorded by the Synoptic Gospels, to limit it to the amount of work mentioned by John, since he omits much of the early ministry, because, it would seem, the others are so full just here. (*c*) The Feast of Purim, moreover, was observed at home in the synagogues, and not by going to Jerusalem. See Esther 9:22 and Jos. Ant. xi. 6, 13. But "the multitude" (John 5:13) seems to imply (Robinson) a concourse of strangers at one of the great festivals. (*d*) It seems hardly probable, besides, that Jesus would go to any feast just a month before the Passover and come back to Galilee and not go to the Passover itself (John 6:4). Least of all would he do this in the case of Purim. (*e*) The man who was healed at this feast was healed on the Sabbath (John 5:9), and this occasioned the outburst among the people. But the Feast of Purim was never celebrated on the

Sabbath, and when it came on a Sabbath it was postponed. See Reland, Antiq. Sacr. 4, 9.

4. Pentecost is held to be the feast here alluded to by many early and some later writers, such as Chrysostom, Cyril of Alexandria, Erasmus, Calvin, Bengel, etc. Norris makes it the Pentecost after the first Passover, but to do this, has to crowd into this short interval Christ's first Judean ministry, the journey through Samaria together with the first part of his Galilean ministry. So this idea has little weight. McClellan argues that the allusions of Jesus in John 5:17–47, "infallibly point to Pentecost," meaning the Pentecost after a second Passover that is not mentioned. He further contends that this best suits the chronological arrangement and the term "a feast of the Jews." This view is certainly possible and cannot be positively disproved, although it is not so "infallibly" clear as McClellan imagines.

5. The Passover has always met with many adherents, being the second Passover in the Saviour's ministry and making four in all (John 2:13; 5:1; 6:4; 12:1). An unnamed Passover may exist in the ministry even if not referred to here. The arguments in favor of this interpretation are the most satisfactory. We cannot consider them as absolutely conclusive, yet the Passover meets all sides of the case better than any of the other feasts. (*a*) The plucking of ears from standing grain by the disciples (Luke 6:1) would indicate a time after the Passover and before Pentecost. This incident appears to have happened after the feast mentioned in John 5:1. (*b*) It is fairly implied (John 5:1) that the feast took Jesus to Jerusalem. The Passover would more likely be the one to lead him there. It is expressly stated that he attended two Passovers and a special reason is given for his not attending a third. If there was another Passover in his ministry, this would naturally be the one. (*c*) This suits best the hostility manifested at this feast, which would have time to become acute (Broadus' Comm. on Matt.) and break out with increased vigor in Galilee and prevent his attending the next Passover (John 6:4; 7:1). (*d*) If this Passover be a second Passover of the ministry, sufficient time is afforded for the great Galilean ministry without artificial crowding. His ministry would be long enough to allow the great work recorded as done by him. Only two serious objections can be urged to this idea. (1) It is objected that the article would be used with "feast," if the Passover were thus mentioned as *the* feast. But to this we can reply: (*a*) The article is sometimes omitted when the Passover is meant (Matt. 27:15; Mark 15:6). (*b*) The absence of the article proves nothing whatever one way or the other. No conclusion can be drawn for or against the idea of the Passover. (*c*) The article does occur in many manuscripts, including the Sinaitic, and is put in the margin of the Revised Version. So nothing can be gained against this theory here. (2) The chief

objection is that Jesus would not have remained so long away from Jerusalem, a year and six months, from the Second Passover till the Feast of Tabernacles after the Third Passover. But (*a*) we do not know that he did not attend any other feast in that time, for silence proves nothing; and (*b*) a good reason is given for his failure to attend the Third Passover, which may have applied to the others, if he did not go, *viz.*, the desire of the Jews to kill him (John 7:1).

Hence it is natural that there should be a variety of opinions as to the length of the Saviour's ministry, varying all the way from one to four years, leaving out mere guesses based on five and more Passovers. McKnight argues that the ministry may have lasted five or more full years, since all the Passovers of Christ's ministry may not be mentioned.

(1) The *Bi-paschal* theory makes the time of the public life of Jesus one year, allowing only two Passovers to the Gospel of John. Browne in his *Ordo Saeclorum* advocates this view. But the words, "the Passover," in John 6:4 must be omitted, and for this there is not enough documentary evidence. If this could be done, Westcott thinks Browne would make out a good case. But with the present text, his view cannot be entertained.

(2) The *Tri-paschal* theory finds only three Passovers in the life of Christ. Hence the public work of Jesus would be from two to two and a half years in length. This view is quite possible, as is shown in the Harmony. These writers usually make the feast of John 5:1 Purim before the Passover of John 6:4, or Pentecost after it.

(3) The *Quadri-paschal* theory contends for four Passovers and a ministry of from three to three and a half years. This theory follows from making John 5:1 a Passover or Purim before or Pentecost or Tabernacles after an unnamed Passover. This seems to be the more probable length of the Saviour's public work on earth. How short a space was even this to compass such a marvellous work. The ministry of Jesus seems crowded beyond our comprehension. It would be certain that the Saviour's public life lasted about three years and a half, if it was admitted that John 5:1 referred to a Passover. Various writers seek to find an allusion to the three years of the Saviour's ministry in the Parable of the Barren Fig Tree (Luke 13:6), but this application of the parable is by no means certain, since three might naturally be used as a round number. But there can very well have been a passover not mentioned. All we can say is that we know that the ministry of Jesus was two and a half years in length with the probability of three and a half.

8. The Four Lists of the Twelve Apostles

It is interesting to compare the four lists of Jesus' chosen apostles as given by Matthew, Mark, Luke, and Acts.

Mark 3:16 f.	Matthew 10:2 f.	Luke 6:14 f.	Acts 1:13 f.
1. Simon Peter	Simon Peter	Simon Peter	Simon Peter
2. James	Andrew	Andrew	James
3. John	James	James	John
4. Andrew	John	John	Andrew
5. Philip	Philip	Philip	Philip
6. Bartholomew	Bartholomew	Bartholomew	Thomas
7. Matthew	Thomas	Matthew	Bartholomew
8. Thomas	Matthew	Thomas	Matthew
9. James the son of Alpheus	James the son of Alpheus	James the son of Alpheus	James the son of Alpheus
10. Thaddeus	Thaddeus	Simon the Zealot	Simon the Zealot
11. Simon the Cananæan	Simon the Cananæan	Judas the brother of James	Judas the brother of James
12. Judas Iscariot	Judas Iscariot	Judas Iscariot	

Let us examine the names here given.

(1) The lists are given some time after the selection was made, and hence represent a later grouping according to later developments in this inner circle. The primacy of Peter in these lists does not mean necessarily that he was the acknowledged leader at first. See discussion under (4) below. The point to note here is that we are not to think of Peter as the formal leader of the Twelve before the death of Christ. Jesus was himself that leader.

(2) One mark of an apostle was that he should have been with the Lord from the baptism of John until the day that he was received up (Acts 1:21 f.). Perhaps no great stress is to be laid on any exact time here, provided it began in the time of John. An apostle must know the Lord. Hence Paul received the vision of Christ. We have some knowledge of seven of these apostles before this time. If we infer from John 1:41 that John followed the example of Andrew in finding his own brother, it was not long till James was a disciple as well as John, Andrew, and Peter. Philip and Nathanael are soon added to the list (John 1:43 f.). Later Matthew hears the call of the Saviour, too (Matt. 9:9; Mark 2:13 f). Of the other five we have no knowledge previous to this occasion. Jesus had "found" them by the same insight that led to his other selections. He chose Judas, though knowing that he was a devil.

(3) Observe the three groups of four, headed by Simon Peter, Philip, and James the son of Alpheus, respectively. The great variety in the arrangement of the other names makes this uniformity significant. It seems

clear that there are three recognized groups among the apostles (Bengel, Broadus, Clark). Each group has the same persons in every list, although there is such a variety in the order. In the first group Matthew and Luke have the same order, while Mark and Acts agree. In the second group Mark and Luke have a like order, while Matthew and Acts agree in putting Matthew at the end of this group. In the third group Matthew and Mark agree exactly, while Luke and Acts are identical save the dropping out of Judas Iscariot from the list in Acts because of his apostasy and death. No great importance can be attached to the precise order within the groups since Luke, in the Gospel and Acts, gives a different arrangement in the first and second groups.

(4) Observe also that Simon Peter not only stands at the head of his group, but at the head of all the groups, while Judas Iscariot is always at the bottom till he drops out entirely. Simon finally occupied a position of precedence of some sort. He was one of the inner circle of three that was so close to the Saviour's heart. Perhaps it was this, rather than any notion of primacy in authority or power. He was the spokesman because of his natural impetuosity. The question as to who should be greatest among the apostles illustrates the spirit of rivalry about precedence that existed among them. In the October, 1916, Journal of Theol. Studies, Dr. A. Wright argues that the critical text in Mark 14:10 means "Judas Iscariot the first of the Twelve." The *Koiné* did sometimes use *heis* as an ordinal (see Moulton, *Prolegomena*, p. 96, and my *Grammar of the Greek New Testament*, pp. 671 f.). But the disputes among the Twelve show that they themselves considered Jesus only as leader till his death. See my article on "The Primacy of Judas Iscariot," the Expositor (London) for April, 1917, and one by Rendel Harris in the June, 1917, issue, and Wright's reply in the November, 1917, number.

(5) There are among the Twelve three pairs of brothers—Simon and Andrew, James and John, James the son of Alpheus and Judas the brother of James. The first two pairs form the first group of the Twelve. It is, however, uncertain whether Judas is the brother or the son of James. The Greek is ambiguous, James's Judas. The Revised Version translated it "Judas son of James," but the Epistle of Jude begins "Judas a servant of Jesus Christ and brother of James." But the Jude of the Epistle and the Judas of the Twelve were hardly the same. Cf. Broadus, Comm. on Matt., p. 216.

(6) There are some apparent discrepancies in the names in the various lists. Bartholomew occurs in every list, but is generally understood to be another name for Nathanael. Thaddeus is also called Judas the brother of James. Matthew and Mark give Thaddeus, and Luke in Gospel and Acts gives Judas the brother of James. It was a very common circumstance

for one to have two names. Lebbeus, given in some MSS. in Matthew and Mark, is only a marginal explanation of Thaddeus. Both are terms of endearment. Matthew and Mark again call Simon the Cananæan, while Luke in the Gospel and Acts speaks of him as Simon the Zealot. But "Zealot" is simply a translation into Greek of the Aramaic "Cananæan." Jesus gave the other Simon the name "Cephas," which was translated into the Greek "Peter," meaning rock. He is called by all three names in the New Testament. Matthew likewise had another name, Levi, and Thomas was also called Didymus, which was a Greek translation of Thomas, meaning "twin."

9. *The Sermon on the Mount*

Do Matthew and Luke record the same discourse? Let us consider the several theories on this subject. My own view will be stated last.

1. Some hold that the two discourses are entirely distinct in time, place, circumstances and audience. The arguments for this theory usually presented are these.

(*a*) The time of delivery of the two sermons appears to be different. Matthew gives the sermon before his call (Matt. 9:9), while Luke precedes his sermon by the call of the twelve. Hence Matthew's discourse comes quite a while before Luke's in the early Galilean ministry. But it may be well replied that, inasmuch as Matthew's arrangement in ch. 8–13 is not chronological, but topical, it is entirely possible, even likely, that the same arrangement should prevail in ch. 5–7. It is perfectly natural that Matthew, writing for Jewish readers and about the Messianic reign, should give at the beginning of his account of that reign the formal principles that rule in this new state of affairs, as proclaimed by Jesus on a later occasion. In the early part of the ministry of Jesus, besides, the hearers would hardly be prepared for so advanced and radical ideas. Besides, Matthew makes no note of time whatever for this discourse.

(*b*) The place appears to be different. One is on a mountain (Matt. 5:1), while the other is on a plain (Luke 6:17). Hence the one is called by Clark the Sermon on the Mount, and the other the Sermon on the Plain. Miller (Int. Stand. Bible Encyclopædia) is uncertain whether Matthew and Luke report the same discourse and so discusses also Luke's "Sermon on the Plain." But his argument is not convincing. If it is necessary that "plain" here shall mean a place away from a mountain, down in a valley, this would seem to refer to a different place. McClellan seeks to show that Luke uses "and" in 6:17–20 by way of anticipation. He presents for effective grouping events that happened after Jesus came down out of the mountain before he gives the sermon delivered to the whole body of disciples up in the mountain. This is possible, but another interpretation is much more likely. The plain here is really simply "a level place" (Rev. Ver.). So then the two accounts of Matthew and Luke will harmonize quite well. Jesus first went up into the mountain to pray (Luke 6:12) and selected and instructed the Twelve. Afterwards he came down to a level place on the mountain side whither the crowds had gathered, and stood there and wrought miracles (Luke 6:17). He then went up a little higher into the mountain where he could sit down and see and teach the multitudes (Matt. 5:1). Matthew gives the multitudes as the reason for his going up into the mountain. By this arrangement any discrepancy between "sat" in Matthew and "stood" in Luke disappears. Waddy has given an admirable arrangement of the material at this point in Note C, p. xix. Many writers affirm that the tradition mentioned by Jerome, making the Horns of Hattin the place where the Sermon on the Mount was delivered, suits this explanation exactly. There is a level place on it where the crowds could have assembled. It is not necessary to insist that this mountain is the Mount of Beatitudes, nor need we contend, as Robinson does, that the mountain must be very close to Capernaum.

(*c*) The audience is different. Matthew (4:25) states that his audience was composed of "great multitudes from Galilee and Decapolis and Jerusalem and Judea and from beyond Jordan," while Luke (6:17) says that there was "a great multitude of his disciples, and a great number of the people from all Judea and Jerusalem, and the sea coast of Tyre and Sidon." Matthew says (5:1) also that "his disciples came unto him." Hence both assemblages were composed of great multitudes from many regions besides many of his disciples, but in neither case is Jesus said to address himself to any save his disciples, his followers (Matt. 5:1 and Luke 6:20). So in both accounts the Saviour seems to withdraw a little from the great outside crowd of curiosity seekers. But the multitudes also must have heard something of what he said, for they were astonished at his teaching (Matt. 7:28). Andrews well shows that the audience in Matthew were not mostly Jews (according to Kraft), and the audience in Luke mostly heathen. Matthew omits Tyre and Sidon, but he had already mentioned Syria (4:24), which includes Tyre and Sidon. Neither list may be complete. Hence nothing can be made out of Luke's omission of Galilee, Decapolis, and beyond Jordan. Great multitudes from the same general regions are alluded to as being present.

(*d*) The contents are radically different. It is objected by Alford, Greswell, etc., that Luke omits large portions of what Matthew has so that Luke has only thirty verses, while Matthew has one hundred and seven. But this leaves out of consideration the several large portions of the same matter which Luke has placed elsewhere, or which Jesus repeated on other occasions (cf. Matt. 6:9–13 and Luke 11:2–4; Matt. 6:25–34 and Luke 12:22–31). Jesus often repeated his sayings on other occasions as all teachers do and ought to do. Neither evangelist gives a complete report of this wonderful discourse. So Matthew omits some things which Luke records (cf. Matt. 5:12 with Luke 6:23–6; Matt. 7:12 with Luke 6:31–40). Nor need we be surprised that Luke, writing generally for all Christians, omits large portions towards the beginning of the sermon that were designed especially for Jews (see Matt. 5:17–27; 6:1–18). These Matthew would be sure to record. Luke adds four woes to the beatitudes. It is unnecessary to remark upon minor variations of language, since the gospels manifestly aim to give the sense of what the Saviour said and not the *verbatim* words. The variations in the Synoptic reports of the sayings of Jesus add much to the interest of the narratives. Moreover, to offset these variations, which admit of explanation, it ought to be remembered that the two discourses begin alike and end alike, that they have a general similarity in the order of the different parts, and that they show a general likeness and often absolute identity of expression.

So these differences all melt away on careful comparison, and it is not proved that there are two distinct sermons.

2. Another theory holds that the two sermons are distinct, but spoken on the same day, and near together. So Augustine, who is followed by Lange. The further points of this theory are two. (*a*) The one (Matt.) was spoken before the choice of the Apostles, to the disciples alone, and while Jesus was sitting on the mountain. (*b*) The other (Luke) was spoken after the choice of the Apostles, to the multitudes, and standing upon the plain. It is not hard to see that these points do not solve the question. In Matt. 7:28 we are told that the multitudes were astonished at his teaching and in Luke 6:20 that "he lifted up his eyes on his disciples, and said." So this distinction vanishes. The question of the mountain and the plain has been already discussed, and another more probable explanation suggested. It is only a conjecture that the discourse of Matthew was before the appointment of the Twelve. This theory has had no great following.

3. Wieseler holds that Matthew has simply brought together detached sayings of Jesus on different occasions and does not mean to present the whole as one discourse; Luke's account being only one of the discourses used by Matthew. But this violates the evident notes of place and audience and surroundings by which Matthew gives local color and cast to the entire discourse. See Matt. 5:1 and 8:1. The case of the grouping of the miracles in chapters 8 and 9 is not parallel, since there Matthew does not state that they occurred on one occasion. The fact that various portions of this discourse are repeated elsewhere by Matthew is immaterial, because this was a common habit of Jesus in his discourses. Votaw in his exhaustive and able discussion of the Sermon on the Mount in the extra volume in the Hastings D B admits the possibility of this hypothesis, but considers it far less probable

than the historical reality of the Sermon as recorded by both Matthew and Luke. Moffatt (Encycl. Biblica) considers it "a composition rather than an actual address," while Bacon (Sermon on the Mount) admits only what is also in Luke. Adeney (Hastings' D C G) holds to the essential integrity of the address in Matthew.

4. Both Matthew and Luke give substantially similar accounts of the same discourse. In that case we have a good illustration of the use of the Logia in Matthew and Luke. Most of the arguments for this interpretation have been mentioned in rebuttal of the previously mentioned theories. (*a*) This is the most natural explanation in view of the large volume of similar matter in both, in the beginning, progress, and close of the discourse. It is always best to give the Scripture the most natural and manifest setting, when possible. (*b*) This theory is the most probable one, since it is hardly likely that Jesus would again make the same sermon to the same audience, and under the same circumstances. (*c*) There are no objections to this theory that do not admit of a probable explanation. See the discussion above. The omissions and additions in each case suit the specific purpose of the writer. The apparent contradictions, when studied carefully, blend into a harmonious whole. Hence we seem to be justified in maintaining the identity of the discourses recorded by Matthew and Luke. For a careful outline of this matchless discourse see Broadus on Matthew. Stalker, *The Ethics of Jesus*, has a very able exposition of the teaching.

10. *The Combination of Luke and John*

We now have to deal with the most perplexing question in harmonistic study, the proper disposal of the mass of material furnished by Luke in 9:51–18:14. McClellan discusses ten schemes, pushes them all aside, and then suggests another which is no more convincing and equally complicated. Nothing can be attempted here but a presentation of the chief points in this endless discussion. All the principal plans for arranging this part of Luke proceed on one or the other of the following ideas:

1. Some hold that this portion of Luke is neither orderly nor chronological. Hence many of the incidents, here recorded as apparently belonging to the last six months of the Saviour's ministry, in reality are to be placed earlier. They are put here as a sort of summing up of things not mentioned elsewhere. So Robinson and others. In favor of this theory it is urged that Luke here speaks of some things that Matthew and Mark put before the third Passover, such as the healing of a demoniac (Luke 11:14–36) and the blasphemy following. But it may be well replied.

(*a*) It is not at all clear that we have here the same events that are recorded in Matthew and Mark. Similar miracles were often wrought in the Master's work and similar sayings were frequently repeated on similar or different occasions. This was a common habit with him, as we have heretofore seen.

(*b*) This portion of Luke is his distinctive contribution to the ministry of Christ in addition to his account of the nativity. He has condensed his account of the withdrawals from Galilee, apparently to make room for the description of another part of Christ's work. Matthew and Mark almost confine themselves to the ministry in Galilee, while Luke thus devotes the bulk of his narrative to what seems to be a later ministry, after Jesus has left Galilee. It is hardly likely that this account should be a mere jumble of scattered details.

(*c*) Especially is this unlikely in view of Luke's express statement (1:3) that he was going to write an orderly narrative. In no real sense could this be true, if this large section is dislocated in time and order of events.

2. Others refer the entire narrative (Luke 9:51–18:14) to the last journey of the Saviour to Jerusalem to the Passover and see a triple reference to the same journey arguing for triplications in Luke. Others prefer to understand it as meaning the journey to the Feast of the Tabernacles or Dedication. Some would combine this idea with the unchronological plan noticed above. In favor of this journey being continuous and the last one to Jerusalem, the following arguments are adduced:

(*a*) The language of Luke 9:51, "when the days were being completed that he should be received up," implies that the end was drawing near, and that he was setting his face towards Jerusalem to meet it. This is true without doubt, for Wieseler's interpretation of "received up" as meaning Christ's reception by man is entirely too forced. The expression points to the end of Christ's earthly career. But what does the vague expression, "the days were being completed," mean? Does it have to mean only a few weeks? May it not include as much as six months? For we know that Jesus had been instructing his disciples on this very subject expressly and pointedly, and at the Transfiguration he had spoken of his "decease." Henceforward this was the uppermost subject in his mind. So the interpretation is correct, but the inference is not necessary. This journey in Luke 9:51 need not be either just before the Passover or the Dedication. It could be as early as Tabernacles and be thus described.

(*b*) It is insisted that this is Jesus' final departure from Galilee, the one described by Matthew and Mark. No place is allowed for a return to Galilee after the departure in Luke 9:51. Robinson urges that Luke 9:51 naturally means a final departure from Galilee. But it may simply mean that he left it as a sphere of activity, not that he never entered Galilee again. And then Luke 17:11 expressly says that Jesus went "through the midst of Samaria and Galilee." This means more than going on the border between the two countries, as McClellan argues. He went through some portions of

Samaria and Galilee. In order for McClellan to carry out his scheme he has to resort to the artificial device of referring part of John 10:40 to the departure from Galilee, and the other half to the Perean ministry after a diversion of considerable length into Samaria and back into Galilee. So the effort is not convincing to place all the material in this large section of Luke in one last journey to Jerusalem.

3. The combination of Luke's narrative with that of John. Wieseler was the first to point out a possible parallel between Luke and John. John gives us three journeys,—the Feast of Tabernacles (John 7:2 ff.), the journey to Bethany at the raising of Lazarus (John 11:17 f.), the final Passover (John 12:1). Luke likewise three times in this section speaks of Jesus going to Jerusalem, 9:51; 13:22; 17:11. Hence it would seem possible, even probable, that their journeys corresponded. If so, John 7:2–11:54 is to be taken as parallel to Luke 9:51–18:14. This plan is followed by various modern scholars.

According to John's chronology, Jesus was in Jerusalem at the Feast of Tabernacles (7:2), at the Feast of Dedication (10:22), and at the Passover (12:1). Just after the Feast of the Dedication we find him abiding beyond Jordan, where John had baptized (John 10:40). From this point he comes to Bethany near Jerusalem at the raising of Lazarus (John 11:17), whence he withdraws to a little town called Ephraim in the hills north of Jerusalem (John 11:54). Here he abides awhile with his disciples away from his enemies till he goes to the Passover. Such is John's outline of these last six months of the Saviour's life.

(*a*) But how is all this to be reconciled with the statement of Luke (17:11) that Jesus went through Samaria and Galilee? If Jesus went back to Galilee, John would have mentioned it, we are told. Not necessarily, not unless it fell in with his plan to do so. Hence no conflict need exist between Luke and John. Luke says he went through Galilee and John permits it by the break in his narrative at 11:54. Various points in the six months have been suggested as the point when the return to Galilee was made. The most natural point is from Ephraim, whither he had withdrawn (John 11:54). It was not far to go up through Samaria and join in Galilee (Luke 17:11) the pilgrims from his own country who were in the habit of going to the Passover through Perea, to avoid passing through Samaria. This supposition is not improbable, as Robinson and McClellan urge, but very natural; it makes Luke and John both agree, and allows Luke 9:51 to mean that Jesus then left Galilee as a field of operations. Various other theories are suggested for this return to Galilee, but none of them appear as fitting as this one. It was just before the Passover, when such a journey from Galilee to Jerusalem would be made.

(*b*) One other point needs to be considered. The theory we hold makes the journey in Luke 9:51 identical with the one in John 7:2–10, *viz.*, to Tabernacles. Many hold such identity to be impossible because of apparent contradictions in the narratives. Andrews makes three objections against this identity: (1) That the Lord refused to go with his brethren (John 7:6). But it was his brothers who were not favorable to him that he refused to go with. He simply wished to avoid publicity. His face was set (Luke 9:51) all the time, but he was not going with them. (2) That the manner of the going is unlike; the one in John is secret, while the one in Luke is public. But the secrecy in John may merely mean the avoidance of the caravan routes and so through Samaria (Luke). The messengers sent before were not to herald his coming to gather crowds simply, but to make ready for him. It was needed, since the Samaritans saw that his face was as if he were going to Jerusalem. (3) That he went rapidly according to John and slowly according to Luke. He does, according to John, appear in Jerusalem before the feast is over, but Luke does not make him move slowly. Nor is it necessary to connect the sending of the seventy (Luke 10:1 ff.) with this journey. It belongs rather to the interval between Tabernacles and Dedication. So the secret going of John and the going through Samaria of Luke agree. John explains, 7:10, that Jesus rejected the advice of his brothers. This theory is held irrespective of this being the final departure from Galilee. It is not necessary to fill out every detail in this programme and show where Jesus was between Tabernacles and Dedication. The main outlines remain clear and harmonious and are fairly satisfactory. This combination of Luke and John preserves the integrity of both narratives and fills up a large blank that would otherwise exist in these closing months of the Saviour's life. Upon the whole, therefore, this view seems decidedly preferable, though nothing like absolute certainty can be claimed in regard to the question.

We do not know what special source Luke had for 9:51–18:14. Some of it may have come from the Logia (Q). Hawkins (*Oxford Studies*, pp. 55 ff.) calls it "the Travel Document." Burton (*Some Principles of Literary Criticism and Their Application to the Synoptic Problem*) suggests "The Peræan Document" and thinks that Luke may have drafted it early out of oral material. But at any rate it is a great and characteristic portion of his Gospel and adds greatly to our knowledge of Christ.

11. Did Christ Eat the Passover?

To put this question in another form, it would be, On what day of the month was Jesus crucified? For the crucifixion occurred on the same Jewish day as the eating of the meal recorded by all four Evangelists. Nearly all agree that the crucifixion occurred on Friday and the meal was eaten the evening before, our Thursday, but the beginning of the Jewish day, counting from sunset to sunset. But what day of the month was it? The Passover feast began on the 15th Nisan, the lamb being slain in the afternoon of the 14th. But the day of the week would vary with the new moon. If Jesus ate the regular Passover supper, he was crucified on the 15th Nisan. If he ate an anticipatory meal a day in advance and was himself slain at the hour of killing the paschal lamb, he was crucified on the 14th Nisan. In that case he did not really eat the Passover supper at all. So then we must seek to determine the truth about this matter, because express statements are made about it in the Gospels.

1. Some sentimental views of the question need to be disposed of first. A great controversy once raged in the early churches about the Passover.

(*a*) In the latter part of the second century some of the churches of Asia Minor, largely composed of Jewish Christians, kept up the Passover on the ground that Jesus had eaten it the night before his crucifixion. Polycarp, the disciple of John, expresses the persuasion that Jesus ate the Passover.

(*b*) But some of the churches were afraid of this example and its application to the discussion about the relation of the Mosaic laws to Christianity. So they took the position that Jesus did not eat the Passover himself, but as the Paschal Lamb, was crucified at the time the lamb was slain. He was our Passover. The Greek churches now hold this position, while the Latin churches hold that Jesus ate the Passover. But those arguments are purely subjective and do not affect the question of fact. Hence we waive this old-time controversy and come to the testimony of the Gospels themselves.

2. The testimony of the Synoptists, Mark, Matthew, and Luke. The evidence they give is abundant and explicit to the effect that Jesus ate the regular Paschal Supper on the evening after the 14th Nisan.

(*a*) Jesus predicted that his death would occur during the Feast of the Passover. See Matthew 26:2, "Ye know that after two days the Passover cometh, and the Son of Man is delivered up to be crucified." See also Mark 14:1 and Luke 22:1, where the fact is alluded to. Passover is used in the general sense of the feast of unleavened bread, as Luke explains. The feast of unleavened bread followed the Passover meal, beginning the next morning and lasting a week. But the one term was used to include the other. The Passover was expanded to mean the entire feast that followed, and *vice versa.*

(*b*) It is true that the Jewish authorities decided not to put Jesus to death during the feast (Matthew 26:5; Mark 14:2). But this decision was reached not because of any compunctions of conscience in the matter, but because they were afraid of a tumult among the people, owing to the great crowds, many of whom were friendly to Christ. But so soon as Judas offered his services, their fears vanished and they proceeded with their murderous designs (Matthew 26:14; Mark 14:11). The rulers did expedite matters at the crucifixion that the bodies might not be exposed on the Sabbath.

But they had often tried to slay Jesus on the Sabbath heretofore. Public executions did take place during the feasts (Deut. 17:12 f.).

(*c*) The Synoptists flatly say (Matthew 26:17, 20; Mark 14:12, 17; Luke 22:7, 14) that on the first day of unleavened bread Jesus sent Peter and John from Bethany into the city to make preparations for eating the Passover, and that on the evening of the same day he ate it with his disciples. Luke calls it "the hour." Now, the first day of unleavened bread was the 14th Nisan. There is no question about this. Josephus speaks of the feast lasting eight days. The lamb of the supper being slain on the afternoon of this day, it was regarded as the beginning of the feast. Besides, Mark and Luke end the whole matter by saying that on this day they sacrificed the Passover. Jesus himself calls it the Passover (Luke 22:15). It is useless to say that Jesus ate the Passover a day in advance. This could not be done, especially by one to whom the temple authorities were hostile. Equally useless is it to say that the Jews ate the Passover a day too late. If a mistake was made about the new moon, they would hardly keep the Passover on two different days, nor would Jesus be apt to make a point about the matter.

3. The testimony of John. If we had only the evidence of the Synoptists, no serious trouble would ever arise on this question. Strauss has strenuously urged that John is on this point in hopeless conflict with the other Evangelists, since he makes Jesus eat the Passover on the evening after the 13th Nisan (Wednesday), and not the evening after the 14th (Thursday). This idea has gained a foothold among many able modern writers who see a clear contradiction between the Synoptics and the Fourth Gospel. Some of these evidently do so because they hold that the Paschal controversy in Asia Minor arose from this supposed conflict of John with the Synoptists, and that this shows John's Gospel to have been in existence when that controversy began. It is not worth while to maintain that John in chapter 13 alludes to a different meal on a different occasion. The points of contact with the Synoptists are too sharp and clear, such as the sop given to Judas. But five passages in John are produced as being in direct opposition to the statements of the Synoptic Gospels. A careful examination of each of these five passages in the Fourth Gospel will show that John does not say that Jesus ate the Passover meal a day in advance of the regular time, but quite the contrary.

(*a*) John 13:1 f., "Now before the feast of the Passover, Jesus knowing, etc." Here, it is alleged, a distinct statement is made that this supper was before the Passover, and consequently twenty-four hours before. But several things are taken for granted in this inference. One is that the phrase "feast of the Passover" is to be confined to this particular meal, and is not to include the entire festival of unleavened bread (*cf.* Luke 22:1). Often by a metonymy of speech the name of a part is given to the whole. Besides, it is not certain that verse 1 is to be connected with verse 2. The best exegetes agree that a complete idea may be presented therein, either a general statement that Jesus loved his own before the Passover and until the end, or that he came into special consciousness of this love just before the Passover. And if the more natural interpretation be taken and the application of this love be made in verse 2, it is not necessary that the "before" be as much as twenty-four hours. Observe also the text adopted in the Revised Version in verse 2, not "supper being ended," but "during supper." With this reading agree the other references in 13:4, "riseth from supper," 13:12, "sat down again," 13:23, "there was at the table reclining in Jesus' bosom." So the natural meaning is that just before the meal began, Jesus purposed to show his love for his own by a practical illustration. So, after they had all reclined at the table according to custom, Jesus arose and passed around the tables, washing their feet; then he reclined again and proceeded with the meal. So nothing at all can be made out of this passage against the view that this was the regular Passover; but, on the other hand, the most natural meaning is that John is here describing what took place at this Passover meal. Else, why should he mention the Passover at all?

(*b*) John 13:27, "That thou doest, do quickly." The objection is made that the disciples would not have thought that Jesus referred to the feast (13:29), if the Passover meal was already going on or was over. So, it is urged, this remark must have been made a day before the Passover was celebrated. But if that were the case, where would be the necessity for hurry, as there would be plenty of time on the morrow? The word "feast" here need not be confined to the paschal supper, but more naturally refers to the whole of the feast, of which the supper was a part. So this haste was needed to provide for the feast of unleavened bread which began on the next morning. No real force lies in the fact that this day was a holy day, being the first day of the Passover festival. The Mishna expressly allows the procuring, even on a Sabbath, what was needed for the Passover. If this could be done on a Sabbath, much more could it be done on a feast day which was not a Sabbath. Hence not only was it possible for the disciples to have misunderstood the remark of Jesus on the Passover evening, but it was far more natural that such misapprehensions should arise then than a day before. So this passage, like the preceding, when rightly understood, really confirms the Synoptists.

(*c*) John 18:28, "They themselves entered not into the palace, that they might not be defiled, but might eat the Passover." At first sight this does look like a contradiction. For this was certainly after the feast of John 13:2, and if they had not eaten the Passover meal, why here is a clear case of conflict of authorities. But it is by no means certain that the phrase "eat the Passover" means simply the paschal supper. This phrase occurs five times in the New Testament besides this, but all in Matthew, Mark, and Luke (Matt. 26:17; Mark 14:12, 14; Luke 22:11, 15). In all of these the reference is to the paschal supper. But the word "passover" is used in three senses in the New Testament, the paschal supper, the paschal lamb, or the paschal festival. The word is used eight times in John besides this instance, and in every case the Passover festival is meant. So we may fairly infer that the usage of John must determine his own meaning rather than that of the Synoptists. This becomes more probable when we remember that John wrote much later than they, after the destruction of Jerusalem, when these terms were not used so strictly. He always speaks of "the Jews" as separate from Christians. And this very expression is used in 2 Chronicles 30:22, "And they did eat the festival seven days." The Septuagint translates it, "And they fulfilled (kept) the festival of unleavened bread seven days." See Robinson. So it is entirely possible for the phrase, "eat the Passover," to mean in this instance also the celebration of the Passover festival. Some have urged that the Sanhedrin had not eaten the Passover at the regular hour because of the excitement of the trial. But this is hardly tenable. And, moreover, since this remark was made early in the morning, how could that affect the eating of the supper in the evening? For whatever impurities one had during the day passed away at evening. Hence this uncleanness must belong to the same day on which it was incurred. If the Passover festival had begun, this would be true, for they would wish to participate in the offerings of that day. So this passage likewise becomes an argument in favor of agreement with the Synoptists.

(*d*) John 19:14, "Now it was the Preparation of the Passover." This is claimed to mean the day preceding the Passover festival. Hence Christ was crucified on the 14th Nisan, in opposition to the Synoptists. The afternoon before the Passover was used as a preparation, but it was not technically so called. This phrase "Preparation" was really the name of a day in the week, the day before the Sabbath, our Friday. We are not left to conjecture about this question. The Evangelists all use it in this sense alone. Matthew uses it for Friday (27:62), Mark expressly says that the Preparation was the day before the Sabbath (15:42), Luke says that it was the day of the Preparation and the Sabbath drew on (23:54), and John himself so uses the word in two other passages (19:31, 42), in both of which haste is exercised on the Preparation, because the Sabbath was at hand. The New Testament usage is conclusive, therefore, on this point. This, then, was the Friday of Passover week. And this agrees with the Synoptists. Besides, the term "Preparation" has long been the regular name for Friday in the Greek language, caused by the New Testament usage. It is so in the Modern Greek to-day. It was the Sabbath eve, just as the Germans have Sonnabend for Sunday eve, *i.e.*, Saturday afternoon. So this passage also becomes a positive argument for the agreement between John and the Synoptists.

(*e*) John 19:31, "For the day of that Sabbath was a high day." From this passage it has been argued that at this Passover the first day of the Passover festival coincided with the weekly Sabbath. But that is an entirely gratuitous inference. This coincidence would, of course, be a "high day," but so would the first day of the feast, the last day, or the Sabbath of the feast. In John 7:37 the last day is called "the great day of the feast." The Sabbath occurring during the festival would be a high day likewise. Robinson's arguments on this point are quite conclusive. Nothing can be made out of the expression against the position of the Synoptists.

McClellan discusses various other passages in John which show that the crucifixion occurred on Friday, and that this was the first day of the feast (John 18:39, 40; 19:31, 42; 20:1, 19, etc.). We conclude then that a fair interpretation of the passages alleged not only removes all contradiction between John and the Synoptists, but rather decidedly favors the view that they have the same date for the Passover meal, and that Jesus ate the Passover at the regular hour and was crucified on Friday, 15th Nisan.

It is reassuring to note that David Smith (*The Days of His Flesh*, Appendix VIII) reaches the same conclusion as that just stated. He makes it out that Jesus ate the regular Passover meal and was crucified on Friday 15th of Nisan and that the passages in John really agree with the Synoptic account.

12. The Hour of the Crucifixion

In John 19:14 it is stated that the time when Pilate sentenced Jesus to be crucified, or rather when he began the last trial in which he sentenced him, was about the sixth hour. We read, however, in Mark 15:25 that it was the third hour when Christ was crucified. The Synoptists all unite in saying that the darkness began at the sixth hour. The Jewish way of counting the hours was to divide the night and day into twelve divisions each, beginning at sunrise and sunset. The hours would thus vary in length with the time of year. Just after the vernal equinox the third hour of Mark would be about 9 A.M., and the sixth hour of the Synoptists would be about noon. The ninth hour, when Jesus gave his piteous cry to God (Mark 15:34), would be about 3 P.M. But how can the sixth hour of John, the time when Jesus was sentenced by Pilate, be reconciled to this schedule? A real difficulty is here presented, but by no means an insuperable one, as Alford and Meyer hold. Let us discuss some of the more usual explanations. Andrews and McClellan give quite a variety of suggested solutions.

1. Some hold that "sixth" in John is a textual error for "third." This could easily happen, since the gamma and the digamma of the Greek are

very similar. Eusebius said that the accurate copies had it "third" in John. But the textual evidence is overwhelmingly against it, and, besides, the difficulty would not be removed. John is evidently speaking of the time at the last trial and Mark of the time after Jesus has been led out to the crucifixion. So nothing is gained by this hypothesis. We should still be confronted with the same difficulty. The change to *third* in John was a mere stupid scribal correction.

2. Others would change the punctuation in John 19:14 so as to make "of the Passover" belong to "sixth hour," beginning from midnight. But there is no evidence that the Passover began with midnight. So Hofmann. This is very forced and unnatural.

3. Views that hinge on the word "preparation." Some would hold that John simply says that about noon the preparation time of the Passover begins. But Preparation here means Friday, and noon is not the hour needed to harmonize with Mark. Equally arbitrary is it to count six hours backward from noon so as to reach six o'clock.

Augustine suggested that the six hours are to be counted from 3 A.M. This would make 9 A.M., and would concur with the hour of Mark. But this is wholly arbitrary and unsatisfactory, and would not relieve the trouble.

4. Equally arbitrary is the solution that makes Mark refer to the hour of the sentence and John to the crucifixion, just the reverse of the Scripture account. Augustine also proposed that Jesus was crucified at the third hour by the tongues of the Jews, and at the sixth by the hands of the soldiers.

5. Others hold that Mark and John both speak in general terms. Hence the crucifixion may have taken place between 9 and 12 in the morning. Mark looks in one direction and John in the other without aiming at definiteness. The Jews, it is true, were not as exact in the use of expressions of time as we are to-day, but this solution hardly meets the requirements of the case. Mark puts his *third* hour at the beginning of the crucifixion, and John his *sixth* hour at the beginning of the last trial. This reconciliation does not reconcile.

6. The most satisfactory solution of the difficulty is to be found in the idea that John here uses the Roman computation of time, from midnight to noon and noon to midnight, just as we do now. Hence the sixth hour would be our six o'clock in the morning. If this hour was the beginning of the last trial of Jesus, we then have enough, but not too much, time for the completion of the trial, the carrying away of Jesus outside the city walls, together with the procuring of the crosses, etc. All the events, moreover, narrated by the Evangelists, could have occurred between dawn (John 18:27) and six or seven.

For a long time it was doubted whether the Romans ever used this method of computing time for civil days. Farrar vehemently opposes this idea.

But Plutarch, Pliny, Aulus Gellius, and Macrobius expressly say that the Roman civil day was reckoned from midnight to midnight. So the question of fact may be considered as settled. The only remaining question is whether John used this mode of reckoning. Of course, the Romans had also the natural day and the natural night just as we do now. In favor of the idea that John uses the Roman way of counting the hours in the civil day, several things may be said.

(*a*) He wrote the Gospel late in the century, probably in Asia Minor, long after the destruction of Jerusalem, when the Jewish method would not likely be preserved. Roman ideas were prevalent in Asia Minor. John evidently is not writing for the Jews primarily, since he constantly speaks of "the Jews" as outsiders. John is writing to be understood by the people, and this is the way it would be understood in Asia Minor.

(*b*) All the passages in John, where the hour is mentioned, allow this computation. John 1:39 would be 10 A.M.; 4:6 f. would be 6 P.M., counting from noon also (as we do). This hour suits best the circumstances. In the evening the women would come to get water, Jesus would have time for his journey thither, and would be tired and hungry. In John 4:52 the hour would be 7 P.M. This hour likewise suits the circumstances better. John 11:9, Are there not twelve hours in the day? is not against this idea, since here obviously the natural day, as opposed to night, is meant. The Romans used both methods and so do we.

(*c*) Moreover, one passage in John (20:19), when compared with Luke 24:29, 36, makes it necessary to understand that John used the Roman method in this instance. It was toward evening, and the day had declined, according to Luke, when Jesus and the disciples drew near to Emmaus. Here he ate supper and, "rising up that very hour," the disciples returned seven miles to Jerusalem and told these things to the eleven who were together. But while they were narrating these things Jesus appeared to them. Now John, in mentioning this very appearance of Jesus (20:19), says that it "was evening on *that day*, the first day of the week," *i.e.*, evening of the day when Mary Magdalene had seen the Lord. But with the Jews the evening began the day. Hence John, here at least, is *bound* to mean the Roman day. It was the evening of the same day in the morning of which Mary had seen Jesus. This appears conclusive. John did use the Roman method here, may have done so always, almost certainly did so in 19:14. Besides, as McClellan shows, the natural meaning of John's phrase is that it was the sixth hour of the Friday (Preparation) of the Passover. But we have just seen that John in 20:19 counts according to the Roman day. Hence the sixth hour of Friday would be six o'clock in the morning.

This is the only solution that really harmonizes John and Mark. The rest make the hours agree, but the hours bring together different events.

This method harmonizes the whole narrative, and seems entirely probable, if we can assume that the Romans or Greeks employed hours in this sense, a point denied by Ramsay.

Sir W. M. Ramsay (*The Expositor* for March, 1893, and Extra Volume, Hastings D B) contends that Mark and John are at variance, but that it is of small moment, since the ancients had little notion about hours. He seeks to show that the martyrdom of Polycarp and Pronius, usually relied on to prove that in Asia Minor the hours were counted from midnight, took place in the afternoon, instead of the morning, the usual time. Hence the eighth and tenth hours respectively would be 2 P.M. and 4 P.M. Ramsay argues that, when hours were counted, they were always counted from sunrise. He holds that John is more accurate about hours than Mark and that hence Mark is in error. He agrees that John "stood on the Roman plane" in the use of time, but denies that the sixth hour can be our 6 A.M. But the evidence is too uncertain for such a dogmatic position.

13. *The Time of the Resurrection of Christ*

1. Mark, Luke, and John say that the resurrection had taken place early on the first day of the week, *i.e.* early Sunday morning. Mark (16:9) says that Jesus, "having risen early, on the first day of the week, appeared, etc." The position of "early" is ambiguous in the Greek and the passage is disputed. Mark (16:2) states that it was very early on the first day of the week, the sun having risen, when the women came to the sepulchre. Luke (24:1) says that the women came to the tomb at early dawn on the first day of the week. John (20:1) says that Mary Magdalene came to the tomb in the morning on the first day of the week. So then, there is no doubt that these three Evangelists mean to say that Jesus rose very early on Sunday morning, and that shortly after that event came the two Marys and some other women to anoint his body with spices.

Much objection is made to some of the details in the accounts of Mark and John especially as being inconsistent. John (20:1) says that Mary comes while it is yet dark, while Mark says (16:2) that the sun was risen. But Mark also says in the same verse that it was very early, which would agree with John's statement that it was yet dark. Hence Mark's other statement, that the sun was risen, must be interpreted in the light of his own words. Two solutions can be offered.

(*a*) We may suppose, as McClellan and others, that John's note of time refers to the starting from Bethany, while it was yet dark or very early (Mark). In a few minutes it would be early dawn (Luke), and by the time the women come to the tomb, the sun would be up. All this is entirely possible and looks even probable, for in the twilight of early dawn, the border line is very narrow between darkness and sunrise. A stiff morning walk would pass through all the stages. It all depends on where you take your stand in this fleeting interim. Mark covers both sides and so includes it all from the first glimmering light till the full light of day.

(*b*) Or the expression, "the sun was risen" (aorist participle), may simply be a general expression applicable to the phenomena of sunrise. The first gleam of daylight comes from the rising sun, though not yet completely risen. Robinson gives several examples from the Septuagint, where the same phrase is used in the aorist tense in a general way for the dawning light of day (Judges 9:33; 2 Kings 3:22; Ps. 104:22). Either of these explanations is entirely possible and removes the difficulty.

2. But Matthew seems to put the resurrection on the evening after the Sabbath, our Saturday evening. He says (28:1), "But late on the Sabbath day, as it was dawning into the first day of the week, came Mary Magdalene and the other Mary to view the sepulchre." If this passage means that the visit was made at the end of the Sabbath day (evening) and after the resurrection of Jesus, then Matthew is in plain contradiction to the other Evangelists. Some have taken the position that Jesus rose at sunset on the Sabbath day, forgetting that Mark (16:9) says that he rose early in the morning. There are several ways of reconciling Matthew with the other gospels.

(*a*) Greswell, Alford and others would translate "late on the Sabbath day" by "late in the week." The Greek word is the same in this verse for Sabbath and week. In both cases, therefore, the translation could be the same. But little sense would result from this translation. "Late in the week" and "dawning into the first day of the week" hardly fit well. By this explanation the latter expression is used for the first part of Sunday and the visit occurred in this dawning part of the day.

(*b*) Others would translate "late on the Sabbath day" by "after the Sabbath day." Godet, Grimm and others contend that the Greek idiom could mean this, and the *Koine* allows it (Robertson, *Grammar of the Greek New Testament*, pp. 645 f.). This rendering is possible, though the papyri have instances of "late on" for this preposition (*opse*), and it is so translated by several English translators. Thus the Greek idiom allows either "late on" or "after."

(*c*) Matthew does not clearly say that this visit was made after the resurrection of the Saviour although his words may mean that. Hence the words may have their natural meaning as sustained by the papyri. Late on the Sabbath day, about sundown say, the two Marys go to view the sepulchre (Matt. 28:1), having rested through the day (Luke 23:56). The women who had come with Jesus from Galilee had gone thither on Friday, after his burial, to see where he was laid and had prepared spices. If they went at nightfall at the close of the Sabbath (Matt. 28:1) "to see the sepulchre," they could have bought spices after sundown (Mark 16:1). Then (Mark 16:2) in the early morning, they rose and took the spices and went to anoint his body. It was then that they saw the angel (Matt. 28:5). Matthew does not say that in the visit of 28:1 the angel appeared to them. He speaks of the earthquake having come, and the resurrection, and then resumes. This view gains some support from the use of the same Greek word in Luke 23:54, "And it was the day of the Preparation (Friday) and the Sabbath drew on (was dawning)." Here the meaning seems to be that the Sabbath *dawned* at the close of the day. So Westcott, McClellan and others. However it may be about the visit of the women in Matt. 28:1, Matthew certainly does not mean to say that Jesus rose at sunset on the Sabbath. The whole course of his narrative in the rest of the chapter shows that it was the morning of Sunday when the angel appeared. While (Matt. 28:11) the women went to the disciples, the soldiers ran to the chief priests (Matt. 28:13) and said that the disciples came by *night* and stole him while they slept, clearly implying that it was now day. Hence Matthew does not teach that Jesus rose at sunset, but the reverse. Besides, Matthew expressly says that Jesus rose on the third day, which would not be true, if he rose on the Sabbath.

(*d*) Sabbath day may be used of the day followed by the night, according to a possible understanding of the language. The Jews originally counted from evening to evening, but this custom did not prevail universally. Jonah (1:17) and Matthew (12:40) speak of three days and three nights, following the day by the night. Meyer, Morison, Clark and others hold this view, and it is possible, but certainly not so satisfactory as the view given under (c). At any rate, it remains clear that Matthew agrees with the other Evangelists in putting the resurrection of Jesus Sunday morning. The chief point of difficulty is Matthew's visit of the women in 28:1, whether this was in the evening before simply "to view the sepulchre," or in the morning to anoint the body of the Saviour. The condensed account of Matthew leaves this question unsettled, and there we too shall have to leave it. And this last matter does not affect the question as to the time of the Lord's resurrection, but only the number of the visits made by the women.

14. The Length of Our Lord's Stay in the Tomb

Quite an effort is made in some quarters to show that Jesus remained in the tomb seventy-two hours, three full days and nights. The effort seems due to a desire to give full value to the expression "three days" and to vindicate scripture. But a minutely literal interpretation of this phrase makes "on the third day" flatly erroneous. A good deal of labor has been expended in the impossible attempt to make three and four equal to each other. There are three sets of expressions used about the matter, besides the express statements of the Gospels about the days of the crucifixion and resurrection. Let us examine these lines of evidence.

1. Luke settles the matter pointedly by mentioning all the time between the crucifixion and the resurrection (Luke 23:50–24:3). The burial took place Friday afternoon just before the Sabbath drew on (Luke 23:54). The women rested on the Sabbath (Saturday) (Luke 23:56), and went to the sepulchre early Sunday morning, the first day of the week (Luke 24:1). There is no escaping this piece of chronology. This is all the time there was between the two events. Jesus then lay in the tomb from late in the afternoon of Friday till early Sunday morning. The other Gospels agree with this reckoning of the time, as we have already seen.

2. But how about the prediction of Jesus, repeatedly made, and once illustrated by the case of Jonah, that he would rise after three days? Are two nights and a day and two pieces of days three days? Let us see.

(*a*) The well-known custom of the Jews was to count a part of a day as a whole day of twenty-four hours. Hence a part of a day or night would be counted as a whole day, the term day obviously having two senses, as night and day, or day contrasted with night. So then the part of Friday would count as one day, Saturday another, and the part of Sunday the third day. This method of reckoning gives no trouble to a Jew or to modern men, for that matter. In free vernacular we speak the same way today.

(*b*) Besides, the phrase "on the third day" is obliged to mean that the resurrection took place on that day, for, if it occurred after the third day, it would be on the fourth day and not on the third. Now it so happens that this term "third day" is applied *seven* times to the resurrection of Christ (Matt. 16:21; Matt. 17:23; Matt. 20:19; Luke 27:7, 21, 46; 1 Cor. 15:4). These numerous passages of Scripture, both prophecy and statement of history, agree with the record of the fact that Jesus did rise on the third day. (Luke 24:7.)

(*c*) Moreover, the phrase "after three days" is used by the same writers (Matthew and Luke) in connection with the former one, "the third day," as meaning the same thing. Hence the definite and clear expressions must explain the one that is less so. The chief priests and Pharisees remember (Matt. 27:63) that Jesus said, after three days I rise again. Hence they urge Pilate to keep a guard over the tomb until the *third day* (Matt. 27:64). This is their own interpretation of the Saviour's words. Besides, in parallel passages in the different Gospels, one will have one expression and another the other, naturally suggesting that they regarded them as equivalent. (Cf. Mark 8:31 with Matt. 16:21, Luke 9:22 with Mark 10:34.) On the third day cannot mean on the fourth day, while after three days can be used as meaning on the third day.

(*d*) Matthew 12:40 is urged as conclusive the other way. But the "three days and three nights" may be nothing more than a longer way of saying three days, using day in its long sense. And we have already seen that the Jews counted any part of this full day (day and night) as a whole day (day and night). Hence this passage may mean nothing more than the common "after three days" above mentioned, and, like that expression, must be interpreted in accordance with the definite term "on the third day" and with the clear chronological data given by Luke and the rest. They seemed to be conscious of no discrepancy in these various expressions. Most likely they understood them as well as we do at any rate.

A LIST OF THE PARABLES OF JESUS

The Sign of the Temple, § 31.
The Physician, § 39 (cf. § 47).
The Three Parables about the New Dispensation, § 48.
The Blind Guiding the Blind, The Mote and the Beam, § 54.
The Wise and Foolish Builders, § 54.
The Children in the Market Place, § 57.
The Two Debtors, § 59.
Parables about Satan's Kingdom, § 61.
The Unclean Spirit that Returned, § 62.
The Sower, § 64.
The Seed Growing of Itself, § 64.
The Tares, § 64.
The Mustard Seed, §§ 64 and 110.
The Leaven, §§ 64 and 110.
The Hid Treasure, § 64.
The Pearl of Great Price, § 64.
The Net, § 64.
The Scribe, § 64.
The Parable of Corban, § 77.
The Unmerciful Servant, § 92.
The Good Shepherd, § 101.
The Good Samaritan, § 103.
The Importunate Friend, § 105.
The Rich Fool, § 108.
The Waiting Servants, § 108.
The Wise Steward, § 108.
The Fig Tree, § 109.
Seats at Feasts, § 114.
Feast for the Poor, § 114.
The Great Supper, § 114.
The Tower and the King, § 115.
The Lost Sheep, § 116 (cf. § 91).
The Lost Coin, § 116.
The Lost Son, § 116.
The Unrighteous Steward, § 117.

The Rich Man and Lazarus, § 117.
Unprofitable Servants, § 117.
The Importunate Widow, § 121.
The Pharisee and the Publican, § 121.
The Laborers in the Vineyard, § 124.
The Pounds, § 127.
The Two Sons, § 132.
The Wicked Husbandmen, § 132.
The Rejected Stone, § 132.
The Marriage Feast and the Wedding Garment, § 132.
The Fig Tree, § 139.
The Porter, § 139.
The Master and the Thief, § 139.
The Wise Servant, § 139.
The Ten Virgins, § 139.
The Talents, § 139.
The Sheep and the Goats, § 139.

A LIST OF THE MIRACLES OF JESUS

The Water Made Wine, § 29.
The Courtier's Son, § 38.
The First Draught of Fishes, § 41.
The Capernaum Demoniac, § 42.
Simon's Mother-in-law, § 43.
A Leper, § 45.
The Paralytic, § 46.
The Impotent Man, § 49.
The Man with a Withered Hand, § 51.
The Centurion's Servant, § 55.
The Widow's Son, § 56.
A Blind and Dumb Man, § 61.
The Stilling of the Storm, § 65.
The Gadarene Demoniacs, § 66.
The Woman with an Issue of Blood, § 67.
Jairus' Daughter, § 67.
Two Blind Men, § 68.
A Dumb Demoniac, § 68.
The Five Thousand Fed, § 72.
Jesus Walking on the Water, § 74.
The Phœnician Woman's Daughter, § 78.
The Deaf and Dumb Man, § 79.
The Four Thousand Fed, § 79.
A Blind Man Healed, § 81.
The Demoniac Boy, § 87.
The Shekel in the Fish's Mouth, § 89.
The Man Born Blind, § 100.
The Woman with an Infirmity, § 110.
The Man with the Dropsy, § 114.
The Raising of Lazarus, § 118.
The Ten Lepers, § 120.
Blind Bartimæus and His Companion, § 126.
The Fig Tree Cursed, § 129.
Malchus' Ear, § 153.
The Second Draught of Fishes, § 180.

Besides these particular miracles numerous general groups must be added, as Mark 6:56; Matt. 4:23 f.; 9:35 f.; Luke 4:40 f.; 5:15 f.; 6:17–19; 7:21 f.; John 2:23; 3:2; 4:45; 20:30; 21:25.

LIST OF OLD TESTAMENT QUOTATIONS IN THE GOSPELS

Mark	1: 2,	from	Mal. 3:1; Isa. 40:3.
"	1: 3,	"	Isa. 40:3.
"	1:11,	"	Ps. 2:7; Isa. 42:1.
"	1:24,	"	Ps. 16:10.
"	1:44,	"	Lev. 13:49; 14:2–32.
"	2:24,	"	Ex. 20:10, Deut. 5:14; 23:25
"	2:25,	"	Lev. 24:9; 1 Sam. 21:1–6.
"	4:12,	"	Isa. 6:9, 10.
"	4:29,	"	Joel 3:13.
"	4:32,	"	Dan. 4:9.
"	6:18,	"	Lev. 18:16; 20:21.
"	7:6, 7,	"	Isa. 29:13.
"	7:10,	"	Ex. 20:12; 21:17; Lev. 20:9; Deut. 5:16.
"	8:18,	"	Isa. 6:9, 10; Jer. 5:21; Ezek. 12:2.
"	8:38,	"	Ps. 62:12; Prov. 24:12.
"	9: 7,	"	Deut. 18:15; Isa. 42:1; Ps. 2:7.
"	9:12,	"	Mal. 4:5.
"	9:13,	"	1 Kings 10:2, 10.
"	9:48,	"	Isa. 66:24.
"	9:49,	"	Lev. 2:13.
"	10: 4,	"	Deut. 24:1.
"	10: 6,	"	Gen. 1:27; 5:2.
"	10:7, 8,	"	Gen. 2:24.
"	10:19,	"	Ex. 20:12–17; Deut. 5:16–21.
"	10:27,	"	Gen. 18:14; Job 42:2.
"	11: 9,	"	Ps. 118:26.
"	11:17,	"	Isa. 5:17; Jer. 7:11.
"	12: 2,	"	Isa. 5:1 f.
"	12:10, 11,	"	Ps. 118:22 f.
"	12:19,	"	Gen. 38:8; Deut. 25:5, 6.
"	12:26,	"	Ex. 3:6.
"	12:29,	"	Deut. 6:4, 6.
"	12:31,	"	Lev. 19:18.
"	12:33,	"	1 Sam 15:22.

Mark	12:36,	from	Ps. 8:7; 110:1.
"	13:12,	"	Mic. 7:6.
"	13:14,	"	Dan. 9:27.
"	13:19,	"	Dan. 12:1.
"	13:24,	"	Dan. 8:10; Eccl. 12:2; Joel 4:16.
"	13:26,	"	Dan. 7:13.
"	14:12,	"	Ex. 12:18–20.
"	14:18,	"	Ps. 41:9.
"	14:24,	"	Ex. 24:8; Lev. 4:18–20; Jer. 31:31.
"	14:27,	"	Zech. 13:7.
"	14:34,	"	Ps. 42:6.
"	14:62,	"	Ps. 110:1; Dan. 7:13.
"	14:64,	"	Lev. 24:16.
"	15:24,	"	Ps. 22:18.
"	15:34,	"	Ps. 22:1.
Matt.	1: 1–17,	"	1 Chron. 1:34; 2:1–15; 3:1–19.
"	1:23,	"	Isa. 7:14.
"	2: 2,	"	Num. 24:17.
"	2: 6,	"	Mic. 5:1 f.
"	2:15,	"	Hos. 11:1.
"	2:18,	"	Jer. 31:15.
"	3: 3,	"	Isa. 40:3.
"	3:17,	"	Ps. 2:7; Isa. 42:1.
"	4: 4,	"	Deut. 8:3.
"	4: 6,	"	Ps. 91:11.
"	4: 7,	"	Deut. 6:16.
"	4:10,	"	Deut. 6:13.
"	4:15 f.,	"	Isa. 8:23; 9:1 f.
"	5: 4,	"	Isa. 61:2.
"	5: 5,	"	Ps. 37:11.
"	5: 6,	"	Ps. 55.
"	5: 7,	"	Ps. 18:25; Prov. 11:17.
"	5: 8,	"	Ps. 24:3–5.
"	5:21 f.,	"	Ex. 20:13; Deut. 5:17.
"	5:27,	"	Ex. 20:14; Deut. 5:18.
"	5:31,	"	Deut. 24:1.
"	5:33 ff.,	"	Ex. 20:7; Num. 30:2; Lev. 19:12; Deut. 5:11; 23:21; Isa. 66:1; Ps. 48:2.
"	5:38,	"	Ex. 21:24; Lev. 24:20; Deut. 19:21.
"	5:43,	"	Lev. 19:18; Deut. 23:6; 25:19.
"	8:11,	"	Isa. 49:12.
"	8:17,	"	Isa. 53:4.

Matt.	9:13,	from	Hos. 6:6.
"	9:36,	"	Num. 27:17; Ezek. 24:5.
"	10:35,	"	Mic. 7:6.
"	11: 5,	"	Isa. 2:18–19; 35:5–6; 61:1.
"	11:10,	"	Mal. 3:1.
"	11:15,	"	Mal. 4:5.
"	11:23,	"	Isa. 14:13–15.
"	11:24,	"	Gen. 19:24.
"	11:29 f.,	"	Jer. 6:16.
"	12: 2,	"	Ex. 20:10; Deut. 5:14; 23:25.
"	12: 3,	"	Lev. 24:9; 1 Sam. 21:1–6.
"	12: 5,	"	Num. 28:9–10
"	12: 7,	"	Hos. 6:6.
"	12:18–21,	"	Isa. 42:1–4.
"	12:40,	"	Jonah 1:17; 2:1–2; 3:5; 4:3; 1 Kings 10:1–10.
"	13:14, 15,	"	Isa. 6:9, 10.
"	13:32,	"	Dan. 4:9–21.
"	13:35,	"	Ps. 78:2.
"	13:43,	"	Dan. 12:3.
"	15: 4,	"	Ex. 20:12; 21:17; Lev. 20:9.
"	15:8, 9,	"	Isa. 29:13.
"	16: 4,	"	Jonah 3:4.
"	16:18,	"	Ps. 89:4, 26, 38, 48.
"	16:27,	"	Ps. 62:12; Prov. 24:12.
"	17: 5,	"	Isa. 42:1; Deut. 18:5; Ps. 2:7.
"	17:11–12,	"	1 Kings 19:2, 10; Mal. 4:5–6.
"	18:16,	"	Deut. 19:15.
"	19: 4,	"	Gen. 1:27; 5:2.
"	19: 5,	"	Gen. 2:24.
"	19: 7,	"	Deut. 24:1.
"	19:18,	"	Ex. 20:12, 13, 14; 21:17; Deut. 5:19, 20.
"	19:19,	"	Lev. 19:18; Ex. 20:12.
"	19:26,	"	Gen. 18:14.
"	21: 5,	"	Isa. 62:11; Zech. 9:9.
"	21: 9,	"	Ps. 118:26.
"	21:13,	"	Isa. 56:7; Jer. 7:11.
"	21:16,	"	Ps. 82.
"	21:33,	"	Isa. 5:1 f.
"	21:42,	"	Ps. 118:22.
"	21:44,	"	Isa. 8:14.
"	22:24,	"	Deut. 25:5.
"	22:32,	"	Ex. 3:6, 15.

Matt.	22:37,	from Deut. 6:5.
"	22:39,	" Lev. 19:18.
"	22:44,	" Ps. 110:1.
"	23:5–6,	" Ex. 13:9; Num. 13:38–39; Deut. 6:8; 11:18.
"	23:23,	" Lev. 27:30; Mic. 6:8.
"	23:35,	" Gen. 4:8; 2 Chron. 24:20–21.
"	23:38 f.,	" Ps. 118:26; Jer. 12:7; 22:5.
"	24:15,	" Dan. 9:27; 11:31; 12:11.
"	24:21,	" Dan. 12:1.
"	24:24,	" Deut. 13:1.
"	24:29,	" Dan. 8:10; Joel 4:16.
"	24:30,	" Dan. 7:13; Isa. 13:9–10; Ezek. 32:7–8; Amos 8:9; Zeph. 1:14–16.
"	24:37,	" Gen. 6:11–13; 7:7, 21–23.
"	25:31,	" Zech. 14:5.
"	25:46,	" Dan. 12:2.
"	26:28,	" Ex. 24:8; Lev. 4:18–20; Jer. 31:31; Zech. 9:11.
"	26:31,	" Zech. 13:7.
"	26:64,	" Ps. 110:1; Dan. 7:13.
"	26:65,	" Lev. 24:16.
"	27: 6,	" Deut. 23:18.
"	27:9, 10,	" Jer. 18:2; 19:2; 32:6; Zech. 11:13.
"	27:24,	" Deut. 21, 6–9.
"	27:34,	" Ps. 69:21.
"	27:35,	" Ps. 22:19.
"	27:46,	" Ps. 22:1.
Luke	1:15,	" Num. 6:3; Judg. 13:4–5; 1 Sam. 1:11.
"	1:17,	" Mal. 3:1; 4:5–6.
"	1:19,	" Dan. 8:16; 9:21.
"	1:31,	" Isa. 7:14.
"	1:32,	" 2 Sam. 7:12–17.
"	1:35,	" Ex. 13:12.
"	1:38,	" Gen. 18:14.
"	1:46 f.,	" 1 Sam. 2:1–10.
"	1:48,	" 1 Sam. 1:11.
"	1:49,	" 1 Sam. 2:2.
"	1:50,	" Ps. 103:17.
"	1:51,	" 1 Sam. 2:4; Ps. 89:10.
"	1:52,	" 1 Sam. 2:7; Job. 5:11; 12:19.
"	1:53,	" 1 Sam. 2:5; Ps. 107:9.
"	1:54,	" Isa. 41:8–9; Gen. 17:7; Mic. 7:20.
"	1:59,	" Lev. 12:3.

Luke	1:68,	from	Ps. 72:18; 111:9.
"	1:69,	"	1 Sam. 2:10; Ps. 18:3.
"	1:71,	"	Ps. 18:4; 106:10.
"	1:72 f.,	"	Gen. 17:7; Lev. 26:42; Ps. 105:8; Mic. 7:20.
"	1:76,	"	Mal. 3:1.
"	1:78,	"	Mal. 4:2.
"	1:79,	"	Isa. 8:22; 9:2.
"	2:21,	"	Gen. 17:12; Lev. 12:3.
"	2:23 f.,	"	Ex. 13:2, 12; Lev. 12:1–8.
"	2:30,	"	Isa. 52:10.
"	2:32,	"	Isa. 42:6; 49:6.
"	2:41,	"	Ex. 23:14–17; Deut. 16:1–8.
"	2:52,	"	1 Sam. 2:26.
"	3:4–6,	"	Isa. 40:3–5.
"	3:22,	"	Ps. 2:7; Isa. 42:1.
"	3:23–38,	"	1 Chron. 1:1–4, 24–28; 2:1–15; 3:17; Ruth 4:18–22.
"	4: 4,	"	Deut. 8:3.
"	4: 8,	"	Deut. 6:13.
"	4:10 f.,	"	Ps. 91:11.
"	4:12,	"	Deut. 6:16.
"	4:18 f.,	"	Isa. 58:6; 61:1 f.
"	4:25–27,	"	1 Kings 17:1; 17:8–9; 18:1–2; 2 Kings 5:1, 14.
"	4:34,	"	Ps. 16:10.
"	5:14,	"	Lev. 13:49; 14:2–32.
"	6: 2,	"	Ex. 20:10; Deut. 5:14; 23:25.
"	6: 3,	"	Lev. 24:9; 1 Sam. 21:1–6.
"	6:21,	"	Isa. 61:2.
"	7:22,	"	Isa. 2:18–19; 35:5–6; 61:1.
"	7:27,	"	Mal. 3:1.
"	8:10,	"	Isa. 6:9 f.
"	10:12,	"	Gen. 19:24.
"	10:15,	"	Isa. 14:13–15.
"	10:27,	"	Lev. 18:5; 19:18; Deut. 6:4 f.
"	11:29,	"	Jonah 3:1–4.
"	11:31,	"	1 Kings 10:1–3.
"	11:32,	"	Jonah 3:5–10.
"	11:42, 51,	"	Lev. 27:30; Gen. 4:8; 2 Chron. 24:20 f.; Mic. 6:8.
"	12:53,	"	Mic. 7:6.
"	13:14, 19,	"	Ex. 20:8–11; Deut. 5:12–15; Dan. 4:10–12, 20 f.
"	13:27, 29,	"	Ps. 6:8; 13:29; 107:3; Isa. 49:12.
"	17:12,	"	Lev. 13:45–46.
"	17:13 f.,	"	Lev. 13:49; 14:1–3.

Luke	17:26,	from	Gen. 6:11–13; 7:7, 21–23.
"	17:28, 33,	"	Gen. 18:20–22; 19:24–25; Gen. 19:26.
"	18:20,	"	Ex. 20:12–17; Deut. 5:16–21.
"	19:8, 10,	"	Ex. 22:1; Num. 5:6–7; Ezek. 34:16.
"	19:38,	"	Ps. 118:26.
"	19:46,	"	Isa. 56:7; Jer. 7:11.
"	20:9,	"	Isa. 5:1 f.
"	20:17,	"	Ps. 118:22 f.
"	20:18,	"	Isa. 8:14.
"	20:28, 38,	"	Gen. 38:8; Deut. 25:5 f.; Ex. 3:6.
"	20:42 f.,	"	Ps. 8:7; 110:1.
"	21:20,	"	Dan. 9:27.
"	21:22,	"	Dan. 12:1.
"	21:25 f.,	"	Dan. 8:10; Joel 4:16; Isa. 13:9 f.; Ezek. 32:7 f.; Amos. 8:9; Zeph. 1:14 f.
"	21:27, 28,	"	Dan. 7:13; Deut. 30:4 (LXX); Isa. 27:12 f.; Zech. 2:6 (LXX).
"	22:37,	"	Isa. 53:12.
"	22:46,	"	Ps. 31:5.
"	22:69,	"	Ps. 110:1; Dan. 7:13.
"	23:30,	"	Hos. 10:8.
"	23:46,	"	Ps. 31:6.
"	23:56,	"	Ex. 12:16; 20:8–11; Deut. 5:12–15.
"	24:46,	"	Hos. 6:2.
John	1:23,	"	Isa. 40:3.
"	1:29, 36,	"	Isa. 53:7.
"	1:49,	"	2 Sam. 7:14; Ps. 2:7.
"	1:51,	"	Gen. 28:12.
"	2:18,	"	Ex. 16:4, 15; Neh. 9:15; Ps. 69:9.
"	3:14,	"	Num. 21:8–9.
"	4: 5,	"	Josh. 24:32.
"	5:10,	"	Ex. 20:10; Deut. 5:14.
"	6:14,	"	Deut. 18:15.
"	6:31,	"	Ex. 16:4; Neh. 9:15; Ps. 78:24.
"	6:45,	"	Isa. 54:13.
"	7:22,	"	Gen. 17:9–14; Lev. 12:1–3.
"	7:38,	"	Prov. 18:4.
"	7:42,	"	2 Sam. 7:12; Isa. 11:1; Mic. 5:2.
"	8: 5,	"	Lev. 20:10; Deut. 22:22–24.
"	8:17,	"	Deut. 77:6; 19:15.
"	8:39,	"	Isa. 6:9 f.
"	10:16,	"	Ezek. 35: 23; 37:24.

John	10:34,	from	Ps. 82:6.
"	12:13,	"	Ps. 118:26.
"	12:14 f.,	"	Zech. 9:9.
"	12:27,	"	Ps. 42:6.
"	12:38,	"	Isa. 53:1.
"	12:40,	"	Isa. 6:9 f.,
"	13:18,	"	Ps. 41:9.
"	15:25,	"	Ps. 35:19; 69:5.
"	16:22,	"	Isa. 66:14.
"	17:12,	"	Ps. 41:9.
"	19:24,	"	Ps. 22:18.
"	19:29,	"	Ps. 69:21.
"	19:36,	"	Ex. 12:46; Num. 9:12; Ps. 34:21.
"	19:37,	"	Zech. 12:10.
"	19:42,	"	Deut. 21:22.

A LIST OF SOME UNCANONICAL SAYINGS OF JESUS

Some of the more important reported sayings of Christ are given which are not found in the Gospels or Acts; whether true words of the Master or not, it is not known. Some certainly are not like the Spirit of Christ, but it will be of service to the student to compare them with the genuine Words of Jesus in our Gospels. The Apocryphal Gospels are passed by as not worth using in this list.

1. The Logia of Jesus (Grenfell and Hunt):

Jesus saith: Except ye fast to the world, ye shall in no wise find the Kingdom of God; and except ye keep the Sabbath, ye shall not see the Father.

Jesus saith: I stood in the midst of the world, and in the flesh was I seen of them, and I found all men drunken, and none found I athirst among them, and my soul grieveth over the sons of men because they are blind in their heart.

Jesus saith: Wherever there are . . . and there is one . . . alone, I am with him. Raise the stone and there thou shalt find me, cleave the wood and there am I.

Jesus saith: A prophet is not acceptable in his own country, neither doth a physician work cures upon them that know him.

Jesus saith: A city built upon the top of a high hill and stablished, can neither fall nor be hid.

2. Readings found in Codex D.

One is concerning a man found working on the Sabbath, and comes after Luke 6:4: O man, if indeed thou knowest what thou doest, thou art blessed; but if thou knowest not, thou art cursed and art a transgressor of the law.

Likewise Codex D has, after Matt. 20:28: But you seek to increase from little, and from greater to be less.

3. Quotations found in various early Fathers.

From Barnabas: Let us resist all iniquity, and hold it in hatred. They who wish to see me and lay hold on my kingdom must receive me by affliction and suffering.

From Origen and others: Show yourselves tried money changers.

Ask great things, and the small shall be added to you; and ask heavenly things, and the earthly shall be added unto you.

He who is near me is near the fire; he who is far from me, is far from the kingdom.

For those that are sick I was sick, and for those that hunger, I suffered hunger, and for those that thirst, I suffered thirst.

From Clement of Rome (Ep. II.): Keep the flesh pure, and the seal unspotted.

When the two shall be one, and that which is without as that which is within, and the male with the female neither male nor female.

If ye kept not that which is small, who will give you that which is great? For I say unto you, that he that is faithful in very little is faithful also in much.

From Justin Martyr: In whatsoever I may find you, in this will I also judge you. Such as I may find thee, I will judge thee.

From Ignatius: Take hold, handle me, and see that I am not an incorporeal spirit.

From Clement of Alexandria: He that wonders shall reign, and he that reigns shall rest. Look with wonder at that which is before you. My mystery is for me and for the sons of my house.

From Papias: The days will come in which vines shall spring up, each having ten thousand stocks, and on each stock ten thousand branches, and on each branch ten thousand shoots, and on each shoot ten thousand bunches and on each bunch ten thousand grapes, and each grape when pressed shall give five and twenty measures of wine. And when any saint shall have seized one bunch, another shall cry: I am a better bunch; take me; through me bless the Lord.

SIMILAR INCIDENTS AND CHIEF REPEATED SAYINGS

Calling Disciples: §§ 28, 41, and 53.
Cleansing the Temple: §§ 31 and 129.
Owning Jesus as Messiah: §§ 28, 35, 41, 76, 82, 118.
Rejection at Nazareth: §§ 39 and 69.
Miraculous Draught of Fishes: §§ 41 and 180.
Parables of Mustard Seed and Leaven: §§ 64 (d) and 110.
The Tours of Galilee: §§ 44, 60, and 70.
Healings on the Sabbath: §§ 42, 43, 49–51, 100, 110, 114.
The Lists of the Twelve: §§ 53 and 70.
Courtier's Son and Centurion's Servant: §§ 38 and 55.
The Model Prayer: §§ 54 and 105.
The Anointing of Christ: §§ 59 and 141.
The Blasphemous Accusation: §§ 61, 68, and 106.
Groups of Parables: §§ 64, 91–92, 108, 114–117, 121, 124, 132, 139.
Sending the Twelve and Sending the Seventy: §§ 70 and 102.
Feeding the Five Thousand and the Four Thousand: §§ 72 and 79.
Tests of Discipleship: §§ 76, 83 and 115.
Jesus Foretelling His Death: §§ 31, 83, 85, 86, 88, 125, 139–152.
The Twelve Contending for Supremacy: §§ 90, 125, 144.
Attacking Jesus in Jerusalem: §§ 31, 49, 96–101, 111, 119, 124–135, 153–167.
Foretelling the Second Coming: §§ 84, 120, 127, 139, 148–151.
Divorce: §§ 54 and 122.
Like Children: §§ 90 and 123.
Rewards of Service: §§ 93 and 124.
Worldly Anxieties: §§ 54 and 108.
The Ninety and Nine: §§ 91 and 116.
Baptism of Death: §§ 108 and 125.
The Pounds and the Talents: §§ 127 and 139.
The Agony of Christ: §§ 130 and 152.
Denouncing the Scribes and Pharisees: §§ 61 and 137.
Lament Over Jerusalem: §§ 113, 128, and 137.
About a Sword: §§ 70, 147, 153.
The Three Commissions: §§ 178, 181, and 183.

In general the Later Judean Ministry and the Perean Ministry, chiefly Luke's contribution to the Life of Christ, furnish many events and discourses similar to those described in the Galilean Ministry. Sections 102 to 127 furnish most of the so-called "doublets" or repeated sayings of Jesus or similar miracles. This is just what we should expect in a popular teacher who journeyed in different parts of the country. Some of these were real doublets, spoken by Jesus more than once. Others may be grouped by Luke in a different place. We have no way to decide the problem.